Barbara Hepworth

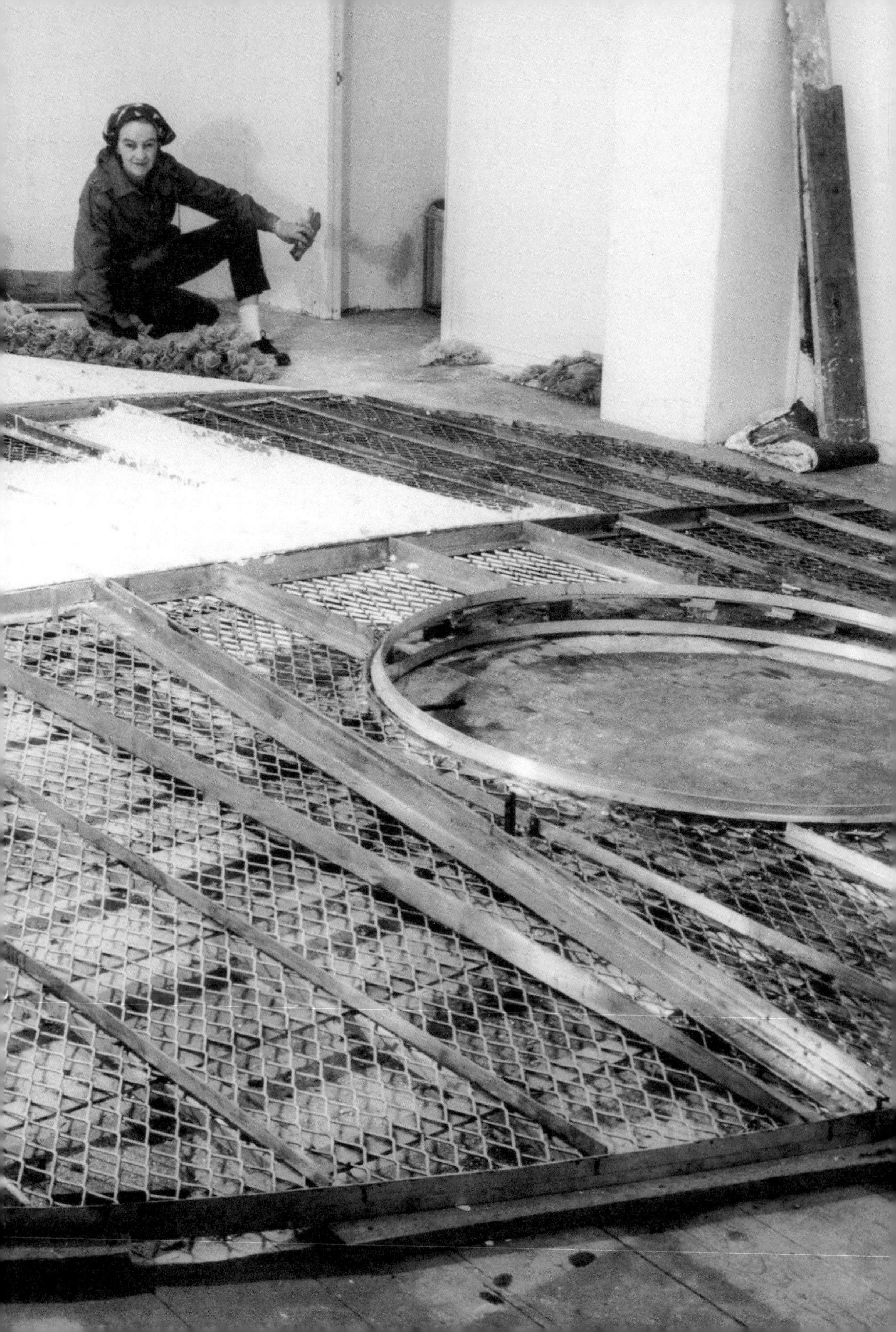

Eleanor Clayton

Barbara Hepworth
Art & Life

Foreword by Ali Smith

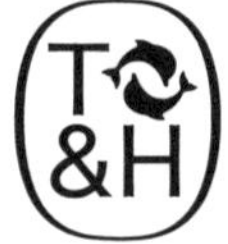

To John and Edith

FRONTISPIECE Barbara Hepworth at work on the first
stage of the prototype for the United Nations *Single Form*,
25 January 1963 (detail). Photograph by Studio St Ives

First published in the United Kingdom in 2021 by
Thames & Hudson Ltd, 181A High Holborn, London WC1V 7QX

First published in the United States of America in 2021 by
Thames & Hudson Inc., 500 Fifth Avenue, New York,
New York 10110

Published on the occasion of the major exhibition *Barbara
Hepworth: Art & Life* held at The Hepworth Wakefield
(21 May 2021–27 February 2022)

Reprinted 2021

British Library Cataloguing-in-Publication Data
A catalogue record for this book is available from
the British Library

Library of Congress Control Number 2020950623

ISBN 978-0-500-09425-9

Printed and bound in Belgium by Graphius

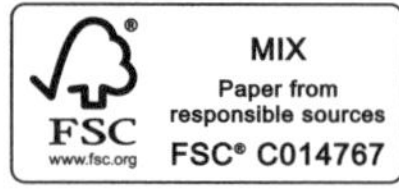

Be the first to know about our new releases,
exclusive content and author events by visiting
thamesandhudson.com
thamesandhudsonusa.com
thamesandhudson.com.au

Contents

Foreword

'Your work is very organic,' an interviewer said to Barbara Hepworth once. 'It's meant to be,' Hepworth replied. 'I'm organic myself.'

This off-the-cuff reply isn't just frank and funny. In it there's a vision that connects every individual to the ground we walk on, the world we inhabit, and the planet's place in something universal. Hepworth saw our own organic relation as connected not just to the landscapes we inhabit or the elements of the physical world from which we're literally made but to the world in outer space, and more. There's a renewing, in encounter with her work, of what words like 'space' and 'world' mean, all the way from the planetary sphere right back to the miniature curvature of the side of a pebble.

Simultaneously ancient and contemporary, concrete and symbolic, earthy and spiritual, her art conjures from two pieces of shaped stone everything from the intimate pull of love between two living beings to the massive power of earth's magnetism.

She opened expectations of figuration to abstraction, and vice versa. She pierced holes in stone, wood and metal, opened her materials to light and to air as if matter itself has eyes or is a window to itself and the rest of the world, waiting for us to understand it inside out, to open our own eyes to what matter is. She made herself open to the life she perceived deep in stone, wood, metal; she sensed that a slab of marble, say, already held form inside it and that it was her responsibility, in a kind of dialogue with her materials and with the working of her head and hands, to find that form. She strung strings across hollows to bring out the music, the underlying rhythm, in the space that a curve can suggest or the depth that a surface will belie.

She lived through two world wars; it's no surprise that she became an early environmentalist, a socialist and anti-nuclear campaigner, and this commitment and her art practice were indivisible from each other and as organic to her as breathing.

This book reads Hepworth's life and art together as an organic symbiosis. Eleanor Clayton traces a biographical timeline that dispenses with anything not integral to the relationship between the artist and the work/s. With access to unpublished letters to friends and people closest to her, she aligns Hepworth's 'private thoughts' with her 'public narrative', treating the life and the work as one and the same and revealing not just the impossibility but the daftness of ever splitting one from the

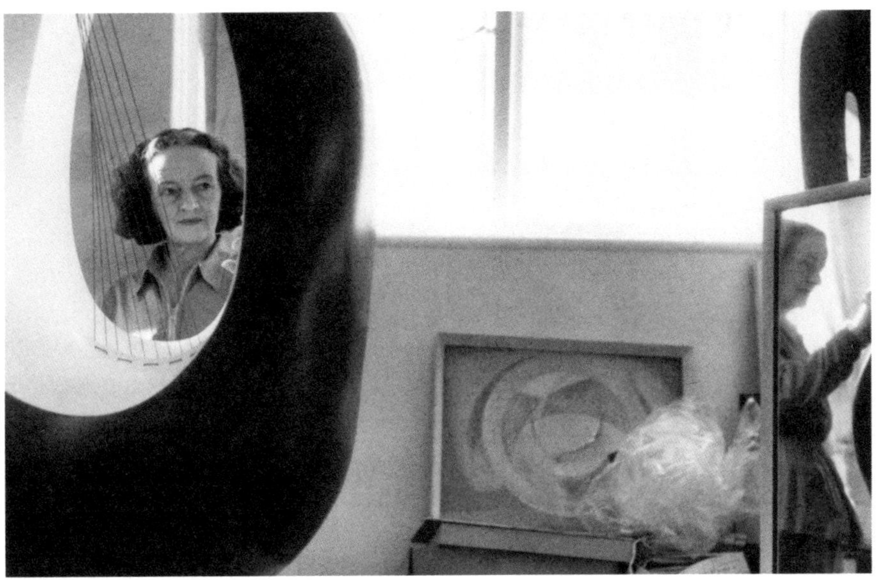

other. The book deals with contemporary fractures in history across the lifetime, shifts and fashions in art history, and the everyday 'continued, insidious sexism' that Hepworth had to withstand from one half of the century to the other. It contextualises all of this by placing Hepworth's own wise voice centre-stage.

What a voice. Hepworth was also one of our most eloquent speakers on time, on life, on what we make of these, and on the art process at the core of both. Fiercely intelligent, always striving against any falsity or pretension both in what she said and what she made, she defined art as the opposite of elitism and was committed to the 'universal language' she knew it to be. This voicing, and this book, make for a new revelation of the underlying rhythm at the heart of the artist and the art, a galvanising vision of both at work in the real world.

'One could really do with 10 lifetimes,' the artist said towards the end of her life, 'to express the variations and subtleties which one lifetime can give.' I wish this book were ten times as long as it is, for the human being it conjures who saw earth, stone, stars and spirit come together as one organic vision, and for the process, the person, the art and the spirit that came together to make Barbara Hepworth.

Ali Smith

ABOVE Barbara Hepworth in the studio in 1956, with *Curved Form (Delphi)* (1955). Photograph by Charles Gimpel

Introduction

*The forms which have had special meaning for me since
childhood have been the standing form (which is the translation
of my feeling towards the human being standing in landscape);
the two forms (which is the tender relationship of one living
thing beside another); and the 'closed form', such as the oval,
spherical or pierced form (sometimes incorporating colour)
which translates for me the association of meaning of gesture
in landscape; in the repose of say a mother & child, or the
feeling of the embrace of living things, either in nature or
in the human spirit.*[1]

Barbara Hepworth is one of the most significant sculptors of the twentieth century. With a career that spanned decades of tumultuous political and social change, she was at the forefront of multiple avant-garde movements. She worked during a period when art writing flourished, and contemporary art permeated both popular press and the public realm. This was concurrent with the increasing appearance of artist statements, and Hepworth wrote extensively on her work throughout her career. From her statement in the 1934 publication *Unit One*, relatively early in her career, to the 1952 *Barbara Hepworth: Carvings and Drawings*, and finally 1970's *Pictorial Autobiography*, she comprehensively articulated the ideas that both motivated her work and were expressed in it, often including many complex concepts in relatively simple statements. The quote above offers a perfect example. Hepworth delineates three forms that are profoundly important to her: the single vertical form, two forms alongside each other, and the 'closed form', explaining further that by the latter she means 'oval, spherical or pierced'. She associates these physical shapes with particular ideas – the human being standing in landscape, the tender relationship of one entity to another, the 'feeling of the embrace of living things'. Such tangible, physical realities – a figure standing at the top of a hill, a mother holding a child – are intrinsically ephemeral, emotional experiences. Much of Hepworth's art and life attempts this synthesis of matter and idea, the singular and the universal, form and content.

Recent access to Hepworth's letters to her closest friend, political activist and author Margaret Gardiner, many of which are previously unpublished, alongside archival research into Hepworth's correspondences with critic E. H. Ramsden, her long-term partner and fellow artist Ben Nicholson, composer Priaulx Rainier, and economist, diplomat and poet Dag Hammarskjöld, among other friends and colleagues, offers personal insight into her life and working practices, and provides the opportunity to interweave her private thoughts and conversations within her public narrative.[2] As this list of names attests, Hepworth's circle of friends invites a look at fields of interest previously under-researched or looked at in isolation, from literature to politics, religion, music, science and technology. Bringing together this wide range of material, looked at in depth and spanning a lifetime, explores more fully the development of Hepworth's artistic ideas and how they both infused and were inspired by all aspects of life. The availability of contemporaneous critical responses to Hepworth's exhibitions through vast online press archives offers a further view on how her works, frequently conveying concepts she considered universal and eternal, were received at a particular moment in time.

Hepworth's case is unusual among artists not only in the availability of extensive archives of correspondence but also in that much of her working process has been preserved through her two studios in St Ives (one of which became the Barbara Hepworth Museum following her death), and through her plaster and aluminium prototypes for bronze sculptures (now on permanent display at The Hepworth Wakefield). These unique works form the core of the Hepworth Family Gift, which also includes tools, technical drawings, notes and materials, giving an insight into the practical processes that Hepworth used to make sculpture. Taken together, these resources offer an unparalleled opportunity to explore the intellectual and physical development of sculpture side by side, echoing Hepworth's synthesising of the ephemeral and the material. Additionally, she kept meticulous records of her work, most notably in volumes of 'Sculpture Records', which illustrate this book and are held at Tate Archive and The Hepworth Wakefield. These folders include details of the work, and its exhibition and publication history, alongside carefully selected photographs.

As well as showing Hepworth grappling with the presentation of sculpture in two-dimensional terms, as the multiple views of sculptures in her monographs also attest, these folders reveal another aspect – the often-unseen labour of the artist in promoting their work and developing their career. As with many artists, there was little separation between Hepworth's professional and personal life: many of her friends were also collectors of her work, critics who championed her career, and curators who included her work within their exhibitions. Similarly, Hepworth herself collected the work of her peers, most often through gifts or swaps, photographed other artists' work for their promotion, and assisted writer friends in the practical aspects of publication. For Hepworth, a thread connected all activities, whether domestic chores, childcare, reading and writing, listening to music or carving. When asked about the difficulties of managing the demands of a large family alongside her work, Hepworth responded in 1973, 'I found it was a great inspiration to me. I loved the family and everything to do with them. I loved the environment and the cooking, I used to cook and go in my studio. I had to have methods of working. If I was in the middle of a work and the oven burned or the children called for me, I used to make an arrangement with music, records or poetry, so that when I went back to the studio, I picked up where I left off. I enjoyed it, you see, it was part of me.'[3] She insisted on the importance of continuing to work despite these other claims to her time, stating in the same interview, 'I found one had to do some work every day even at midnight because either you're professional or you're not.'[4] This is reflected in her letters to friends, which show her snatching time to scribble pencil notes from her studio so as not to break her working flow, writing to Ramsden, 'Please forgive a pencil note – I find that if I write like this in my studio it does not interfere with my carving – settling down upstairs with pen & ink does,'[5] and to Gardiner, 'I will try to write a nicer letter when I have done some carving. I'm not fit to live with unless I can do some work – even an hour a day keeps me civilised.'[6]

The underlying assumption in the interviewer's question is that, as a married woman and mother of four children, working was a choice rather than a necessity. This was something that Hepworth objected to both on pragmatically financial grounds and for her own well-being, noting in her *Pictorial Autobiography*, 'I had nearly thirty years of wonderful family life; but I will confess that the dictates of work are as compelling for a woman as for a man. Not competitively, but as complementary, and this is only just being realised.'[7] Hepworth encountered continued, often insidious, sexism throughout her career, frequently being identified by her gender as apart from her male contemporaries through the term 'sculptress', which she loathed. Often sexist comments were couched as praise: an early piece in the *Yorkshire Evening News* on one of her first exhibitions described her as 'a lovely girl with whom nobody would associate a hammer and chisel',[8] while others were less complimentary, the *Yorkshire Post* commenting in 1937, 'if no other consideration were relevant, it would still be remarkable that a year's sculpture of such force and determination could come from a woman's hands'.[9] Even at the peak of Hepworth's success, the *Observer* noted, 'it's all the more surprising that one of the most internationally famous sculptors of our time should be a frail and reserved Yorkshirewoman in her late fifties'.[10] These perpetual comments led Hepworth to state in 1968, 'I am constantly plagued by this little-woman attitude. There is a deep prejudice against women in art.'[11]

She fought against this prejudice as fervently as she strived to make a positive impact on society in general, relentlessly believing that clarity of thought and communicating this through art could bring about a better world in all aspects. She wrote to Gardiner, amid the turmoil of the immediate post-war period, 'each day I feel more energetically opposed to ideas which underestimate the innate beauty & goodness in people. To be consistent one should be without fear. Fear of a "new aristocracy" is the prevailing fear & perhaps that is what one should try to grapple with – in all its forms – whether it is an aristocracy of C[ommunist] P[arty] members, artists, business men, atom bomb holders, or writers.'[12] Later, in 1959, as the threat of nuclear war loomed, she insisted, 'life will always insist on begetting life. By upholding this faith in life we strengthen those who are flagging and becoming cynical because they fear for their lives. They fear for the continuity of life. This continuity contains a tremendous and impelling force. In autumn all the dynamics are laid for spring [...] The artist who understands this is feeling his way to an understanding of the structures underlying these impulses. I believe that this is true not only for the artist but for the scientist and the healer as well.'[13] The subtitle of this book, 'Art & Life', is then not merely descriptive of the contents but aims to convey something of the further synthesis for which Hepworth constantly strived; to infuse life with art, and art with life, to express the realities of her interactions and environment in such a manner that her particular experience echoed universal human truths. Perhaps this is what makes her work so continually potent today.

I was told when I began this project that biographers often end up resenting their subjects. I write as a curator who loves the artist she is presenting, a fan writing of her hero. Hepworth's work and words have continually helped me to gain balance and perspective through challenging times and to see the world with wonder and delight. As a young woman I empathised with her struggles to be serious and to be taken seriously on her own terms. When I became a mother, I identified with her frustrations in trying to combine childcare and work, and was motivated by her ability to embrace these difficulties as an integral and valuable part of lived experience. As the Covid-19 pandemic shook the structure of our society, I was inspired by Hepworth's celebration of community, and her faith in the ability of people to come together and build something new, and potentially better. Hepworth wisely noted, when it was suggested that ancient civilisations lived in more peaceful times, 'I don't think that anyone's lived in a very tranquil, pastoral civilisation. I think that those times, that each time of living people must have been beset by the most urgent and terrifying problems.'[14] The world continues to be urgent, terrifying, and inspirational. When asked, towards the end of her life, about the role of contemporary sculpture, Hepworth responded with typical eloquence and idealism: 'today when we are all conscious of the expanding universe, the forms experienced by the sculptor should express not only this consciousness but should, I feel, emphasize also the possibilities of new developments of the human spirit, so that it can affirm and continue life in its highest form'.[15] I hope that reading about her remarkable art and life can offer something of the same.

Eleanor Clayton

Chapter 1

The Shadow
Dance

*Perhaps what one wants to say is formed in childhood and
the rest of one's life is spent trying to say it. I know that
all I felt during the early years of my life in Yorkshire is
dynamic and constant in my life today.*[1]

A small painting Barbara Hepworth made when she was seventeen
(opposite) shows two figures, standing in contemplative stillness, apart
from one another on a beach. Mottled rocks on the left give way to a
sweep of cliff and expanse of calm, pale blue sea. The painting conveys
a romantic and intimate connection between humanity and landscape,
highlighting elements of nature – rocks and sea – that would be present within Hepworth's work throughout her life. These elements also
represent facets of Yorkshire, the huge county in the north of England
where Hepworth was born: traditional fishing communities on the east
coast, and rural farming communities and dramatic rocky outcrops in
the Yorkshire Dales. But Yorkshire, and the relationship of its people to
its landscape, also influenced Hepworth in more subtle ways. The county
was at the heart of the industrial revolution, with prominent coal-mining
communities, and technological innovation led to its centrality in the
wool and cotton trade. This was particularly present in the West Riding,
the area where Hepworth grew up, which had significant coal pits and
wool mills, and a canal that was a conduit to national and international
trade. Hepworth's awareness of the power of collective productivity,
and her socialist political viewpoint, grew from these early experiences.
A mixture of aesthetics and politics infuses her childhood memories:

*I observed the granite sets, the steep hills of industrial Yorkshire,
the scurrying of mill girls in their shawls huddled against the
cold and wind – the lonely figure against a street gas-lamp, the
squatting miner outside his door, and the gleaming 'withinness'
of his sparkling ugly house [...] The position of man in relation
to this country, and the horror of the approaching slump and
then the First World War, absorbed all my thoughts. The
exploitation of man, the image of human dignity in spite of these
horrors, obsessed me. I would imagine stone 'images' rising out
of the ground, which would pinpoint the spiritual triumph of
man and at the same time give the sensuous, evocative, and
biologically necessary fetish for survival.*[2]

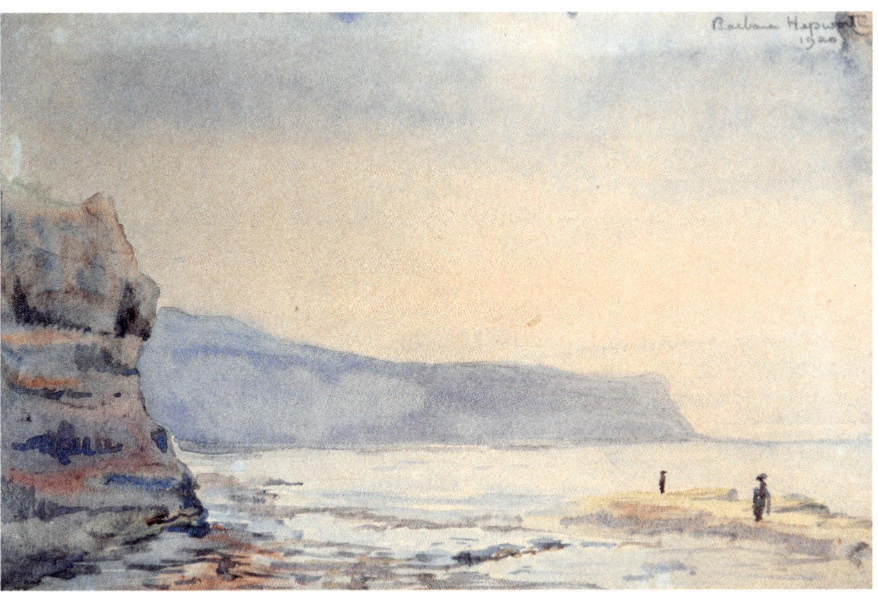

This fusing of opposites – land and sea, nature and industry, physical and spiritual – is a powerful aspect of Hepworth's artistic and personal vision. It is perhaps this spirit of synthesis above all else that can be understood as significant in her formative years.

Jocelyn Barbara Hepworth was born on 10 January 1903 into a middle-class family in the city of Wakefield. While her extended family had their roots in the wool trade, her father Herbert was a civil engineer for the local authority who was promoted through the ranks during her childhood, eventually becoming the County Surveyor for the West Riding. She described him as 'gentle, kind and very intelligent', and her mother Gertrude ('Gerda') as 'beautiful and gay', and she considered their approach to family management to be a combination of 'lavish love and their necessary stern frugality'.[3] Hepworth was baptised and confirmed at Wakefield Cathedral, a building that still holds a significant place within the architectural landscape of the city and, which Hepworth remembered, 'played a large part in my early life'.[4] During her childhood, however, her parents became committed to Christian Science, a relatively new religious movement that had recently spread from America. Based on an alternative reading of the Bible, the founder Mary Baker Eddy's *Science and Health with Key to the Scriptures* was published in 1875, its popularity became widespread, and by the turn of the century a new Christian Science church was being erected every four

ABOVE Barbara Hepworth, *Robin Hood's Bay*, 1920, watercolour on paper, 19 × 28 cm (7½ × 11 in.)

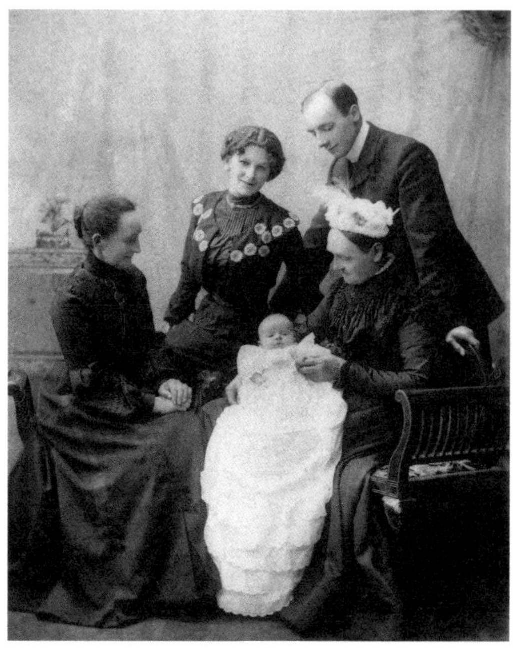

days.[5] As a teenager, Hepworth owned and inscribed her own copy of *Science and Health*. This text distinguishes between the 'mortal mind', which perceives – and can falsely prioritise – the physical world, and the 'divine Mind', or God, which represents the true nature of existence, a spiritual singularity of which everything is a part.

Despite this emphasis on the spiritual and ephemeral world, Hepworth's father was keenly focused on material details in his work as County Surveyor. Hepworth accompanied her father on his inspections around the county, her recollections also a reminder of the world as it was then, in the throes of technological innovations, a motorised vehicle still being a relative rarity:

> *[...] my father would mention very quietly the stresses and strains of roads and bridges and we would then continue to float through the landscape in our private thoughts. It was an early and very high car, which enabled us to see over hedges. At the furious pace of about 25 miles per hour, and being very careful not to disturb the horses and drivers of their carts, we roamed through the dales and valleys and up the moors, and through the Pennines. From the deep indigo and blacks and scarlets of the industrial heart we sailed through unimaginable beauty of unspoiled countryside.[6]*

ABOVE Barbara Hepworth as an infant, with her parents, her paternal grandmother and her paternal great-grandmother, 1903

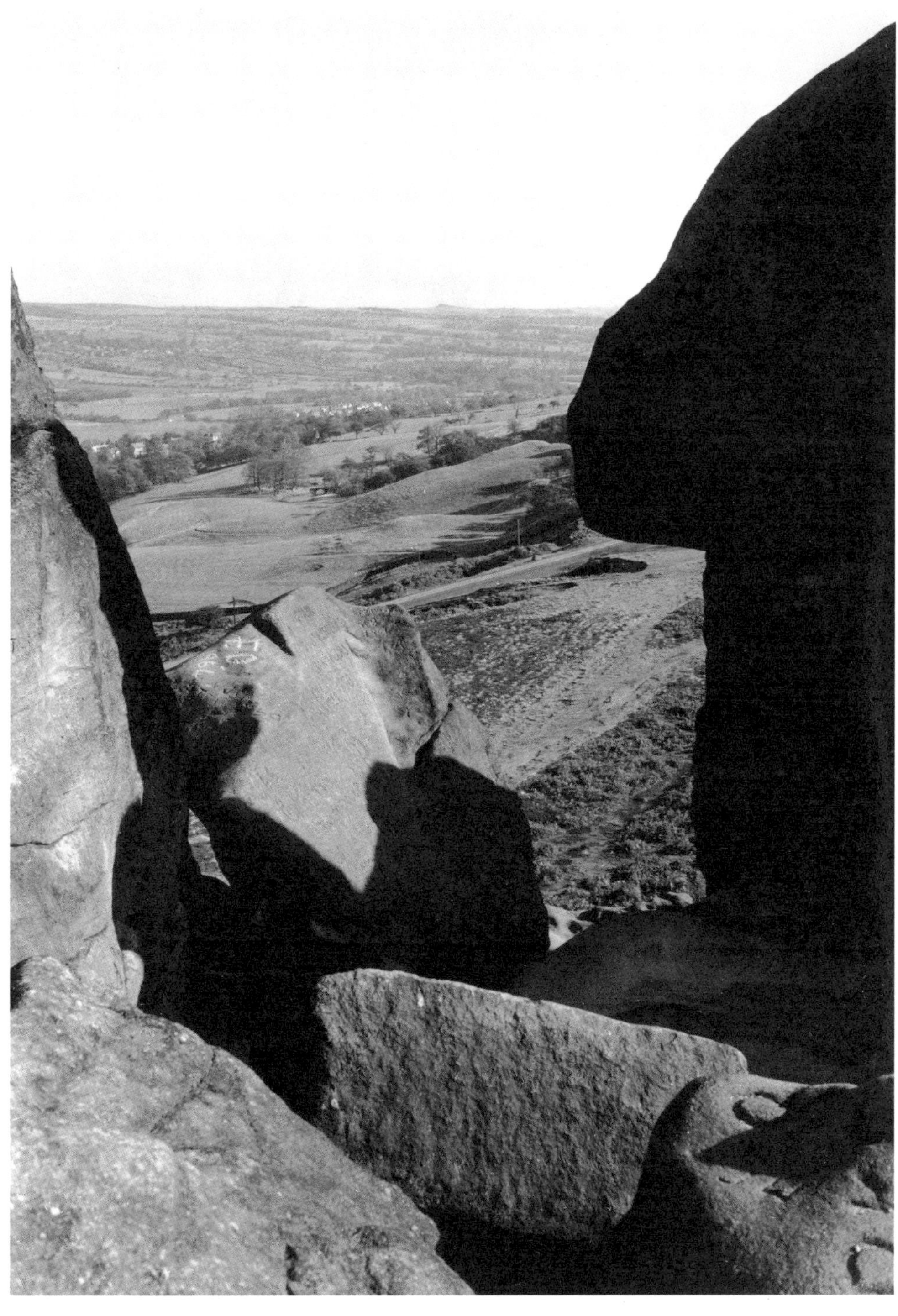

 Cow and Calf rocks above Ilkley, West
Yorkshire. Photograph (commissioned by Barbara
Hepworth): Lee Sheldrake/Penwith Photo Press

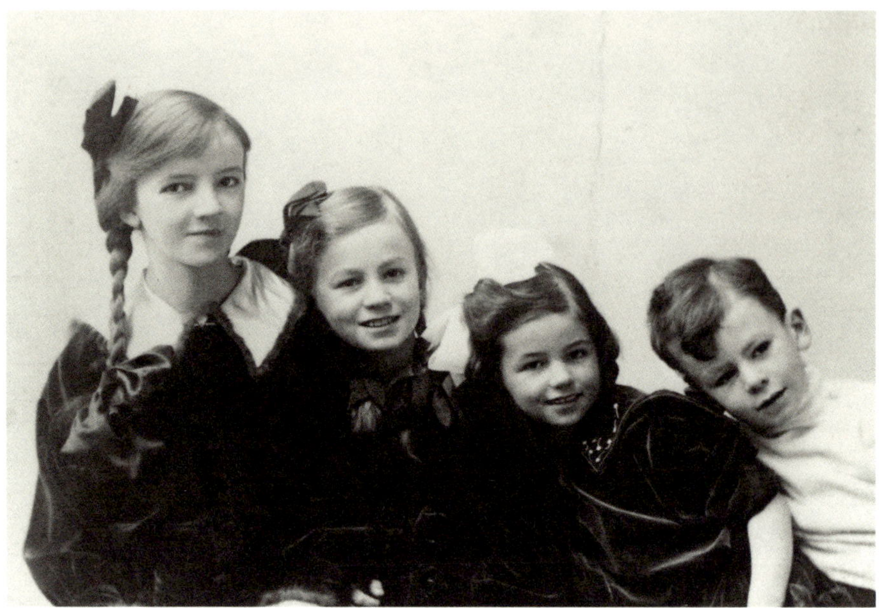

The visual impact of these trips resonated throughout Hepworth's life, and she expressed the impression in her 1970 *Pictorial Autobiography* in sculptural terms: 'moving through and over the West Riding landscape with my father in his car, the hills were sculptures; the roads defined the forms'.[7] Yorkshire remained an important touchstone for Hepworth: she defined her no-nonsense temperament as that of a Yorkshirewoman (writing, for example, to friends of her 'constitutional Yorkshireman's belief in calling a spade a spade'[8]), and in her sixties she commissioned photographs of key landscapes within the county that continued to inspire her, like the large rock formation known as 'The Cow and Calf' in Ilkley (see previous page).[9]

As her father's career progressed, her family also grew and Hepworth became the eldest of four children: Joan, born in 1906, Anthony in 1909, and Elizabeth in 1911. That Hepworth accompanied her father on his trips rather than her younger brother showed the progressive attitude of her father, who valued education for his daughters as much as for his son – a relatively unusual approach at a time when middle-class women were expected to be housewives and mothers. Hepworth attended the Wakefield Girls' High School, where she credited the headmistress, Miss McCroben, with introducing her to Egyptian sculpture in a particularly memorable slide-show: 'at the age of 7 I sat in the lecture hall of a school of 600 girls with tightened nerves & muscles gazing on slides

ABOVE Barbara, Joan, Elizabeth and Anthony (Tony) Hepworth, *c*. 1915

of the Pyramids, Greek temples & ancient sculptures. That first vision of "form" between heaven & earth never leaves me.'[10] She recalled, 'My headmistress knew I detested sports and games. I loved dancing, music, drawing and painting. And wonderfully, when all had departed to the playing fields, I found myself miraculously alone with easel, paints and paper in the school.'[11]

There are few surviving sculptures from this period, although Hepworth remembers modelling heads of her siblings in clay in the cellar, the mucky material not being permitted in the upstairs rooms.[12] An early modelled sculpture in glazed porcelain, *The Pond (Two Figures)* (*c.* 1922), shows a female figure lifting her skirt as she stands within the water, her feet already submerged beneath the surface and a companion leaning over her shoulder (below left). The subject chimes with Hepworth's reminiscences of her early life, the figures immersing themselves in nature, and conveying a close human bond. Surviving teenage drawings, such as *The Shadow Dance* (1919) (below right), reflect Hepworth's interest

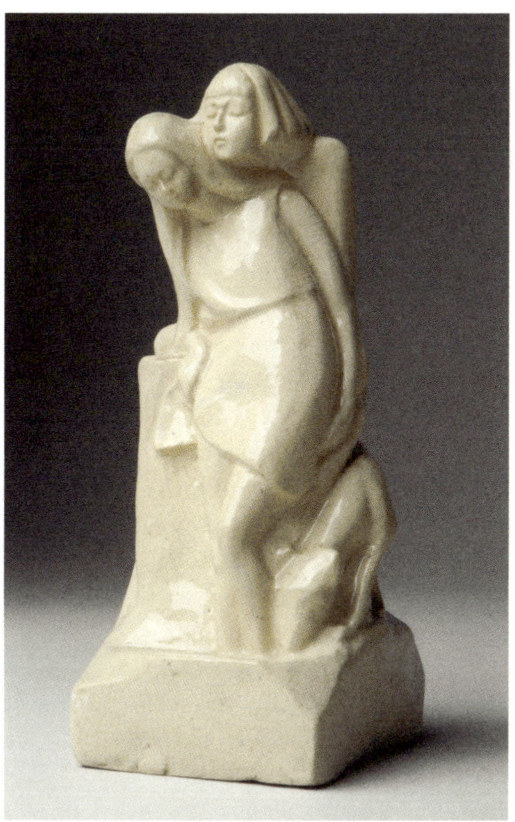

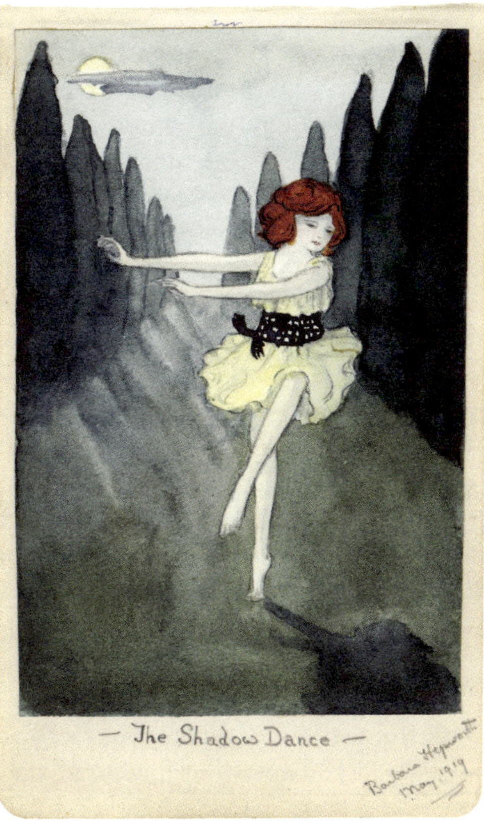

ABOVE LEFT Barbara Hepworth, *The Pond (Two Figures)*, *c.* 1922, glazed porcelain, 18 × 6.5 × 8.5 cm (7 × 2½ × 3⅜ in.)

ABOVE RIGHT Barbara Hepworth, *The Shadow Dance*, 1919, watercolour and ink on paper, 13 × 8 cm (5⅛ × 3⅛ in.)

in music and dance: she played the piano as a child and won several prizes at school as well as a Junior Music Scholarship in 1915. Hepworth attributed this love of music to her mother, who 'saved and scraped to inspire me to further effort in music and dance'.[13] The school also encouraged dance as an integral part of learning, and in 1914 McCroben introduced Dalcroze Eurhythmic classes for the students, in which the concepts of rhythm, structure and musical expression were taught using physical movements.

Hepworth's accomplished draughtsmanship had caught the eye of McCroben, who encouraged Hepworth to take the Junior County Scholarship exam to attend Leeds School of Art, having passed her School Certificate Examination in 1918. Hepworth began her studies at Leeds in 1920 at the age of 17, where she met fellow artist Henry Moore, who was studying there on an ex-serviceman's grant. The education programme at Leeds focused on drawing, '7 to 9 [am] life drawing, and in the day modelling',[14] drawing from the antique, drawing figures in action, drawing from memory, and studying architecture, perspective and anatomy.[15] The drawing master W. B. Pearson drilled his students with the aim of passing the Board of Education examination and securing a place at the Royal College of Art in London. He had, as Moore recalled, 'learnt what the Inspector wanted and insisted on a style of drawing which he found was successful with them'.[16] The days were long, and it was common for Hepworth to catch the 9.30pm train home from Leeds to Wakefield.

Hepworth painted the seaside scene that opened this chapter (see p. 15) in Robin Hood's Bay, North Yorkshire, where her family spent their summer holidays 'in a house on rock rising out of the beach', she recalled. 'I had an attic room and would get up at dawn to go painting all by myself and undisturbed in a world of fantastic beauty. The rocky

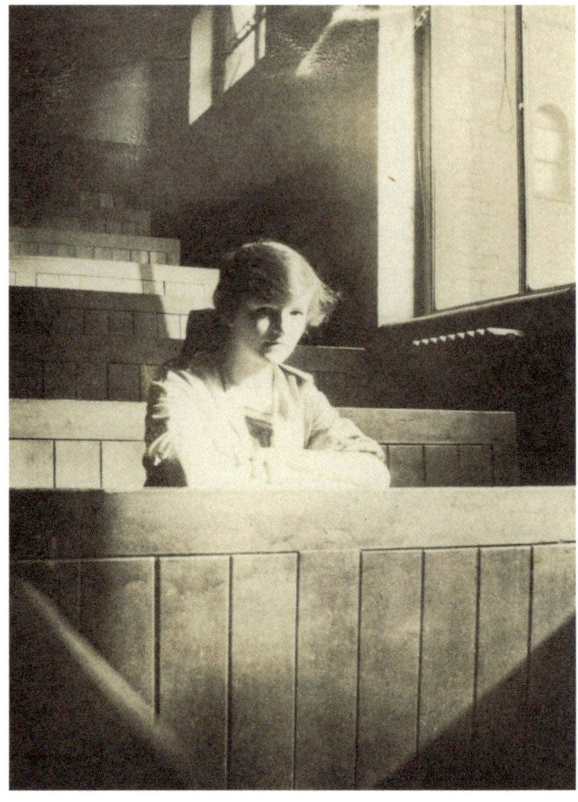

ABOVE Barbara Hepworth, Leeds School of Art, *c.* 1920

scars, the boats, sea and cliffs inspired me continuously.'[17] The house, including the attic room, can be seen in another surviving watercolour from 1920 (below), alongside the rocks, cliffs and sea as Hepworth describes. In addition to furthering a love of landscape, these summer holidays introduced Hepworth to a community of artists. As she recalled, 'artists lived in Robin Hood's Bay and I was able to go and sniff the smell of paint and canvas and explore this wonderful free world of changing light and tide and colour'.[18]

One of the artists she encountered was Ethel Walker. Walker was a painter of the older generation, born in 1861, who was based in London with a studio in Chelsea but spent her summers in Robin Hood's Bay. She painted Hepworth's portrait twice in the early 1920s (see following page), exhibiting the paintings in 1922 and 1923, respectively, with the London-based New English Art Club. The NEAC was a contemporary exhibiting society founded to present work deemed too avant-garde for the conservative Royal Academy, and Walker had become their first female member in 1900. *The Sunday Times* art critic Frank Rutter praised Hepworth's portrait in the 1922 exhibition for its 'charm of colour and delicacy of conception'.[19] Contact with a significant female contemporary

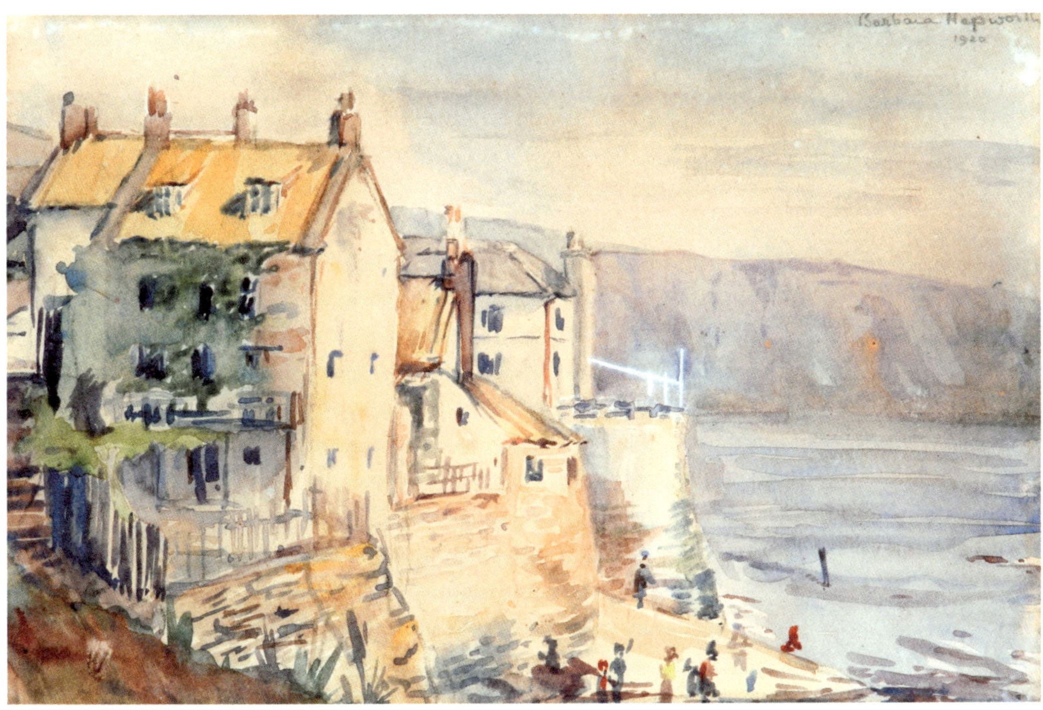

ABOVE Barbara Hepworth, *Study of Robin Hood's Bay*, 1920, watercolour on paper, 14 × 21 cm (5½ × 8¼ in.)

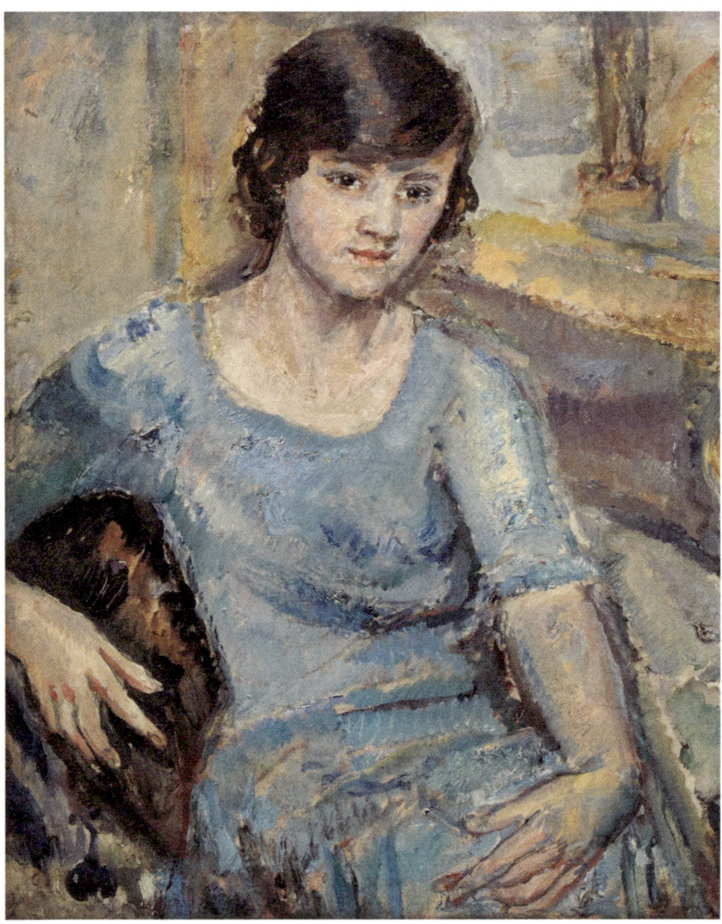

artist succeeding in a male-dominated field may have further fuelled Hepworth's ambitions to become a professional artist. Although Walker's painting looks fairly traditional now, at the time she was considered to be avant-garde; she was later described in *The Telegraph* as 'one of the foremost of British Impressionists'.[20] This enticing contact with London's avant-garde was extended in 1921 when Hepworth won a senior scholarship to study at the Royal College of Art, entering, as she described, 'an expanding world'.[21]

ABOVE Ethel Walker, *Portrait of Barbara Hepworth*, *c.* 1920, oil on canvas, 76.5 × 64 cm (30⅛ × 25⅛ in.)

Chapter 2

An Expanding World

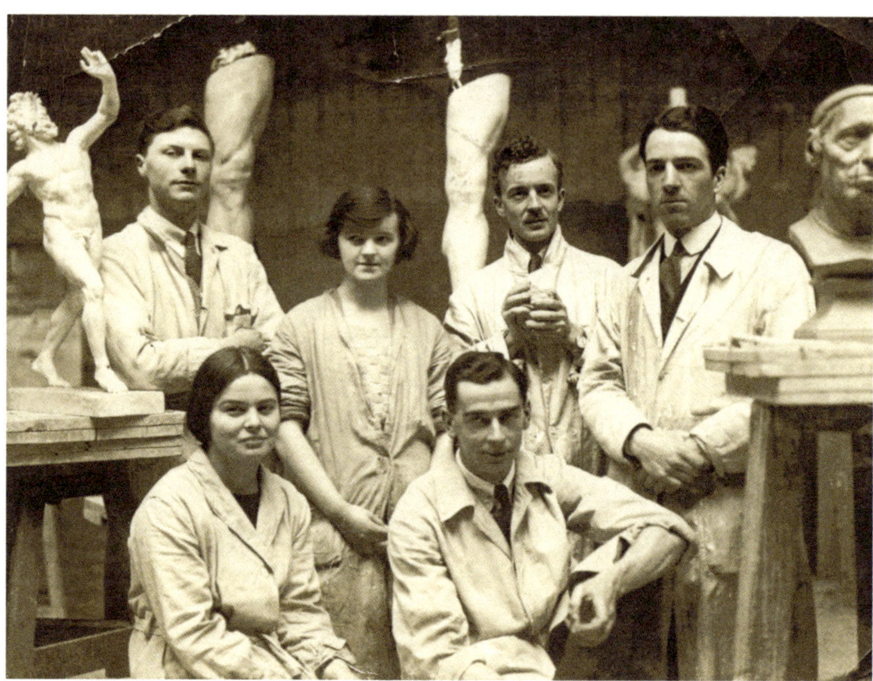

In 1921, Hepworth arrived in London to study at the Royal College of Art. Although still dominated by Victorian sensibilities, London's art scene had been slowly catching up with new developments from Europe. By the end of the nineteenth century, artists such as Paul Cézanne and Claude Monet had made Paris a centre for contemporary art. While a London exhibition of Impressionist art organised at the Grafton Galleries by the main dealer of the group, Paul Durand-Ruel, in 1905 sold nothing,[1] in 1910 critic, writer and artist Roger Fry organised a seminal exhibition that finally brought these paintings and more to the attention of the British public. Under the title *Manet and the Post-Impressionists*, the show presented a progression of modern art, from the realism of Édouard Manet, through the Impressionism of painters including Monet, to the work of 'the Post-Impressionists'. This latter term was coined by Fry for the exhibition to describe Vincent van Gogh, Paul Gauguin, and younger artists including Henri Matisse and Pablo Picasso. The show received a largely outraged critical response and, as P. G. Konody described in *The Observer*, sent 'the great majority of London art-lovers into fits of laughter, whilst finding enthusiastic defenders among a small circle of indiscriminating intellectual snobs'.[2] Criticism of the banal or risqué subject choices of everyday scenes and nudes, respectively, was compounded by the abstract

ABOVE Barbara Hepworth (centre), studying on a Yorkshire Senior County Art Scholarship, with fellow students at the Royal College of Art, London, *c.* 1921–23

manner in which these subjects were depicted, experimenting with form or colour. As the *Manchester Guardian* put it, 'their vice seems to be the modern one of specialisation. They detach and project one aspect of life and nature, and torture it to its shrillest expression; then they cry that "here is truth at last".'[3]

Fry summarised the coverage well when he recalled in 1929, 'the artists were roundly accused of sexual perversion and moral depravity: This of course was only the Englishman's way of saying that he disliked the pictures.'[4] However, this wealth of negative attention had the effect of driving visitors to the show, and between 8 November 1910 and 15 January 1911 around 25,000 people attended. It was a commercial success, and a version was presented in Liverpool in 1911, followed by Fry's *Second Post-Impressionist* exhibition in London, in 1912. The latter included English artists: as one critic noted, 'younger men and women, our flesh-and-blood contemporaries, [who] have taken up the running'.[5] Contemporary art was gaining momentum: 1913 saw the establishment of the London Group, which brought together several exhibiting societies of artists pioneering the 'post-impressionist' style of painting, and the Omega Workshops, which aimed to fuse contemporary fine art with craft and design, bringing art into the home while providing paid work for young artists. Several of the latter broke away to form another group, the Vorticists, whose manifesto and magazine *Blast*, published in 1914, celebrated industry and the machine age.

However, war intervened, and with the death of many exponents and promising careers interrupted, the vitality of the British art scene took time to recover. One champion of contemporary art was painter William Rothenstein, who had become the Principal of the Royal College of Art in 1920, the year before Hepworth arrived. Moore, who moved from Leeds School of Art to the Royal College alongside Hepworth, recalled that Rothenstein was particularly encouraging towards his new cohorts, giving 'the feeling that there was no barrier, no limit to what a young provincial student could get to be and do'.[6] He had invigorated the somewhat stuffy programme of the Royal College by introducing a degree of informality, and he invited young contemporary artists to appear as guest lecturers. Painting was taught by Paul Nash, who had worked at the Omega Workshops before the war and become known for his innovative war paintings for the Ministry of Information. Drawing was taught by Leon Underwood, who was also a carver and, as Hepworth praised, 'made one see in depth'.[7] His style of draughtsmanship conveyed volume and mass on the flat page with minimal but judiciously applied marks, and its influence can be seen in Hepworth's portrait of George Henry Butler (1922), made at Robin Hood's Bay the summer before her graduation (right).

While drawing remained a mainstay of all art education, Hepworth enrolled on the sculpture course and recalled, 'at the Royal College it was all a question of modelling from life. I would spend a whole term on half a figure.'[8] This academic manner of teaching is present in the photograph of Hepworth and her fellow students, surrounded by plaster casts of classical statues (see p. 24): identifiable to the left of the image is a *Dancing Faun* plaster, cast from an original bronze excavated in Pompeii in 1830. The practice of casting copies of classical statues was hugely popular in the Victorian era, which established the study of casts as an educational principle. Plaster could also be carved, and Hepworth's report from the Royal College of Art's 'School of Modelling. Upper Division' dated 25 June 1922 notes that she 'shows considerable talent – has made great progress in life work. Design good. Carving improving.'[9] Hepworth carved a relief in plaster of her cousins, Jill and Peggy Hepworth (1923), while staying with her uncle Arthur, a doctor, during her student years, using Plaster of Paris from his surgery to make the relief (opposite).[10]

At this time, the majority of sculpture made in England was modelled in clay and then given to a master craftsman to produce. The clay model would often be cast in plaster, and then the plaster cast would be used to make the final work in either stone or bronze. Bronze sculptures were made in a foundry, while stone sculptures were made using a 'pointing machine', a measuring device to make a copy of the model. As a text of 1895, *The Technique of Sculpture*, noted, 'the important projections and depressions are marked in this cast by metal pins, called points, and an ingenious device called the pointing machine makes it possible to mark the corresponding points in the block of marble. The marble is then cut away to all the points marked. The number of points may be very great, in which case the statue is nearly finished when all the points are reached. In fact, many sculptors of modern times are merely modellers. They send their models to the stone-cutter, who, with the help of the

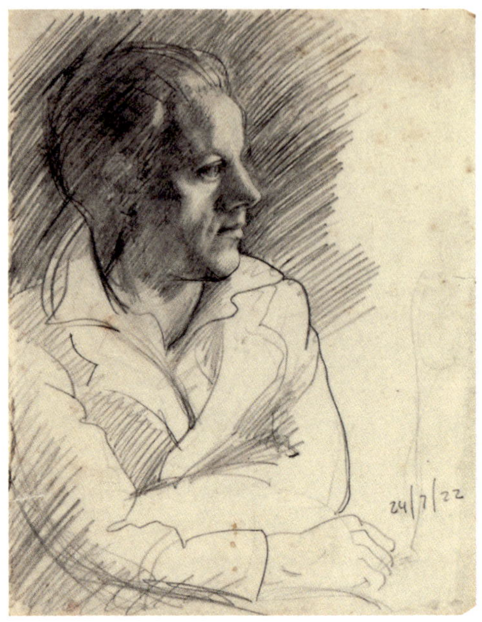

ABOVE Barbara Hepworth, *Portrait of George Henry Butler*, 1922, pencil on paper, 23 × 18 cm (9 × 7 in.)

pointing machine and other contrivances, makes an accurate copy. The more careful sculptors add the finishing touches themselves, but very few do any great amount of chiselling.'[11]

Despite her recollections, it is likely that Hepworth was taught some stone or wood carving as well as modelling. Both Leeds School of Art and the Royal College of Art had wood-carving programmes, although they were vocational courses under the umbrella of craft, and the Royal College's 1920–21 syllabus for the School of Sculpture included stone carving.[12] This reflected the rise in what was widely known post-war as 'direct carving'. Instead of modelling in clay and having the final work produced by a craftsman, the artist cut directly into stone or wood to make their sculptures, keeping complete control over the finished work. This approach was influenced by carved sculptures of non-Western civilisations, which Hepworth also encountered in London, most prominently in the British Museum. However, while at the Royal College, Hepworth's sculptural output adhered to the academic style, perhaps, as critic J. P. Hodin would later suggest, 'to keep her scholarship at all costs'. He continues: 'her personal style and direction of mind were formed more by discussing problems with her colleagues than by listening to her teachers, in the Common-room rather than in the sculpture class [...] In the

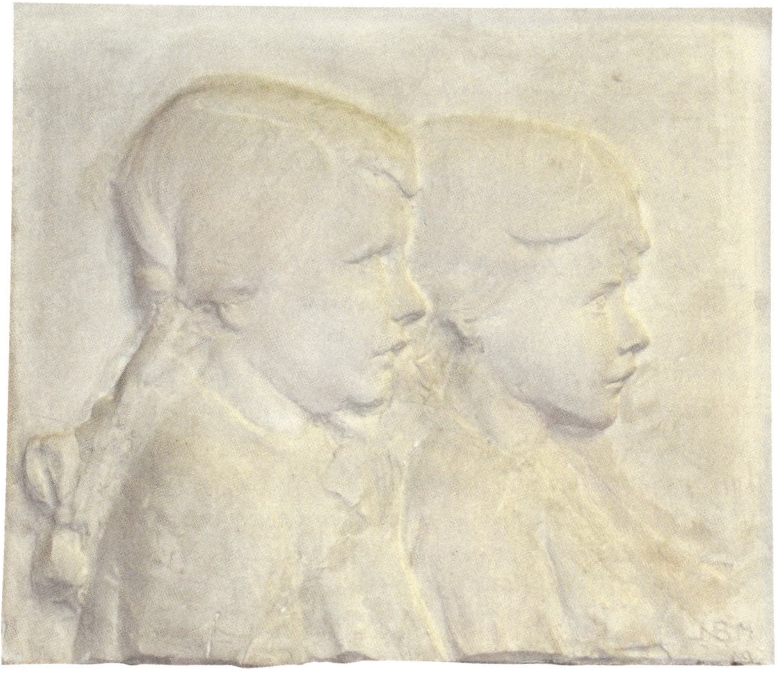

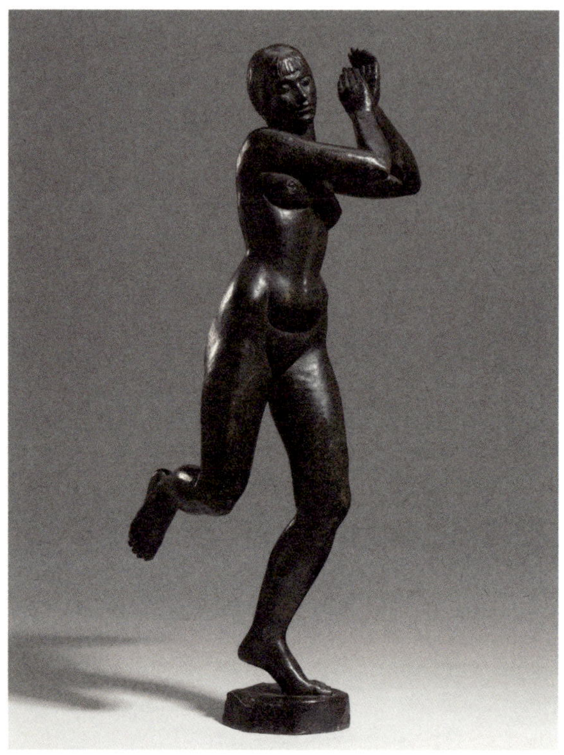

common room the *Cahiers d'art* were eagerly studied and Cubism was the great revelation [...] Paris was the centre of interest.'[13] Hepworth and her fellow students visited Paris several times, and a photograph from her student years shows her on the banks of the Seine alongside Moore and Edna Ginesi, another student who had moved from Leeds School of Art to the Royal College (opposite). The photo was most likely taken by Raymond Coxon, the fourth member of the 'Leeds table', as the quartet was known. Coxon remembers that Parisian outings would follow visits to public and commercial galleries, with free life-drawing classes at the Colarossi and Grande Chaumière academies. A series of figures that Hepworth modelled from life in clay around 1922–23 were subsequently cast in bronze in 1925 (see above).

Hepworth left the Royal College of Art in October 1924, having spent the previous year preparing for the Prix de Rome, an annual competition that afforded the winner two or three years of study in Italy, with lodgings at the British School in Rome and a stipend of £250 (some £15,000 today). Following the Open Examination in October 1923, Hepworth was shortlisted for the Final Competition the following year.

ABOVE Barbara Hepworth, *Venus (Figure II),* *c.* 1922–23 (cast 1925), bronze, height 52.7 cm (20¾ in.)

OPPOSITE Edna Ginesi, Henry Moore and Barbara Hepworth in Paris, 1922 or 1923

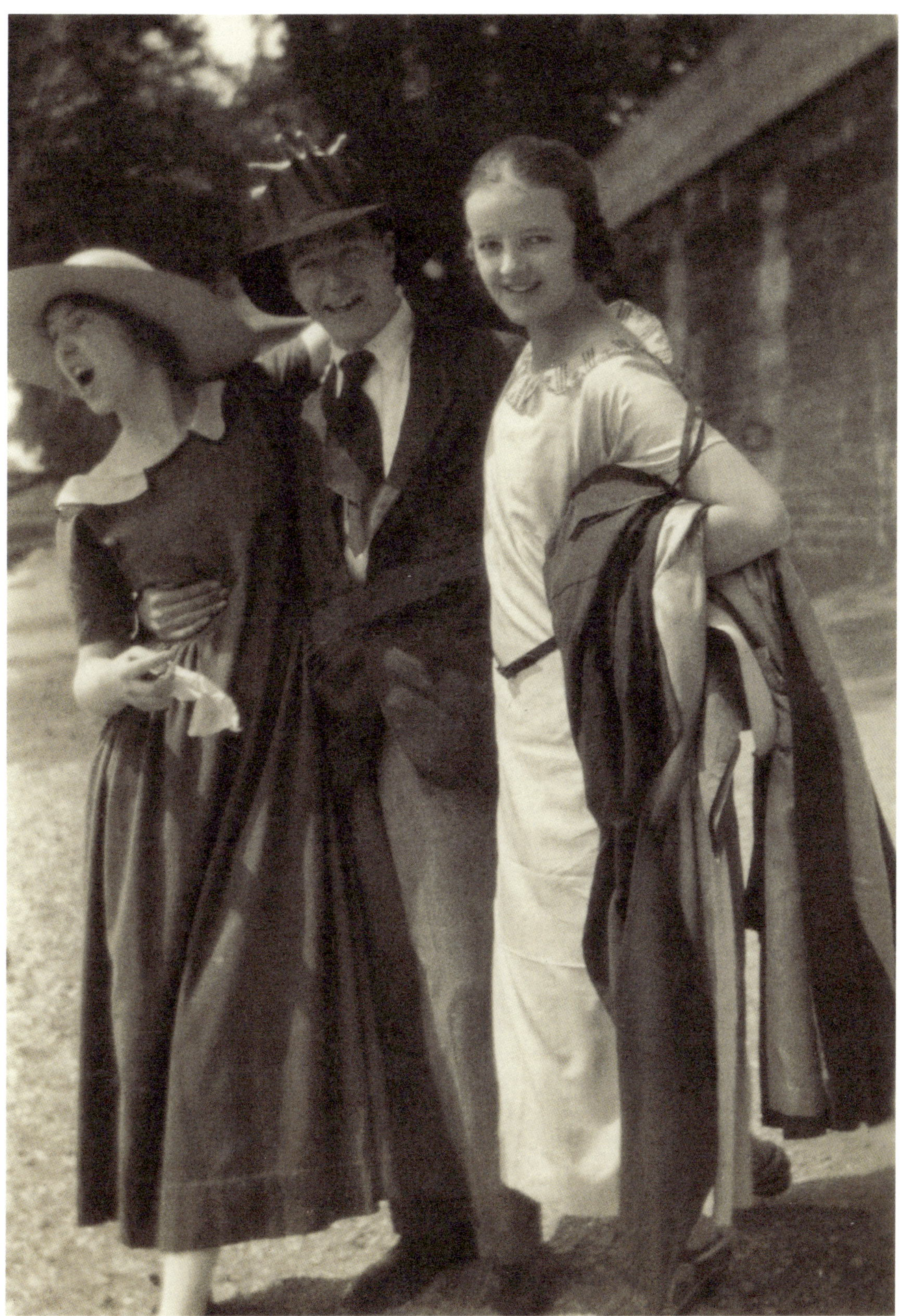

She exhibited 'a finely executed frieze and four strong figure drawings in pencil' alongside the other finalists in the competition's Royal Academy exhibition in February 1924.[14] The applicants had to make a sculpture to given specifications: 'a panel in high relief 5' × 3' for a hospital entrance', modelled in clay and then cast in plaster, to be suitable for bronze casting.[15] A glimpse of Hepworth's entry can be seen behind the backing screen in a full-length portrait from the mid-1920s (below), showing the bare chest of a man with his head turned in profile, drapery hanging over

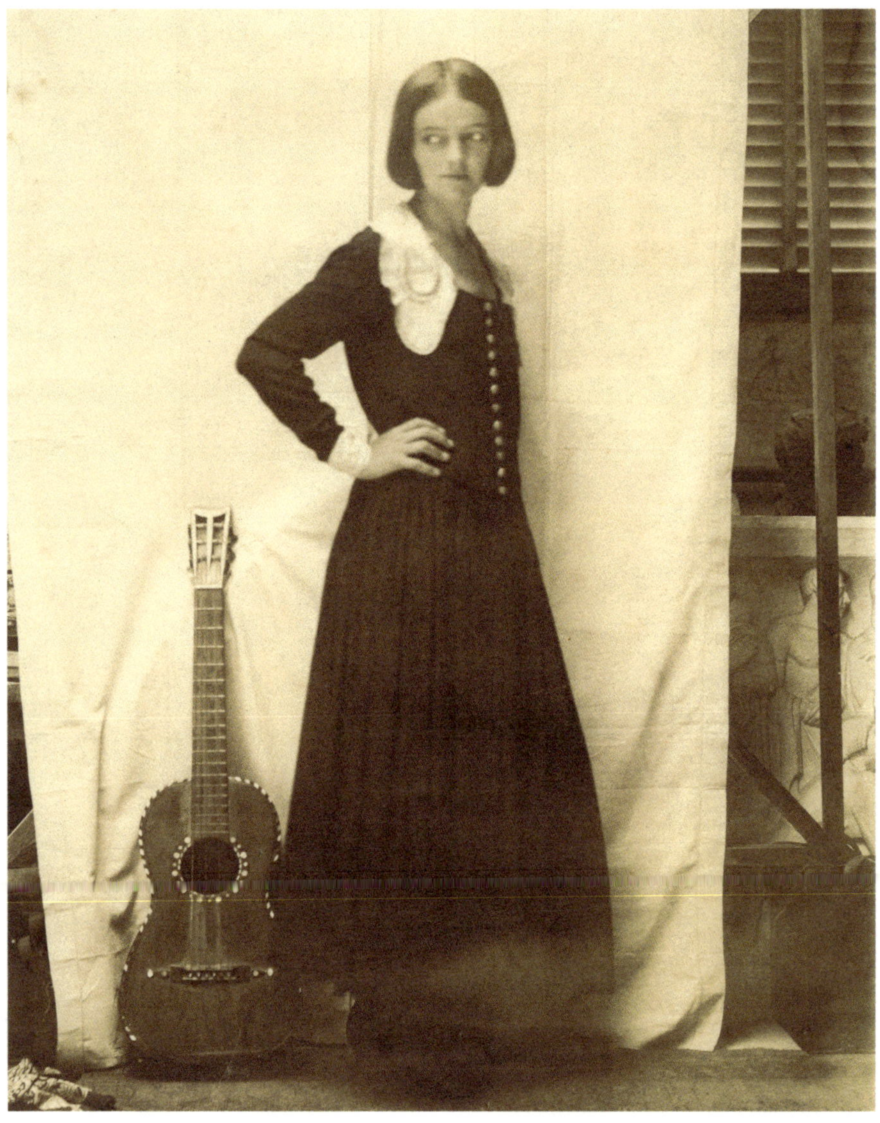

ABOVE Barbara Hepworth in the mid-1920s, with her Prix de Rome scholarship relief in the background

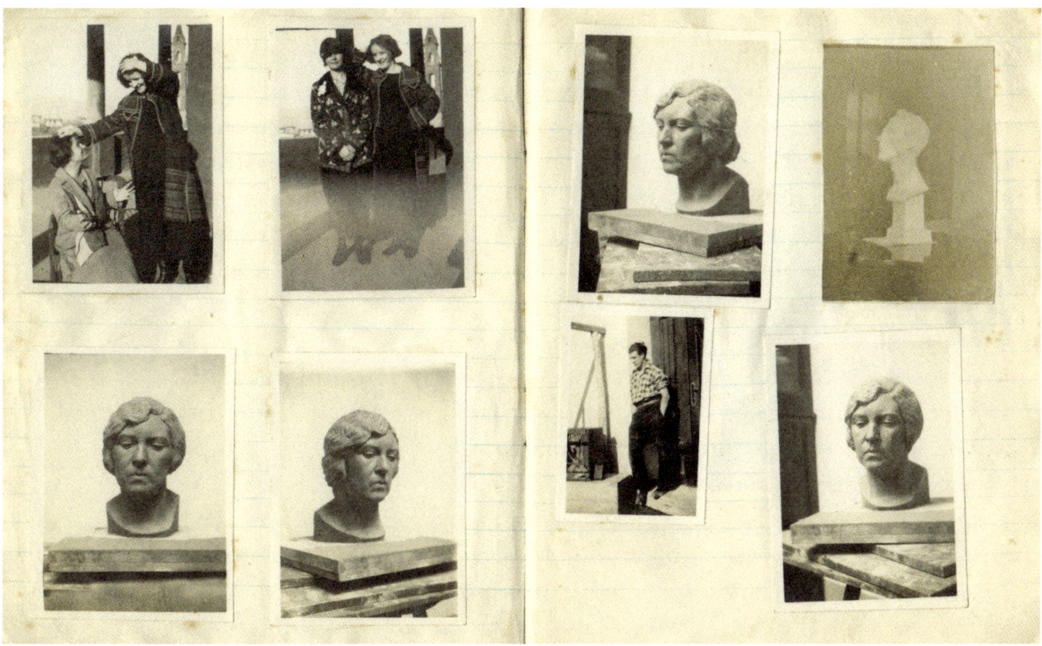

his arm. This formed part of an intricate composition of ten overlapping, draped figures surrounding a central, bare-chested, haloed Jesus Christ. The complex composition showcased Hepworth's masterful grasp of anatomical representation and modelling, alongside impressive technical abilities in depicting drapery. Despite these qualities, and a headline in *The Daily Chronicle* praising, in qualified terms, 'British Woman's Fine Sculpture',[16] the prize went to John Skeaping, a recent graduate from the Royal Academy.

Hepworth was, however, granted a West Riding Scholarship for one year's travel, which she decided to use to go to Italy, embarking on what she described in 1952 as her 'most formative year by far':

There had been something lacking in my childhood in Yorkshire, and that was light. In my early experiences the sun never shone enough, the atmosphere rarely cleared, shadows were never sharp, surfaces never brilliant. Italy opened for me the wonderful realm of light – light which transforms and reveals, which intensifies the subtleties of form and contours and colour, and in which darkness – the darkness of window, door or arch – is set as an altogether new and tangible object.[17]

ABOVE Photographs of Barbara Hepworth with Mrs Richards in Florence, winter 1924–25, and the clay original *Head of Mrs A.R.T. Richards (Quita)*, c. 1924–25, from Hepworth's mother's photograph album

Hepworth arrived in Florence in the autumn of 1924, and spent her first months studying Romanesque and early Renaissance art and architecture in Tuscany, with a short visit to Rome in November. The couple she was staying with, Mrs A. R. T. ('Quita') and Captain Richards, offered her one of her earliest commissions, to sculpt a portrait bust of Quita (see previous page). As Hepworth recalled, 'I worked the head in clay, and then the process of casting is to make moulds and make a plaster replica within the mould, which is then used to make the bronze.'[18] The bust is a somewhat dour, although impressively physically accurate, representation of a lively character, and photographs of Quita and Hepworth together convey a convivial relationship between the two. In Rome she had met with her former competitor John Skeaping, and in early 1925 the two travelled together through the Tuscan countryside to Siena. Photographs from this trip reflect Hepworth's fascination with the Italian architecture and its shadowy interplay with the Mediterranean light (see below). They also document the burgeoning romance between the two sculptors, who shared a love of animals, dancing and music, alongside, perhaps most powerfully, 'the same philosophy of life and art'.[19] Having known each other for only six months, Hepworth and Skeaping were married at the Palazzo Vecchio, Florence, in May 1925.

Hepworth joined Skeaping at the British School in Rome. The Prix de Rome afforded Skeaping free lodgings, and under the new Director of the British School, Bernard Ashmole, the rules had just been changed to allow prize winners to bring their spouses. A photograph from this time shows Hepworth and Skeaping in high spirits outside the British School, where they shared a large studio in which they kept doves (opposite, left). Hepworth's drawn studies of Skeaping show her continuing commitment to her art practice (see opposite, right). The incorporation of increasing light and shade into her drawing technique was achieved through use of crayon, chalk and charcoal to render every contour and volume of Skeaping's face. In addition to advancing her drawing practice, Hepworth credited her time in Italy with

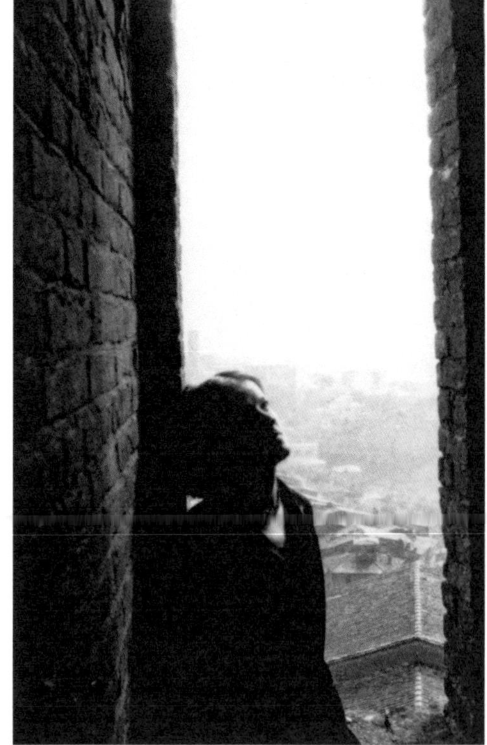

ABOVE Barbara Hepworth in Siena, 1924

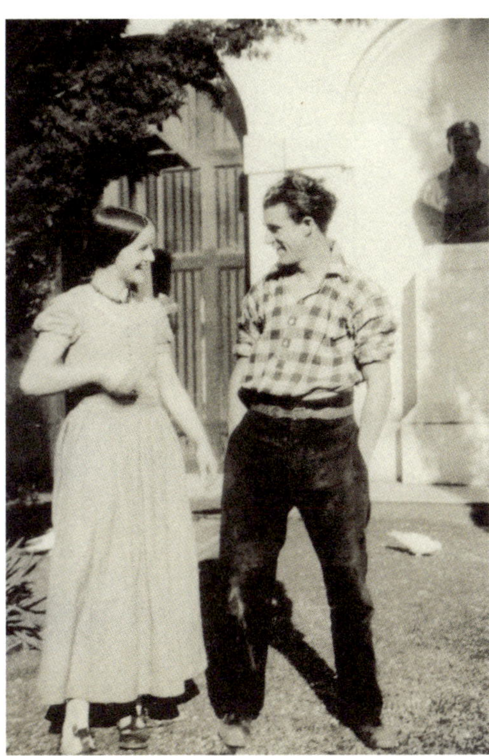

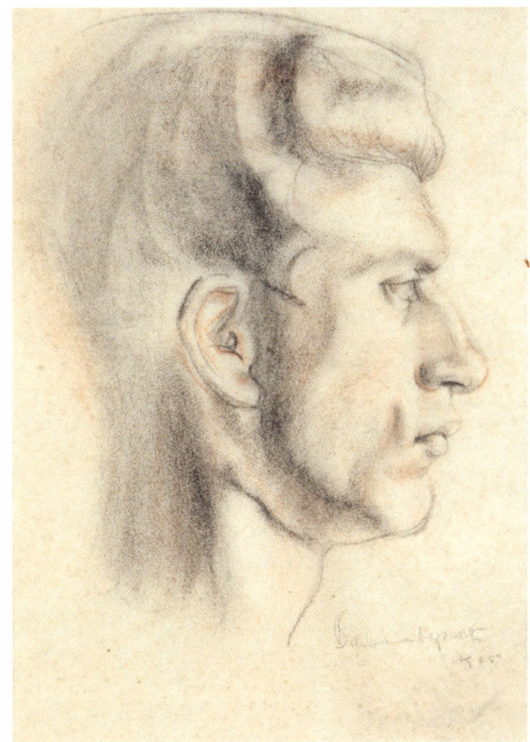

providing her most significant introduction to stone carving, and a life-
long love of marble. Skeaping had been training with a marble craftsman
called Giovanni Ardini, and through Skeaping's translations, as Hepworth
spoke little Italian and Ardini no English, Hepworth became fascinated
with the process of carving. A particular phrase resonated years later:
the fact 'that "marble changes colour under different people's hands"
made me decide immediately that it was not dominance which one had
to attain over material, but an understanding, almost a kind of persua-
sion, and above all greater coordination between head and hand'.[20] The
communication between head and hand, thought and physical material,
would become a central tenet of Hepworth's artistic practice. Her first
carvings from *c.* 1925–26 were of doves, capturing in static form the lively
birds from her Rome studio. Although since destroyed, they were obviously
of great significance to Hepworth as, when compiling a complete record
of her sculpture in later life, these carvings are listed as her first works.

ABOVE LEFT Barbara Hepworth with John
Skeaping at the British School in Rome,
c. 1925–26

ABOVE RIGHT Barbara Hepworth, *Portrait of
a Man in Profile [John Skeaping]*, 1925, crayon
on paper, 33.5 × 23.5 cm (13⅛ × 9¼ in.)

Chapter 3

Material
Harmony

Hepworth and Skeaping returned to London in November 1926. They lived at first in the basement flat of a house owned by their friend, the writer Leo Walmsley, in St Ann's Terrace, St John's Wood. Walmsley described it as 'three rooms, one of which gave on to what originally would have been the garden. Some tenant however had built this over to make a billiard-room with a top light. The Skeapings had the basement rooms to live in, and the billiard-room was their studio.'[1] The skylight offered the natural light that Hepworth found so crucial; and the couple also built an aviary that ran down one side of the studio to keep an array of birds, including budgerigars, canaries and doves. Hepworth and Skeaping continued the practice of direct carving, and were by no means alone in this endeavour. In Britain, sculptors including Jacob Epstein and Henri Gaudier-Brzeska had pioneered the practice before the war, inspired as Hepworth was by the forms of carvings from a range of non-Western civilisations. Artists could view carvings from Africa, Central America, China and more, first-hand, in London's encyclopaedic museums such as the British Museum and the Victoria and Albert Museum (V&A), enabled by the British Empire's enthusiasm for exhibiting the visual cultures of the people it colonised. By the mid-1920s, the once avant-garde practice of direct carving had steadily become more mainstream: critic Kineton Parkes referred to it in his book *Sculpture of To-day* as early as 1921,[2] Epstein was commissioned to carve the monumental public sculpture *Memorial to W. H. Hudson (Rima)* in London's Hyde Park in 1922, and 1926 saw a wood carving exhibited in the annual Royal Academy exhibition – once seen as the bastion of conservatism – and acquired by the Tate.[3]

Hepworth and Skeaping needed to find collectors to buy their work and support their careers, and, as young artists without the backing of a commercial gallery, they took the initiative and held a studio exhibition at their flat in 1927. It was nearly a disaster: Hepworth recalled, 'nobody came until the fourteenth day', but 'then Richard Bedford of the Victoria and Albert Museum brought the late George Eumorfopoulos who bought about three works from each of us'.[4] Bedford had worked at the V&A since 1911, and was both a carver and an academic. In a 1928 article, 'Chinese Animal Sculpture', he acknowledged these specific works, and carvings of non-Western cultures more generally, as 'possible sources of inspiration for modern artists'.[5] This close connection was reflected in the collecting circle who supported Hepworth and Skeaping in these early years. Eumorfopoulos was a collector of Chinese, Korean and Near Eastern art, who co-founded the Oriental Ceramic Society in 1921, and whose collection became part of the V&A and the British Museum's holdings in the mid-1930s. He also collected the work of modern carvers such as Henri Gaudier-Brzeska and Leon Underwood, Hepworth and Moore's former drawing master. Other early buyers of their work included George Hill and Laurence Binyon, who both worked at the British Museum.

Perhaps buoyed by these sales, Hepworth and Skeaping moved from their basement flat into 7, The Mall Studios in Hampstead in January 1928. The studios had been designed for 'gentlemen artists' living in the adjacent Parkhill Road, and each comprised a small waiting room, 'costume rooms' and a lobby, in addition to the open studio.[6] Crucially for Hepworth, they each had three skylights and large north-facing windows, providing consistent and plentiful natural light. Her next exhibition was held in June 1928 at Beaux Arts Gallery, with Skeaping and engraver William Morgan, who was also a Prix de Rome winner. This gathering of Prix de Rome winners and finalists appealed to the press: as *The Times*'s critic wrote, it 'gives to the exhibition a circum-stantial importance, as it undoubtedly accounts for certain affinities in the work, of classic firmness and purity'.[7] The classical Roman art that Hepworth had encountered in Italy, supplementing her academic training at the Royal College, could also be found in the plaster courts of the V&A and in the permanent display of sculptures from Athens's *Parthenon* in the British Museum. Several armless and headless torsos at Beaux Arts Gallery, such as *Torso* (1927), carved in Irish fossil marble, showed these classical and academic influences.[8] Of Hepworth's thirteen sculptures, two were busts cast in bronze, while the others were carv-ings in an array of precisely designated materials – from 'pale Sienna Marble' [*sic*] to 'Mexican White Onyx' and the 'Pentelicon Marble' of *Mask* (1928; opposite). The array of sculptural material was commented upon in the press, with *The Times* also noting Hepworth's particular sen-sitivity to the materials of her sculptures, suggesting that 'most of her carvings are designed within the cubical – or cuboid – mass as if they had been "found" in it'.[9] Hepworth recalled in 1952 that 'at this time all the carvings were an effort to find a personal accord with the stones or wood which I was carving. I was fascinated by the new problem which arose out of each sculpture, and by the kind of form that grew out of achieving a personal harmony with the material.'[10]

The subjects Hepworth 'found' within these materials were all representational and drawn from nature – either figurative studies such as torsos or busts, sometimes designated as dancers or musicians, or dif-ferent types of birds. *The Sphere* newspaper illustrated two of Hepworth's works from the Beaux Arts Gallery under the headline 'Life Created from

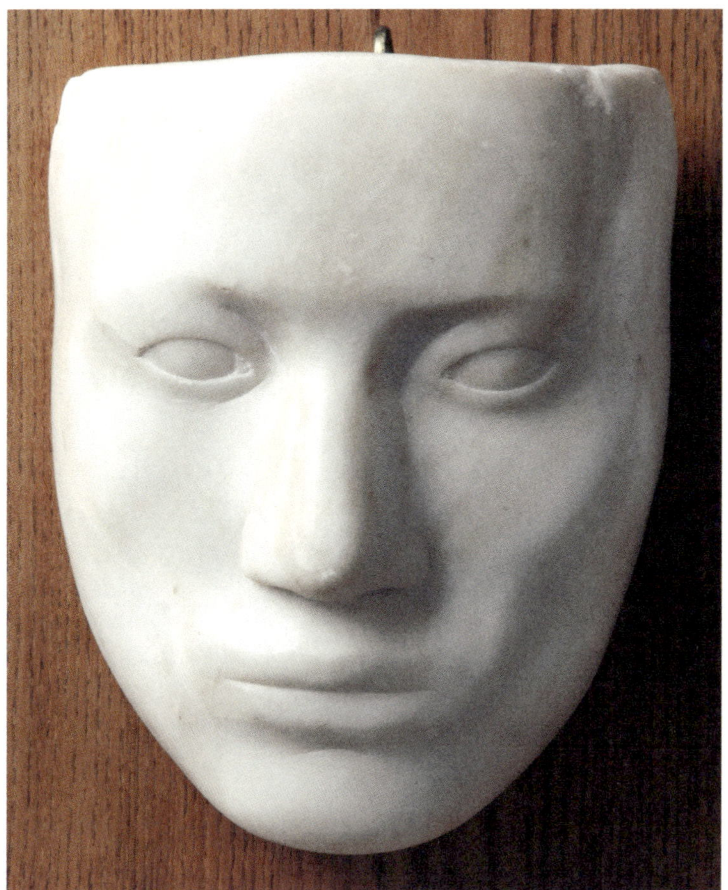

Lifeless Stone', but for Hepworth the material did have a life of its own, the finished subject arising through the process of carving, a metaphorical conversation between artist and material. Her aesthetic interests are also visible in her drawings of this time, and ten largely figurative drawings were exhibited alongside her sculpture at the Beaux Arts Gallery.[11] Works such as *Standing Girl* (1928) and *Crouching Nude Woman* (1929; see following page) offer a sculptor's view of the human body, depicting volumes through line, light and shade. The variety of poses convey movement, the figure folding into a kneel or shifting weight from one leg to another.

The Beaux Arts Gallery exhibition was a commercial as well as critical success. Skeaping recalled, 'the exhibition was a sell-out',[12] and a second show with Morgan and Skeaping was held at Alex Reid & Lefevre Ltd (known as the Lefevre Gallery) in September 1928. Hepworth

ABOVE Barbara Hepworth, *Mask*, 1928, Pentelicon marble, 22 × 17 × 7 cm (8⅝ × 6⅝ × 2¾ in.)

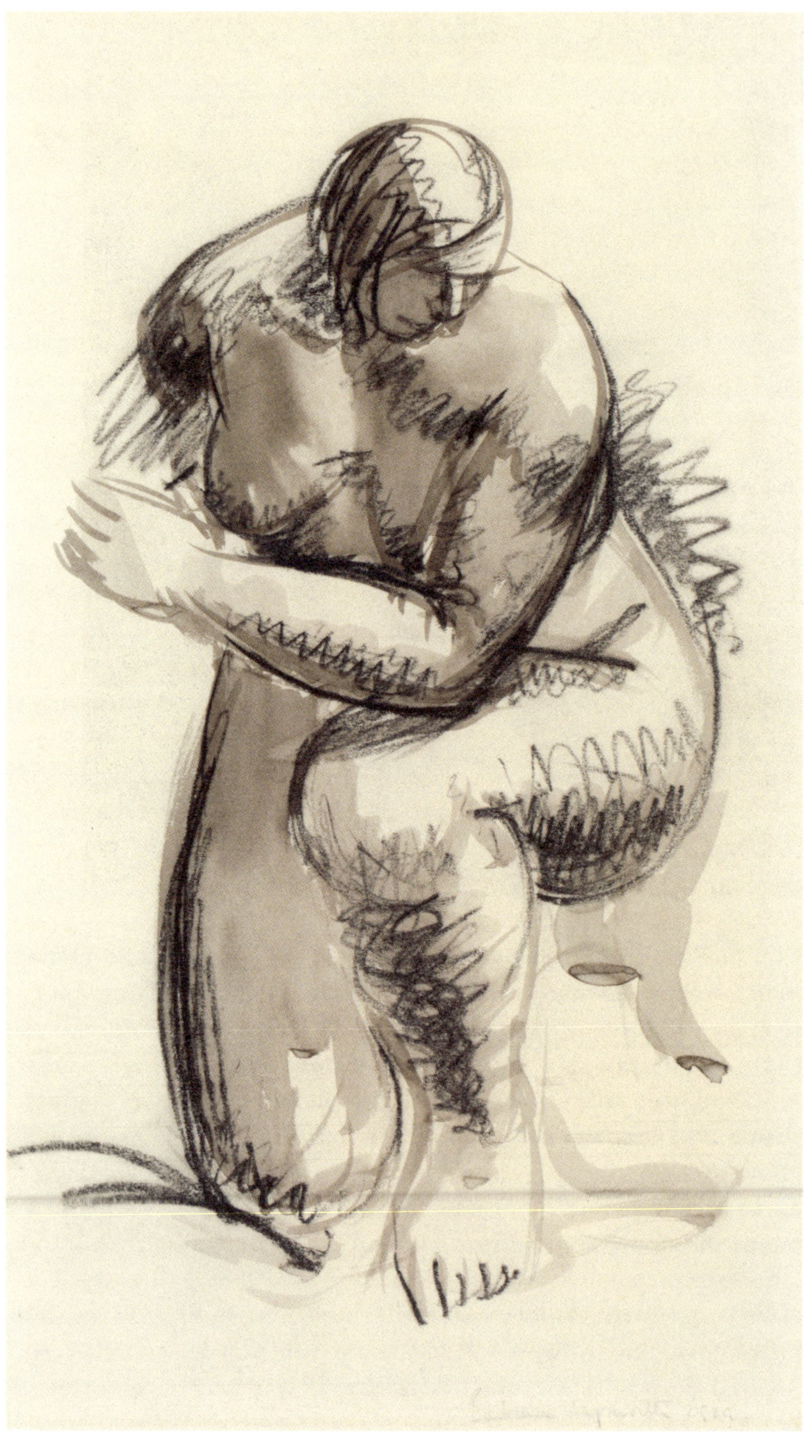

ABOVE Barbara Hepworth, *Figure Study of
a Crouching Nude Woman*, 1929, charcoal
and wash, 43.8 × 25.4 cm (17¼ × 10 in.)

continued to exhibit carvings in group exhibitions, and was included alongside Epstein and Skeaping in *Modern and African Art* at Sydney Burney Gallery in November 1928. The show emphasised formal connections between European and African sculpture, a review in *The Times* lamenting the 'confessed imitation' of the latter by the former, but noting 'what the exhibition really brings out is the traditional character of all good sculpture, independent of place and period', particularly praising Hepworth and Skeaping.[13]

As her reputation grew, so did her family with Skeaping; their son Paul was born on 3 August 1929. Hepworth remembered this as 'a wonderfully happy time. My son Paul was born and, with him in his cot, or on a rug at my feet, my carving developed and strengthened.'[14] Employing a nanny to assist with childcare, she continued to live and work in 7, The Mall Studios, where she was in close contact with other modern artists. Painter Cecil Stephenson, who had also studied at Leeds School of Art and the Royal College, moved into No. 5 in 1919 and lived there until 1965. In 1929, Hepworth helped find a nearby studio for Henry Moore and his wife Irina, who had also studied at the Royal College, and the two artist couples would often hire a model for an evening of life drawing.[15] They also holidayed together, the Skeapings, the Moores and painter Ivon Hitchens captured in photographs taken in Norfolk in the early 1930s (see following page). Hitchens had been a founding member of progressive exhibiting society The Seven & Five in 1920 alongside Underwood, and Hepworth, Moore and Skeaping were elected to the group in 1931. Hepworth wrote of Happisburgh, where they stayed in Norfolk, 'the country is quite flat but for a little hill with a tall flint church and a lighthouse. The trees are all bowed to west and birds seem to dominate all. I feel as though I too have wings on such flat earth. The beach is a ribbon of pale sand as far as the eye can see.'[16] Her sensitivity to the visual impressions of landscape, and the sensations of being within it, remained with her from her time in Yorkshire and Italy.

Hepworth and Skeaping continued to be exhibited as a husband and wife duo, a useful tool for garnering press interest, and they negotiated a joint contract with Arthur Tooth & Sons Galleries.[17] A press clipping accompanies an image of Hepworth carving, with the caption, 'Mrs. J. R. Skeaping, who with her husband is shortly holding an exhibition of carving in rare stone, at work in their studio', promoting their joint exhibition at Arthur Tooth & Sons in October 1930. Featuring 'sixteen remarkable works' by Hepworth, the show drew strong praise from *The Sunday Times*'s art critic Frank Rutter, who stated that the exhibition:

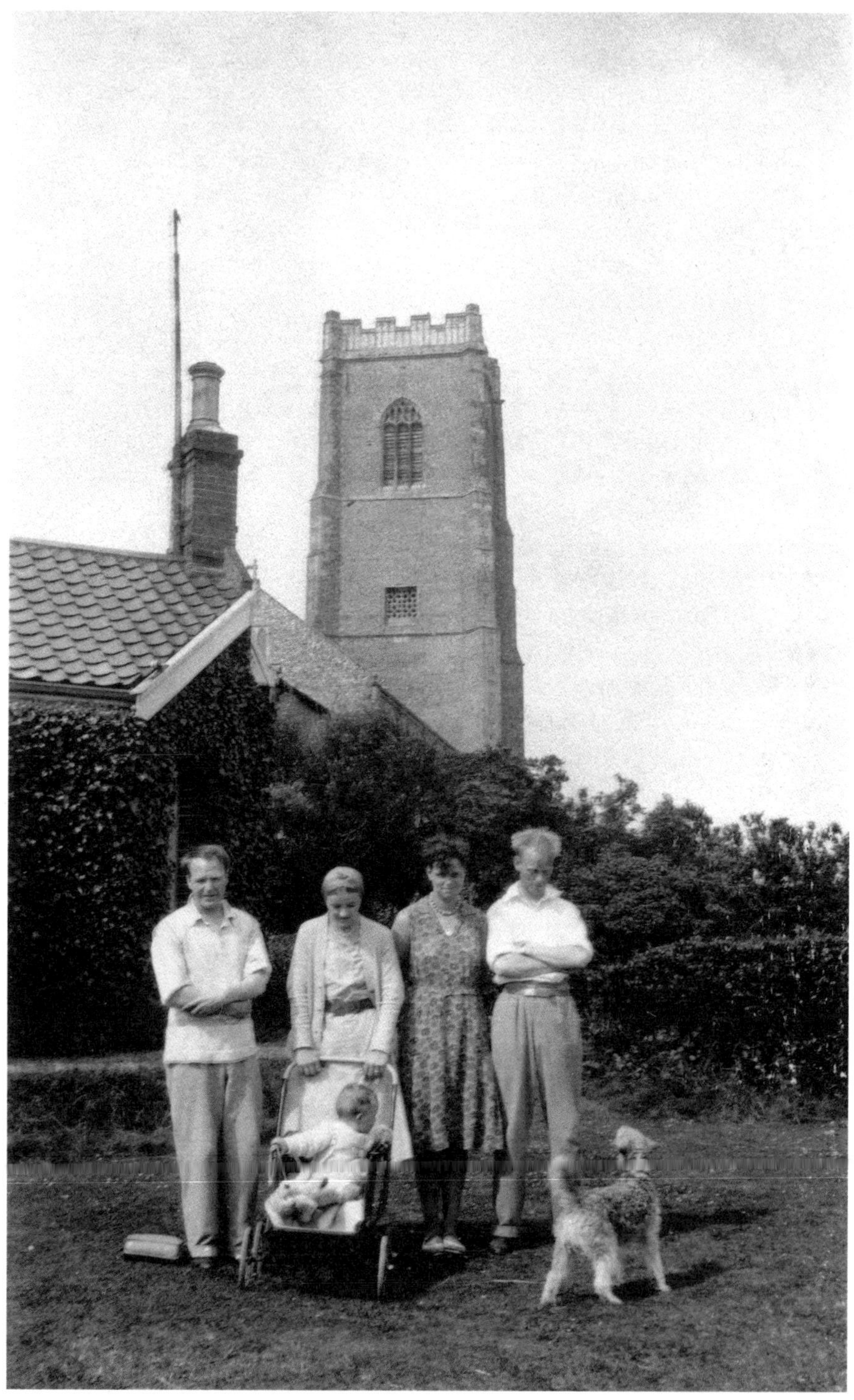

ABOVE Barbara Hepworth at Happisburgh, Norfolk, with Henry Moore (left) and Paul Skeaping in pram, 1930. The figure on the far right may be Ivon Hitchens.

[...] establishes the reputations of John Skeaping and his wife, Barbara Hepworth, as two of the most important young sculptors, most interesting artists, and finest craftsmen of the time [...] The Skeapings are carvers, not modellers. Their technical accomplishment is such that they can handle with complete success a great many different and most recalcitrant kinds of material [...] One peculiarly sculptural virtue both these artists possess is that they never allow themselves to lose sight of the special qualities of the material on which they are at work [...] Moreover, the material itself is frequently allowed by each of them to suggest the actual form the finished work of art will take. Reversing the usual procedure – that of imposing a shape on a piece of raw material – they allow the shape which to their sculptor's minds lies inherent in every block of stone or piece of wood to assert itself [...] A true marriage between material and concept results in a very satisfying and subtle harmony of line and form.[18]

This exhibition included Hepworth's first carvings in wood, after several years of solely working in stone.[19] The particular wood she used distinguished her practice from amateur wood-carving, a popular hobby among middle-class women at the time.[20] The wood carvings Hepworth exhibited in 1930 were in pinkardo, African ivory wood, teak, Burmese wood and ebony, all extremely hard woods, requiring, as Rutter noted, significant technical skill and strength to carve, as distinct from softer woods like pine that were associated with female hobbyists.

Elements of Rutter's review chimed with Hepworth's own thoughts on carving. Earlier in the year, in a series titled 'Contemporary English Sculptors' in *The Architectural Association Journal*, Hepworth had written of the symbiotic relationship between material and concept afforded by carving. Celebrating the 'unlimited variety of materials from which to draw inspiration', she noted that such a diversity meant that 'it would be possible to carve the same subject in a different stone each time, throughout life, without a repetition of form'.[21] The emphasis on the form inherent within the materials must be considered alongside the artistic choices Hepworth made – both the chosen subjects that she 'found' within the material, and the way these were portrayed. The sculptures shown at Tooth's again depicted figures and animals, although in increasingly abstracted form. Hepworth's thoughts on representation and abstraction, and their expression in sculptural form, were also articulated in the journal:

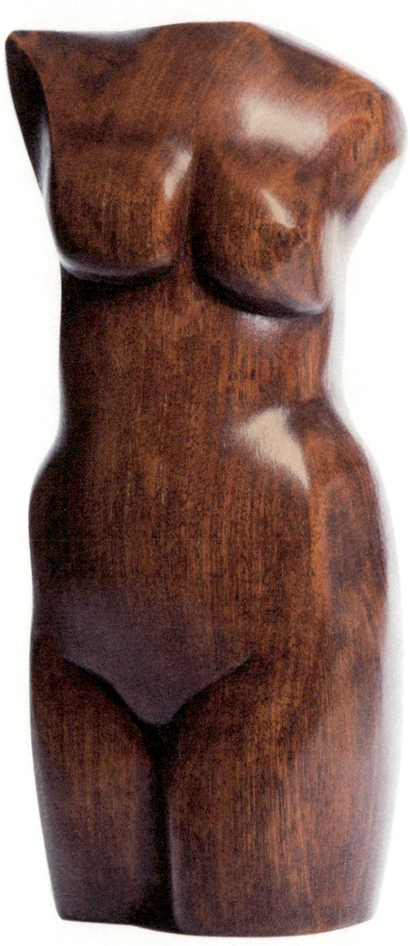

*There are, however, degrees between pure representation and
the abstract. Generalisation, by which I mean an accumulative
assertion of the emotion of a thing, is nearer to the abstract
than particularisation which is a faithful portrayal of an
individual object.*

*My trend is towards generalisation; but I have not dispensed
with representation entirely; as I find that it is possible to take a
pebble of fine and simple shape and carve in addition a sequence
of planes suggestive of the human form, thus giving it an added
significance of emotional value.*[22]

ABOVE Barbara Hepworth, *Torso*, 1929,
pinkardo wood, height 36.5 cm (14⅜ in.)

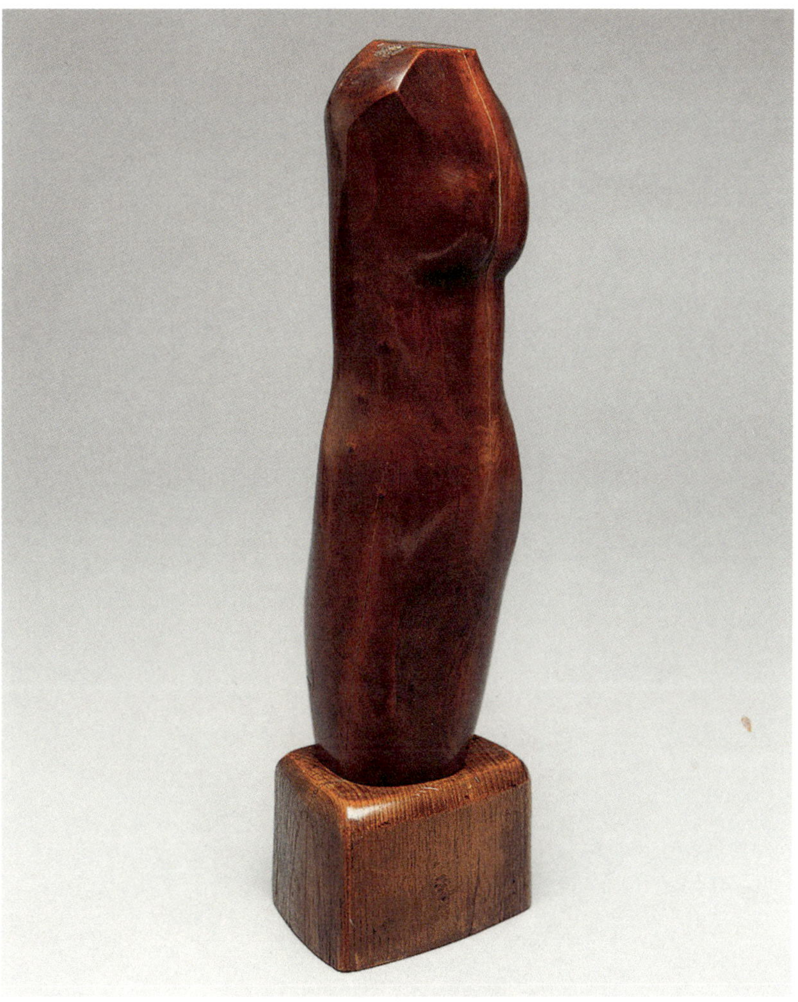

Two torsos from 1929 exhibited at Tooth's, numbers 43 and 44 in the catalogue, exemplify this trend towards generalisation (opposite and above). Again armless and headless, both figures are stripped of details that would identify them as particular individuals; instead, they are presented as a universal human form. They exemplify the process that Hepworth outlines of observing the natural form of the material – in this case, the vertical of a tree trunk – and rendering it human through considered, minimal, carved interventions. In the first torso, this includes the outline of breasts, waist, pelvis and legs, while the second's undulating curves read as breasts from the front, but a simple organic column from the back.

ABOVE Barbara Hepworth, *Torso*, 1929, African
ivory wood, 42 × 11.5 × 10 cm (16½ × 4½ × 4 in.)

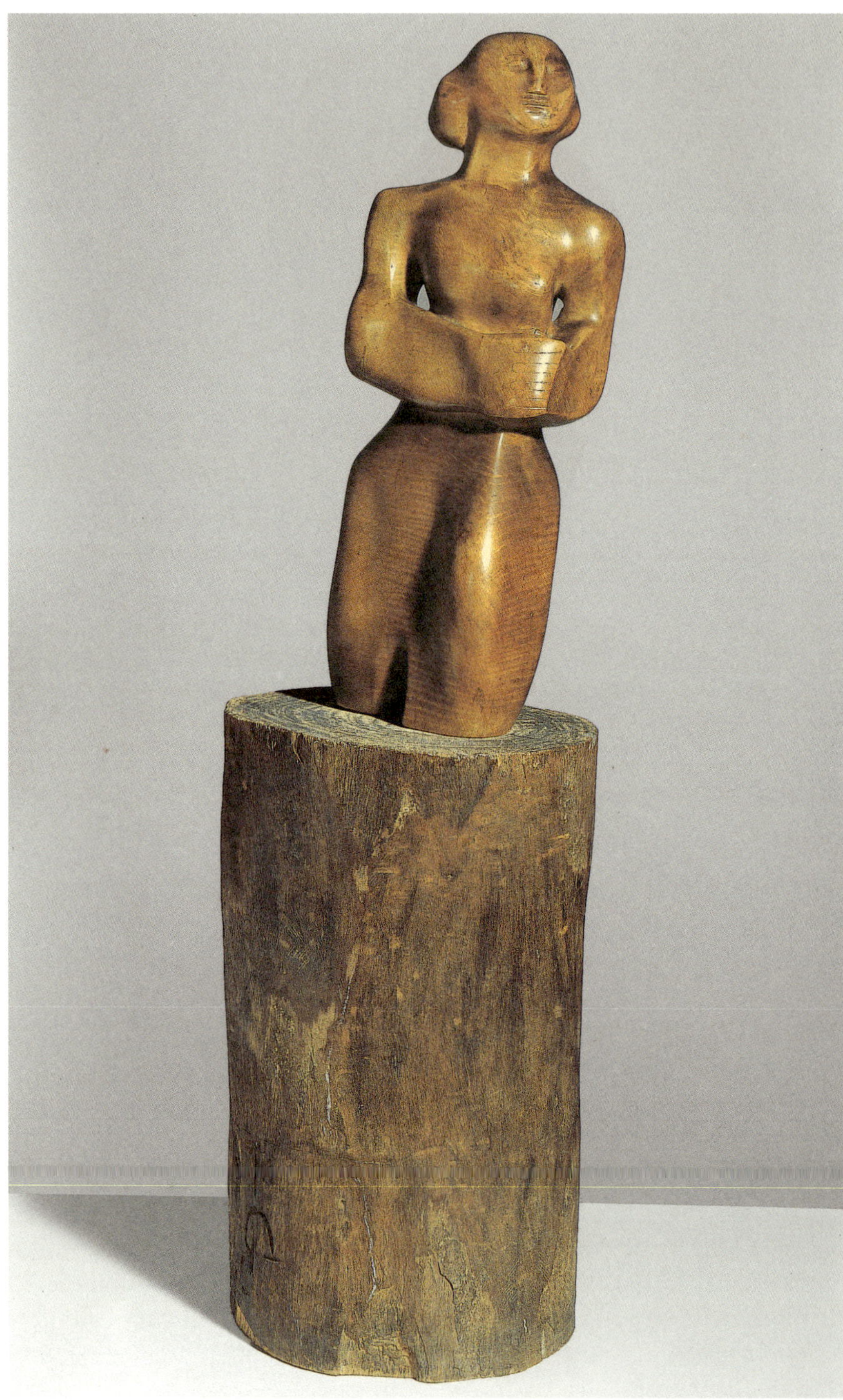

ABOVE Barbara Hepworth, *Figure
in Sycamore*, 1931, sycamore,
118 × 33 × 33 cm (46⅜ × 13 × 13 in.)

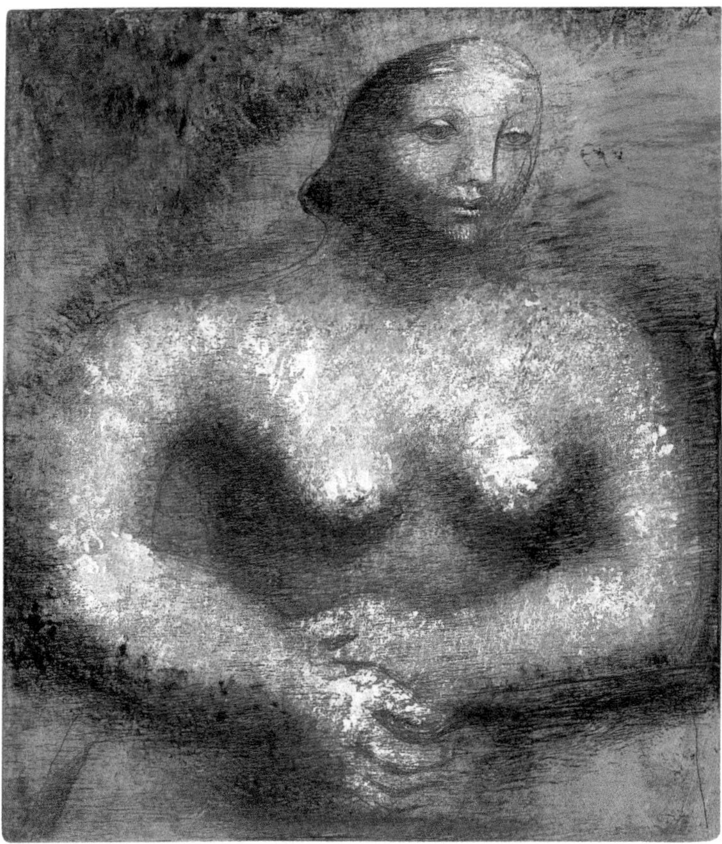

Figure (1929–30) (above) shows the development of Hepworth's figurative work in two dimensions beyond life drawing, perhaps also part of this trend toward generalisation. Unusually for this period she used oil paint alongside pencil on board, the thickness of the paint giving additional depth to the volumes of a figure with clasped hands that emerges from a darkly ethereal ground. The painting bears a striking resemblance to several carvings of this time, suggesting that Hepworth worked through ideas in both two and three dimensions concurrently.[23] It is a peculiarly sculptural drawing, as emphasis is placed on the absences around the figure – the holes between the torso and the arms that would be crucial in carving a figure. When one looks at the most closely associated carving, *Figure in Sycamore* (1931) (opposite), the importance of these absences to the design of the three-dimensional form is even clearer. The base of the sculpture – nearly the same height as the figure itself – is left as a tree trunk, rough and darkly solid, making the lines and elegant form

ABOVE Barbara Hepworth, *Figure*, 1929–30, oil and pencil on board, 30.5 × 26 cm (12 × 10¼ in.)

of the figure above seem more delicate in contrast. This juxtaposition highlights the polished contours, twist and lean of the standing figure, light shining through the spaces under the arms. That the form of the figure emerged from the shadows in an earlier painting suggests that Hepworth was thinking of this subject before she began to carve the wood. Separating idea from material moved away from the notion that the sculptural material dictated the form of the sculpture, giving greater priority to Hepworth's artistic agency. For Hepworth, this separation occurred with the work *Head* (1930) (see right). As she later acknowledged, 'The Head carved in 1930 expressed that feeling of freedom, and a new period began in which my idea formed independently of the block. I wanted to break down the accepted order and rebuild and make my own order.'[24]

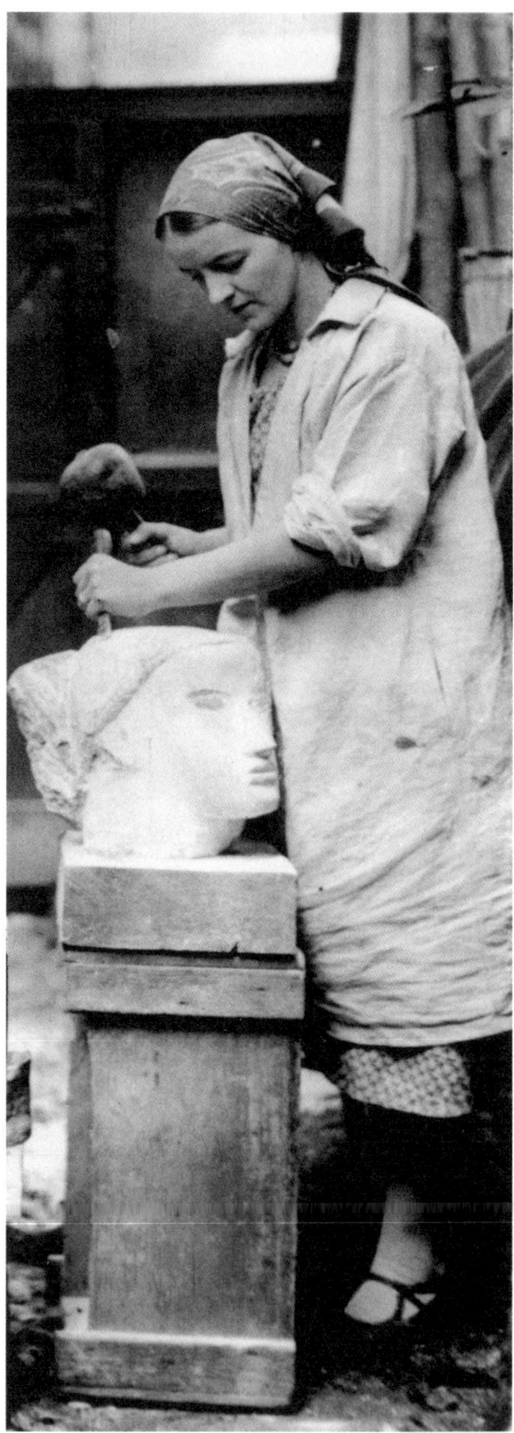

ABOVE Barbara Hepworth carving *Head*, 1930

A New Order

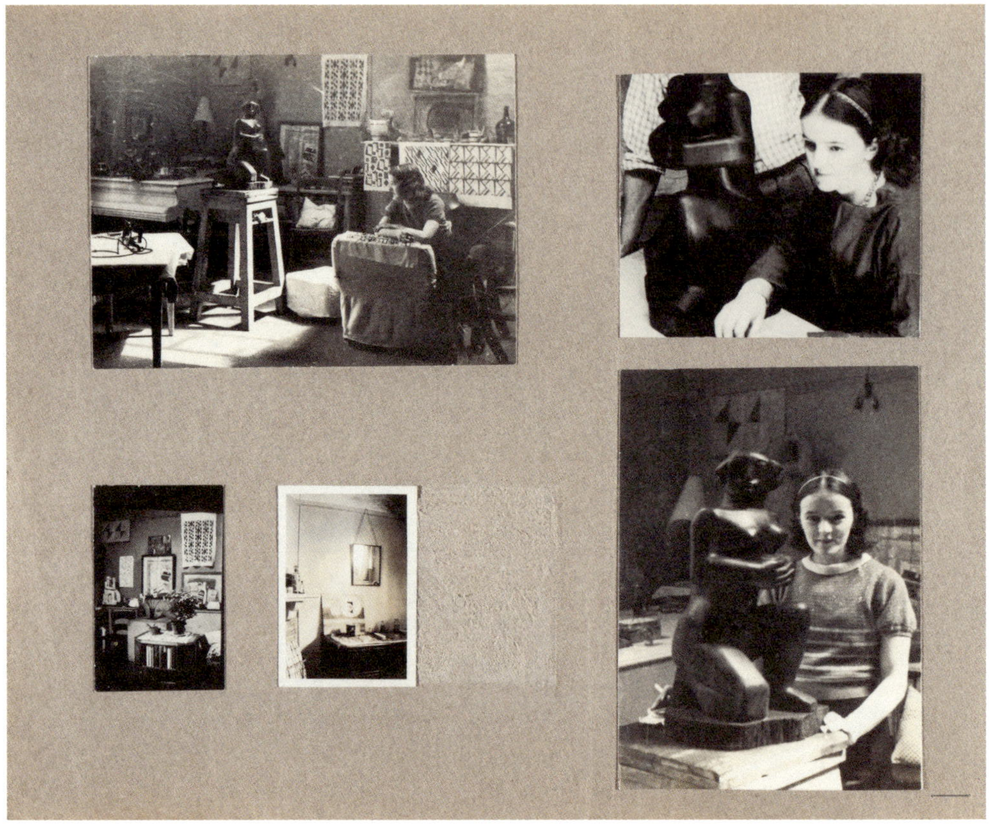

The early 1930s were a period of considerable change for Hepworth. Her marriage with John Skeaping broke down and she began a relationship with another artist, Ben Nicholson, with whom she shared a studio for most of the decade. Photographs of their joint living and working space (see above) hint at the multitude of mutual concerns and influences that shaped Hepworth's life and work during this period, from spirituality to the Parisian avant-garde, disintegrating the boundaries between sculpture and painting, fine art and other disciplines, and indeed between art and life. Mid-way through the decade she would write, 'I think the thing to work at is that work & living is the same thing [...] All is one movement'.[1]

In September 1931, Hepworth returned to Happisburgh with Skeaping, Ivon Hitchens, the Moores, and Skeaping's friends Douglas and Mary Jenkins, and wrote to Nicholson inviting him to join them: 'the Moores and ourselves should be so pleased if you came'.[2] She and Skeaping had only met Nicholson earlier that year, although he and his wife Winifred had been integral to Britain's contemporary art scene

ABOVE A page from Ben Nicholson's photograph album of the 1930s, showing the interior of 7, The Mall Studios, London

throughout the 1920s, exhibiting as part of The Seven & Five at the same galleries as Hepworth.[3] In January 1931, the Nicholsons exhibited with the group at the Leicester Galleries alongside Skeaping, who showed work as a non-member, and in April the four artists spent an evening together at 7, The Mall Studios. As well as being part of the same modernist milieu as Hepworth and Skeaping, the Nicholsons also had small children, their second child Kate born just a month before Paul. Hepworth was clearly struck by meeting both artists, writing to Ben, 'it has been wonderful meeting you and Winifred and the children. We have felt as though something momentous happened the last few weeks and a feeling of Power.'[4] The capitalisation alludes to another common interest – their shared faith in Christian Science, where this terminology refers to the transcendental force of the divine Mind. Ben had first encountered Christian Science in 1918 and had written enthusiastically about it to his mother.[5] Winifred was also a fervent Christian Science practitioner, attributing both the conception of their first child in 1926 and her recovery from a serious fall in 1927 to the power of Christian Science thought.[6] Hepworth had kept her faith into early adulthood, recording her name and the date 1924 in a pocket-sized edition of the central text *Science and Health*, and inscribing a copy for Skeaping 'with all love', dated 'April 19 1925', with the place name 'Firenze'.[7]

Hepworth's invitation to Nicholson to join the holidaying modernists made clear that making art was on the agenda, writing, 'we are reinventing the 7 & 5 [...] I shall take a small piece of stone with me to Leiston [further south from Happisburgh on the East Anglian coast] but working away is terribly difficult – one never has the exact tool or stands & other wretched appliances for carving!'[8] She recalled that she and Moore carved while two-year-old Paul played on the beach.[9] She also sent Nicholson photographs that indicated how she was thinking about sculpture at the time:

> *I am enclosing one or two snaps for you – my camera is*
> *eleven years old and now no good. The ones of rocks are off*
> *Scilly – when I see you, I must show you some good photos*
> *of them and tell you about them. They have moved me more*
> *than anything I have ever seen sculpturally. We took a boat out*
> *into the western islands and there were purple rocks, groups of*
> *rocks, hundreds of rocks all worn by the water and yet retaining*
> *their fundamental thrust and we sailed round watching the*
> *changing aspects and the revealing of surprising movement.*[10]

In Nicholson she saw a kindred spirit, with whom she wanted to discuss these inspirational sights. He joined the group in Happisburgh (see right) without Winifred, who remained at their home in Cumberland, having just given birth to their third child, Andrew, in July. Skeaping and Hepworth's relationship had already begun to deteriorate by this point, as her letters to Ben and Winifred earlier in the summer attest,[11] and he stayed in London for the first week of the holiday during which time Ben and Barbara's relationship grew.

By the end of September, Hepworth had fallen passionately for Nicholson, expressing her feelings in terms of stone and landscape in a letter of 24 September 1931: 'Dear I must write just once to tell you how I love you [...] your dear head is like the most lovely pebble ever seen and your thoughts clear as the pebbles just left by the sea and I love all you are and do, and all you wear just as I love the leaves on the trees.'[12] The boundary between art and life dissolved as Hepworth found herself equally artistically invigorated by the new relationship, writing, 'never have such lovely things happened Ben and all the time I am longing to work because of them. I have never felt like this before. You have given me so much and new things keep coming to me.'[13] Hepworth and Skeaping separated, although they remained friends and co-parents, and in October Hepworth informed Arthur Tooth & Sons that they would no longer be exhibiting jointly. She wrote to Nicholson, 'they offered to give <u>me</u> a contract separately and then I said they might not really want to tie themselves to me until they'd seen enough work of the sort I was doing now – & they said what sort & I said it was tending to become more abstract etc.'[14] Keen to pursue the new artistic avenues prompted by her conversations with Nicholson, Hepworth found herself restricted by the time required for both childcare and the laborious task of carving:

I took Paul up to the lovely nursery school this morning he loves it so. It is a very long walk and we went under trees most of the way and leaves were falling all round us and he was so happy, catching them in his hands. Such lovely people look after the children. I fetch him at four and it gives me 5 hours work and ½ hr for lunch [...] It is lovely for you to be able to get all this work done so quickly. I am having to keep all the very very

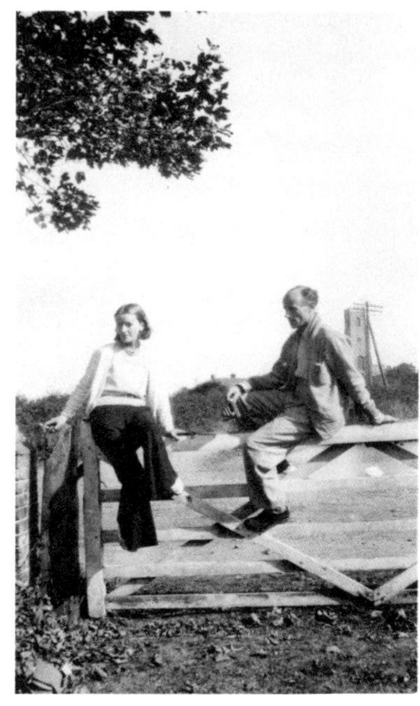

ABOVE Barbara Hepworth with Ben Nicholson at Happisburgh, Norfolk, 1931

*beautiful things you gave me strong and clear inside because
it takes a long time for them to come out in sculpture and
I haven't yet made a start.*[15]

By the following spring, Hepworth's turn towards abstraction
was evident in her new carving, *Torso* (1932) (below). Working again in
challenging materials, this time African blackwood, Hepworth noted, 'I
sawed the bottom off that piece of blackwood to make it stand up – it was

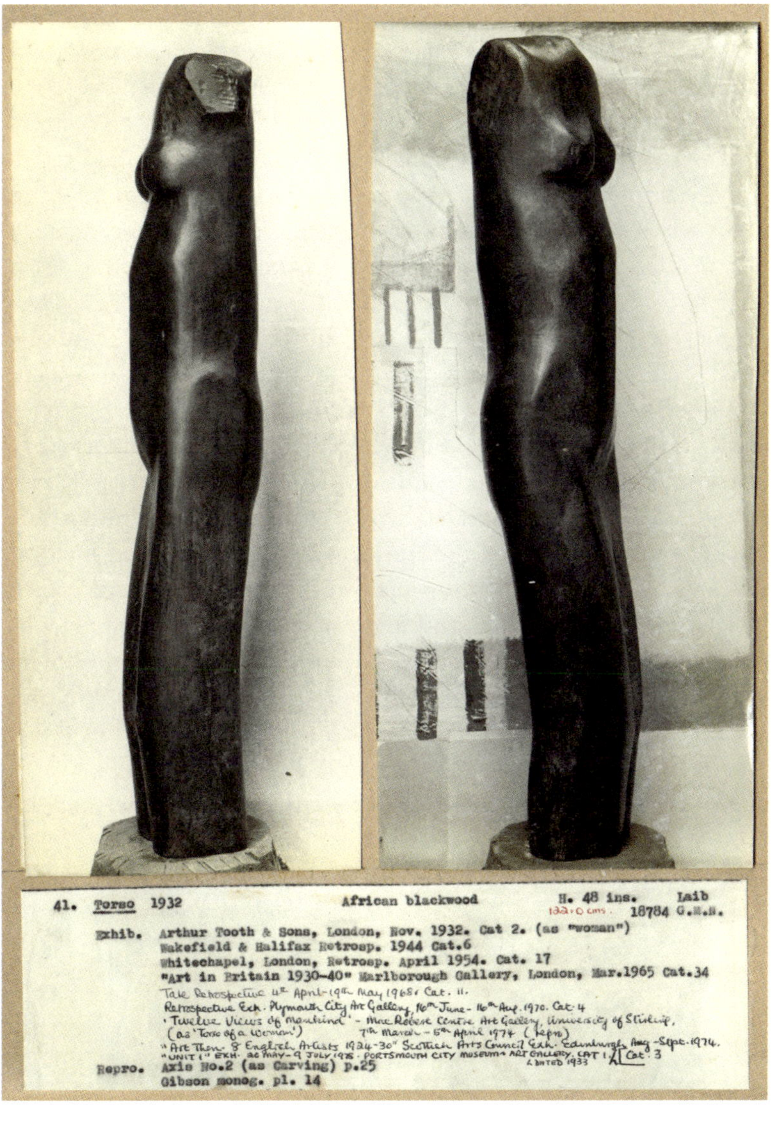

ABOVE Barbara Hepworth's sculpture record for *Torso*
(1932). Photographs by Paul Laib. These records,
initially compiled in the 1960s under Hepworth's
supervision, often included several views to adequately
capture the three dimensions of sculptural form.

the hardest work I have ever done. I almost couldn't do it.'[16] The slender figure of the armless and headless torso is unrealistically elongated, a taut vertical column, almost a line instead of a human form. It rises up from a trunk of wood left rough in its natural state. This can be read as a metaphor for the central tenets of Christian Science, the priority of the transcendental world of ideas or thoughts over the physical world. Hepworth's increasing faith in Christian Science, prompted by her interactions with Nicholson, is evident in letters written while working on this sculpture. She notes, 'I found some most lovely things, reading [*Science and Health*]. You know that Science Thought as I know it is the very core of my being – the lovely Genesis of perfect creation and unfolding of spiritual ideas. How beautiful it has been working with you dear. You make such loveliness and clearness.'[17] 'Working' in this context probably means the spiritual work of Christian Science, rather than artistic practice. As the faith believed that true reality was immaterial, physical experiences were regarded as manifestations of beliefs. Ailments were therefore best addressed through the work of thought, akin to prayer, as Hepworth would later write to Nicholson about a sore throat, 'you have given me a good help with my throat belief – Please could you give me one more – it is not quite cleared up',[18] and when her mother was ill, 'her arm has not healed & they want to try skin grafting – I have written to her asking her not to let them and I am working for her. It would be lovely if you could give her a good think.'[19]

However, Hepworth struggled with the implications of a philosophy that placed absolute emphasis on the spiritual rather than material world. This was an anathema for a sculptor who embraced the physical world through intense interaction with organic materials and was engaged with all its aspects, from bucolic landscapes to sex. In a letter to Nicholson of 22 July 1932, she elaborated:

> *Science will not admit the necessity of sex harmony. It says*
> *we must get above it if we are in disharmony. How can we*
> *cut out the most lovely thing that God has created – the quiet*
> *strength and urge that makes a flower force its way out of*
> *the beaten earth or raise its head after much trampling –*
> *that makes all that quiet still movement in the night of*
> *things growing – growing to new loveliness and light. It is*
> *the rhythm of the seasons and the heart of the earth and*
> *sea and sands and the very stillness of understanding as*
> *deep as the blue of sky in the night.*[20]

OPPOSITE Barbara Hepworth, *Kneeling Figure*, 1932, rosewood, 67.5 x 32 x 28.8 cm (26½ x 12⅝ x 11⅜ in.)

Ever seeking synthesis and harmony between opposing forces, Hepworth felt a connection between the intellectual elements of Christian Science, 'friendship, science – theory – moral citizenship', and the instinctive physical world, which she saw as encompassing both the 'warmth, creativeness, humanness' of art and the elemental forces of reproduction, 'new life – and creation and children. Surely that last can develop into the first, and the first continue on to even higher planes even from a science point of view.'[21] This oscillation between the physical and ephemeral worlds is reflected in her shifting between abstract and figurative sculptures at this time. Although more abstract in form, *Torso* was made before *Kneeling Figure* (also 1932), a more detailed figure, with facial features, hair, fingers and a carved navel (below), which recalls the life drawings that Hepworth made in 1929.

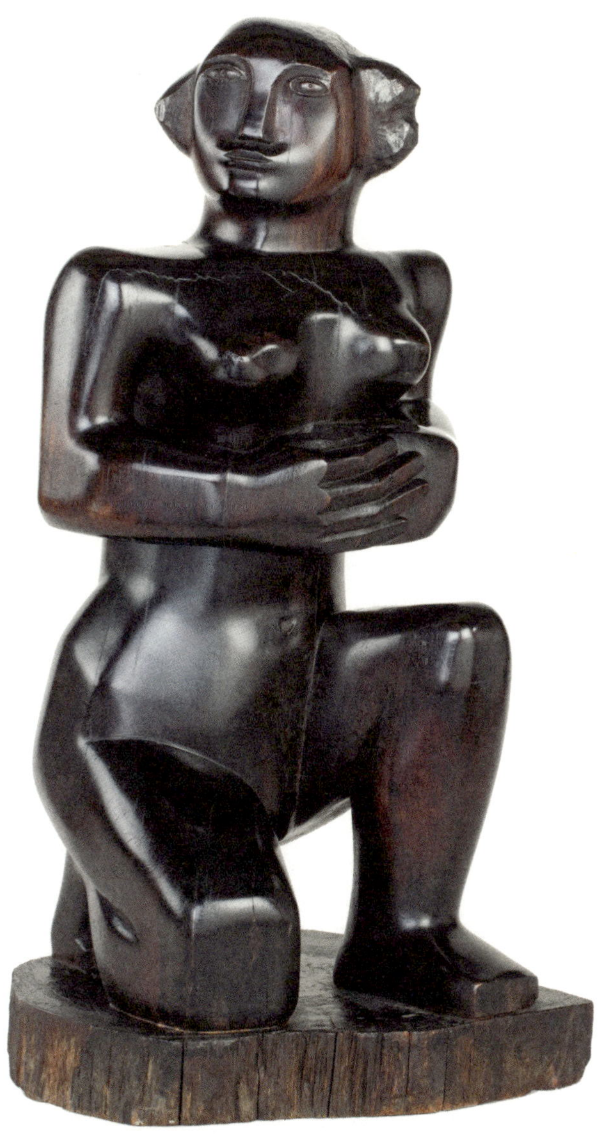

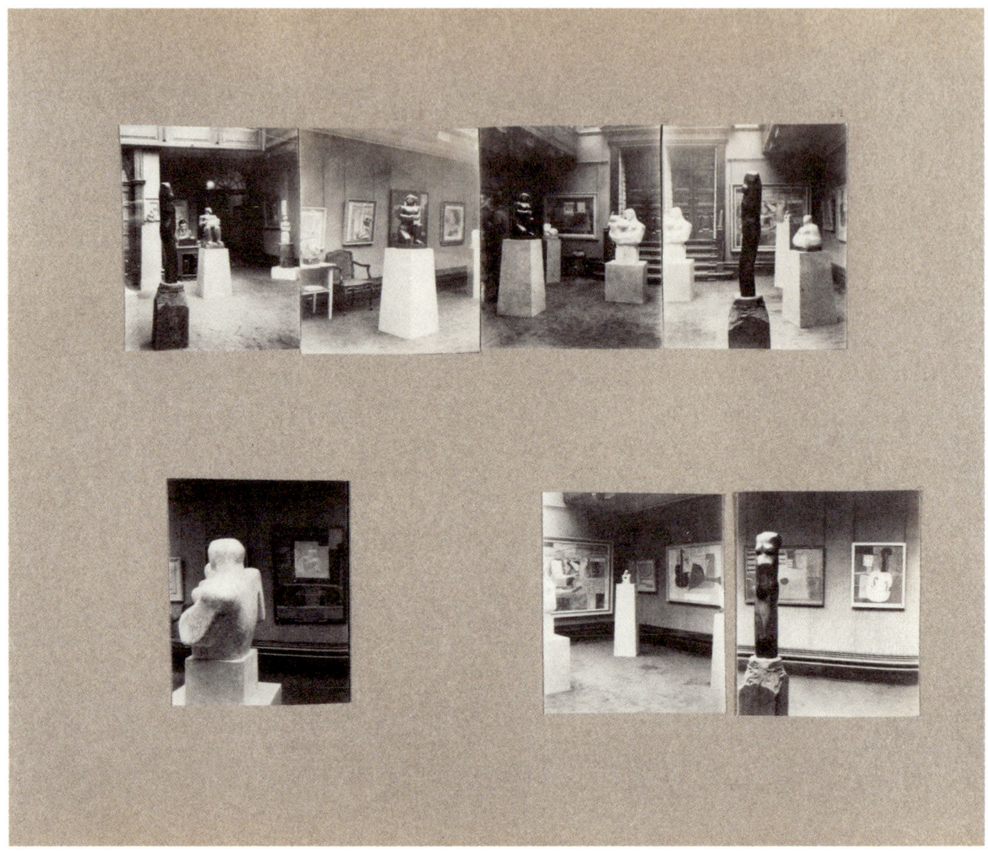

The increasing range of Hepworth's sculptural language was evident at her joint exhibition with Nicholson at the end of the year, held at Arthur Tooth & Sons (above), which included both *Kneeling Figure* and *Torso*.[22] The detailed *Head* (1930–31) showed the more figurative side of her output, while *Abstraction*, now lost but visible in installation photographs, was an entirely abstract biomorphic form, the first carving that Hepworth pierced with a hole to explore mass and light in purely sculptural terms, later titled *Pierced Form*. Nicholson began sharing Hepworth's studio in March 1932, but split his time between Hepworth and his family with Winifred, first in Cumberland and then in Paris, where they moved in September of that year. Hepworth's letters to Nicholson during these periods of separation offer insight into the development of her work in the lead-up to their joint exhibition. In September, she wrote, 'I do so miss you but I am having fun and working hard [...] we were deciding bases for about 2 hrs – the little one I sent to the 7 & 5 is to have a new <u>brown</u>

ABOVE A page from Barbara Hepworth's photograph album showing views of the exhibition *Carvings by Barbara Hepworth, Paintings by Ben Nicholson* at Arthur Tooth & Sons Galleries, London, November– December 1932

stone base (I have polished it and darkened it) and the light stone carving looks marvellous on a slat of grey purple blue slate of irregular shape.'[23] Installation photographs of the exhibition show that Hepworth's attention to the sculptures' bases extended to the plinths as well. Considering the encounter between the viewer and the sculpture, Hepworth displayed works on plinths of a variety of heights and styles, some square and others tapered at the top, giving an altar-like appearance. *Head* is shown on a table next to a chair, encouraging intimate viewing, while *Torso* enters the viewers' space, standing directly on the floor.

Hepworth's letters also reveal her practice of working concurrently on multiple sculptures in a variety of materials. Shortly after writing about bases, Hepworth wrote again:

> *I had a lovely day's work yesterday – the head is good now – I've learnt <u>such a lot doing</u> it I feel as tho' I can't have known anything before. The idea in it <u>was</u> a good one – it still is, only it has freed itself. I realise now that the idea was hardly developed at all – it was only hinted at – suggested mistily and the real surface was another such[?] under the wood. I worked from 1pm to 9.30. Had a great go on the stone girl in the shed. Yes, I will leave the wooden torso till we are working together – I know exactly what I want to do.*[24]

Hepworth was still questioning whether the sculptural idea came from the artist or the material. In some cases she noted that the process of carving 'frees' the idea, while in others she had a clear idea of what she wanted to do before approaching the material. By the time the exhibition opened she had determined, as she wrote in *Studio* magazine, that 'an idea for carving must be clearly formed before starting and sustained during the long process of working'.[25]

Hepworth's sculpture in the exhibition catalogue was accompanied by an essay written by Herbert Read,[26] a poet and art critic also from Yorkshire who would become a close friend, supporter, and soon neighbour of Hepworth, Moore and Nicholson, moving to The Mall Studios in 1933.[27] His text stated the importance of Hepworth, who, in 'the revival of the art in our own time [...] occupies a leading position'.[28] Of the less figurative work, he reassured the reader: 'that some of Miss Hepworth's creative conceptions should recede into a symbolic world of abstractions is not a feature that should deter the disinterested spectator [...] modern artists like Barbara Hepworth step boldly in a new venture which may succeed in redeeming art from its present triviality and insignificance [...] such art is to be enjoyed: it is perfect in its freedom, its force and its contemporaneity.'[29] Paul Nash, writing in *Weekend Review*, similarly attempted to ease the shock of the abstract works: 'if the layman may think these paintings and carvings unusual, he may be comforted to know that quite a few professional eyes have blinked before them [...] there is no denying their sensuous appeal. Each is alive with a physical and mental charm, part instinctive, part infinitely calculated.'[30]

Read had also interpreted Hepworth's sculpture as balancing between instinct and intellect, but he used more psychoanalytical terms, describing 'this marginal world between consciousness and unconsciousness from which emerge strange images of universal appeal'.[31] This terminology reflects the influence of contemporary art practices in Paris (also seen in the biomorphic forms that Hepworth was beginning to create) where the Surrealist movement, closely connected with the development of Freud's theories on the unconscious, had become prominent in the late 1920s. At the end of 1932, following a short visit to Dieppe with Nicholson in August of that year, Hepworth considered relocating to Paris, asking Nicholson, 'will you please find out the cost of a small flat – 2 rooms adjoining – that is with communicating doors and a place to cook? Please. This is important. If you can get the approx. cost while you are there – the least poss. rent for a place where we could work, we could then reckon it out more easily here, and perhaps let this furnished for enough money for the surplus to pay the Paris rent.'[32] In the event, she remained based in London but returned to France with Nicholson in Easter of 1933, where a trip to Avignon and Saint-Rémy-de-Provence was bookended by visits to the studios of Brancusi, Picasso and Jean Arp.

Although Arp was not at home, Hepworth was shown round by Sophie Taeuber-Arp, his wife and fellow artist, and recalled the impact of the studio: 'seeing his work for the first time freed me of many inhibitions and this helped me to see the figure in landscape with new eyes. I stood in the corridor almost all the way [on the train to Avignon] looking out on the superb Rhone valley and thinking of the way Arp had fused landscape with the human form in so extraordinary a manner. Perhaps in freeing himself from material demands his idea transcended all possible limitations. I began to imagine the earth rising and becoming human.'[33] She could be describing *Seated Figure* (1932–33), where the form is more mountain than figure, made human by an incised profile in its uppermost protuberance (see opposite). Collages from this time, *Composition* and *St. Rémy* (both 1933) (see p. 58), seem to repurpose the biomorphic

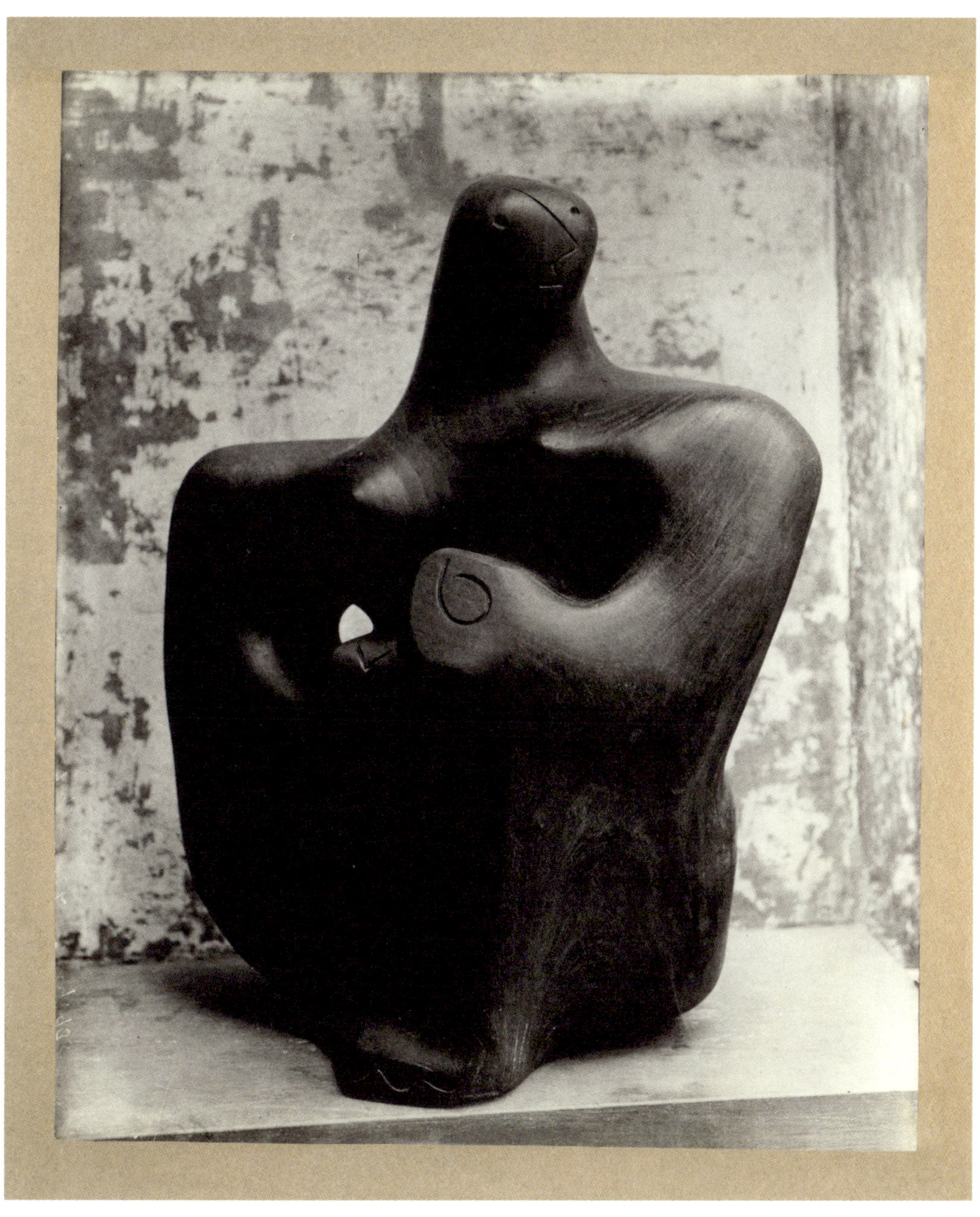

ABOVE Barbara Hepworth's sculpture record for
Seated Figure (1932–33). Photograph by Paul Laib.
The photographs used in Hepworth's sculpture
records often staged the works in interesting ways.
Here, the rough background highlights the surface
of the wood, and the lighting draws attention to
the sculpture's incised profile and hand.

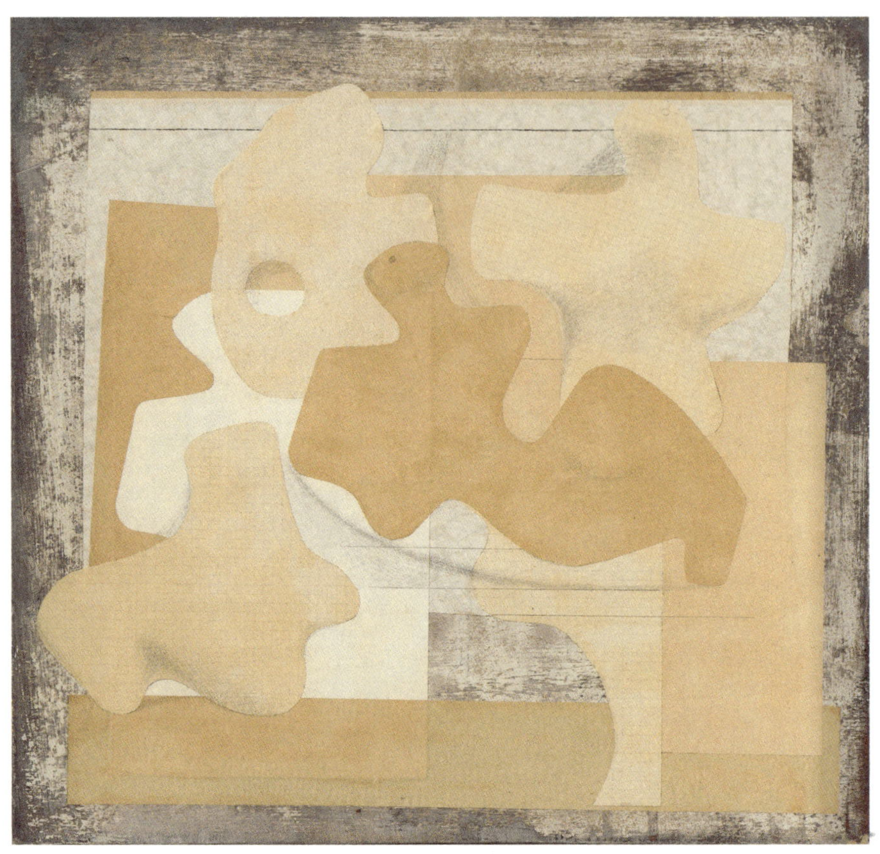

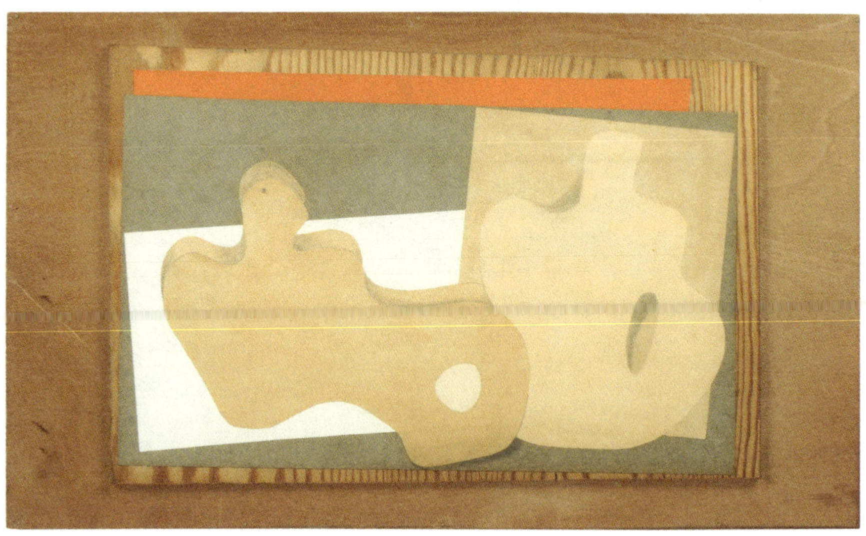

TOP Barbara Hepworth, *St. Rémy*, 1933, collage on oil ground, 25 × 35.5 cm (9⅞ × 14 in.)

ABOVE Barbara Hepworth, *Composition*, 1933, pencil and collage on wood, 28.5 × 44.5 cm (11⅛ × 17½ in.)

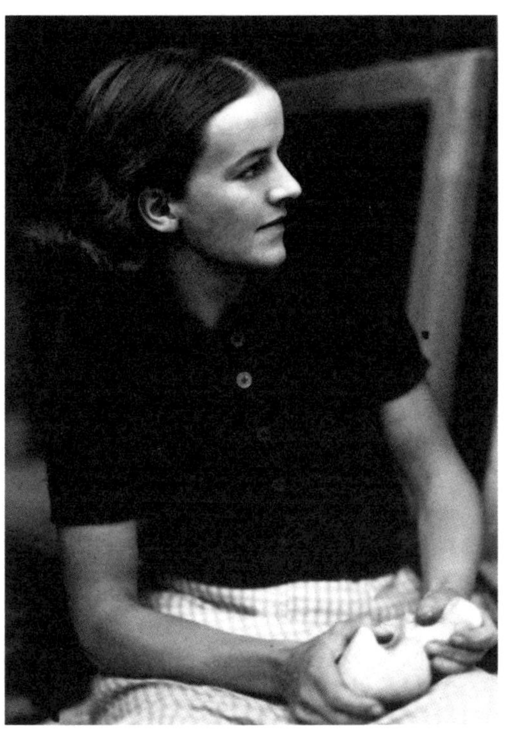

forms of the sculptures *Seated Figure* and *Reclining Figure* (1933) to create imagined landscapes, layered on top of sharp geometric shapes cut from assorted papers.

Hepworth wrote of sourcing materials for these: 'I am v. busy doing constructions & searching London for the things I need for my ideas (coloured things of course).'[34] Her terminology suggests an increasing awareness of abstract groups, particularly Constructivism, a Russian movement brought to Western Europe in the 1920s by Naum Gabo and Antoine Pevsner. Taeuber-Arp had introduced Hepworth and Nicholson to the painter Auguste Herbin, who invited them to join the Paris-based abstract group Abstraction-Création, of which Gabo and Pevsner were also members.[35] Hepworth joined in April 1933, exhibited with the group from 1933 to 1935, and wrote an essay for the second issue of the associated publication *Abstraction-Création: art non-figuratif*, featuring alongside Arp, Gabo and Pevsner among others who would become close friends, including Alexander Calder and Piet Mondrian. Two images of *Abstraction* (see p. 54) from different angles illustrated Hepworth's essay, which considered music as abstract art, comparing the 'mathematical and rationalised' compositions of Bach with 'the most abstract moments in the oeuvre of Richard Wagner [...] in which the wilful and non-"representational" music sets out to convey to us his optimistic-idealist understanding of the world'. This praise is set against a study of the compositions of Claude Debussy, whose 'evocations of the sea, moonlight, rustling trees' are seen as 'reflections and images that can never match up to nature in its divine imperceptibility and superior creativity'. She concludes, 'reality exists only within ideas; and all tangible or acoustic forms strive "invisibly" for dimensions that our spirits alone can understand'. Pure abstraction is the representation of true reality, as she resolves: 'let us, then, extract the eternal laws of nature and of the harmony of the spheres'.[36]

Hepworth returned to France in September 1933, visiting Dieppe and Cubist Georges Braque in nearby Varengeville. By the end of the year,

ABOVE Barbara Hepworth in The Mall Studios, London, 1933. Photograph by Paul Laib

Hepworth's letters to Nicholson allude to their shared network and how each helped its development from their respective positions in London and Paris. She wrote on around 8 December, 'send my love to Braque, and to Paris and my love to Tauber Arp [...] it is so nice of you to show my photos to people – it is such a help'.[37] On 22 December, Nicholson wrote back with news of Jean Arp's response to seeing photographs of Hepworth's work: 'He said he'd heard that Harry [Henry Moore] was v. good – but this (you!) is much better. <u>He wants to meet you very much</u> & asked a lot about how you worked.'[38] Hepworth, in turn, supported Nicholson's career in London, showing work to potential collectors who visited the studio, discussing it with critics, and sending him materials – crucially, razor blades, with which he made his first reliefs, a major development in his work, prompting Hepworth to write, 'I am very interested in your new work idea (carving out) <u>naturally</u> – I've been longing for it to happen for ages.'[39] Connections between Paris and London were strengthened in 1933 with the reopening of the Mayor Gallery in April, where the programme brought British and Continental artists together.[40] Hepworth met many of these artists when they visited London for exhibitions, including Braque, Calder and László Moholy-Nagy. Moholy-Nagy had been associated with the Bauhaus, a German art school established in 1920 with the aim of reimagining the material world through integrated art practice, unifying fine art with design and commercial mass production. Hepworth revelled in the exchange of ideas with her new artist friends: 'Moholy phoned me – he is sweet – not going to Paris – talked of his new book [*60 Photos*] a bit and also of consulting me about the sculpture – I 'spose he means mine.'[41]

Her letters to Nicholson during their periods of separation give a glimpse into a range of interests and preoccupations, from politics to music and architecture. A letter from December 1932 describes going to the cinema with a male friend and the subsequent discussions on 'communism and a woman paying for herself [...] it took all dinner time to get as far as to arrange that in future I paid my share!'[42] They also reveal the financial hardship that Hepworth found herself in as a single parent, though she shared the care of Paul with Skeaping and Nicholson contributed to the rent. She explored all avenues for making a living through art, however tangential. In December 1932 she took on a tutoring job, writing that 'Jim [Ede] has got me a job teaching a child of 6 years. Every other day for the next 2 or 3 weeks. I need the money tho' and I should think I shall have to work v. hard for it.'[43] She and Nicholson also tried print-making, attempting to sell designs commercially. Writing in December 1932,

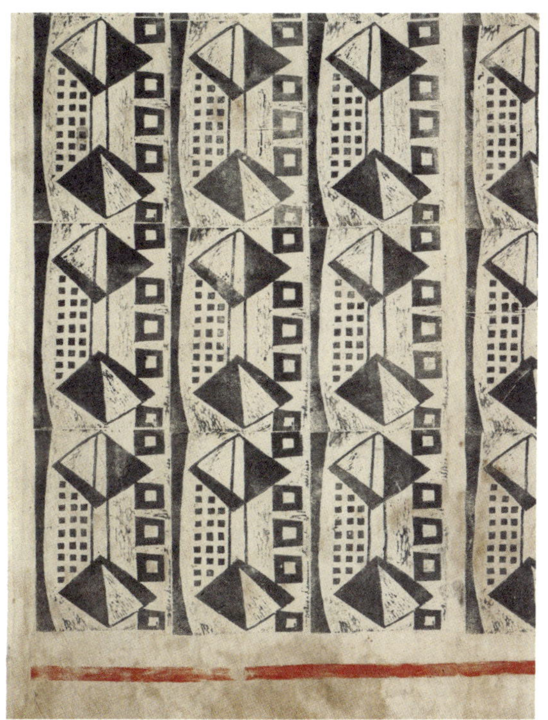

ABOVE Barbara Hepworth, detail of curtains, 1932–33, height 103 cm (40½ in.)

she tells him that Fortnum & Mason will 'probably buy some of our designs sometime. They pay £10 for a <u>paper</u> design. Whether is a Nash or a student. Rather a nice idea.'[44] The process of lino printing delighted her and she enthused, 'I'm absolutely bitten by this printing business, can't get on with carving at all! I've just done one for 2 colours and tonight superimposed a third just for fun [...] Jack [Skeaping] is going to try and help me sell some prints. It would be fun if I could do one as good as your diamond one [...] here is a bit of lino for you. It is not so jolly and cut as the other but you might get something jolly out of it.'[45]

Photographs of their studio show experiments in fabric printing, and several of Hepworth's designs were realised as furnishing fabrics and curtains, some of which she exhibited in a joint show with Nicholson at the Lefevre Gallery in October 1933. In contrasting light and dark hues, like the curtains (1932–33) (above), Hepworth's designs are more geometric than her concurrent sculptures, with diamonds, squares and grids exploring an interplay between absence and presence. The studio photographs also show the couple's cultural interests jostling alongside one another: fabric designs, plants and books sit beside Hepworth's sculptures, Nicholson's paintings, art materials, and works by other artists they knew – both originals and reproductions, including Braque's *Zao* (1931) – with Hepworth's white baby grand piano in the corner. As is clear from her text in *Abstraction-Création: art non-figuratif*, she had come to feel a great affinity between music and the abstract form of art she was developing. She frequently went to concerts, experiences which confirmed these connections:

In Bach the visual sense is always delighted because every movement made by the orchestra is beautiful all the bows of 1ˢᵗ fiddles, 2ⁿᵈ fiddles, and violas, cellos and double bass working lovely rhythmic movement [...] The wind instruments

*support – what a lovely vision – so complete – perfect
construction and understanding if you knew just a little more
about the construction you would see the likeness to Picasso –
in fact no difference at all hardly.*[46]

Hepworth uses the term 'rhythm' visually as well as musically, describing, for example, a 'v. nice house – conceived sculpturally' that a friend, Marshall Sisson, had designed: 'it has a circular rhythm and is only experienced fully by walking round it'.[47] Just as she had experienced the Yorkshire hills of her childhood as sculptures, so she was beginning to see rhythm and balance in all creative endeavours.

This outlook chimed with artistic developments of the time. The ideas of the Bauhaus began to infiltrate Britain's cultural scene alongside the increasing influence of Surrealism and a burgeoning group of abstract artists. These were brought together with the 'composition of a new

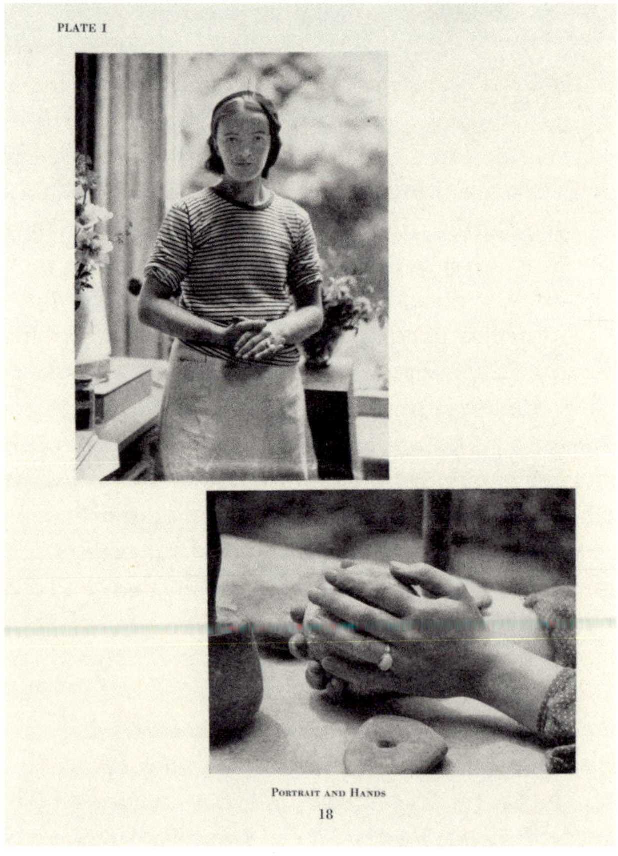

ABOVE Photographs in *Unit One: The Modern Movement in English Architecture, Painting and Sculpture*, 1934

society of painters, sculptors, and architects under the name Unit One', announced by Paul Nash in the 'Letters to the Editor' section of *The Times* on 12 June 1933. Acknowledging the disparate beliefs and individuality of the eleven members, Nash claimed their unity came from 'a quality of mind, of spirit, perhaps, which unites the work of these artists [...] Unit One may be said to stand for the expression of a truly contemporary spirit, for that thing which is recognised as peculiarly *of to-day* in painting, sculpture and architecture.'[48] The group met weekly at the Mayor Gallery, and their work was included in an exhibition of contemporary British art at the Anglo-German club in mid-December 1933. Hepworth described the show to Nicholson: 'Unit One is a room by itself – the cocktail Bar – all the other English art in the Ballroom. Unit One looks v. nice – shiny cocktail shakers & sparkly glasses. 3 [Edward] Wadsworths, 2 [Edward] Burras – 2 of yours, a mask of Harry's [Moore] and my big carving.'[49] This was followed by a Unit One exhibition at the Mayor Gallery in April 1934, which toured to Liverpool, Manchester, Henley, Derby, Swansea and Belfast. The intervening months were filled with preparations for the show and accompanying book, edited by Herbert Read, in which each artist was represented by an artist statement alongside photographs of their studio and hands (see opposite).

Hepworth worked hard on her statement, expressing concern to Nicholson: 'I seem to have written a lot of rubbish. How I am going to give it all form and some sort of balance of writing I don't know. I <u>have</u> thoughts that are worth putting into carving but apparently none that are of sufficient importance to take their natural shape in writing.'[50] She was also juggling the writing alongside creating work for the show and caring for Paul, and wrote somewhat rebukingly to Nicholson:

I am very busy with my constructions. I have to do all my work between 6.30 at night and 3 am in the morning as the rest of the day is children & housework. As I have to be up at 8 for Paul's breakfast I feel rather sleepy.

Herbert liked my article, he said people like me always did it well! Also he said he thought the book would be exciting. Please will you send <u>something</u> yourself straight away as Herbert has to write 6,000 words conclusion drawn from our articles etc. in the next fortnight. Your delay is holding everything up. Of course I see your point about preferring to work – so do we all but we <u>did</u> all voluntarily join together for the production of this book – and I do *feel we must all pull our weight I think. This sounds like a sermon! but even I have managed it <u>with</u> all the housework and Paul.*[51]

Hepworth had reservations about the finished book, writing, 'Oh dear – I do think English productions are boring. I 'spose it <u>is</u> marvellous that a firm like Cassells should have put a book out as good as Unit 1 – but it bores me so – I think perhaps it is the respectable matt paper [...] However it is all a step in the right direction and one should not be too disappointed.'[52] She also noted that, although the painters and architects were listed in alphabetical order, the sculptors were not: 'they have put Harry first on the dust cover tho' I start the book inside – just like the [private view invitation] card'.[53] Despite these reservations, Hepworth's entry beautifully encapsulates a vibrant moment in her life and work:

The present moment is the only real time [...] There is freedom to work out ideas and today seems alive with a sense of imminent new discovery.

In an electric train moving south I see a blue aeroplane between a ploughed field and a green field, pylons in lovely juxtaposition with the springy turf and trees of every stature. It is the relationship of these things that makes such loveliness –

The sounds of unseen birds and droning aeroplanes in the sky, part hidden by the leaves of a tree so very much older than I am the feeling of easy walking down the street with green red traffic lights, the earth revealing its shape to the feet and eye [...]

At the present moment we are building up a new mythology which is more easily understood when the things we care for are seen. Small things found and kept for their lovely shape, their weight, their texture and intense pure colour. Objects that we place near to each other, in their different aspects and relationships create new experience. A scarlet circle on the wall, a slender white bottle on a shelf near it, a bright blue box and lovely-shaped fishing floats that rest in the hand like a bird, weighty pebbles, dull greys, some gleaming white, all these move about the room and as they are placed, make the room gay or serious or bright as a frosty morning and nearly always give a tremendous feeling of work [...] the predisposition to carve is not enough, there must be a positive living and moving towards an ideal.[54]

Chapter 5

Mother
& Child

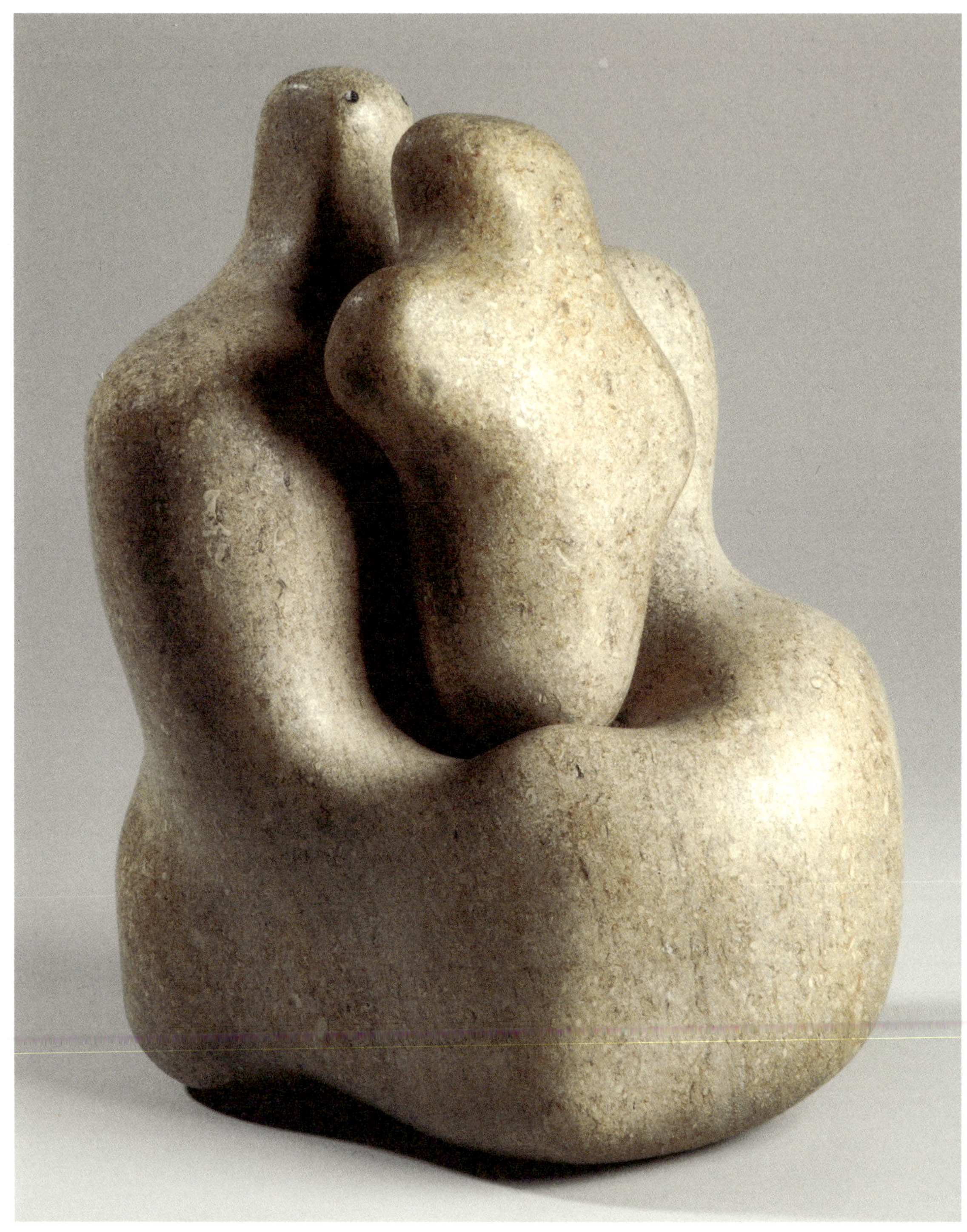

 Barbara Hepworth, *Mother and Child*, 1934, pink Ancaster stone, 30.5 × 26 × 22 cm (12 × 10¼ × 8⅝ in.)

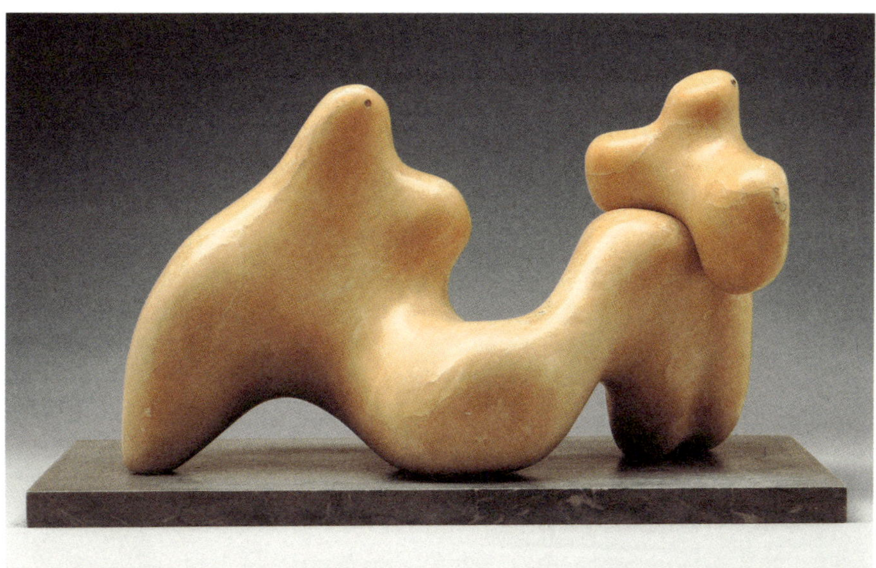

In late 1933, Hepworth and Nicholson exhibited together at the Lefevre Gallery in London. A review of the show by Adrian Stokes in *The Spectator* paid particular attention to Hepworth's 'Mother and Child' stone carvings:

> *It is not a matter of a mother and child group represented*
> *in stone. Miss Hepworth's stone is a mother, her huge pebble*
> *its child. A man would have made the group more pointed:*
> *no man could have treated this composition with such a*
> *pure complacence. The idea itself is a spectacular one, but*
> *it gains from Miss Hepworth's hands a surer poignancy.*[1]

Hepworth made several more 'Mother and Child' sculptures in 1934. As with the earlier *Seated Figure* (see p. 56), she combined biomorphic forms akin to landscapes with figurative allusions. *Mother and Child* (1934) comprises two separate stones, the larger 'mother' stone with two carved eyes cradling the smaller 'child', which, while safely rooted in its mother's lap, leans slightly forward with little outstretched arms (opposite). *Large and Small Form* (1934) continues the theme (above), with pin-prick eyes given to both the large amorphous horizontal form – which recalls the *Reclining Figure* of 1933 (see p. 59) – and the separate small pebble perched on its knee. For both works, Stokes's description is apt: there are concavities or absences in the large forms where the small forms once were – the stone is, indeed, a mother. Positioned on the hinge between

ABOVE Barbara Hepworth, *Large and Small Form*, 1934, alabaster, 23 × 37 × 18 cm (9 × 14½ × 7 in.)

abstraction and figuration, Hepworth would later describe these works as 'turbulent [...] but I stand by them. They mattered a lot emotionally & sculpturally.'[2]

Although maternal subjects were a familiar trope in modernist circles, Hepworth's focus on this subject in 1934 was possibly due to her own pregnancy with Nicholson. Early in their relationship Hepworth had discussed the prospect of their having children with Margaret Gardiner, a writer and political activist, whom Hepworth would describe as her '<u>one</u> intimate friend'.[3] She wrote to Nicholson in 1932, 'Margaret said we must have a child because it would be such a lovely beautiful thing. I do think it was so sweet of her.'[4] In May 1934, this musing had become a reality, and she wrote, 'It is such a lovely idea, this baby. So beautiful & mysterious.'[5] The singular baby turned out to be triplets, who were born on 3 October 1934, and named Simon, Rachel and Sarah – collectively termed in letters as 'SRS'. Having triplets was an unpredictable event several decades before ultrasound was used in a clinical setting. Hepworth and Nicholson had intended to expand their household to the neighbouring No. 3A, Church Road (now Tasker Road, adjacent to The Mall Studios), and Hepworth recalled, 'we had only a basement flat, no washing in the garden, and a kitchen-bathroom, and £20 in the bank and only one cot'.[6] Reflecting on the impact of the birth in 1952, she noted, 'we were only prepared for one child and the arrival of three babies by six o clock in the morning meant considerable improvisations for the first few days [...] when I started carving again in November 1934, my work seemed to have changed direction although the only fresh influence had been the arrival of the children. The work was more formal and all traces of naturalism had disappeared.'[7] In 1943, she summarised the evolution of her forms at this time to E. H. Ramsden: 'the Torso or figure became the Single Form, The Mother & Child or "group" became a Two Form'.[8] Very few singular form sculptures exist from this year, as the multi-part groups dominated Hepworth's production. An exception is the diminutive *Standing Figure* (1934) (right), in whose bulbous torso it is tempting to read an expanding pregnant bump.

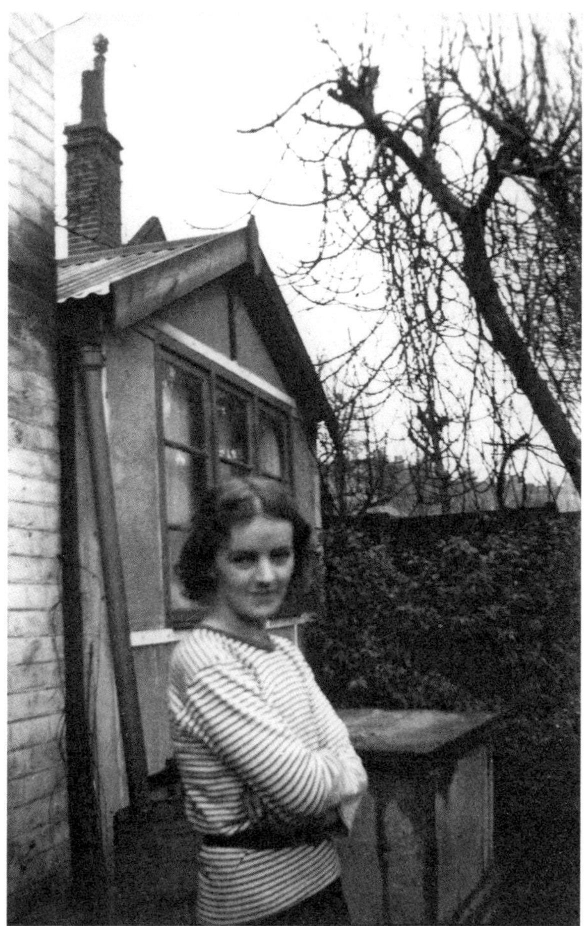

Although Hepworth later recalled the arrival of the triplets as a creative boost, her letters from the time reveal a fraught reality alongside astonishing resilience. By mid-December, just twelve weeks after the birth, Nicholson had returned to Paris, leaving Hepworth with the triplets and five-year-old Paul. She details at length in a letter to Nicholson her struggles to run the household and to find suitable support to look after the children, the triplets needing individual and round-the-clock care, concluding, 'the one thing I cannot do is do more than I am doing – I am too tired and need every bit of sleep I can get & should be no good to S. S. R. & Paul if I am not well'.[9] The task at hand was considerable and Hepworth was torn between unwillingness to lose the career she had worked hard to establish, and intense love of her new babies: 'I am v. happy & not worrying at all – I am just working at the problem as tho'

it were a carving [...] I am certain of this tho' that it will work out for the best & equally certain that I am not going on from week to week & month to month being separated from carving by nurses, under nurses & cooks. I am going to work in the New Year. It is 5 months or more since I did any. It has gone into these babies & I am pleased and happy about it because they are so beautiful.'[10]

Hepworth's doctor suggested that Wellgarth, a nearby nursery training college, might take care of the triplets, and Hepworth visited just before Christmas 1934. She was impressed by both the environment and the staff, writing to Nicholson that 'the Creche is well designed the rooms are on a balcony with the whole of one wall which slides back so that the children have maximum sheltered air. Rather lovely. Matron of the home seemed awfully clear – she's had babies of 2lb 10 oz from the beginning.'[11] The latter was particularly important as, like most triplets, the babies were born very small and needed particular care to build them up. In addition, Wellgarth offered a substantial discount to the triplets' care fees, inclusive of all expenses, Hepworth noting, 'it was jolly decent of them. That would be exactly half what it is costing us now.'[12] As the triplets grew bigger, the situation reached crisis point and Hepworth wrote in early January 1935, 'The babies are lovely & so well: everything else is bloody hell [...] I do wish you were here, the responsibility of making decisions alone is awful.' She further noted:

> *Logic says put the babies in Wellgarth for a year at £250 &*
> *get insured & save & <u>do some work</u> & let flat furnished.*
> *Another part of me says struggle on – I don't know which part*
> *of me it is maybe the sentimental part. I certainly can not work*
> *under these conditions & if they go on I shall just be ill.*
>
> *I could do some lovely work now I know. If you have any*
> *ideas on the baby question please ring me up from Jeans. My*
> *head is going round & round. Wellgarth is perfectly designed for*
> *rearing <u>healthy strong babies</u>. If they go they will be well looked*
> *after – we can see them any time. But they are <u>entirely</u> in hands*
> *of Matron and we should have to be content to have it so & do*
> *our Science work carefully all the time. Personally I would rather*
> *they were in a good creche now & with us later when they need*
> *to be taught Science & other things by us – than with us now &*
> *away later [...] I think they would be better at Wellgarth than*
> *No. 3 – they'd get much hardier – more sun & air & skilled diet*
> *& No. 3 is <u>very</u> damp & dreadfully difficult to arrange – Sarah*

*has to be put in the sitting room now she's so noisy (!) & there's
not room to swing a cat round. The gas is leaking the boiler's
leaking & the window falling in!!!!*[13]

By mid-January she had decided:

*I am entirely convinced that these 3 babies will have to go
to Wellgarth. It is not going to be possible to work things at
3a so that I can work. I just can't work & <u>never shall again</u> if
I have all that to see to. I'll stick it out until you come back so
that you can help over decisions and arrangements. I know I can
do some lovely work now I've never felt <u>so clear</u> or <u>so full of ideas</u>
but I cannot get one hour to myself with any peace. The flat is
totally inadequate now they are larger & noisier & the expense
& difficulties terrific. The babies are <u>lovely</u> – so large & so
smiling. They ought to be out all the time but it is very difficult
to get them out enough. I'm trying to get Rachel out today
for the first time.*[14]

As is clear from the letters, the issue of how to best care for her
children occupied Hepworth's thoughts constantly, as she 'tried to look
at it from all points of view'.[15] She needed to continue working in order
to earn a living to support them, and her work was bound to her sense
of self. She also feared she was unable to provide the specialist care that
three small babies required, but she did not want to part with her children:

*I think it's the hardest thing I've ever had to think about. I am
so deeply happy about the babies & want them with me all the
time but I am also so deeply unhappy about not working. They
are such marvellous creatures, absolutely lovely. But somehow
since they came I have felt so completed with you that my one
desire is to work & work & work for the rest of my life. I feel
more poised, more clear & serene than ever before & have not
only one idea but 20 waiting to be worked out. The ultimate &
greatest use we can be to the children is in our clarity [...] There
must be the right place that makes a full rich life for all of us.*[16]

The solution offered by Wellgarth allowed Hepworth time and
space to work, while giving close and regular contact with the babies,
and reassurance that their physical needs were being expertly met.

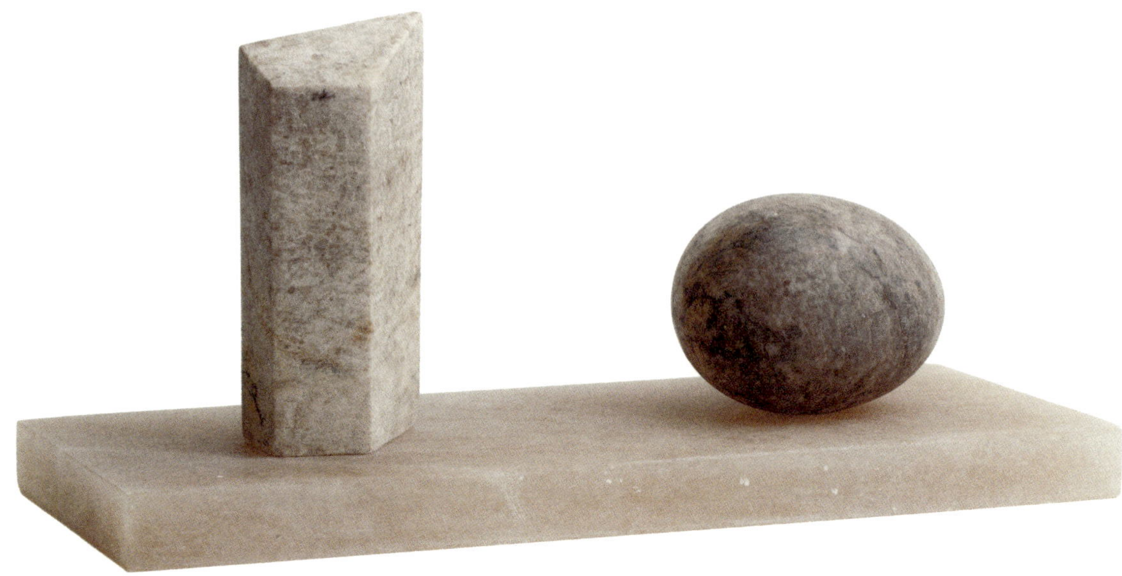

This was not unusual at the time, and was approved of in left-leaning circles, as Hepworth noted: 'Herbert [Read] says he would not hesitate because he believes in the Russian method entirely.'[17] Hepworth was also supported in this decision by Margaret Gardiner, who offered to contribute to the cost of Wellgarth.

The clarity and serenity that motivated Hepworth to work post-triplets is evident in sculptures such as *Two Forms* (above), listed in Hepworth's sculpture records as dating from 'late' 1934. When viewed alongside her earlier 'turbulent' multi-part works like *Large and Small Form*, the biomorphic shifting forms give way to stillness and geometric shapes. However, the two forms are not strictly geometric – a cuboid with unequal sides and a slanted top, and an uneven, egg-like ovoid. These idiosyncrasies, combined with the textured warmth of the alabaster surface, give the sculpture a character that is tactile and human, rather than purely geometric and mechanical. Hepworth explicitly connected these abstract forms to interpersonal experiences, noting that through exploring 'the relationships in space, in size and texture and weight, as well as in the tensions between the forms [...] I hope to discover some absolute essence in sculptural terms giving the quality of human relationships'.[18] The tension between these two forms could reflect the push and pull of the maternal experience that Hepworth so deftly described in her letters – the desire to care for and be close to her children, and yet retain her own identity and agency.

ABOVE Barbara Hepworth, *Two Forms*, 1934–35, grey alabaster, height 16.5 cm (6½ in.)

Taking Hepworth's instructive interpretation further, *Three Forms* (1935) (below) reflects the relationships and tensions – in formal terms – between the three babies. Three white marble rounded forms of varying sizes and character are placed asymmetrically on a rectangular base of the same material. Extending Adrian Stokes's reading of Hepworth's earlier 'Mother and Child' sculptures (see p. 67), the base functions as the mother of the group, providing support and unbreakably connected by common physicality. The bases of these group sculptures were given particular attention in an article on Hepworth published in

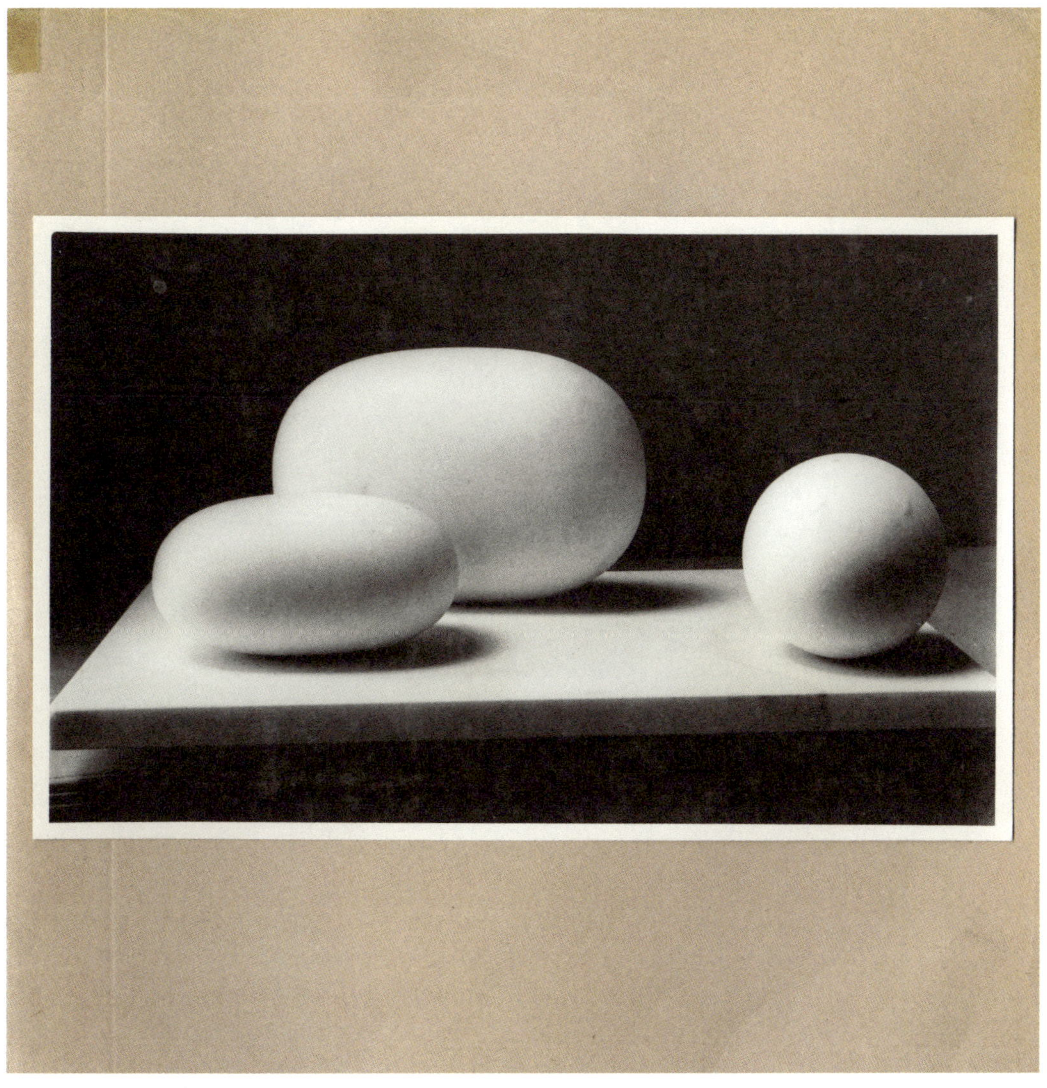

ABOVE Barbara Hepworth's sculpture record for
Three Forms (1935). Hepworth took this photograph
herself. The heightened contrast emphasises the
forms' shadows on the base, highlighting this important
supporting structure.

Axis, a journal that had been established by critic Myfanwy Evans and painter John Piper in 1935 to celebrate abstract art, conceived as a British alternative to *Abstraction-Création*.[19] In a letter to Nicholson accompanying a copy of the second issue of *Axis*, Hepworth shows characteristic attention to detail: 'the type for the printed matter is an improvement. Far better than before – less "obvious" & easier to read – not so flashy and more serious in feeling. The written matter is much, much better than before. Herbert's article on you is splendid I think. Jean's long article very good indeed. The whole production is a normal development – it is more mature than No. 1, less amateur, but with a loss of clarity in many ways. No. 3 ought to be a beauty, uniting the professional appearance of this no. & the clear thing John and Myfanwy stand for.'[20]

Hepworth's work was featured in No. 3, in an article titled 'New Works by Barbara Hepworth', written by archaeologist Henri Frankfort. His text accompanied four reproductions of the new geometric group sculptures:

> *They each consist of a rectangular slab upon which two or three distinct elements are presented. One hesitates to call the slab a base, for it is by no means an accessory, but, on the contrary an essential part of each carving; and it requires little contemplation to discover its function [...] each carving contains, besides the base and the exquisitely modelled elements upon it, a third constituent of equal importance. Even as in music, not only the sounds but also the silences enter into the rhythm of the composition, so matter and empty space form in their harmony these carvings. But space unlimited, [sic] cannot enter into the order which is a work of art. It is the function of the oblong slab to give it definition, to delimit with precision the spatial individuality of each work as a whole.*[21]

This picks up on Hepworth's articulation of the close relationship between abstract art and music, while the description of sculptures in terms of **matter and empty space** hints at her interest in geometry and mathematics. In 1935, she discovered mathematical models, writing, 'John Summerson [her future brother-in-law] says there are some marvellous things in a mathematical school in Oxford – Sculptural working out of Mathematical equations – hidden away in a cupboard. I think I shall go to Oxford as soon as I get back from Leeds.'[22] This enthusiasm for an expression of mathematics through sculptural form echoes her suggestion in *Abstraction-Création* for a dialogue between science, art, maths and music. As she wrote: 'forms generated from scientific data and spiritual conjecture, they can move towards the nature of numbers [...] let us be "musicians" of numbers; we will then become pure spirits'.[23]

The connection of abstraction with spirituality was amplified by meeting both Wassily Kandinsky and Piet Mondrian during a brief visit to Paris with Nicholson just after Christmas 1934. Hepworth later recalled the impact of visiting Mondrian's studio, in particular:

> *When I first went there it made me gasp with surprise at its beauty – it seemed to be literally suspended over the main railway lines into Paris (Gare Montparnasse). Inside the studio everything gleamed with whiteness. The walls, furniture, easels, were all immaculate with white paint – except I remember, for a blue box and a red gramophone. Far up on the white walls were placed different sized rectangles of primary colours, red, yellow, and blue, all movable and all placed with conscious visual purpose.*[24]

Like Hepworth, Mondrian aimed to express a transcendental reality through his abstraction, carefully positioning primary colours in geometric shapes against white backgrounds to focus attention on movement and balance, structural continuity and flux, a fusing of seemingly opposing forces central to the true nature of the universe and our experience of it. The beginnings of a friendship between Mondrian and Hepworth can be seen in her letters to Nicholson at the time: 'so glad Mondrian said nice things about me & work. Goodness I did learn a LOT.'[25] Inspired by Mondrian, in early January 1935 Hepworth painted their studio entirely white, writing, 'the studio is <u>marvellous</u> all white – it is v. roughly done – ought to have a 3rd coat but that can wait till we are richer. I can really <u>think</u> & I've hidden so many things I don't like now <u>it is so peaceful</u>.'[26] Her letters at this time, while focused on childcare, also continued to communicate the business and movement of contemporary art, from assisting with Nicholson's sales to discussing the many avant-garde artists with whom they had become friends. An image of the studio painted white shows Hepworth and Nicholson's work alongside a mobile by Calder, which was a gift from the artist (see following page). This photograph, taken by Hepworth, emphasises the points of dialogue between the works: light and shade – presence and absence – are notable in Hepworth's sculpture and Nicholson's relief, both in white, while a fine sense of balance

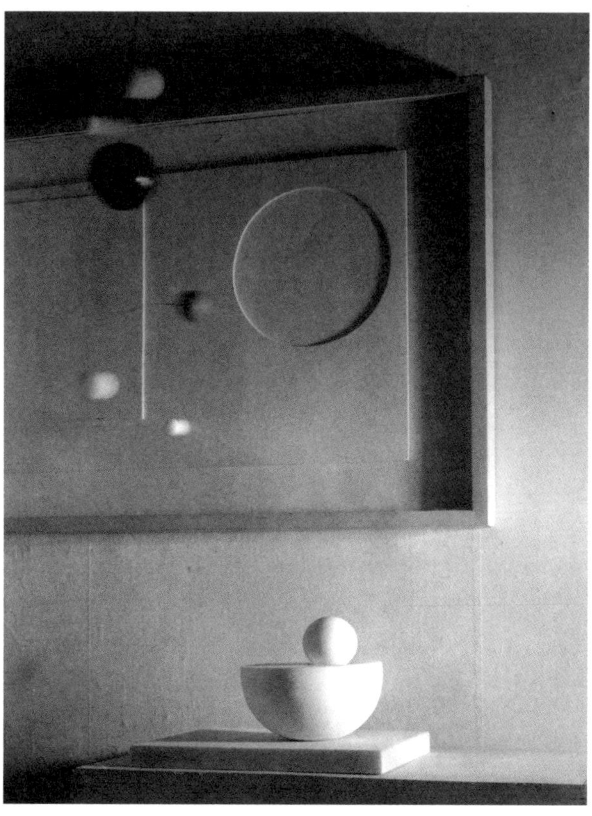

connects her stacked forms with Calder's, and repeated circles appear in all three, the 'harmony of spheres' that Hepworth had called for in *Abstraction-Création.*[27]

Hepworth largely kept in touch with the Paris-based avant-garde through Nicholson, passing messages to, and hearing news of, Arp, Mondrian, Jean Hélion and Alberto Giacometti among others, with occasional brief visits. Back in London she met regularly with Moore and Read, as well as designer Sadie Speight and her husband architect Leslie Martin, scientist J. D. Bernal who was in a relationship with Margaret Gardiner, and surrealist artist and collector Roland Penrose, who purchased a sculpture from Hepworth for the garden of his new Hampstead house.[28] Sales like this were important, and social events at the studio clearly functioned as a commercial tool, as Hepworth wrote to Nicholson: 'you know the sort of party that leads to unexpected sales [...] I don't seem able to cope with that sort of thing when you're not here, I can only try all avenues leading to my own sales.'[29] Money was tight, so

ABOVE The interior of 7, The Mall Studios, with Ben Nicholson's *1935 (white relief)*, Barbara Hepworth's *Cup and Ball* (1935), and part of the mobile by Alexander Calder given to them in 1935. Photograph taken by Hepworth

in addition to creating her own opportunities for sales, Hepworth invoked Christian Science thought: 'Supply is difficult. Bills for electricity & one thing & another billing in & I have v. little left – 3 or 4 £. Will you try to hold the right thought about supply all the time dear? & I will try too.'[30]

In addition to living costs, there were expenses associated with the promotion of work. In early 1936, Hepworth and Nicholson were included alongside many of their peers – Arp, Calder, Gabo, Giacometti, Hélion, Kandinsky, Miró, Moholy-Nagy, Moore and Mondrian – in a significant exhibition, *Abstract and Concrete*, which brought together British and European abstract artists. It was organised by Nicolete Gray, who had bought one of Hepworth's early figurative drawings, *Recumbent Nude*, in 1929. Opening in February 1936 at 41, St Giles in Oxford, it toured to Liverpool's School of Architecture, the Lefevre Gallery in London, and Gordon Fraser's Gallery in Cambridge. Photographs of the exhibition (see below) show *Two Segments and Sphere* (1935–36) installed between a large Nicholson *White Relief* and three recent paintings by Mondrian, gleaming white canvases dominated by vertical and horizontal black lines which, rather than forming a strict grid, created unequal squares

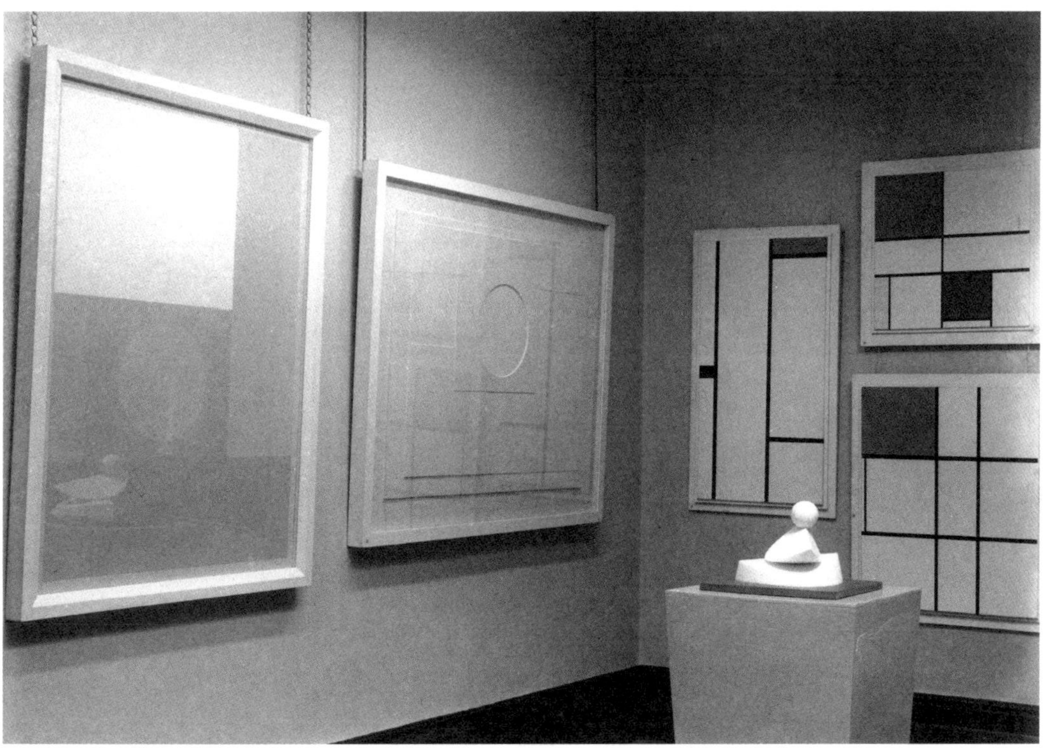

ABOVE The touring exhibition *Abstract and Concrete*, as installed at the Lefevre Gallery, London, in 1936, featuring work by Piet Mondrian, Ben Nicholson and Barbara Hepworth. Photograph by Arthur Jackson

unevenly spread across the compositions and occasionally painted in bold primary colours. These syncopated compositions are mirrored in the asymmetric balance of *Two Segments and Sphere*, each part seeming to implausibly balance on the one below, as if the inevitable rocking of each form dictated by the laws of physics has been frozen for a moment in time.

The exhibition was a fantastic opportunity for Hepworth to show and promote her sculpture alongside artists with whom she felt an affinity. However, it proved to entail a lot of work, as the artists were responsible for the insurance of their works, in addition to 'an endless sequence of jobs concerned with this show – packing cases, measurements & the Lord knows what'.[31] Hepworth disliked the way the exhibition was framed, and the title ('I <u>hate</u> the title Abstract & Concrete – it's just a wisecrack – Herbert hates it too [...] Helion said he would not exhibit if show was called Abstract only & so Abstract & Concrete came into being'), and the advertising ('they intend to use the Mondrian as a poster with red lettering all over it – if this is true I will move all I can to stop it. It makes me disgusted with the English point of view. Such a misunderstanding of everything').[32]

The Times review of the exhibition confirmed Hepworth's fears, asking 'is the "concrete" in the title of the Lefevre Galleries exhibition a sly joke?', and deriding the works generally for being 'too solemn'. The philosophical content of the exhibits was largely ignored. Hepworth's 'Carving, 1936' (in white marble, *Two Segments and Sphere*) was singled out for faint praise – 'though carefully finished, [it] does not go beyond the capacities of the monumental mason' – and Mondrian's carefully balanced black grids were likened to windows.[33] The *Manchester Guardian* took a different view: 'their works are not windows; they are uncompromisingly a part of the wall, and therefore a part of the prison. Or rather, they imprison the eye, however much they invite and stimulate the spirit to wander. It is perhaps for this reason that a whole roomful of them is so difficult to look at. The spirit (unlike the eye) cannot undertake in quick succession a series of violent flights into the world of pure form and colour without becoming intensely fatigued and a little irritated.'[34] *The Telegraph* was equally damning. Although noting, 'in sculpture, ingenious methods are used to convey the qualities of balance and proportion', its review concludes: 'the lack of association and suggestion tend to a fatal sameness'.[35] Stripped of recognisable references to the physical world, the artists' aim to present true reality through shape and form was altogether missed, or, as Hepworth had already lamented, misunderstood.

Chapter 6

Artists for Peace

In November 1936, a spherical wood carving by Hepworth prominently illustrated Naum Gabo's article on 'Constructive art', published in *The Listener*. Gabo, who had settled in London near Hepworth in March that year, wrote:

> *Constructive ideas in general are not rare in the history of ideas; they accompany every creative urge of human development. They always appear on the borderline of two consecutive epochs at the moment when the human spirit, having destroyed the old, demands the creation and assertion of the new [...] the constructivist has renounced the representation of natural forms as he is convinced that the external aspect of Nature does not enable us sufficiently to penetrate its hidden depths: this external aspect of Nature represents only the superficial part, the skin of its immense body; it only conforms to the obvious and petty side of our impulses and is not qualified to manifest the most essential and vital subsistence.*[1]

Gabo went on to explain that, instead of mimicking reality, or imitating the forms of machines as some critics claimed, Constructive art aimed to 'create or enrich' reality, using 'elementary, accurate and primary shapes'.[2] The forms of functional machines were as admirable as the beauty of landscape, but both were secondary surface realities that a Constructive artwork comprised of elemental shapes attempted to penetrate.

Hepworth's alignment with these Constructive principles is evident in the concurrent *Ball, Plane and Hole* (below). The planes are angular with sharp corners, and while the ball has a corresponding absence like the

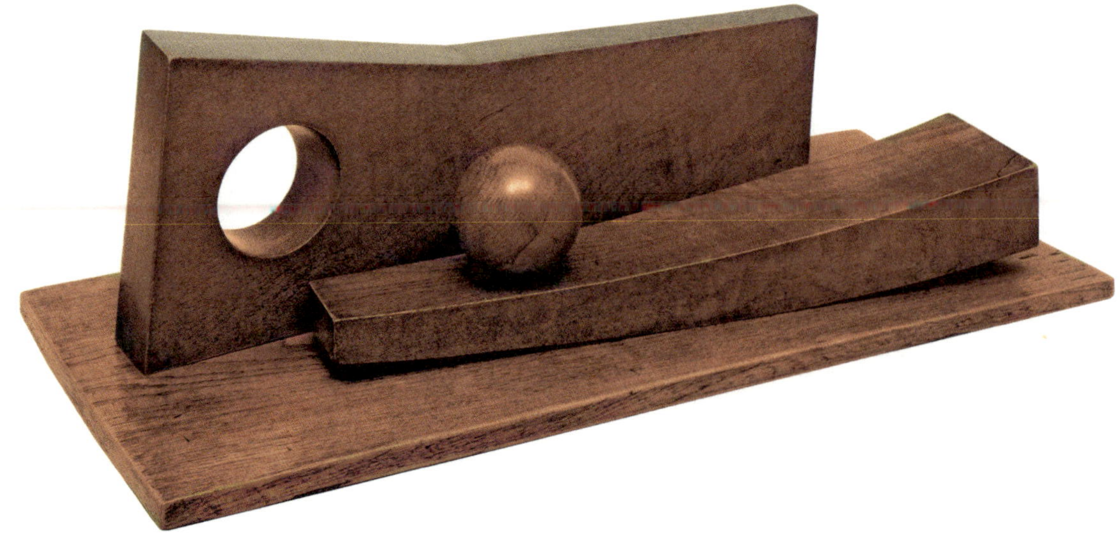

ABOVE Barbara Hepworth, *Ball, Plane and Hole*, 1936, teak on wooden base, 21 × 61.1 × 30.5 cm (8¼ × 24 × 12 in.)

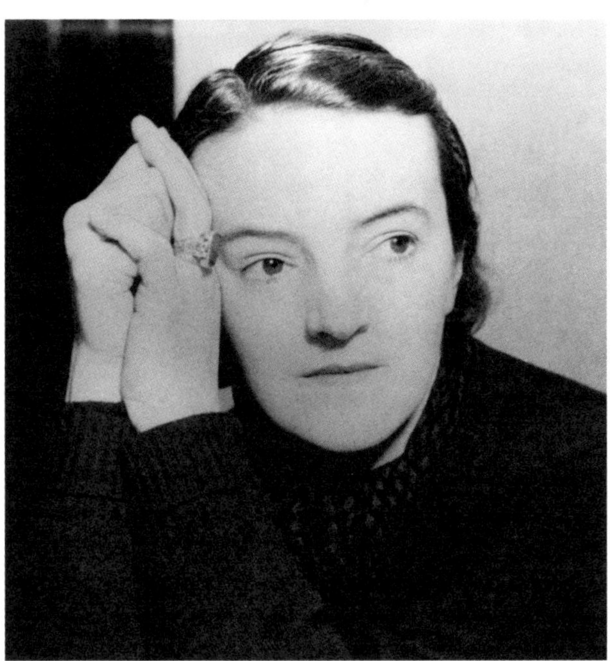

earlier 'Mother and Child' multi-part compositions (see p. 67), it seems to allude more to functionality, or even children's games, than to the 'birth' of form. There is also a stark contrast between the process of carving earlier works, where form was 'discovered' within the material and the organic sculptures seemed to emerge like weathered pebbles, and the creation of *Ball, Plane and Hole*. Two of the elements of the latter were made using a saw, and the pieces are held together with brass screws – a shift in technique to a more mechanical form of construction. Hepworth exhibited *Ball, Plane and Hole* in April–May 1937 with the Artists International Association, an anti-fascist, politically left organisation that aimed for the 'unity of artists for peace, democracy, and cultural development'. The exhibition was wide-ranging, bringing established artists such as Stanley Spencer and Walter Sickert alongside contemporary artists of both abstract and surrealist persuasions, and many more. Herbert Read, writing in *The Listener*, saw the breadth of the exhibition as an 'impressive demonstration of unity in diversity', with 'a more-than-aesthetic aim [...] to discuss the status of the artist in the political world'.[3] Read's article ran alongside 'My Meeting with Hitler', an article by the Rt Hon George Lansbury, MP, following his 'two-and-a-half-hour conversation with Herr Hitler' on the measures required to 'turn the minds of nations away from armaments and force as a method of settling disputes and grievances'.[4] The mounting threat of fascism gave an urgency to the cause of finding a place for artists within the political world. For Hepworth, as for many of her peers, the ideas that motivated the new abstract art were political as well as aesthetic and philosophical, and not to be confined to the realm of fine art. She recalled of these years: 'because of the danger of totalitarianism and impending war, all of us worked the harder to lay strong foundations for the future through an understanding of the true relationship between architecture, painting, and sculpture'.[5]

ABOVE Barbara Hepworth at The Mall Studios, London, *c.* 1938. Photograph by Hans Erni

These ideas were made tangible with the publication of *Circle: International Survey of Constructive Art* in July 1937. The book was co-edited by Gabo, Nicholson and Leslie Martin, who, with Sadie Speight, had become friends with Hepworth after the Unit One exhibition had prompted them to visit The Mall Studios. They also collected her work, purchasing *Ball, Plane and Hole* in 1937. Speight and Hepworth took on the production and layout of *Circle*, working round the clock as the publication date neared. In May, Hepworth wrote to Nicholson, who was staying with Martin and Speight in Hull, 'I must now write to the printers. Also Leslie's article which I am now forwarding to him. Please do all you can to help him to complete corrections of his article – also all the others by Saturday. If this is not done I doubt whether Circle will be out for the Exhibition. I must have Sunday and Monday to complete the corrections myself on the proofs indicated or I must come to Hull for the weekend & bring them back with me so that I can deliver them first thing Tuesday morning.'[6] The book was split into four sections; painting, sculpture, architecture, and 'art and life'. The painting section reproduced the works of twenty-two painters, followed by essays by Mondrian, Winifred Nicholson (writing under an old family name Dacre), Read, architect Le Corbusier, and Ben Nicholson. The architecture section followed the same principle, with illustrations of works – photographs of completed buildings alongside annotated designs – by luminaries of modern architecture, including Bauhaus founder Walter Gropius, who had moved to London fearing Nazi persecution,[7] followed by essays covering subjects from town planning to materials ('Architecture and Material' was written by Marcel Breuer, another Bauhaus associate). The section concludes with a trio of images showing the connection between disciplines: a painting by Moholy-Nagy, the modernist concrete Landquart Bridge by Robert Maillart, and plywood chairs designed by Alvar Aalto.

The sculpture section begins in a similar format, reproducing four works by Hepworth, followed by images of sculptures by nine other artists and essays by Gabo, Moore, scientist J. D. Bernal, and Hepworth herself. Hepworth's essay is astonishing in its breadth, bringing together many ideas that she had been developing throughout the 1930s: the dialogue between form and content, mind and material, and universal and individual experience, encompassing religion, spirituality and society. She begins with a statement on the variety of materials that can be used to express a sculptural idea, and the importance of 'a perfect unity between the idea, the substance and the dimension'.[8] From materials, or substance, she then underscores the priority of the immaterial idea within this unity:

> *Vitality is not a physical, organic attribute of sculpture –*
> *it is a spiritual inner life. Power is not man power or physical*
> *capacity – it is an inner force and energy [...] Vision is not*
> *sight – it is the perception of the mind. It is the discernment*
> *of the reality of life, a piercing of the superficial surfaces*
> *of material existence, that gives a work of art its own life*
> *and purpose and significant power.*[9]

Hepworth then brings these two aspects, the material and the immaterial, together, considering 'it is the sculptor's work fully to comprehend the world of space and form, to project his individual understanding of his own life and time as it is related universally' into sculpture, which she describes as a 'particular plastic extension of thought'.[10] Just as all of the sculptor's experience of the world can be encapsulated in a sculpture, so too can a sculpture relate to all aspects of experience. Hepworth describes this as 'form consciousness [...] the consciousness and understanding of volume and mass, laws of gravity, contour of the earth under our feet, thrusts and stresses of internal structure, space displacement and space volume, the relation of man to a mountain and man's eye to the horizon, and all laws of movement and equilibrium – these are surely the very essence of life, the principles and laws which are the vitalization of our experience, and sculpture a vehicle for projecting our sensibility to the whole of existence.'[11]

Having established that a comprehension of the world can be communicated through sculptural form, Hepworth's essay begins to allude to the socio-political backdrop against which she writes. Constructive art, she claims, 'moves us profoundly because it represents the whole of the artist's experience and vision, his whole sensibility to enduring ideas, his whole desire for a realisation of these ideas in life and a complete rejection of the transitory and local forces of destruction'.[12] These 'forces of destruction' refer to the rise of fascism across Europe, from the Spanish Civil War to the mounting war rhetoric from Hitler's Germany. She continues:

> *These formal relationships have become our thought, our*
> *faith, waking or sleeping – they can be the solution to life*
> *and to living. This is no escapism, no ivory tower, no isolated*
> *pleasure in proportion and space – it is an unconscious manner*
> *of expressing our belief in a possible life. The language of colour*
> *and form is universal and not one for a special class [...] it is a*

thought which gives the same life, the same expansion,
the same universal freedom to everyone.[13]

Constructive art, then, is more than a simple expression of an individual's experience of the world in universal terms. It attempts, through the act of creation, to influence reality and bring about a possible life which is free, in contrast to fascist oppression. Opposite the concluding page of Hepworth's essay are three images of Stonehenge (see below). While they are not a direct illustration, their placement – given Hepworth's responsibility for the book's layout – suggests a connection with her text. The images most aptly relate to a passage where Hepworth states that the Constructive artist 'is bent on discovering a solution to human difficulties by solving his own thought permanently, and in relation to his medium. If we had lived at a time when animals, fire worship, myth or religion were the deepest emotional aspects of life, sculpture would have taken the form, unconsciously, of a recognisable god.'[14] The Neolithic monument of Stonehenge chimes with this statement – a tangible example of how belief can shape, and has in the past shaped, physical experience.

The intensity of the book production impacted on Hepworth's sculptural work: 'I felt today that my carving was looking a little "tired" with having been worked on so spasmodically & so I feel I must really complete it now without another break. I ought to finish in 2 days I think [...] I have made a lovely hole in my carving now.'[15] This possibly refers to *Pierced Hemisphere I* (1937) (opposite). The hole bored into the centre of this work is given particular meaning by Hepworth's *Circle* essay. Piercing the solid marble orb brings immaterial space in dialogue with the physical material, while the hemisphere itself is a metaphor for the tangible world, which seems, because of the recessed plane on one side and the spiralling hole, to be turning. In 1943, Hepworth wrote to E. H. Ramsden that the shape of *Pierced Hemisphere I* evolved from her

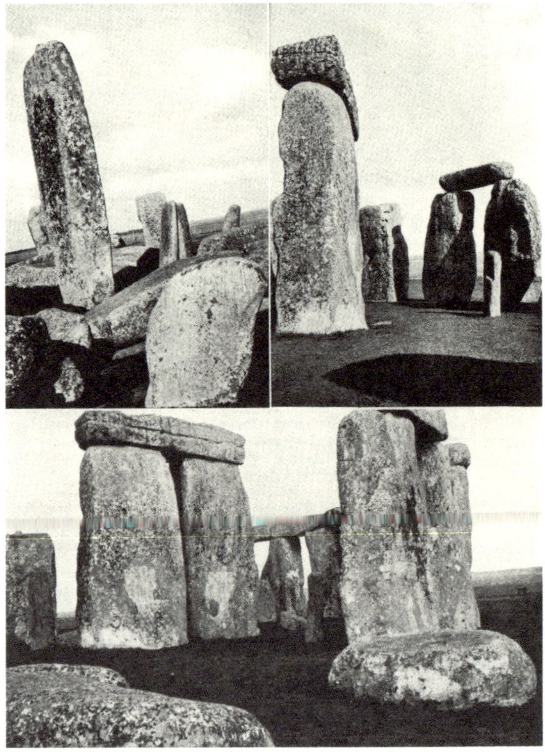

ABOVE Three views of Stonehenge, as reproduced in *Circle: International Survey of Constructive Art*, 1937. Photographs by Carola Giedion-Wecker and Walter Gropius

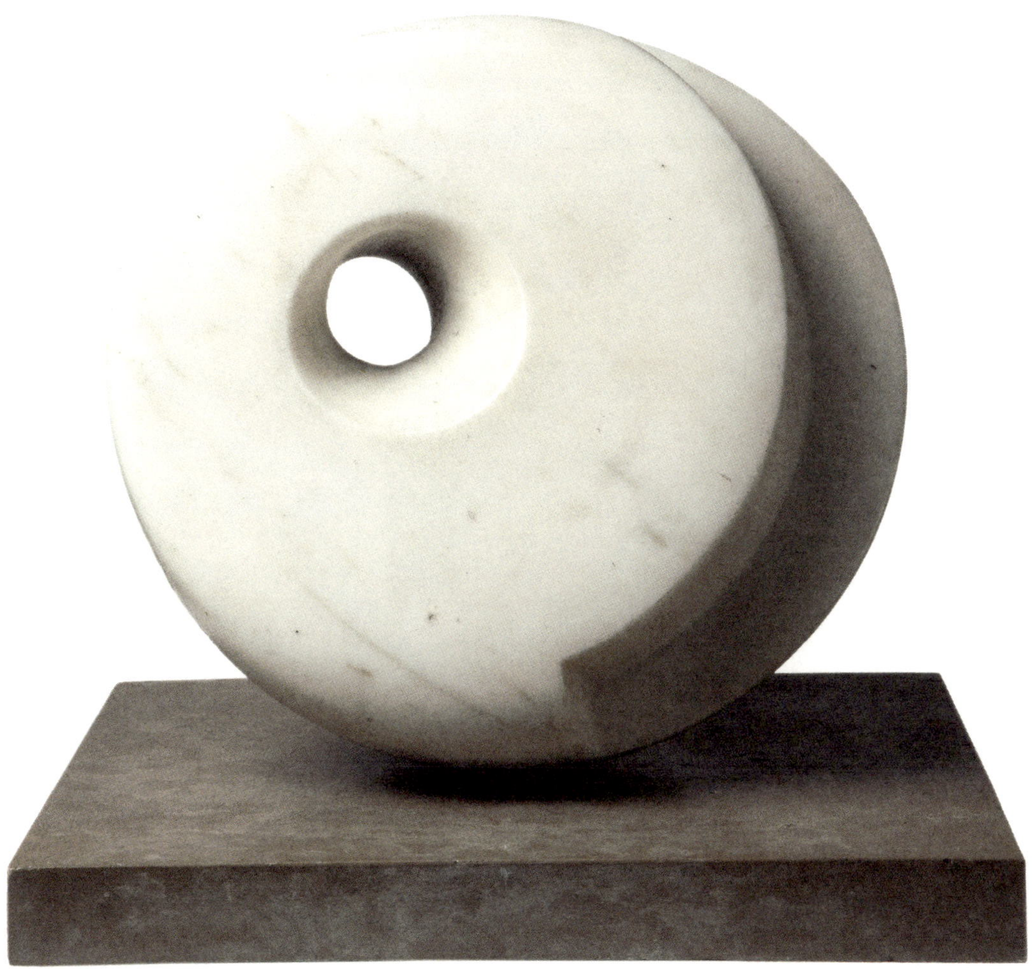

earlier 'head' carvings. This suggests its central piercing can be read as a symbolic eye, recalling Hepworth's assertion that vision 'is the perception of the mind' and encouraging the viewer to 'see' the intangible. *Pierced Hemisphere I* synthesises seeming opposites within one singular form – the material and ephemeral, the individual and the universal – offering above all an instructive approach to life that promotes dialogue and unity over discord and opposition.

J. D. Bernal's essay on 'Art and the Scientist' brings Hepworth's sculpture in direct contact with the physical world again. An illustration of 'Equi-potential surface of two like charges' is placed alongside a photograph of Hepworth's sculpture *Two Forms* (figs. 5a and 5b) (see following page). The former is an image of atomic elements – the building

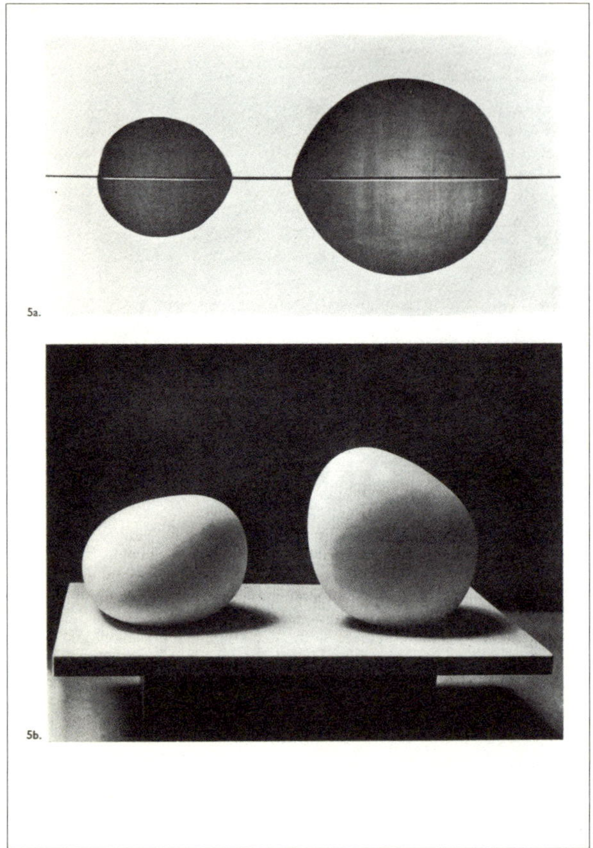

blocks of the physical world which are invisible to the naked eye – in an electro-magnetic field where 'like' charges repel, while 'unlike' charges attract. The comparison gives truth to the unity of the ephemeral and tangible, highlighting that in many proven cases they are the very same. That the 'like' charges repel one another recalls Hepworth's statement that her multi-part abstract sculptures explored the tension and relationship between living things. For Bernal, the juxtaposition conveyed how both the mathematician and the sculptor shared an 'extraordinary intuitive grasp of the unity of a surface even extending to surfaces which though separated in space and apparently disconnected yet belong together'.[16] Bernal saw the laws of physics expressed in Hepworth's sculpture, universal and undeniable. These ideas were picked up in the final section of *Circle*, on 'Art and Life'. Alongside subjects that Hepworth was passionate about (Gropius on 'Art Education and State', Léonide Massine on 'Choreography') was 'A Note on Biotechnics' by Karel Honzik. Honzik

ABOVE 'Equi-potential surface of two like charges' and Barbara Hepworth's *Two Forms* (1935), reproduced in *Circle: International Survey of Constructive Art*, 1937

illustrated, as Bernal had indicated, the closeness of biological, organic forms to those of modern design. He outlined 'two branches of technology in constant process of evolution, one human and the other phytogenical', noting instances where modern design mirrors the functional forms of nature. In conclusion, he observed that in nature a form persists and repeats through 'its craving for an ideal perfection expressed in the harmony of an ultimate balance'.[17]

This statement could aptly describe the sculptures exhibited in Hepworth's first solo exhibition, held at the Lefevre Gallery in October 1937.

The twenty-three sculptures largely fell into three types of form – single upright forms, two forms in dialogue, and oval forms – each repeated in seeking harmony and balance. Hepworth was clearly struck by Bernal's writing in *Circle*, and the feeling was mutual, as she boasted to Nicholson: 'by the way, Des told Marg. I was v. intelligent – high praise Marg. says!'[18] Bernal wrote the foreword for Hepworth's exhibition catalogue, an 'appreciation of the sculptures exhibited by Miss Hepworth', which again drew connections between Hepworth's forms and the laws of physics.[19] Of the single forms, such as *Single Form* (1937; cat. 16) (above) and the slightly later *Single Form* (1937–38) (left), he writes, 'though at first sight similar, comparison brings out subtle differences of entasis and change of section. They may indeed be considered to introduce a fourth dimension into sculpture, representing by a surface the movement of a closed curve in time.'[20] Of the two-form sculptures he writes, 'their separate surfaces are made to belong to one another by virtue of their curvatures and their precise distances apart much as two sheets of a geometrically defined single surface', such as an electromagnetic field. Hepworth's experimental photograph of *Two Forms* (1937; cat. 21) illustrates this perfectly (see following page), as the double exposure blurs the distinction between the surfaces, merging the two forms into one. Oddly absent from Bernal's

LEFT Barbara Hepworth, *Single Form*, 1937–38, holly wood, 89.8 × 28 × 17.6 cm (35⅜ × 11 × 6⅞ in.)

ABOVE Barbara Hepworth, *Single Form*, 1937, lignum vitae, 58 × 16 × 16 cm (22⅞ × 6¼ × 6¼ in.)

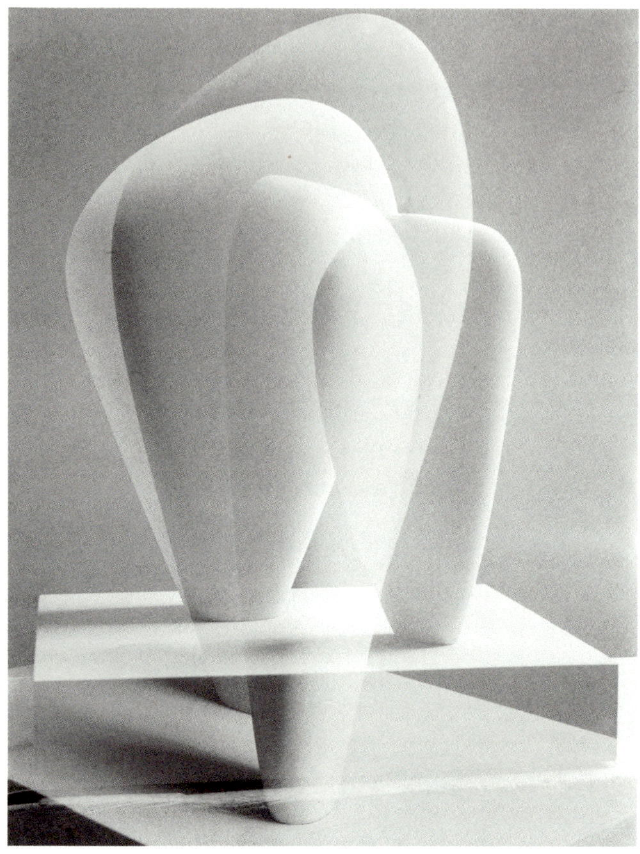

introduction is mention of *Form* (1936), which shows Hepworth's increasing interest in the forms of crystals.[21] Bernal's area of expertise as a physicist was crystallography, and he pioneered the use of X-ray crystallography to understand atomic and molecular structures of biological materials. In *Form* (opposite below), as in the related but later drawing *Sculptural Forms* (1938) (opposite above), Hepworth prioritises the linear structure defining the forms over mass or surface, a photograph of the sculpture emphasising these lines through high contrast of light and shade.

In addition to relating particular sculptures to scientific forms, Bernal felt that 'the first impressions of the present exhibition suggest very strongly the art of the Neolithic builders of stone monuments',[22] and described the different groups in these terms:

> *The largest group of sculptures are the upright blocks*
> *corresponding to the Neolithic Menhirs which stand through*

Above Barbara Hepworth, double-exposure photograph of *Two Forms* (1937)

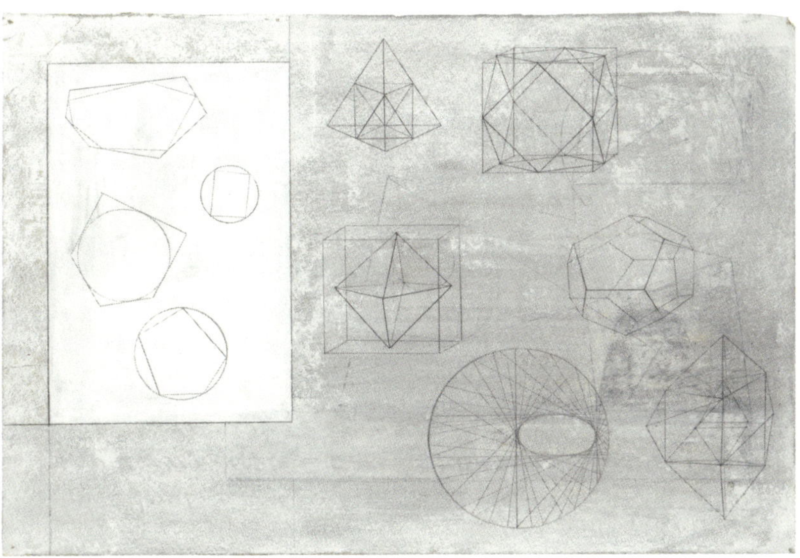

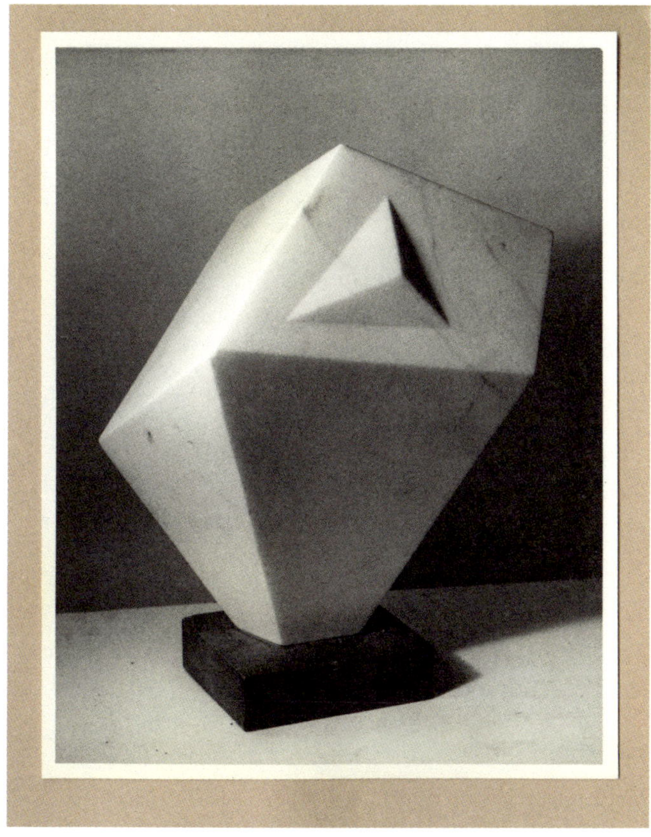

TOP Barbara Hepworth, *Sculptural Forms*,
1938, gouache and pencil on paper,
24.1 × 34.3 cm (9½ × 13½ in.)

ABOVE Barbara Hepworth's sculpture
record for *Form* (1936)

*Cornwall and Brittany as memorials to long forgotten dead.
Another group represents stones pierced in one way or another
with conical holes. Such stones occur in the Dolmens themselves,
supposedly to furnish a means of egress for the soul [...] Finally,
the problem of the relation of two uprights or two spheres, many
solutions to which are offered in Miss Hepworth's art, correspond
on a limited scale to the great alignments and rings of stones
which mark the central shrines of the Megalithic world.*[23]

Hepworth clearly approved of this reading of her work, as is attested not only by the images of Stonehenge that accompanied her essay in *Circle*, but also by a comment to Nicholson on similar monuments at Avebury: 'thank you so much for the things about Avebury. I expect I helped to put up some of the stones, perhaps you did too [...] It all seems very familiar.'[24] Bernal made clear that the parallel he drew with Neolithic art was more than purely formal. In addition to his scientific work, he and Gardiner had founded a society in 1936, For Intellectual Liberty, as 'a rallying-point for intellectual workers concerned with the active defence of peace, liberty and culture in the present conditions of the world'.[25] Like Hepworth, Bernal believed strongly in the integration of art in society, noting of Hepworth's exhibition, 'such abstract works as we have here can plainly not exist in a vacuum'.[26] Just as the prehistoric monuments 'represented the centre of a ritual', so Hepworth's sculptures 'call for some form of social utilisation'.[27]

Rather less ambitiously than Hepworth's utopian wish to reform the world through her beliefs and sculptures, Bernal's pragmatic suggestion is that 'one step to it might be the use of such pieces as are shown here in modern domestic architecture'.[28] The fusion of art and life could thus be achieved, with the benefit that Hepworth might also earn a living through selling sculptures for modernist homes. Perhaps with both these aims in mind, Hepworth made photomontages in collaboration with landscape architect Christopher Tunnard that placed her works around modernist houses, including one that collaged a photograph of the sculpture *Forms in Echelon* (1938) (opposite) onto a garden. Illustrated in *Architectural Review*, this work is described by Hepworth in the accompanying interview as having 'an upward growth but the curves of the two monoliths make a closed composition [...] in the open, with light all round, they create a quietness, a pause in the progress of the eye'.[29] The connection between sculpture and nature remained strong for Hepworth, even as she sought to express an intangible, spiritual world in her work. As she noted in contrast with her Constructive peers, '[Mondrian's] studio and Ben's were most austere, but my studio was a jumble of children, rocks, sculptures, trees, importunate flowers and washing'.[30] In 1937, Hepworth and Nicholson had holidayed with Calder and his family in Varengeville, where Braque was working in his studio and Miró and his family were staying nearby. Hepworth saw art created in and from nature, recalling, 'I have always found people's hands an absorbing interest; watching their movement and gesture reveal their inner thoughts and purposes. I was fascinated by Miro's unique way of picking up pebbles on the beach and arranging them swiftly so that his gesture revealed a Miro painting in movement.'[31]

By the end of 1938, the precarious political situation in Europe caused Winifred to return from Paris with Mondrian, with whom she had become friends. Ben Nicholson found a studio for Mondrian near The Mall Studios on Park Hill Road, and he wrote on 30 September, 'First I would thank you and Barbara so much for having lend me the bed. Gabo and his wife has helped me to buy the rest, copboard etc. The whiting has very well succeeded/ only the paper have had to be taken off. I am very happy with the room only ... the war [*sic*].'[32] Hepworth remembered Mondrian recreating the magic of his Parisian studio, 'starting from an old grey room in a Victorian house and buying cheap unpainted furniture in Camden Town. Very soon the same intensity and clarity of whiteness glowed in his new surroundings.'[33] She and Nicholson were married on 17 November 1938 at the nearby Hampstead Register Office, following the dissolution of Nicholson's marriage to Winifred. Hepworth recalled, 'by early 1939

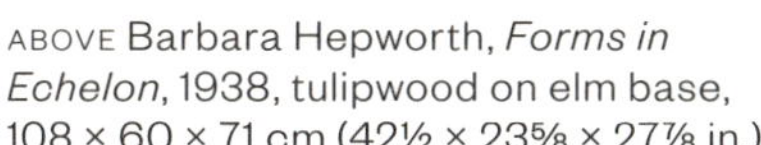

ABOVE Barbara Hepworth, *Forms in Echelon*, 1938, tulipwood on elm base, 108 × 60 × 71 cm (42½ × 23⅝ × 27⅞ in.)

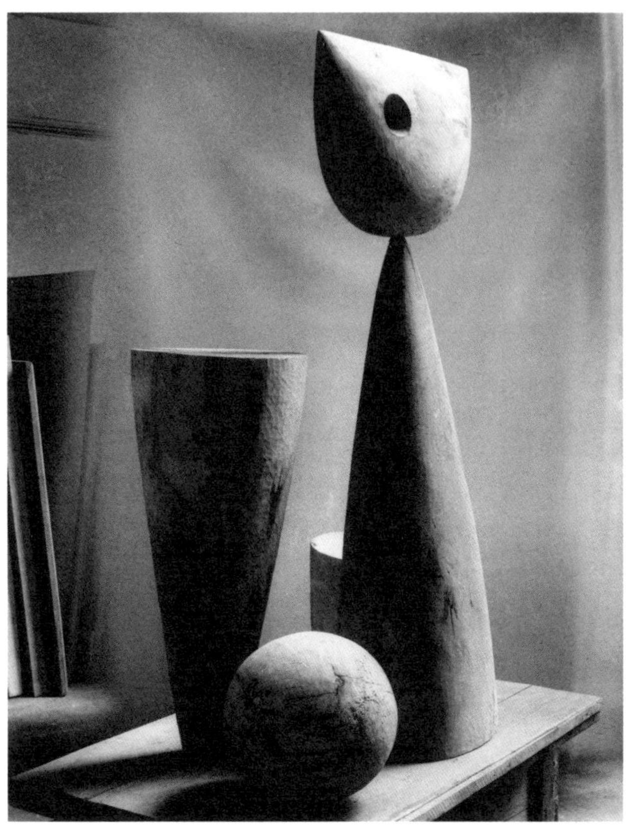

the Spanish War, Munich, and the ever increasing threat of a European war not only absorbed most people's energy, but it seemed to extinguish for a while the interest which had been growing during the previous years. From late 1938 until war was declared it became increasingly difficult to sell a painting or a sculpture and make a bare living.'[34] The utopian spirit of *Circle* was being challenged by depressing world events, evident in rare poetic writing by Hepworth, which she dated 1938–9, and which was perhaps influenced by the Munich Agreement and subsequent German aggression:

> *Dull beats the heart*
> *darkly in the softening shadows*
> *walks the ghost of liberty*
> *the pallid air of dawn is on his lips*
> *out of the deep pools of history*
> *gleam the eyes that pierce the act*
> *of self-deception*[35]

ABOVE Barbara Hepworth, *Project –
Monument to the Spanish War* (1938–39).
Photograph taken by Hepworth

While for Hepworth all her abstract work was political in its inherent engagement with lived experience, 1939 saw the creation of her most explicitly political work so far. Like many of her peers, including those in the Artists International Association with whom she exhibited, Hepworth supported the anti-fascist Republicans in the Spanish Civil War. *Project – Monument to the Spanish War* (1938–39), now destroyed, comprised five carved wooden forms. A photograph taken by Hepworth of this work (opposite) shows a 'cylinder, sphere and cone', the building blocks through which Cézanne claimed to reconstruct the world,[36] surrounding a poised figure made of the remaining two forms, overseeing the construction with a single, deeply staring 'eye'. Hepworth recalled of the time this was made, 'lacking money, space and time I became obsessed by ideas for large works [...] for the first time I had to work imaginatively in maquette form and dream up some future monument'.[37] *Project – Monument to the Spanish War*, along with the contemporaneous plaster maquette *Project for Sculpture in a Landscape*, was lost in the war. As Hepworth and Nicholson moved with their children away from London at the outbreak of war, Mondrian wrote to Hepworth with sympathy over her lack of opportunity to work and asserted their shared utopian ideals: 'I do understand that you are longing to take up your work. In this imperfect world we – imperfect too – must find our life by work, and we have a great privilege that our work is a nice and good work. You know my idea is that art won't be necessary when life has grown to its full development.'[38] Hepworth's poem ends on a hesitantly hopeful note of balance and harmony overcoming conflict and chaos:

> *The thrusting & expanding equipoise*
> *defeats the aggressor; and*
> *In darkness the root springs circular expansion*
> *of concentrated power*
> *delicately concealed in tonal grace, evolving substance*
> *now from yesterday.*[39]

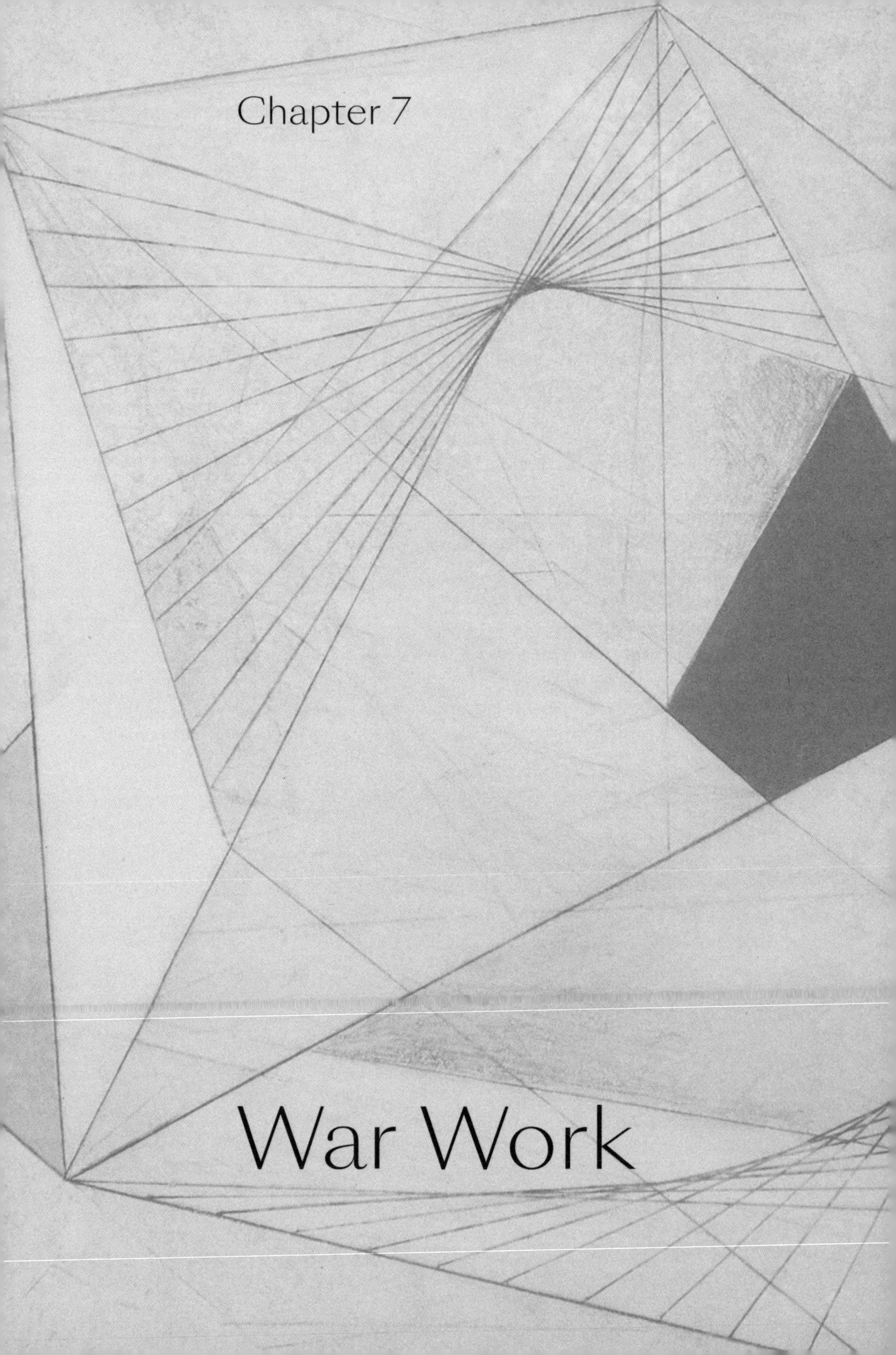

War Work

In late August 1939, Hepworth and Nicholson took their children to stay with Adrian Stokes and artist Margaret Mellis in their house 'Little Park Owles' in Carbis Bay, accepting the invitation to remove their family from London as war approached. Hepworth's departure from London is bound up with the introduction of vibrant colours into her work. As she recalls: 'I did the maquette for the first sculpture with colour, and when I took the children to Cornwall five days before war was declared I took the maquette with me, also my hammer and a minimum of stone carving tools.'[1] Compared to the serenity of her earlier sculptures, these works with colour, such as *Sculpture with Colour (Deep Blue and Red) [3]* (below), are dramatic in palette, the internal dark blue here in stark contrast with the white outer shell and red strings. The uncharacteristically bold colours may have been due to Hepworth's proximity to Stokes at this time, who had written in his book *Colour and Form* (published in 1937), 'carving colour gives the interior life, the warmth, to composition',[2] while the use of strings in tension displays her closeness to Naum Gabo, who moved nearby with his family shortly after Hepworth. Their shared

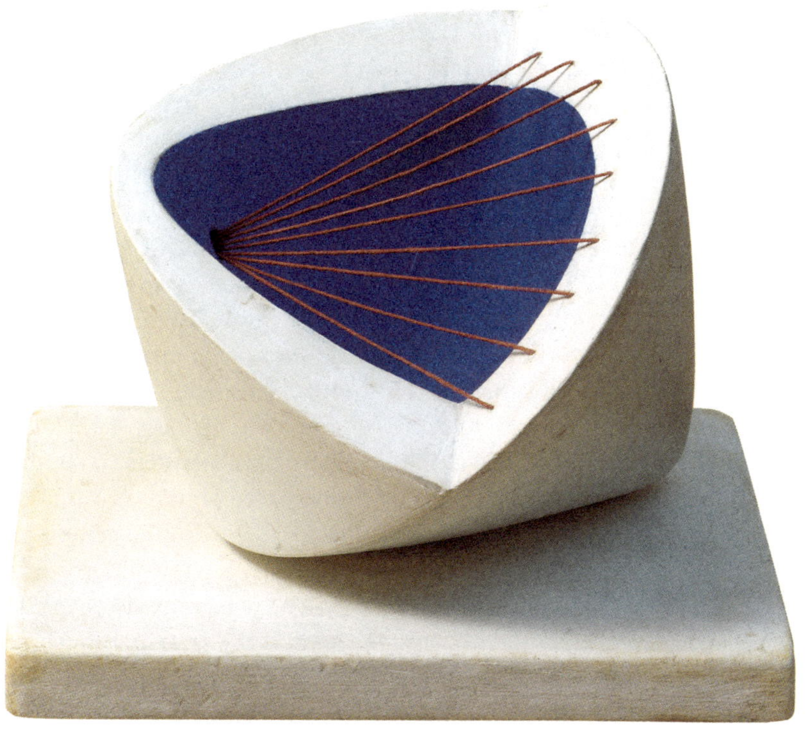

ABOVE Barbara Hepworth, *Sculpture with Colour (Deep Blue and Red) [3]*, 1940, painted plaster and string, height 14 cm (5½ in.)

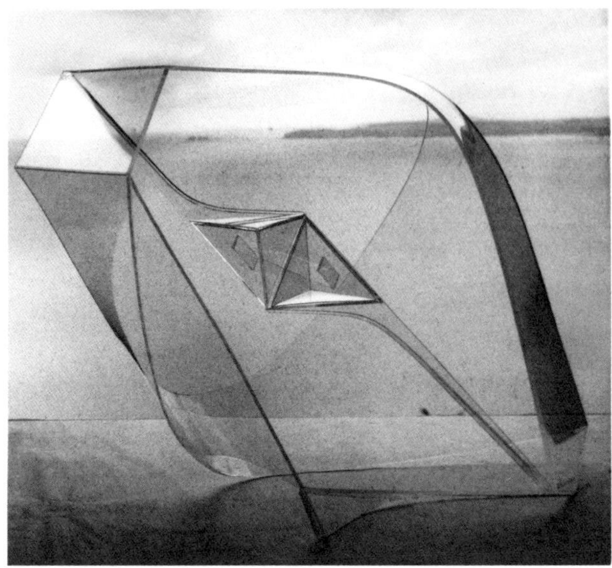

interest in the scientific forms of nature evident in *Circle* is encapsulated in Hepworth's photo of Gabo's *Construction in Space with Crystalline Centre*, set against St Ives Bay (above).

Sculpture with Colour (Deep Blue and Red) introduced two elements, strings and colour, which appeared in Hepworth's work in the 1940s, particularly in the drawings and paintings made during the war. Just as these were in part prompted by the scarcity of sculptural materials and a need to sell affordable work, so Hepworth made several plaster maquettes of *Sculpture with Colour (Deep Blue and Red)*, thinking that they might be sold affordably. Despite the fact that the first of these was initially made in London, Hepworth would later associate this work with the new landscape she found herself in, writing in 1952, 'the colour in the concavities plunged me into the depth of water, caves, of shadows deeper than the carved concavities themselves. The strings were the tension I felt between myself and the sea, the wind or the hills.'[3] The idea of strings as lines of connection echoes Hepworth's efforts to retain and build her network of personal friendships and professional contacts. Since she had no phone at home in the early years of the war, her contact with close friends and peers was confined to letters. A letter to Herbert Read in 1940 indicates the dispersal of the modernist group that was at one point so close, and Hepworth's efforts to keep the network in touch: 'I can't remember when I wrote & what I said to you – but Mondrian has arrived in U.S. safely & 60 Parkhill Rd blown to bits I hear. Hélion is a

ABOVE Naum Gabo's *Construction in Space with Crystalline Centre*, in front of St Ives Bay, photographed by Barbara Hepworth, 1942

prisoner working in the fields in Germany, Leger at Lisbon, Picasso at Royen & we have only recently heard that Klee died. No news of Pevsner. Can you amplify any of this.'[4]

Hepworth and her family stayed at Little Park Owles through the autumn while they sought somewhere to live nearby, moving into Dunluce, also in Carbis Bay, on 27 December 1939. The house was small and did not allow room for Hepworth to have a studio. She would later recall, 'I could only draw at night and make a few plaster maquettes. The day was filled with running a nursery school, double-cropping a tiny garden for food, and trying to feed and protect the children.'[5] The war came at an inopportune time for Hepworth. Just as she had been establishing her career in a strongly abstract direction, she now found herself with a lack of time or space to work. Near the start of the war she wrote to Nicholson, 'I want to be free to grow – to do the sort of work I ought to do – free to explore & free to develop my relationship with the children & free to <u>give</u> [...] I feel life is just beginning for me.'[6] Hepworth took responsibility for managing the household and their finances, writing in 1941, 'we only need a <u>little</u> money – say £1 or £2 a week – if we are careful we can easily manage. The garden is most productive & most of the bills are paid. There's lots of food here now the visitors have gone – great fun, we have splendid meals & my tomatoes are grand.'[7] Nicholson spent stints in London throughout the war, while Hepworth largely stayed in St Ives with the children, writing somewhat enviously, 'It was very exciting getting your bits of news. Please give my love to Sadie & Leslie, & Jack & Herbert & Ludo & so on. It all sounds so gay & exciting seeing such nice people. <u>Please remember all the news – even the v. smallest bits.</u>'[8] Hepworth and Nicholson rented their London studio to Henry Moore soon after the outbreak of war, as it was cheaper than his studio and money was increasingly scarce all round.[9] Nicholson often stayed in No. 3, The Mall Studios, where the triplets had lived after leaving Wellgarth nursing college, and his visits allowed Hepworth to obtain some materials, and toys and books for the children, having left London in such haste.

Hepworth worked hard to continue developing her career despite the adverse circumstances. An important contact during the early years of war was the critic E. Hartley Ramsden, who, with her partner Margot Eates, became close friends, collectors and promotors of Hepworth's work. Hepworth had first written to Ramsden from The Mall Studios in late May 1939 to offer 'a second photo of a more recent sculpture, to give you a choice', for inclusion in Ramsden's 1940 book, *An Introduction to Modern Art*. Hepworth appears in this survey of artists ranging from

Turner, Cézanne and Matisse to Dalí, Braque, Brancusi, Mondrian, and British contemporaries Nash and Moore (including 'English Engineers' and 'Chinese Craftsmen'), and is thanked along with Nicholson in the preface for 'their helpful advice on technical details'.[10] By the following year, a friendship had been formed, and Hepworth wrote on 7 May 1940 giving an insight into her daily life:

Dear Hartley,

I am ashamed because I have not written to you before – my letters are never much good in peace time but now I am usually so tired with so many various jobs I have to do that they often don't make sense at all. I postpone writing until I get a quiet moment – which is about once every 2 months.

I enjoyed reading your book so much. I like the way it is written & I found it most interesting. The format is rather successful too – are you pleased? I enjoyed reading the bits about sculpture particularly [...]

Life is very strenuous these days – the business of keeping going, feeding the family, gardening, mending etc.etc. It is just another negative side of the war – waste of time, energy, life. What are you doing & thinking? There are so many things to be thought out now – thought out v. concisely. I feel we are entering a new phase of existence & we must grasp everything very firmly. I'm not interested in 'when the war stops'. It is an empty phrase – the war is, & psychological needs are dynamic – what are we to do about it? Especially women.

Ben is working v. hard. The children flourish.

I have been painting & have achieved a good new sculpture I think. Material is almost impossible to get hold of – maybe that in itself will produce new ideas & vitality.[11]

In noting issues affecting women especially, Hepworth alludes to the fact that, in war-time, with money scarce and paid help hard to find, traditional roles asserted themselves and the labour of the household – cooking, cleaning and childcare – largely fell to women. Hepworth and Nicholson had a live-in nanny who moved with them from London and provided crucial childcare for the triplets, although a later letter to Ramsden shows Hepworth still grappling to combine work with domestic chores, seeking inspiration from the poet Rainer Maria Rilke:

*I've slowly discovered how to create for 30 mins, cook for
40 mins, create for another 30 & look after children for 50 &
so on through the day. It's a sort of miracle to be able to do it –
I think the secret lies in not resisting the chores & drudgery &
in carrying the creative mood on within oneself while cooking
so that it's unbroken. Rilke helps too (most grand & beautiful
work don't you think?) reading him I'm immediately in the
right frame of mind. Normally I used to need 8 hrs continuous
work to really create something.*

*Things of course will soon be desperate – Nanny may get
whisked away – though I shall put up a fight to keep her because
schooling is so terribly expensive & the local elementary is a poor
one & a long way off. So I'm rather putting up a last struggle
for my own work.*[12]

With materials hard to get hold of and a lack of time and studio space, Hepworth turned to drawing and painting as a creative outlet, recalling, 'in the late evenings, and during the night I did innumerable drawings in gouache and pencil – all of them abstract, and all of them my own way of exploring the particular tensions and relationships of form and colour which were to occupy me in sculpture during the later years of the war'.[13] At Dunluce, Hepworth painted her room as she had the studio in London, creating a better space for work, and writing to Nicholson during one of his visits to London, 'my room looks grand all white. Feel right on to work (both drawing & carving) – weather perfect.'[14] She wrote with increasingly specific requests for drawing materials, showing a deepening of interest and a complexity of methods: 'I enclose a sample of paper which I used to get from Colley – there's a bit of a trademark showing on it & before I painted it, it was a dull fawn, see corner. I do good drawings on this paper – see if Colley can trace it & get me some <u>please</u>. Also razor blades I've used 4 pckts this week!'[15] This is swiftly followed by requests for paints, 'Bring me 2 peculiar colours from Lechertier Barbe – something neutralish (I've got grisjaune, gris parquet & gris bleu) perhaps a queer green?';[16] and for specific supports several months later, 'I hope you can bring lots of ply & board & canvasses back'.[17] In 1952, Hepworth recalled her process in creating these works: 'first there is only one's mood; then the surface takes one's mood in colour and texture; then a line or curve which, made with a pencil on the hard surface of many coats of oil or gouache, has a particular kind of "bite" rather like incising on slate; then one is lost in a new world of

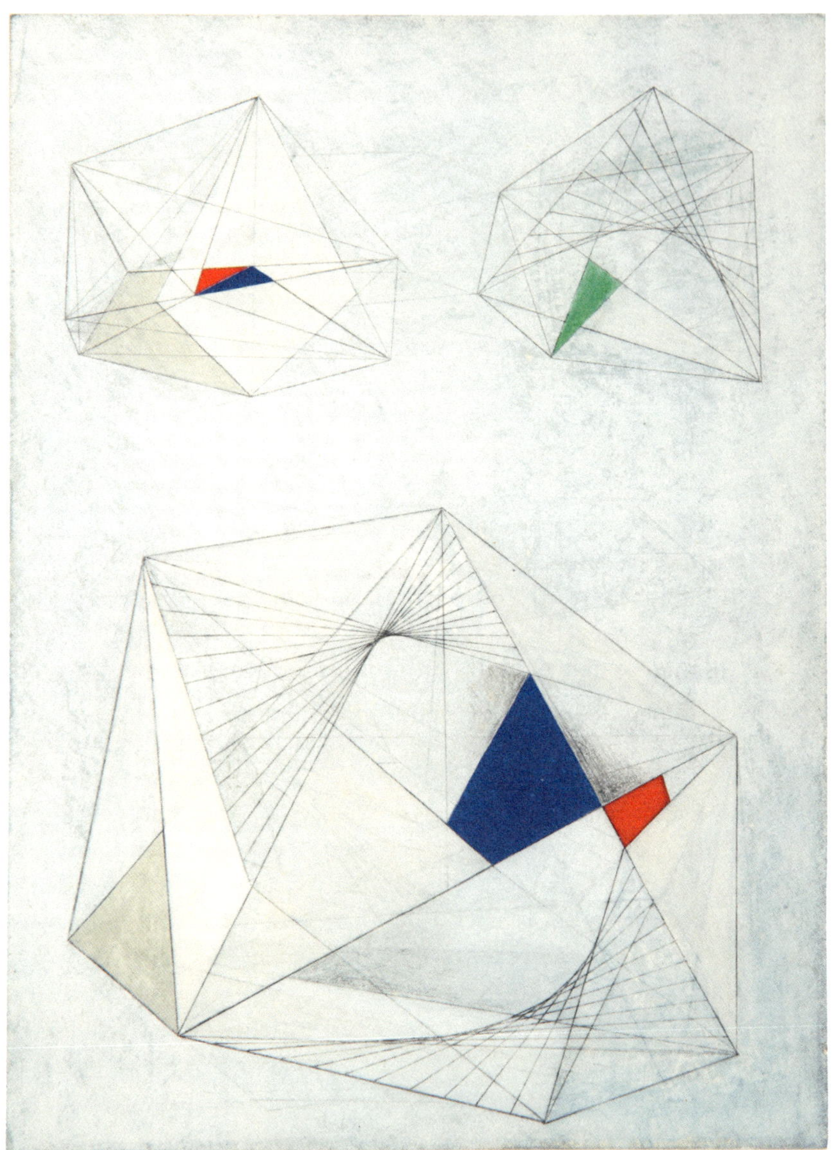

a thousand possibilities because the next line in association with the
first will have a compulsion about it which will carry one forward into
completely unknown territory.'[18]

Three drawings from 1941 show an array of crystalline forms,
incorporating curves created from overlapping straight lines (opposite
and above). *Drawing for Sculpture* is closest to *Sculpture with Colour
(Deep Blue and Red)* in its palette, with sections painted bold red and

ABOVE Barbara Hepworth, *Drawing for
Sculpture*, 1941, pencil and gouache on
paper, 26.2 × 18.6 cm (10⅜ × 7⅜ in.)

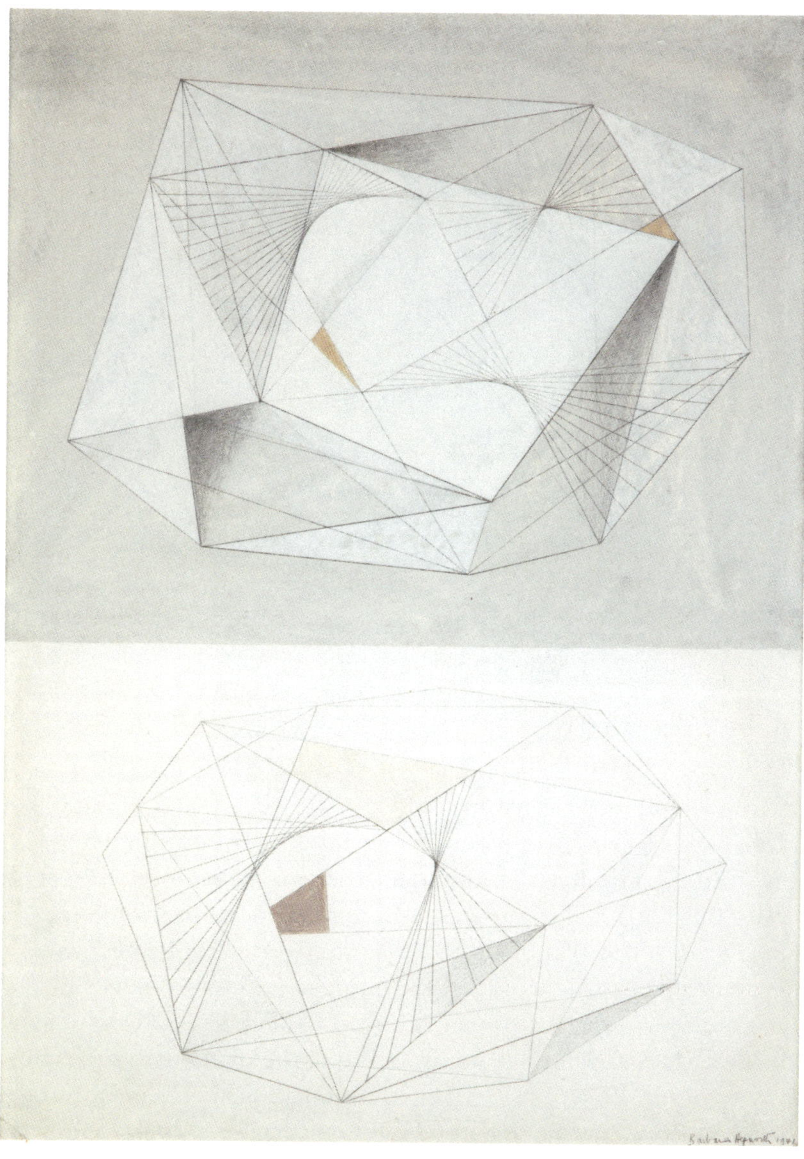

blue recalling Mondrian's gridded compositions. Painted on board, lines barely visible beneath thick layers of gouache hint at the origins of the emerging forms, ghostly tethers connecting the upper and faintly suggesting the 'back' of the lower. In *Forms (Brown, Grey and White)*, the sharp lines and muted colour palette draw greater attention to the depth of the crystalline facets rendered in darker and lighter greys, at times the gradation of tone creating Escherian illusory forms. This impossibility

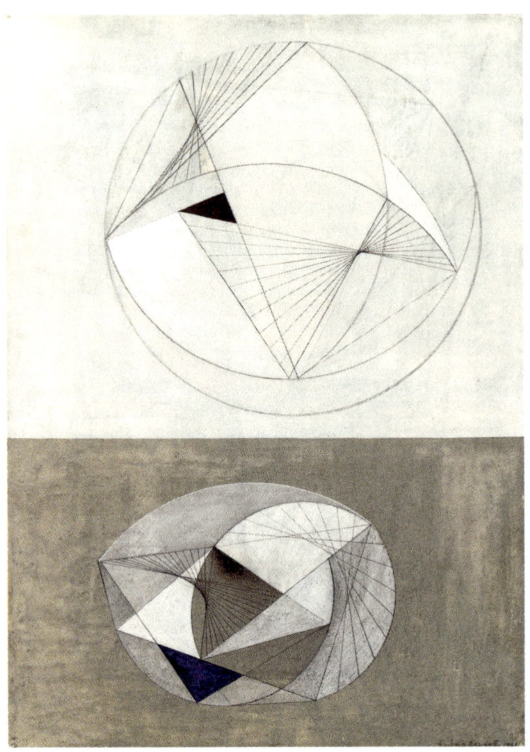

of form aligns with Hepworth's description of drawing: 'suddenly before one's eyes is a new form which, from the sculptor's point of view, free as it is from the problems of solid material, can be deepened or extended, twisted or flattened, tightened and hardened according to one's will.'[19] *Two Forms* (above) shows the continuation of sculptural forms from Hepworth's pre-war work. In the upper section a perfect circle with curves inset into the side recalls *Pierced Hemisphere I* (see p. 85), while the lower section shows a continuation of the oval form of carvings such as *Conicoid* (1939) (opposite). The inner curves of *Conicoid* are suggested through a combination of curved lines and straight, overlapping 'strings', while the central shading echoes the piercing of the form. Razors incised the thick gouache to reveal underlayers of paint and to emphasise the crispness of line.

In addition to offering a creative outlet, the drawings provided a form of income, as they sold well, and Hepworth soon wrote to Nicholson, 'I'm thinking of having a show of drawings in Leeds, Oxford & London as soon as I can make it and am most anxious that the Leicester Galleries should have one of my best ones – I think the largest one – a pale one

ABOVE Barbara Hepworth, *Two Forms*,
1941, bodycolour and pencil on paper,
50.5 × 35.3 cm (19⅞ × 13⅞ in.)

with 2 forms [...] is the best one & the one most likely to sell. Please let them have that. What's the position over Leslie & the white one? Has he bought it or just taken it or what?',[20] and later, 'I think the place for me to show my drawings would be Leicester Galleries – tell him I've sold 12 in as many weeks!'[21] One of these sales was to Ramsden's partner, Margot Eates, as a present for Ramsden, and Hepworth wrote, 'How sweet of you to want to get that drawing – I'm really delighted that Hartley likes it so much & love to think of it belonging to her. Of course £6 is heaps of money – too much for you to pay really. Please make it less if £6 leaves you short & pay when & how you like.' While offering flexible payment to friends, Hepworth was also hesitantly raising her prices, given the popularity of these works: 'tell Hartley I'm going to put them all up on her advice! But it's a risk I feel.' Hepworth clearly felt the artistic importance of the drawings, as she noted, 'I should like to have it to show if I have a show. I hope Hartley would also lend me hers, I'm sure she would', with the caveat, 'of course a show may never come off as the war is gaining such momentum'.[22]

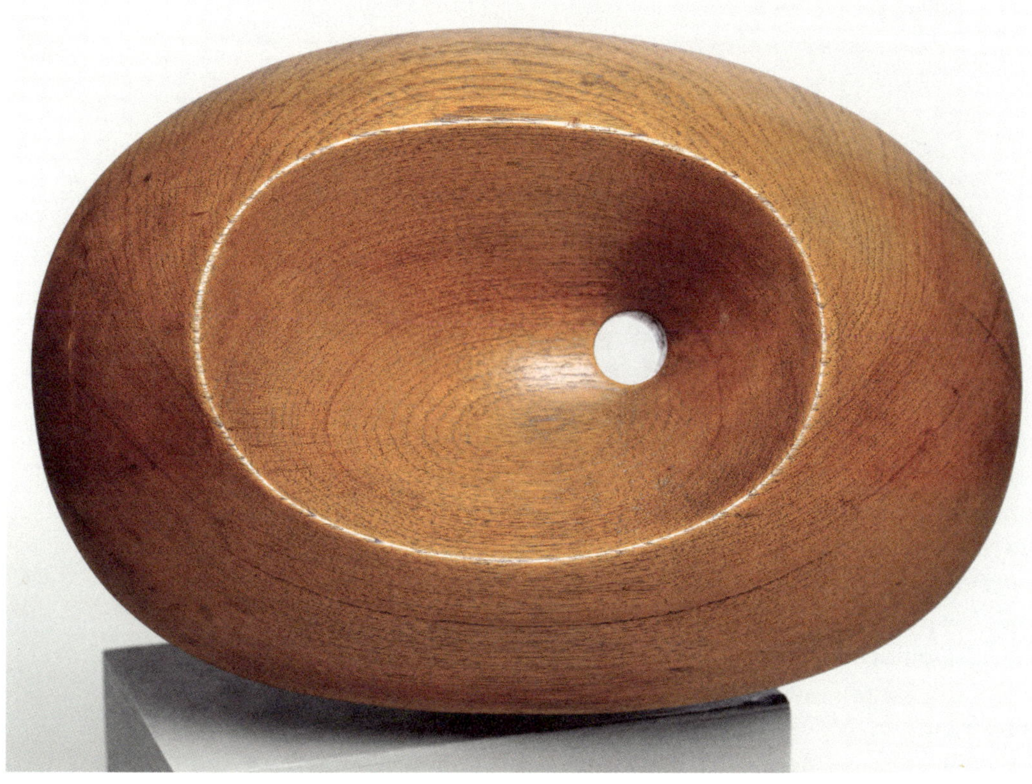

ABOVE Barbara Hepworth, *Conicoid*, 1939,
teak wood, 22 × 30 × 15 cm (8⅝ × 11⅞ × 5⅞ in.)

Hepworth was right. As the war gained momentum, it was several years before she was able to mount significant exhibitions. However, she found the new experience of living in the countryside enriching, as she wrote to Margaret Gardiner:

I feel that contemporary writing is that which gives the full flavour of the present day values which contain complete germinating capacity for life tomorrow. That excludes all reactionary present day thought, all mysticism practically except the strong faith in the resilient power of human nature. (This of course is entirely my personal idea!) I don't think one is nearer to this aliveness in London necessarily. The experience of household chores & menial work brings one quite a bit nearer a true insight though of course London & travelling about gives one more contacts. But I have been so grateful for this St. Ives experience – I had no knowledge before of how a small town works – what forces there are in clubs, in religion, in static & floating population. How the Town Council works & local MP & the relationship of the Boro' to County etc. London seems v. impersonal & irresponsible now as I remember it.

I write v. much for myself because we are v. much preoccupied (all of us) in thoroughly working out the living status of artist to society & that will never be solved by a commission of fine arts but only by the artist being allowed to take his place along with other workers.[23]

Hepworth's political awareness from before the war was heightened by the experience of living in a smaller community, where individual action had a direct impact. In 1942, she campaigned with Gabo and Stokes to raise funds for an X-ray unit for the Russian Red Cross. The people of St Ives, 'a town of only 8,000', writes Hepworth, raised over £1,600.[24] The personal connection to Russia through Gabo was compounded by national sentiment. Winston Churchill had broadcast a rousing speech when Germany invaded the Soviet Union in 1941, stating, 'the cause of any Russian fighting for his hearth and home is the cause of free men and free peoples in every quarter of the globe',[25] prompting Hepworth to write, 'Don't get cigs. I have a few & I'm trying to save a £1 for Russian Red + fund out of my personal money.'[26] She also sent work to an exhibition organised by the Association of Architects, Surveyors and Technical Assistants to raise money for the 'Aid to Russia Fund'. This show was held in émigré architect Ernő Goldfinger's modernist house in Hampstead, and fifty per cent of sales and all entrance fees went to the cause. Hepworth wrote to Nicholson in London for his help: 'I have just got an invitation to show at Goldfinger's house in connection with the AASTA. This is a group I'm most interested in & I should like to send something.'[27]

However, the experience of war was wearing. In early May 1942, Hepworth wrote to Nicholson in London, 'we had 5 alerts during 12 hours [...] I haven't done any work yet except drudgery – it just doesn't seem possible to do it under these conditions though I'm just bursting with ideas.'[28] Hepworth was increasingly worried by a series of health complaints from the children and herself, writing to Gardiner in early 1943, 'I'm afraid the war conditions are beginning to tell – I've never known such fatigue before & more people say the same. We shall have to conserve every ounce of energy to pull through & fight for the building of peace.'[29] The 'fatigue' was perhaps as much feeling dispirited by the news of Nazi atrocities that were being made public, causing Hepworth to write in uncharacteristically negative terms:

> *The world was almost becoming civilised in some ways & we have been within an inch of all reality – all knowledge, all love & creative energy being exterminated for perhaps ever. In its place there would be a ghastly paganism & withering of the spirit. Too ugly to contemplate. One does not need to be in a concentration camp to imagine the murder, rape, lust, torture & lying which the Nazi & Fascist doctrine would impose upon the world [...]*
>
> *Unless we hate with passion [...] every Nazi Fascist thinking man & woman & punish them accordingly after the war we are guilty of treachery <u>now</u> in allowing our men, our airmen & men at sea to lose their lives in this war.*
>
> *Further – we must continue to hate for years after the war until every Nazi potentiality is torn right out of our own country & our own souls. The Nazi doctrine is evil – sheer concentrated evil. We cannot love good if we tolerate evil – We've tried that between 2 wars & look at Spain & the smirch on our own spirits.*
>
> *My own fear is that we shall consider ourselves too gentlemanly if we win the war to exercise the law on such a vast scale but if we fail to do so our own children will die & their children would be better not born [...] I honestly believe that unless we hate evil with passion – sustained, logical & ruthless – we shall ourselves sink into suicidal apathy.*

She concludes, 'I love the great sympathy & understanding in you dear Margaret which makes it impossible for you to hate. It is part of your own creative beauty – but it cannot, in itself I feel, meet reality today. We are too far gone to be saved by gentleness.'[30]

Throughout the ups and downs of war-time life, Hepworth's work – however briefly snatched – provided her with great solace. As she urged Gardiner, 'do carry on working – whatever the cost. Although one so easily gets apparently exhausted, the work itself is nourishing in a durable way, unlike every other sort of activity.'[31] A significant boost came in July 1942, when Hepworth and her family moved into Chy-an-Kerris, a seven-bedroom house in Carbis Bay. She recalled, 'there was a sudden release from what had seemed to be an almost unbearable diminution of space and now I had a studio workroom looking straight towards the horizon of the sea'.[32] Her work was included in the exhibition *New Movements in Art*, organised by Ramsden and Eates, which toured from London to Leicester, Manchester and Doncaster over 1942–43. Hepworth selected works to send, including a sculpture and a drawing that she chose 'specially because it tells well at a distance because it is almost a mobile'.[33] Early in 1943, Hepworth was invited by curator Philip Hendy to show with Paul Nash at Temple Newsam, 'a retrospective exhibition which means all the work I can get hold of. (I'm <u>delighted</u> to be showing with Paul) [...] I'm quite childishly pleased about showing in Yorkshire.'[34] Hepworth was pleased with the range of work she managed to gather for the exhibition, and further delighted when Leeds bought *Conicoid* for their collection: 'it is a small one but I'm so glad Hendy chose such a good one of recent date'.[35]

Hepworth was less pleased with the review of the show by William Gibson, a friend of Ramsden, in *The Listener*. After observing the influence of Moore and Arp, Gibson wrote of *Sculpture with Colour (Deep Blue and Red)*:

> *[It] is coloured and includes the use of string: the first version was made in 1941 and it seems to mark a new development. It is wise to express no opinion at this stage. This, however, should be said: Miss Hepworth has, I understand, made few carvings recently; both her previous sculpture and the increasing beauty of her drawings, many of which are shown, make it fervently to be hoped that she will soon provide full opportunity of studying the newer style. If this is a period of gestation good and well. Miss Hepworth, as we have seen, is an artist who develops*

her art slowly after considerable private experience and cogitation. If, on the other hand, it is the result of external circumstance, it is a tragedy, for there is no doubt that her work is a permanent contribution to the art of sculpture.[36]

Although fatigued by comparisons with Moore, Hepworth acknowledged to Ramsden, 'actually there will always be a bond between Moore & myself because we are carvers in contrast to others who build up mould & fit together forms in space. But you are the only one who appreciated the period when influences were most at work – in my case & in others – & the only one who knows how essentially different Moore & I are – when he finally matured on the surrealist side & I on the constructive side in 1934.'[37]

Hepworth was more outraged by the suggestion that her lack of work was due to a period of lengthy cogitation, writing indignantly, 'He <u>must</u> <u>know</u> why I haven't produced many carvings – it's the WAR-WORK. He must know that. If I didn't have to cook, wash up, nurse children ad infinitum I should carve, carve & carve. The proof of this is in the drawings. They are not just a way of amusing myself nor are they experimental probings – they are my sculptures born in the disguise of 2 dimensions.'[38] A related point in the article rankled, and she continues, 'it would be nice (I did appreciate it when you called me a sculptor [instead of sculptress]) if people could abandon Miss, Mr. & M. & so on. I should almost prefer to be called comrade Hepworth! I suppose W.G felt that he was not free to drop the Miss et. in his position. I don't mind my sex as being exposed by my Christian name because the only way (I feel) for women to get an equal square deal with men is to openly fight as women for the fact that art is "not biological" as you say. I'm sorry PH [Philip Hendy] made the mistake about your name if you dislike it so much. But I think nevertheless that you aid the common cause (if not your own) better by being known as a woman.'[39]

The question of gender was clearly on Hepworth's mind, not least due to her increasing frustration with juggling the traditionally feminine domestic labour with her own artistic practice. Writing to Gardiner in mid-1943, she noted: 'it is really time I tried to write to you properly but I seize a pen when it's convenient such as tonight when, although v. weary, I have a fire going in order to cook for tomorrow. Physically we are managing ok & SRS are fine – the only stumbling block is the spiritual or psychological difficulty of my new & wholly repulsive working hours. I have always felt creative from midday onwards, getting more & more subconscious towards night. Now I must work 1½ to 2 hours in the morning & do lunch at the same time & 2 hours after lunch before SRS come back from school. After that my duties to SRS & house don't finish till 9pm & I'm simply too tired. Perhaps I shall change & adapt myself – or perhaps the house & family will!'[40] Alongside living the realities of her gender role, Hepworth was also engaging with the subject cerebrally, as she had been approached by Dr Helen Rosenau to feature in 'a book on "Women & art theory all the ages", she wants a photo of mine & a few notes'.[41] As Hepworth would later write to Ramsden, 'I like Dr. Rosenau's little book (pity they made such a mess of my blocks!) because it presents a difficult subject in an easy manner. Of course the whole idea touches very close on my own personal problems which I've been up against since I was 16.'[42]

Despite the struggle to be taken seriously as a woman artist in a male-dominated world, and on top of the practical battle for time, Hepworth took pleasure in the challenge and the multifarious experience, writing to Gardiner on the subject:

> I've always felt that if I renounced responsibilities I should lose something. I have always believed in doing _everything_ & my only advice to you about the house, Martin [Gardiner's son with Bernal], the garden & writing is _do_ _it_ _all_. The only proof I can offer of the success of my philosophy is that
>
> 1) the birth of SRS which seemed on the face of it a knock out blow improved & _matured_ my work to an incredible degree.
> 2) the fact that I've tried to do gardening & house as war work has (although it has limited concrete production of sculpture) given me a new angle on things & I feel today, after 3 years of it – exceptionally able to face correctly the post war world. Also I feel more _intensely_ & _passionately_ than ever before.
>
> But whether this is because of these hazards or only because I have won a battle with myself I just don't know. I work to a very simple & single-minded philosophy & always tell myself that I must, & will, do everything. You say you feel tired – too tired to write – for me there is a special creative pleasure in letting or forcing my mind to surmount tiredness – of course this makes one _more_ tired but on the other hand the victory is so exciting it makes it possible to surmount even that![43]

With this single-mindedness, Hepworth continued to develop her carving even though materials were scarce. In 1943 she made *Oval Sculpture* (below), writing to Gardiner, 'I have been getting on with my new carving nevertheless but it is a complex one & will take <u>ages</u>.'[44] It is a remarkable achievement in sculpture, an interweaving exploration of inner and outer form, and the push and pull of space and matter. Interviewed in 1946, Hepworth talked of the evolution of her forms, noting, 'I have always been interested in oval or ovoid shapes. The first carvings were simple realistic oval forms of the human head or of a bird. Gradually my interest grew in more abstract values – the weight, poise, and curvature of the ovoid as a basic form. The carving and piercing of such a form seems to open up an infinite variety of continuous curves in the third dimension, changing in accordance with the contours of the original ovoid and with the degree of penetration of the material. Here is sufficient field for exploration to last a lifetime.'[45] The complexity of the form is perhaps made possible by many earlier drawings, such as *Oval Form No. 2* (1942)

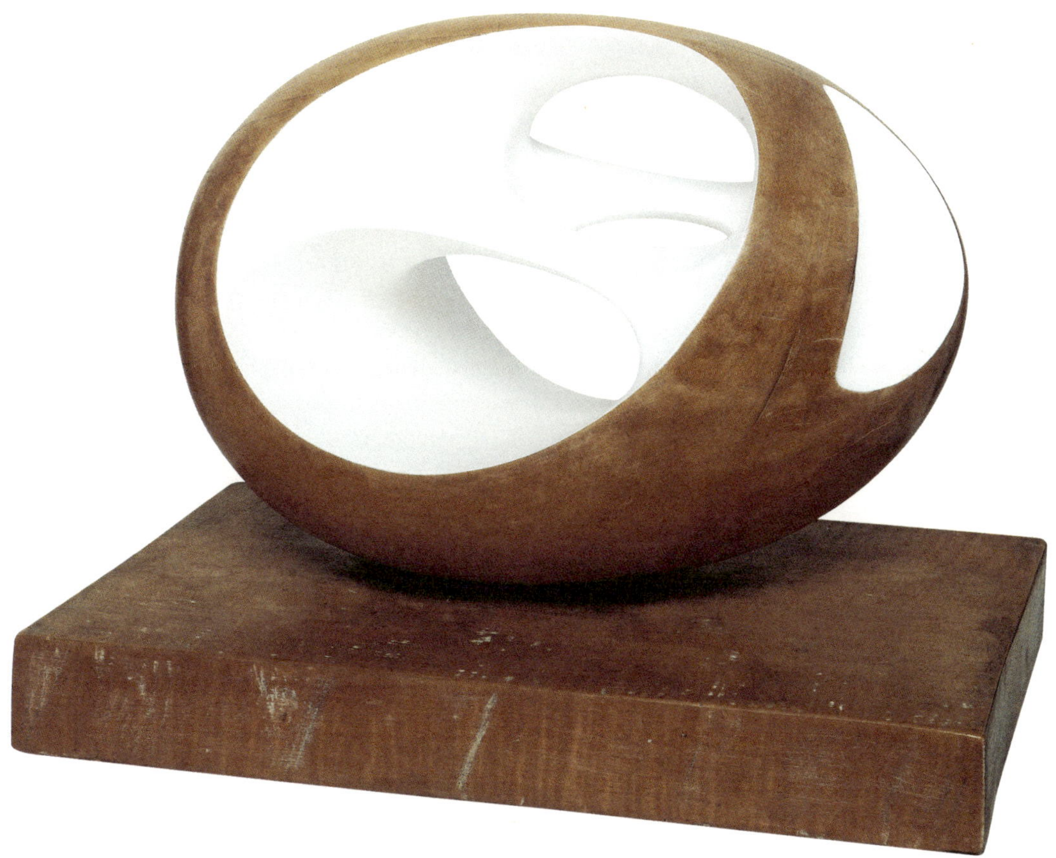

ABOVE Barbara Hepworth, *Oval Sculpture*, 1943, planewood with painted concavities, 34.9 × 46.2 × 29.9 cm (13¾ × 18⅛ × 11¾ in.)

(opposite above). As Hepworth explained, 'I spend whole periods of time entirely in drawing (or painting as I use colour) when I search for forms and rhythms and curvatures for my own satisfaction. These drawings I call "drawings for sculpture"; but it is in a general sense – that is – out of the drawings springs a general influence. Only occasionally can I say that one particular drawing has later become one particular sculpture. I like to think of the drawings as a form of exploration and not as a two-dimensional representation of a particular three-dimensional object.'[46]

In 1944, Hepworth had her first solo exhibition in a public gallery, held in her hometown of Wakefield. Less than a decade earlier, the *Yorkshire Post* had dismissed her work in a group show, *Living British Artists* at Wakefield City Art Gallery, saying 'Barbara Hepworth's carved alabaster head do[es] not invite the interest of the uninitiated'.[47] The idea for a solo show had first been broached in 1942, when Hepworth replied to the gallery's director, Ernest Musgrave, 'I should like to have an exhibition at Wakefield – I think I'm less known in Wakefield than anywhere! Partly because I have never been back there & don't know anybody living there except you, & partly because sculpture is so difficult for most people to understand.'[48] Hepworth helped to gather sculptures from across her career, writing in detail to Musgrave over the installation, 'I am delighted that the Torso can be shown belonging to the Sadler collection. I think that the contrast between it & the "Single Form" in lignum vitae is important & both the tall sculptures will make the hanging of the exhibition much more complete [...] it really ought to be placed higher than the Torso – it looks best when placed on a stand 2 ft 6 inches to 3 ft high. The curved lines are conceived for placing at that height in relation to eye level, whereas the Torso is meant to be only a little above human level.'[49] Hepworth wrote to thank Musgrave, following the opening: 'my mother wrote & told me how very beautifully you had arranged the exhibition [...] I wanted to thank you for what you have done & for all the hard work it must have entailed.' She also referred to the negative press the exhibition received: 'I saw the Wakefield Express notice on Saturday & I think it is, without any doubt, the worst press notice I've had in 16 years',[50] giving credence to her fears over the acceptance of her work by a general public.

Hepworth had been unable to attend the opening because her daughter Sarah had been hospitalised in Exeter with osteomyelitis, a rare bone infection, in January 1944. The final year of war was extremely tough for Hepworth as the family was plagued by ill health from all sides. She wrote to Ramsden: 'I'm terribly tired – Ben, Simon & Rachel all in

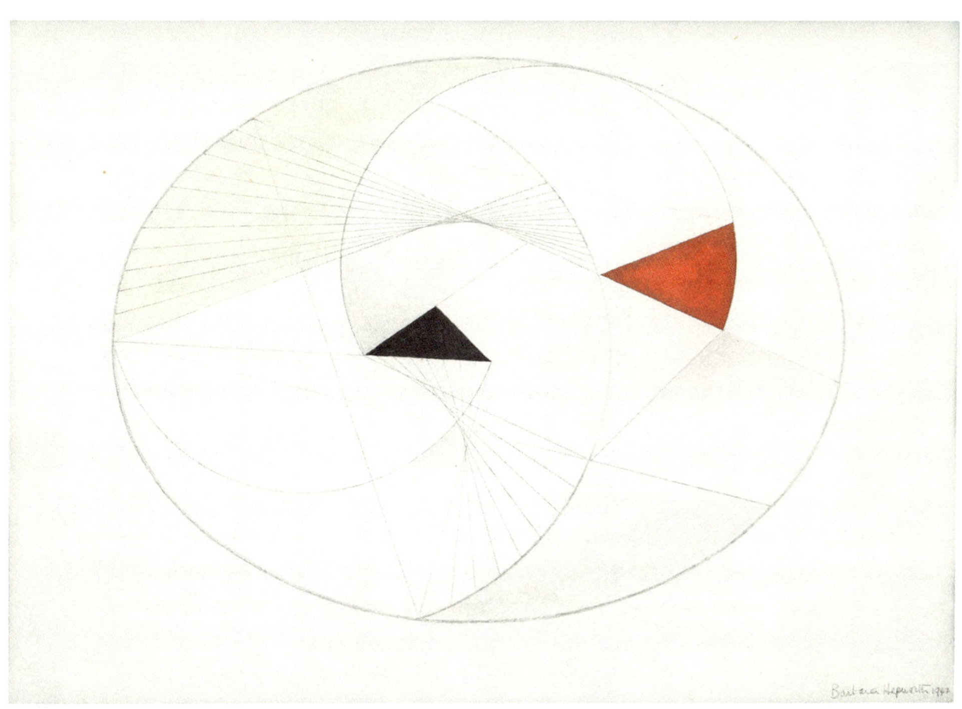

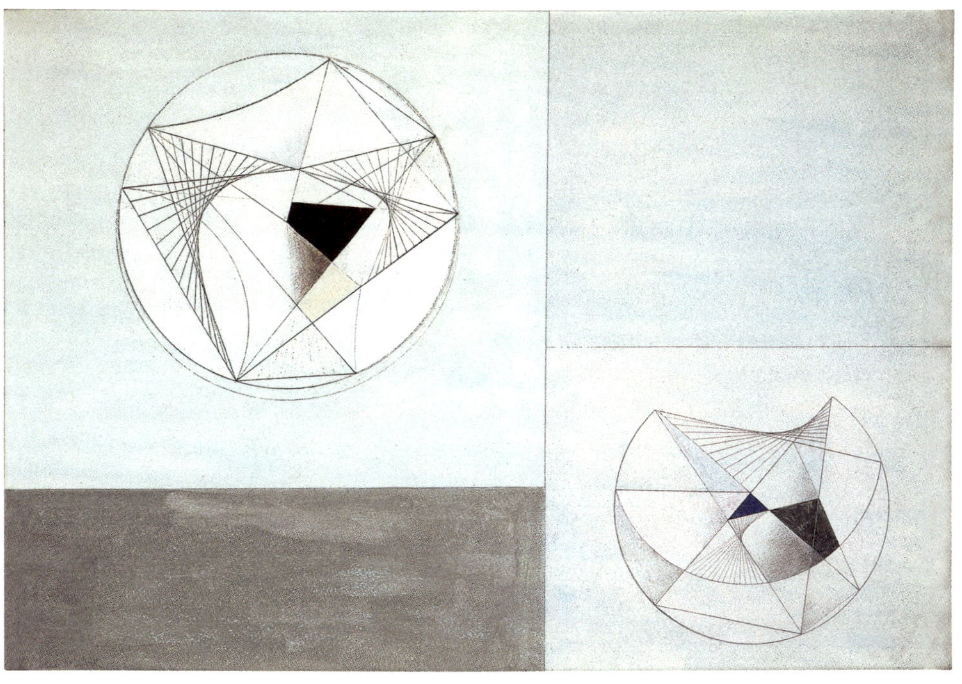

TOP Barbara Hepworth, *Oval Form No. 2*, 1942, pencil
and gouache on paper, 26.7 × 37 cm (10½ × 14½ in.)

ABOVE Barbara Hepworth, *Drawing for Sculpture*, 1942,
gouache and pencil on paper, 37 × 52.7 cm (14½ × 20¾ in.)

bed with asthma, tonsillitis & bronchitis (please don't say it!) Goodness knows one tries to think rightly about these things – maybe the great tension, the sense of imminent & awful loss of life hanging over everything has something to do with it. I don't know. Anyway, I fly into the studio every available moment – there again there is this sense of urgency. I have never seen things look so beautiful as this last week – perhaps the most beautiful Spring there has ever been – and a suspension of sound, a thing to remember these days.'[51] Six years of rations, air raids and general hardship were taking their toll, although Hepworth found solace in her work, and the curved, open forms she began to carve seemed to be a direct response to these conditions. As she wrote revealingly to Eates at this time:

> *[...] thank you for all the nice things you said about the sculpture in your last letter. You are right when you say that it has been wrested in the very face of adverse fate – fate still goes on rather adversely – & one does certainly get an intensity of vision under such conditions. But the odd thing is that I have discovered in myself (or won?) an 'easy flow' for the first time in my life. I am carried along in a rhythm which seems to turn hundreds of thousands of hammer blows into a fluid movement & I am carried on the crest.*
>
> *Perhaps joy & grief are now rightly mixed. Carving is for me simply an act of the appreciation of living, a joyful act, but one is torn & driven by alternating hope & despair.*[52]

Despite continuing exhibitions, the family were also struggling financially. Hepworth wrote of a visit by curator and art collector Jim Ede: 'Jim was charming – so nice to the children & so refreshing to be with. He enjoyed all the work, the stones, the shells & crystals & he's lent us a delightful deep blue Miro which looks wonderful in the studio with the sculptures. He bought 3 <u>little</u> paintings of Bens & though he may not realise it completely saved our life – we were at bottom & could not pay either school bills or grocer!'[53] Sales were scarce in the uncertain political climate, and illness cost money at this time, before the National Health Service was established in Britain. Sarah's continuing hospital bills were so high that Hepworth had to ask for financial support from Gardiner, writing, 'asking you for more seems a bit unfair – you've done so much – without security of any kind it seems the devil – but I think if we can survive to the end of the war & Sarah is cured, there is a real hope of Ben & I doing better. Our reputations have increased colossally during the last year.'[54]

Hepworth's letters allude to her concerns over political events during this time. She worried for her sister Joan and her children near London and tried to get them evacuated; agonised over Sarah, still in hospital ('very worried about Sarah in Exeter – they say she is progressing slowly but she is so far away & I'm terrified of possible bombing & find I miss her more & more');[55] and was troubled by the continuing war. As she wrote to Gardiner:

> *I said I would write when I felt more cheerful – it's no good waiting for that so you'll have to forgive me. The weather puts one to rock bottom. It gets more savage every day. Shrieking winds, torrential rain, heavy seas, raw damp cold. It out does January. We've all had awful throats and colds & we never stop thinking about Normandy.[56]*
>
> *I'm glad you are writing – you must – one can easily expire bothering about moths & cleanliness & cabbages & so on & for what purpose? I am full of ideas for new carvings – when I'm working & thinking of them I'm quite sane really, but the rest of the time I doubt whether I am – you see the feeling that emanates from the war activity, everything that is thought & written is so violent in essence just now, so changed in its quality since six months ago, that philosophy or ethics of the last years may not be valid.[57]*

Hepworth was able to carve more as she had received a government permit allowing her to purchase English hardwood, although, as she wrote to Nicholson, 'the outlook for my wood looks bad. I can get the wood but seasoned wood is extinct. Newly felled timber will split to hell. Therefore its <u>very</u> important to get any seasoned wood I have in the Mall send down here. Not only will it cost much less but it will be worth carving.'[58] Her wood arrived and she wrote to Ramsden late in the summer of 1944, 'I have carved every day.'[59]

Around this time, Hepworth wrote to Gardiner at length, hinting at the dramatic backdrop of world events, while discussing the fine details of personal experience alongside broader political concerns:

> *About clothes & our personal appearance. I've been thinking a lot about it lately & I think it's a very real problem for people*

*like you & me. I never thought it was going to be – in fact I used
to look with scorn on people who fussed about growing older &
bothered about this & that. But I can see now that we (in a large
sense because there are many like us) have got to think it out.
I suppose 90% of women quite simply grow into older women &
grow into older women's clothes & hats & hair 'dos'. Especially
when they have children & they lose their figures & look forward
to grandchildren! But chaps like us are a different sort of shape!
Physically & mentally – we have always worn odd sort of clothes
& done odd sort of things – we don't feel in the least bit settled
down, or contented or stable. And, I, for one, am not at all
interested in grandchildren! I feel most definitely that when I
have got the children safely through to adolescence that a new
period will start for me, a period of freedom & activity when
there will be such a <u>lot</u> to be done. The children must make their
own lives & I've no doubt that they will.*

*<u>But</u> feeling this way I have some resentment about growing
older & faded – also I'm not quite sure how to do it gracefully!
The average older women's clothes are appalling at the same
time there is nothing more painful than dressing in clothes too
young or too obvious in colour & form. And yet I adore bright
colours & definite shapes. So do you! Practically speaking then
what does one do – how to dress one's hair, what make up to
use, how to go grey elegantly – choice of clothes, shoes, jewellery
are so much greater problems for us. I look at Mrs. Backhouse
(you remember her?) with her good tweeds, pearls, careful waves
& shingle, & fur round her neck – she looks elegant & right.
But I should look like an idiot in such clothes. Vogue is no
help at all. We have to evolve some personal style that is an
inspiration to <u>ourselves</u>. Inspiration is a necessity otherwise
one is overcome by tiredness.*

*How silly to talk & write like this when one's mind is so
turned towards France & the weather & winds & sea! Yet one
must keep silent about the main events of our lives.*[60]

*I'm sick of everybody praying in the national sense. If they
must pray I wish to goodness they'd pray for political guidance.
I think as a nation we have got a sense of human rightness –
but rather than give it a label politically we would give it the lie.
I can't forget even in sleep the <u>awful</u> loss of life. What a hideous
payment for deaf ears & blind eyes. I think all of us over 40 have*

*a great debt to pay after the war – we simply must act clearly
to save our children having to pay it for us. The difficulty is how
& where to act – where is the power & virility? I know so many
people who talk or believe Socialism, who recognise Russia in
the full sense, who sense hypocrisy & hate it, & yet who will
indubitably, as in hypnosis, vote Tory next time.*[61]

In 1944, the interim war government made moves towards what would become the post-war welfare state, forming the Ministry of National Insurance and publishing 'white papers' on social insurance and a national health service. Hepworth was increasingly supportive of the Labour Party and these developments, debating the proposals with Ramsden: 'I think we have all got our particular & individual aversions & phobias – insecurity & financial worry over the children happen to be ours – so it doesn't seem to us so bad to pay out 7/6 a week & get back 10/- for the children & be fully insured! It's a bit of a comfort in fact. On the other side I should be stark crazy if I had to do work which I did not like by compulsion.'[62] Defining her political position more clearly, she wrote, 'I happen to be atheist & vaguely socialist (as Margot calls it Comm. cum Lab. cum Lib.), _definitely_ left but unformed in doctrine.'[63] Clarifying further on the point of religion, she wrote, 'This does not mean I am not religious – I am rather specially so & I feel personally everything has to be worked out _here_ & _now_ [...] A thousand discussions could not change my "beliefs" – only experience could do that as everything, with me, has to come through the heart & emotions. To make matters worse I cannot write or use words with any ease at all & it's only through living & feeling, reading & feeling, carving & feeling that I believe and have faith.'[64]

Hepworth's letters show an increasing concern for the post-war world and arts' place alongside what she called 'the cold power of a machine age'.[65] Having previously believed in the power of art to influence the world through expressing an intangible but truer reality, Hepworth now found that the war brought these ideas in dialogue with both technological innovations and ethical horrors. She felt that good could come of both these developments if art could be an active influence, writing, 'I think there will be a new form of ethics – social to political – very _much_ to the good & what we had hoped for – but the speed is out of proportion in the world of invention to the detriment of poetry and aesthetic vision.'[66] She was not unthinkingly positive, however, and fervently felt the need to somehow address the negative impacts of the war:

*I have been carving, but mentally I have felt a hopeless sort
of tiredness, just not caring what happens apart from sculpture.
There is such vitality & beauty in poetry, music, form & colour
that the devastation & suffering everywhere is almost beyond
comprehension. One has either to face the 2 things side by
side & be torn asunder by the extremities – or turn away &
just enjoy what comes along which is what a lot of people
have to do I suppose.*

*I saw 12 mins of that Paris film[67] there was a strange beauty
in the mix up of death & joy, of dogs, bicycles, many, many
women, barricades, fearlessness – but the suffering & corpses are
only too real to me – the hand grenade thrown in the lorry of
Germans that set them alight so that men crawled away burning
like torches – that is the crucifixion – the extremity of suffering
but made <u>unclean</u> by science. Nature is brutal, very brutal, but
cleanly so. Science has turned the Leonardo vision of flight into
a hard bright explosion passage through the air, bodies burn &
crash burning through space, flesh is filled with bullets or torn
up with bits of iron, & then Science uses penicillin or skin graft
& sends them back for more [...] When the Nazis first burnt
books & paintings, the jet-propelled plane, which is a monster of
ugliness, was inevitable. I cannot see any hope of stopping this
suicidal impulse unless art & science stand firm together.[68]*

Strengthening the connection between art, science, and all forms of life, which Hepworth aimed to express and amplify within her work, seemed more urgent than ever. She would later write, 'the worse the international scene became the more determined and passionate became my desire to find a full expression of the idea which had germinated before the war broke out [...] I do not think this preoccupation with abstract forms was escapism; I see it as a consolidation of faith in living values, and a completely logical way of expressing the intrinsic "will to life" as opposed to the extrinsic disaster of the war.'[69]

Hepworth began 1945 with a positive spirit, writing to Gardiner in December 1944: 'to create one lasting thing in a lifetime is an affirmation of what we are all fighting for. Of course there are other things to do – politics, social & family, but they must be welded into a coherent wholeness & into our experience. My show is definitely fixed for 14 months hence. I hope 1945 will be a bit easier. I've got into such a good rhythm of work. I feel I would rather die than be stopped.'[70] She concludes, 'it seems 1000 years since I saw you – I miss you so much & I feel v. lonely at times, particularly these days when there are such political rifts & a sense of urgency'.[71] The year 1945 brought the end of the war, and resolution of several family issues. Having spent the previous year in and out of hospital, Sarah returned home and her health continued to improve. Rachel and Simon were offered the maximum 50% scholarships for progressive boarding school Dartington Hall. Despite this, Hepworth wrote, 'it will mean colossal sacrifices for Ben & I, as you will realise, as its more than ½ our income but it will leave Ben & I more free for the next 5 years to work & earn. I was rather overwhelmed by S&R's keenness to get away but delighted to see how much they'd observed & appreciated about the school.'[72] The financial situation was exacerbated by William Rothenstein, then Director of the Tate, selecting a work for acquisition which was subsequently turned down by the Trustees, one of whom was Henry Moore. Hepworth was stung: 'I can't help feeling a bit sore as well as fed up about the financial disappointment considering what they <u>do</u> buy.'[73]

As the allied troops advanced, accompanied by journalists and filmmakers, the fullness of Nazi atrocities became known. On 1 May 1945, Hepworth wrote, 'tomorrow I'm going unwillingly & deliberately to see the "Belsen film" or is it Buchenwald? I don't want to but I feel I must not shirk it.'[74] The film, showing the Belsen concentration camp at the end of the war, had a huge impact on Hepworth:

I was absolutely <u>right</u> (for myself) to go to the Belsen film. I gained a whole lot philosophically. The actual thing is quite different to imagination. It's much more terrible but much more easily coordinated to one's actions, philosophy & one's creative impulses. The 'imagination' of horrors is, for me, of a nightmare quality which cannot be digested. (surrealist)

The crucifixion can no longer be a dominant of human suffering or divine suffering. In the nameless thousands of Belsen, the depths of human suffering – I can find the heart of things which was perhaps missing for our civilisation before the war. I don't want to charge in a crusade of only abstract qualities – but a crusade which is fully religious. Belsen was not a war episode – it was the result of Fascism. The end of the war does not wipe it out or make it impossible. It is part of history & part of religion – it should, I feel, be recorded in book form & in every home for everybody over 16. At any rate that

is how I feel, badly explained. I have no words really, but in the
cinema everybody absolutely still & tears running unchecked.
There was an <u>absence</u> of fear & a lot of profound understanding.
It's the absence of fear which is important for everybody really,
for solving peace.[75]

Victory in Europe was announced on 8 May, but it took some time for the reality that war was over to sink in. On 15 June 1945, Hepworth wrote to Gardiner, 'After S&R left for school I did a complete flop – fearful melancholia & inertia. Just beginning to come to life again. Seems a silly thing to do when I had leisure, first time for 6 years. It was glorious to take the blackout down last Fri. Such a feeling of light & air in the house; revealing alas! Many cobwebs.'[76] To Nicholson she captured her mood succinctly: 'at last I feel that VE is actual & feel like work again. I have never seen things look more lovely. Sailing boats are appearing again.'[77]

Chapter 8

Landscape
Sculpture

Hepworth's war-time retrospectives had offered her opportunity to reflect on her work, and this was compounded by an article E. H. Ramsden wrote concurrently for the magazine *Horizon*. Ramsden had written about Hepworth's work previously, in both her survey of modern art in 1940, and an article for *World Review*, a monthly journal of 'contributions by some of our leading thinkers, to cast light upon the pattern of the modern world', in 1941.[1] Hepworth had written positively of the latter: 'I liked your article very much. Personally I never believe in simplifying for the general public – but all these men say it's essential.'[2] Hepworth clearly valued the intellectual rigour that Ramsden brought to her writing, and sent a series of lengthy letters on the evolution of her work to inform the article:

> *The early work – which you say you don't know much – contains all the same ideas of form, emotion, tension & so on in a less mature way than the later. As I put in my last letter the Torso or figure became the Single Form, The Mother & Child or 'group' became a Two Form. The Head evolved into Single Form [drawing of sphere] & Pierced Hemisphere [drawing of Pierced Hemisphere I] & Two Heads became Darkwood spheres. The birds were the embryo [drawing of Two Forms]. There was a turbulent period 1933–34 but that was just before the triplets were born. You will see how all the forms flew quickly into their right places in the first carving I did after SRS were born.[3]*

Hepworth describes total coherence and continuity between her early representational figurative work and later geometrically abstract sculpture, going on to explain the source of all her work: 'emotionally I've always thought of everything related to landscape – scale, tension, poise, everything for me comes from the contours & feel of the earth & the relation of man or woman in this landscape [...] whenever I've made a carving – however small it's always been born of landscape & for me brings the outside world into the palm of ones hand or into ones room'.[4]

By talking of the 'outside world', Hepworth does not restrict the notion of landscape solely to nature, and speaks more expansively of landscape as one's surroundings as she continues:

> *I think there's only one standard of sculpture, ptg, writing, music – I hate female or male work. The only equilibrium seems to be the fusion of strength & tenderness. As a woman*

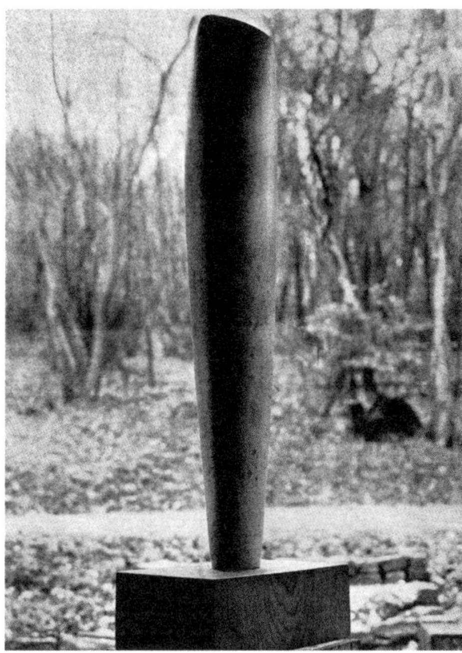

*I've nothing to say – only as a sculptor & what one has to
say as a sculptor at this point could be most easily understood
by working in direct contact with society & architecture –
by being given actual sculptural problems to solve. I don't
mean that anything else hasn't direct influence – it has & it
flows on. But the full flowering of sculpture must come out of
doors with nature & a collective society [...] Here, where people
respect a stone in a field – one gets the direct impact of man's
spiritual reaction to sculpture.*[5]

Landscape refers both literally to nature, and figuratively to the societal environment in which one lives, as Hepworth would later expand: 'I think of landscape in a far broader sense. I extend its meaning to include an idea of the whole universe.'[6] Hepworth recalls the ideas related to Stonehenge that she alluded to in *Circle* (see p. 84) – that sculpture must spring from and serve society in both the people it comprises and the landscape, or environment, they inhabit.

However, she also wanted to convey the strong fusion of her work with the natural world. Ramsden's article was illustrated by Hepworth's own photograph of *Single Form* (1937–38) (above), which she insisted on quite firmly:

ABOVE Barbara Hepworth's photograph
of *Single Form* (1937–38), as reproduced
in *Horizon*, vol. 7, no. 42 (June 1943)

I took this photo myself down at Herbert [Read]'s place in Bucks because when I conceived Single Form it was born of this particular sort of landscape. All my sculpture comes out of landscape – the feel of the earth as one walks on it, the resistance, the flow the weathering the outcrops the growth structure, ice-age, flood – the longer I live & the more constructive my work becomes, the more passionately I feel this. I'm sick of sculptures in galleries & photos with flat backgrounds. I don't refute the validity of either or indeed the truth & strength of the tactile & architectural conception either – but no sculpture really lives until it goes back to the landscape, the trees, air & clouds [...] So you see the idea of Single Form being 'dramatized' by young birch trees & soft rain really upsets me because I long for people to see this way about <u>all</u> sculpture. Sculpture will never be a real part of our lives until this natural unity occurs again. No wonder so many people are afraid of sculpture when for so long it has been trapped indoors & caged in a gallery on a stand.[7]

The image is striking in articulating the unity of sculpture and landscape that Hepworth had alluded to in previous writings, given tangible weight in the photograph, where the grain of the wood is in sympathetic dialogue with the backdrop of trees. The sympathy is not purely aesthetic or material, as her description above makes clear. Bringing sculpture into a living landscape connects the static artwork with the temporal world that produced it, which, in Hepworth's expansive philosophy, associates individual immediate experience with the history of the planet, its cyclic consistencies and its shifting evolutions. She also noted practically, 'I really wanted to present quite a different aspect of my work, one which is not so well known but just as important. People get so sick of seeing the same repros (especially as Horizon public would be familiar with Axis, Circle, Carola Giedion & Cahiers d'Art) [...] To improve on this aspect (if I could have all my own way) I should like to reproduce a drawing as well, as they are not known very widely.'[8]

Ramsden did include an image of a drawing alongside Hepworth's photograph, and wrote eloquently on the affinity of Hepworth's work with nature in all its facets:

[...] there could, perhaps, be no finer tribute to the magnitude of her achievement than that in face of it one should be drawn

*both to the contemplation of those cosmic relationships which
exist between the order of Nature and the mind of man, and to
a consideration of the basis and origin of the sculptural instinct
itself. In other words, the character of her work is such that
it not only satisfies the intellectual passion it excites, but, by
the sureness of its plastic quality, which might be said almost
to reunite the stone with the earth from which it is taken, it
stimulates an understanding of that fundamentally creative
impulse from which the will to carve springs [...] [Hepworth
writes] 'here, where people respect a stone in a field, one gets
the direct impact of man's spiritual reaction to sculpture'. It is
true that the 'here' in this case happens to refer to Cornwall and
not to Yorkshire, the county to which she belongs, but this is
immaterial since the Cornish countryside has much in common
with the North, where the conformation of the land is rugged
and of a type that might be expected to produce the woodcarver,
the stone mason and the sculptor and to foster his instincts
[...] for Hepworth, whose feeling for landscape and for man's
relationship to it is equally assured, it is not the organic element
that is important, but the idea or intellectual construction which
lies beyond it and is, therefore in the Platonic sense, precedent.*[9]

Hepworth loved the article, writing enthusiastically to Ramsden, 'I <u>do</u> like the thing you've written for Horizon. I think it's beautifully written & actually I feel it's one of the best things you've done from the point of making one like sculpture <u>more</u>. It almost makes me like it more! I suppose it is difficult writing about friends; but it shouldn't be because an artist is never offended or worried by attacks upon his work or person – he is only furious when the larger issue, i.e. sculpture, painting, music etc. is misunderstood or presented in a dreary manner. The true slight is being ignored or having some dreary article written that makes one almost hate the world.'[10] The parallel that Ramsden drew between Cornwall and Yorkshire rang true, and a decade later Hepworth would note the connection herself: 'the barbaric and magical countryside of rocky hills, fertile valleys, and dynamic coastline of West Penwith has provided me with a background and a soil which compare in strength with those of my childhood in the West Riding'.[11]

The Cornish landscape made a significant visual impact on Hepworth. She recalled:

The sea, a flat diminishing place, held within itself the capacity to radiate an infinitude of blues, greys, greens, and even pinks of strange hues: the lighthouse and its strange rocky island was an eye; the Island of St. Ives an arm, a hand, a face. The rock formation of the great bay had a withinness of form which led my imagination straight to the country of West Penwith behind me – although the visual thrust was straight out to sea. The incoming and receding tides made strange and wonderful calligraphy of the pale granite sand which sparkled with felspar and mica. The rich mineral deposits of Cornwall were apparent on the very surface of things; quartz, amethyst, and topaz; tin and copper below in the old mine shafts, and geology and pre-history – a thousand facts induced a thousand fantasies of form and purpose, structure and life which had gone into the making of what I saw and what I was.[12]

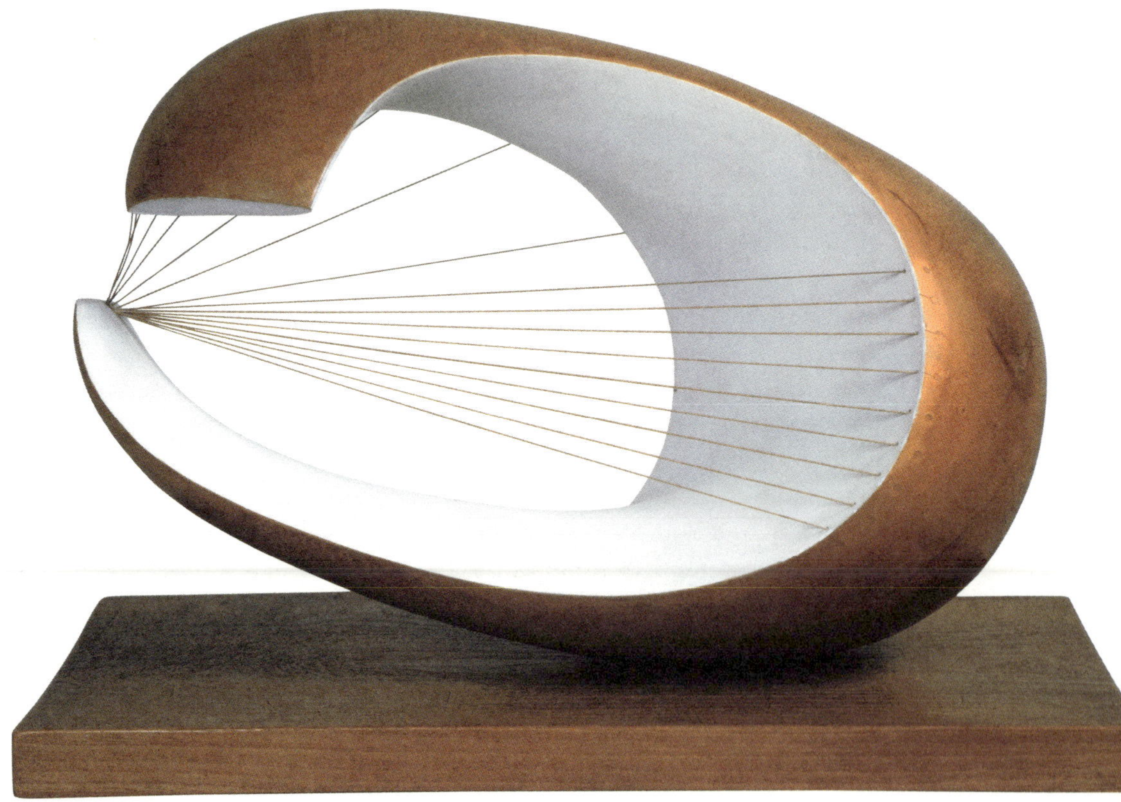

ABOVE Barbara Hepworth, *Wave*, 1943–44, wood, paint and string, 30.5 × 44.5 × 21 cm (12 × 17½ × 8¼ in.)

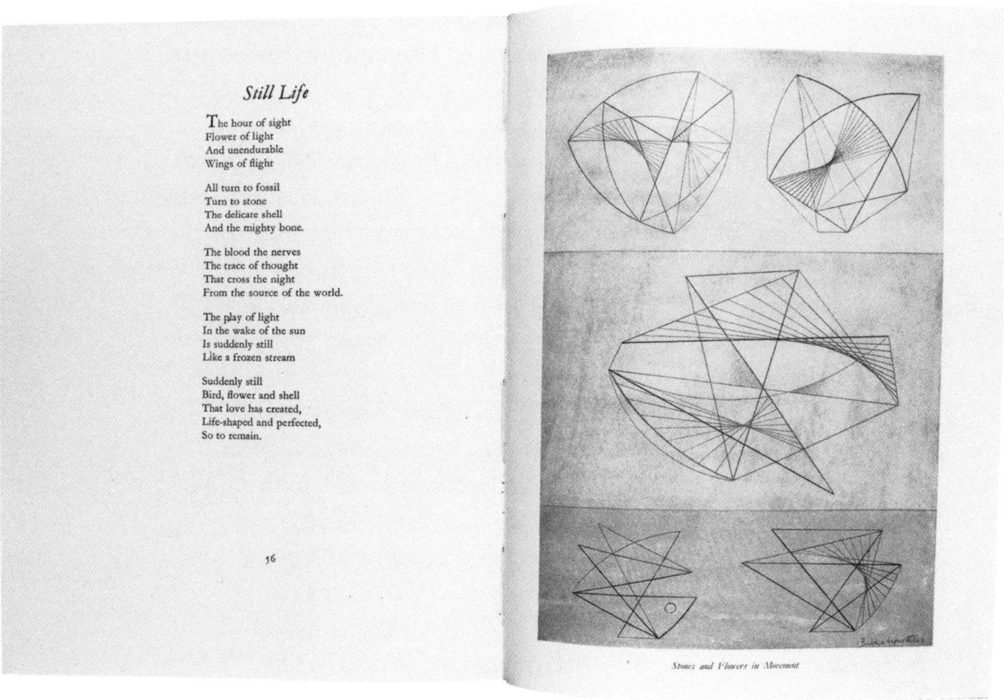

The first direct reference to this landscape came in the sculpture *Wave* (1943–44) (opposite), which literally depicts the movement of the sea that Hepworth describes above. Two views of the work in Hepworth's sculpture records show how faithfully she created the form of a wave, the upper curve of the wood thinning as it curls, frozen at the point of breaking. The inside is painted pale blue, leaving the narrowest edge of outer wooden skin, and Hepworth's choice of colour corresponds to her description of the sea in a letter to Margaret Gardiner at the time *Wave* was made: 'I have never seen things look more lovely – the sea is a pale shimmering blue.'[13] The sculpture is almost completely open on one side, and strings attach the crest of the wave to the base, highlighting the oval form of the work by casting, as Hepworth described, 'transparent curvatures against the colour of the concavities'.[14] The strings are fishing line, connecting materially with the sea and the human community whose livelihoods are bound up with this elemental force.

The strings in *Wave* also drew attention to the space inside the form, as Hepworth's crystalline drawings had done (see p. 100). These found a new outlet in 1943, illustrating a collection of poems by Kathleen Raine, titled *Stone and Flower*. One colour plate introduced the book,

ABOVE Barbara Hepworth's *Stones and Flowers in Movement* (1942), reproduced alongside the poem 'Still Life' in Kathleen Raine's *Stone and Flower: Poems 1935–43*, 1943 and, within, several drawings were set alongside poems that chimed with Hepworth's own philosophical outlook. This is most overt in the poem 'Still Life', which muses on the eternal cycles of nature and the persistence of living things retained in the earth through fossils, accompanied by Hepworth's *Stones and Flowers in Movement* (1942), in which five geometric crystalline forms are at once static and seemingly shifting (see previous page). That Hepworth was representing the natural world, even in abstract works like these, was reiterated in Herbert Read's catalogue foreword for her 1944 solo retrospective in Wakefield, where he wrote:

> *We all know that appearance is not necessarily reality, and that beneath all the changes which our senses record there is a permanent structure which is far more essential to an understanding of life or the universe. We might say that the aim of an artist like Barbara Hepworth is to give us some understanding of this essential structure. That, of course, is also the aim of modern science [...] Once a form is taken from nature – and it may be taken from the properties of crystals as well as from the properties of flowers or human figures – then the 'theme' so selected can be developed into a series of 'variations', strictly comparable to the variations which a composer makes on a musical theme. The form which the sculptor may finally select for representation in the solid substance of wood or stone may have been mentally evolved from an earlier form taken directly from nature. In art it is the life of forms that matters, not the form of life.*[15]

While Read's foreword suggests an almost academic, impersonal engagement with nature, for Hepworth the reality was more vibrant, particularly as the war ended and country life resumed. She wrote to E. H. Ramsden in 1945, 'I feel refreshed today because I went with the children to a horse & cattle show – set in a <u>vast</u> field surrounded by sea, Trencrom & all the lovely landscape. It was sheer joy to see the movement & form of exquisite hunters, trotting horses, cart horses, bulls & human beings in the brief sunlight. Absolute nourishment after ships, planes, war & robots [...] I've got ideas for about 20 sculptures & scarcely know where to begin [...] I think I'm slightly intoxicated these days by the beauty round us here in living things. Too great a contrast to "all the rest" but thank God for it.'[16] The forms of nature inspiring Hepworth were not just

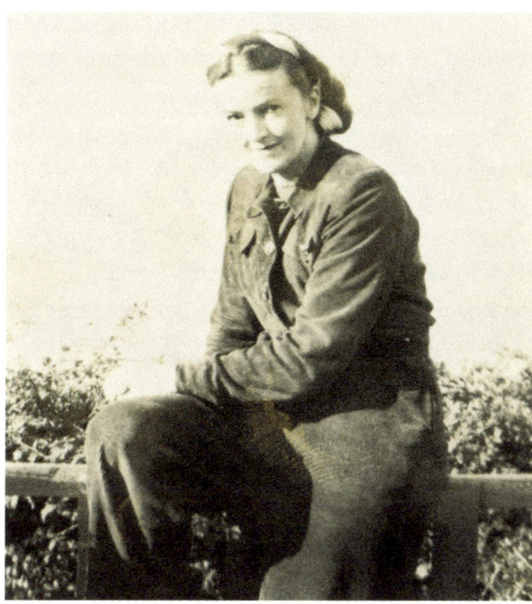

the microscopic structures that built up the physical world, but also the living, breathing flesh of animals and humans – all part of one organic whole. With the end of the war came increased opportunities to find inspiration in her surroundings in many ways, as she wrote to Nicholson: 'It is a sublime day – quite incredibly clear & warm. I really want to go out drawing now. So much to draw & freedom to do it. Last night I hung out of your st[udio] window till v. late just watching the lights spring up for the first time.'[17] She acknowledged the war-time difficulties, and the new challenge of adjusting to peace-time:

> *It is a fortnight since S + R left & I don't seem to have anything to show for that time of leisure. I didn't know how tired I was until the necessity for constant action was removed. Soon I shall feel quite different & be able to work & move easily. So much to be enjoyed now & so many things to be discovered. All these years I have tried to count my blessings each day but looking back – it wasn't really a life at all – factory life would have been only slightly worse. But the children are reared & Sarah getting well & some good sculptures done – that is something.*[18]

With Hepworth's new-found freedom she discovered more of her physical surroundings, exploring the sensations of being in the landscape.

ABOVE Barbara Hepworth at Carbis Bay, Cornwall, 1943

Just as she perceived 'form' in the animals and humans at the county show, so she became attuned to the visual correspondences of her lived sensations. As she recalled in 1952:

> *From the sculptor's point of view one can either be the spectator of the object or the object itself. For a few years I became the object. I was the figure in the landscape and every sculpture contained to a greater or lesser degree the ever-changing forms and contours embodying my own response to a given position in the landscape. What a different shape and 'being' one becomes lying on the sand with the sea almost above from when standing against the wind on a high sheer cliff with seabirds circling patterns below one, and again what a contrast between the form one feels within oneself sheltering near some great rocks or reclining in the sun on the grass-covered rocky shapes which make the double spiral of Pendour or Zennor Cove; this transmutation of essential unity with land and seascape, which derives from all the sensibilities, was for me a voyage of exploration.*[19]

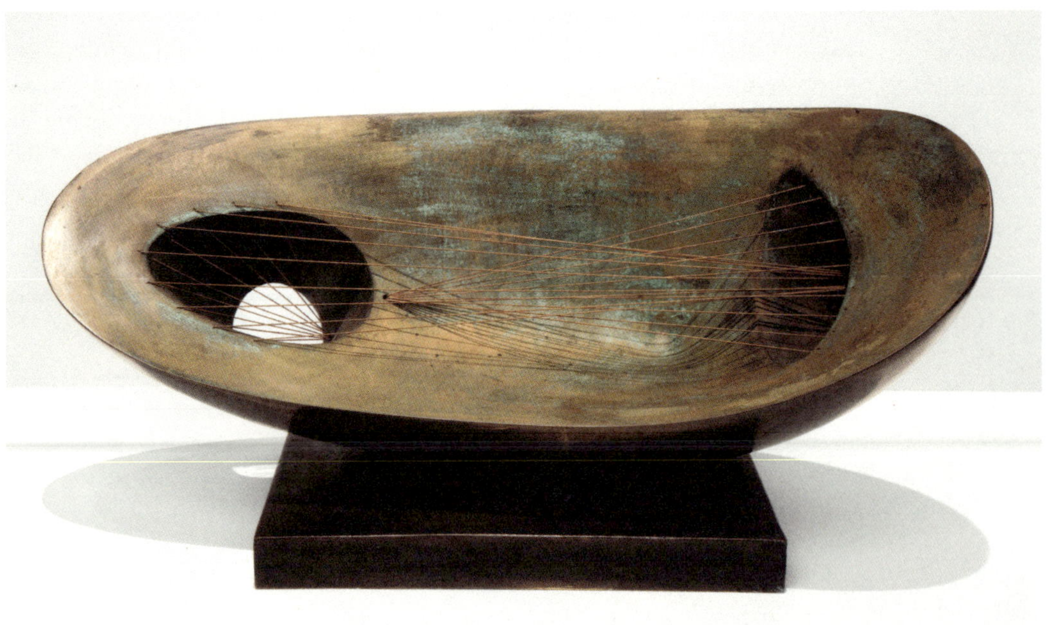

ABOVE Barbara Hepworth, *Landscape Sculpture*, 1944 (cast in 1961), bronze, 27.1 × 65.5 × 26.8 cm (10⅝ × 25¾ × 10½ in.)

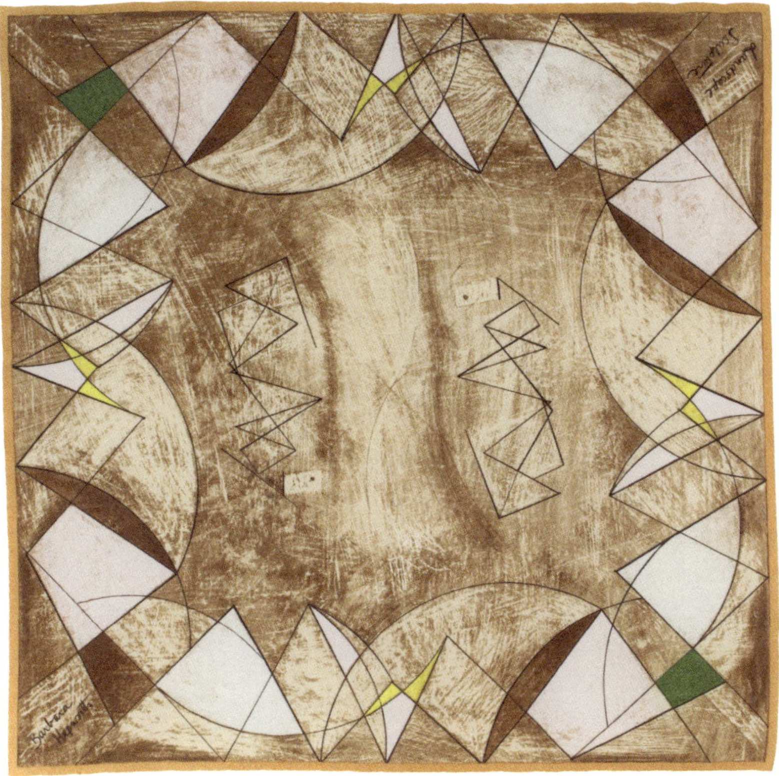

Hepworth's *Landscape Sculpture* (opposite) is one such 'embodied' work, carved in wood in 1944 and cast in bronze in 1961. The form is a hollowed-out oval with two pierced concavities, the created space intersected with a complex lattice of interweaving strings. Hepworth would describe the oval or pierced form as expressing 'the feeling of the embrace of living things, either in nature or in the human spirit'.[20] The sculpture curves up on both sides, conveying the experience of being nestled within a bay: Ramsden proposed that a specific location inspired this work, describing it as 'a transcription of the felt "pull" existing between two hills, in Uny Lelant',[21] near to Chy-an-Kerris.

    While the original wood carving was left unpainted, the later bronze casts were coloured with green, mottled patination on the inner surface, suggesting the grass-covered hills of West Penwith. Several years later, Hepworth was commissioned by Zika Ascher to design a scarf in the series of silk Ascher squares, and gave the fabric design the same title as this work, 'Landscape Sculpture' (1947) (above). In writing a short text to accompany the design, intended for an unrealised book, she explained, 'textile designing is more than patterning. Colour and form go hand in hand – brown fields and green hills cannot be divorced from the earth's shape – a square becomes a triangle, a triangle a circle, a circle an oval by the continuous curve of folding: and we return, always, to the essential human form – the human form in landscape.'[22]

Colour was increasingly important in Hepworth's work at this time, and her letters to Nicholson show her sensitivity to the range of hues in her surroundings: 'there must be magic in this country round here. Yesterday it was grey & vivid emerald & black. Today it is the brightest blue & white & gold & autumn brown. Small white flecks on the sea all over it.'[23] In 1946, she discussed colour in a Q&A published in *Studio*, titled

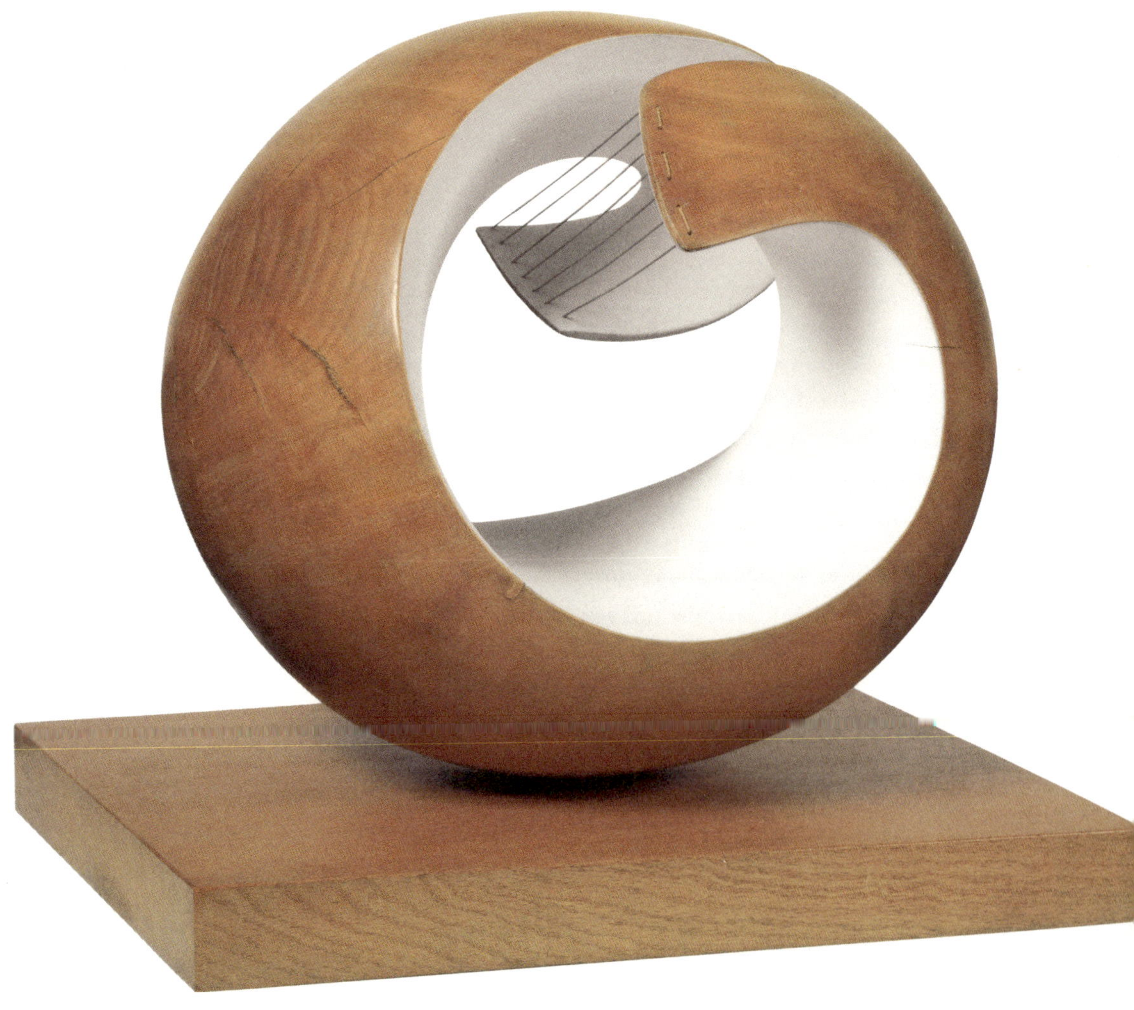

ABOVE Barbara Hepworth, *Pelagos*, 1946, elm and strings on oak base, 43 × 46 × 38.5 cm (16⅞ × 18⅛ × 15⅛ in.)

'Approach to Sculpture': 'I have been deeply interested during the last ten years in the use of colour with form. I have applied oil colour – white, grey, and blues of different degrees of tone. Except in two instances I have always used colour with concave forms [...] becoming inherent in the formal idea.'[24] *Pelagos* (1946) exemplified this fusion of form and colour (opposite), and was reproduced on the cover of *Studio* as well as illustrating the article within. Its title means 'sea' in Greek, and, as with *Landscape Sculpture*, it relates to a specific landscape, in this case the view from Hepworth's studio at Chy-an-Kerris, 'looking straight towards the horizon of the sea and enfolded (but with always the escape for the eye straight out to the Atlantic) by the arms of the land to the left and the right of me. I have used this idea in *Pelagos*.'[25]

While described by Herbert Read as a 'Constructive image',[26] *Pelagos* exhibits Hepworth's personal embodied response to her organic being and environment. The two spiralling arms of the hollowed-out ovoid suggest the encirclement of the landscape, which Hepworth also suggested as a metaphor for a mother's nurturing embrace: 'the "closed form", such as the oval, spherical or pierced form (sometimes incorporating colour) [...] translates for me the association of meaning of gesture in landscape; in the repose of say a mother & child'.[27] Although still deeply committed to many of the Constructive ideals of *Circle*, Hepworth infused these ideas with her own lived experience. As she wrote to Ramsden in 1946:

> *For me there is a huge realm of unconscious relationship between*
> *material & thought & emotion – which holds all the joy &*
> *gives 'life'.*[28] *Every piece of wood or stone has a different life of*
> *its own which one has to come to terms with. I could, for the*
> *rest of my life, take an egg form & in <u>different</u> materials carve*
> *an infinite number of sculptures all giving different sort of*
> *'life'. The sensuous joy of material & touch, hardness, softness,*
> *colour, weight, texture are all bound up (for me) in the emotional*
> *experience of past & present. That is, I only have a partial*
> *idea of what I'm going to do. Constructive seems to imply a*
> *clean & total idea of what is going to be done coupled with a*
> *strict adherence to certain laws & principles. I want to be free*
> *to impose my own discipline. I don't like theories or doctrines*
> *because I wish to be free to break laws if necessary!*[29]

She echoed these sentiments to Gardiner, writing, 'I hope my work will always be constructive but I don't want to be called "c-ivist" any more

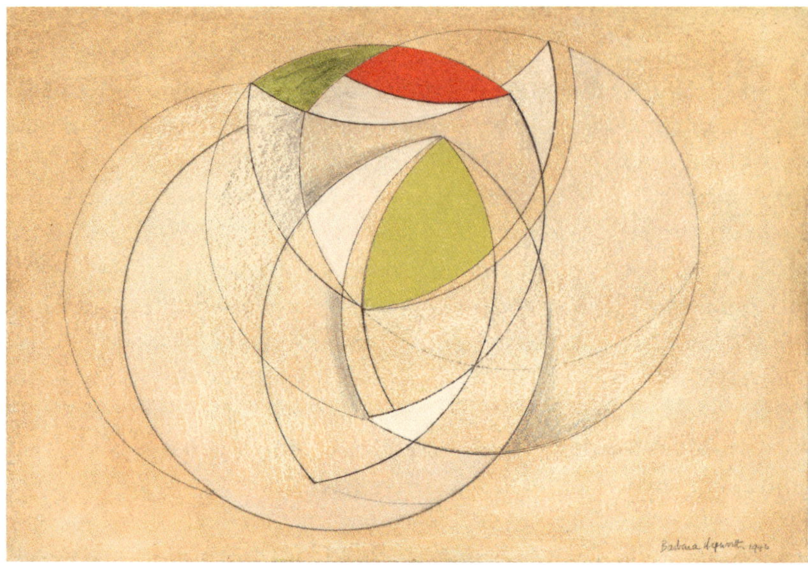

than "Nicholson"! [...] I'll never belong willingly to group or party that represses the natural flow of enjoyment & love for all the facets.'[30] Her drawings and paintings of this time echo this shift, angular and crystal-line cuboids giving way to the sensuous curves and movement of works such as *Curved Forms with Red and Yellow* (1946) (above).

Despite the immense inspiration of the landscape, after the war Hepworth considered returning to London, at least for the winters, to work in No. 3: 'I must work in London this winter – I'm saving all my stone-carving for then – I can't carve stone in a small room & anyway I want to be in London & plan to leave here in Oct when the kids have gone to school.'[31] Not all of the problems Hepworth faced during the war were resolved in peace-time, and a range of children's inevitable sick-nesses and colds, financial worries and household management caused Hepworth to write in frustration, 'I dream all day about being alone, able to sleep & eat when I want to, work when I want to, go out when I feel inclined to.'[32] Both Hepworth and Nicholson wanted to devote time to their careers, and this caused friction as they attempted to balance their work with childcare:

> *I agree with you entirely that one of us should work over*
> *Xmas but I intend to work anyway so it only remains for*
> *you to fix up for yourself – which you have done by saying*
> *you will be in the studio in London. It is nice of you to offer*

ABOVE Barbara Hepworth, *Curved Forms with Red and Yellow*, 1946, oil and pencil on board, 37.5 × 26.7 cm (14¾ × 10½ in.)

*to give up your work so that I could go away to work. I should
like to reserve that offer – if you will let me – until nearer my
show when such help might be invaluable to me. I should hate
'not seeing the children' during the hols. I should never have
countenanced them going to Boarding School unless I had felt
I could rely on a good & healthy contact with them during the
holidays [...] So we just come back to where I started from.
That in my considered opinion a place must be found where
'work' & children are compatible.*[33]

These tensions were set against the backdrop of immediate post-war society, where political in-fighting and civil wars across Europe led Hepworth to lament, '½ the world is going crazy, the other ½ is dying. The only thing to do is to live simply & make as many good sculptures or paintings as one can before one dies.'[34] On a practical level, rationing was still in place and resources were limited. Hepworth wrote to Ramsden, thanking her for a food parcel and giving an insight into these harsh realities: 'we have all been eating the lovely food & are most grateful to you. Food is really scarce here even if one has time to queue up for it.'[35]

In the lead-up to Hepworth's show at the Lefevre Gallery in 1946, her first solo exhibition after the war and her first in London since 1937, tensions increased. She wrote to Gardiner:

*The last 3 days have been sheer hell & I feel that our marriage
is really foundering. 4 children, all seedy, quarrelling like hell in
the house from morning till night because of bad weather & Ben
with asthma behaving like a demented creature because of the
hellish domestic scene. I have 10 mins in the studio & 30 rushing
round the house calming everybody if I can, the chores are never-
ending, the work to be done in the studio piles up & Ben is so
irate he blames me for everything [...] 2 months summer hols
with an irate husband & father in the house all day & all night
is a most desperate strain. My back is fairly broad & I can stand
most things & even work in spite of things but I can't bear his
unhappiness & his reproaches.*

*He has so little energy these days for love, love of life, love
of me, love of the children & all the things that build up life
apart from things being amusing & fun when things go quite
smoothly. Such exhaustion must have obvious physical causes &
I still hope to persuade him to see some good doctors in London.*

*You know how difficult that will be with Ben! The worst of
these Christian Science people is that when that belief fails
them they cannot transfer their faith to medical cure & so they
flounder about getting worse & more wretched & helpless about
everything – still expecting some miracle to occur instead of
taking practical steps.*[36]

Although Hepworth was still committed to Christian Science thought, she
rather typically married this belief with a practical approach to healthcare
and consulted medical doctors when she or her children were unwell.

Finding time to work, alongside managing family life, meant that
preparing for an exhibition to be held in October dominated Hepworth's
year. Writing in the spring, she noted:

*I have been deep in work – the difficulty is that, although I'm
not coming up to London till early Oct, I have only got 6 more
weeks in which to work! It sounds silly – but you see all the
children come back about July 20th – life will be somewhat hectic
till Sept. 21st & during that time all their winter outfits have to
be prepared – then when they get off I shall have a hectic 2 wks
packing up this house & my tools & work. So you see every
moment now (while my sister is here) is of greatest value. I've
got about 7 unfinished sculptures on the go & am trying to
resist the temptation to start 7 more!*[37]

This echoed a statement in *Studio* about her sculptural working process:

*[...] all the time I am not working I am thinking about
sculpture. Looking out of a window or walking down the road
it is impossible not to be aware of form and colour. Then a new
project suddenly appears, and demands realisation as a result
of accumulated emotional experience. The carving process is a
slow process and the conceiving of a project seems to spring out
of a general and sustained experience than one particular
incident. Consequently the carrying out of one idea and
the conception of new idea usually run concurrently.*[38]

The lengthy process of developing and producing new work, compounded
by the logistical practicalities of showing sculpture, did not lend itself to
easy commercial success, as Hepworth was aware, writing, 'I ought to be

showing work here there & everywhere but the packing is so formidable a job & takes me such ages that I put off & off tackling it – it is silly of me because people are buying now & I need the money & by next spring there may be a slump! Still I must finish the work I've started.'[39]

Her Lefevre exhibition led to Hepworth considering the titles of her works more deeply. Already the 1940s had seen the introduction of more lyrical titles, moving away from purely descriptive 'Single Form' or 'Two Forms', and mathematical terms such as 'Conoid' or 'Sphere', towards titles that communicated landscape associations. Hepworth wrote to Ramsden, giving an insight into both the emotions that were contained in the work and the way she hoped that these were communicated:

> *I've been sitting up late at night trying to fix my catalogues & titles. I'm more than ever convinced that the right title is absolutely necessary to me. Can you help me? I've forgotten all my Greek now & haven't a dictionary. I know the feeling & intention of each carving but the exact words are elusive & also I'm very fussy about names & words generally – say some of them often & they become silly – without music. I will list you the ones I'm sticking on. If you agree with Greek word please tell me, correct spelling & punctuation!!*
>
> 1) *Small white marble with yellow – intention is 'flower' – lyric. Can I call it 'Anthos'? How do you pronounce?*
>
> 2) *Large stone with colour. Feeling is Genesis – (obviously impossible) also the 'genesis' is very peaceful. I had thought of 'Arkhe' but don't feel satisfied – though 'the beginning' would be the right idea. 'Origin'? 'Source'? (not quite right?) 'Eirene'? I like Arkhe written but perhaps you will have an idea.*
>
> 3) *Is there a word for 'evolution' – I could cut out the spirit & call it 'penetration' [drawing of Oval Sculpture] but that implies a physical act in some way & I don't like it. The form is evolving & the idea.*
>
> 4) *The grey elm has acquired a word – it is female & sad. A Spaniard the other day said she was crying. It really is 'lamentation' I think that will do – or do you prefer 'lament'? He suggested the equivalent to 'pesar' Spanish word for sadness.*[40]
>
> 5) *Have kept your suggestion & called new one 'Tide'. Is it right? Movement in it is as you say – 'tide'*

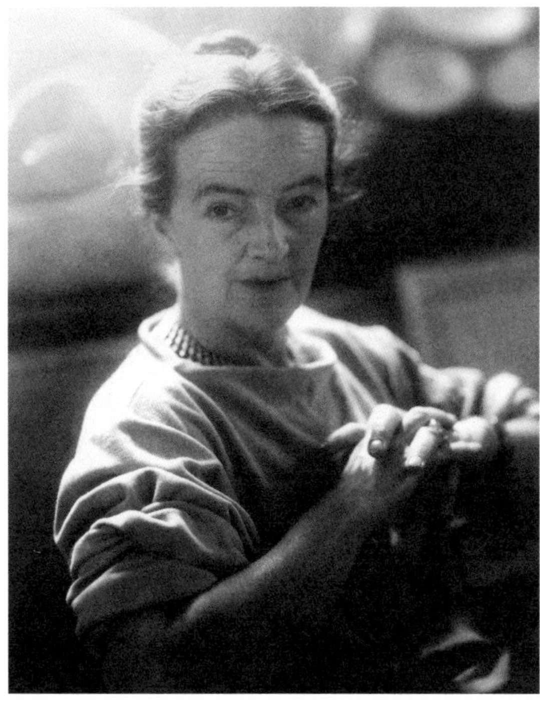

> *6)* *The tall wood – still unfinished – is 'watching'*
> *or guarding – I don't know really. 'Person' seems*
> *silly – 'figure' equally so. Any suggestions?*[41]

This list gives a range of Hepworth's interests – the tangible forms of flower and figure, alongside ephemeral concepts of beginnings and evolutions. Running throughout is a central notion that the works are active, not static. The figure does not passively observe, it is watching or guarding; the form <u>is</u> evolving.

The Lefevre show, comprising thirty sculptures alongside drawings and paintings, was a commercial success. Many of the drawings sold, and the gallery was so confident that it kept the large part of the unsold ones. This commercial element drew criticism from Wyndham Lewis, reviewing in *The Listener*, who wrote that 'the possession of one of these "involutes", "convolutes", or "conoids" would improve the scene in any living room or study [...] if there is, for me, a fault in Miss Hepworth's work, it is to be found in its resemblance to commercial objects, turned out with an industrial sleekness and slickness'.[42] Eric Newton, reviewing for *The Sunday Times*, seemed similarly to miss the emotional or philosophical

 Portrait of Barbara Hepworth at
Chy-an-Kerris, Carbis Bay, Cornwall, 1948

associations that Hepworth aimed to convey, writing rather dismissively of 'explorations on paper, of what could roughly be called the geometry of the egg'.[43] Maurice Collis in the *Observer* was more attuned to her intentions:

> *While it would be easy to compose a paragraph in obscure*
> *explanation of Barbara Hepworth's art, I prefer to describe the*
> *impression which her pierced ovals and involutes made upon me.*
> *On entering one seemed at once to be beside the sea in a*
> *lonely place. Some of the sculptures looked like stones worn*
> *into shapes that suggested the power behind weather, sea, wind,*
> *and time, and which also in a strange way reflected the essence*
> *of a surrounding marine panorama. The hidden and opposing*
> *stresses of nature were hinted at in 'Tides', which resembles the*
> *classical Yin-Yang symbol of the Chinese for the interaction*
> *of the powers of earth and heaven. Into this landscape*
> *interpenetrated by the ultimate springs humanity [...] A vast*
> *calm lies over all, and silence and awe and a remote magic.*
> *Barbara Hepworth is an extraordinary artist.*[44]

Both *The Times* and *The Telegraph* reported that the Queen had visited the exhibition, and Hepworth 'was deeply touched by the Queen liking the sculptures'.[45] While Ramsden had assisted in the titling of works, her partner Margot Eates had helped with the shipping and even the sourcing of plinths ('the Lefevre stands are fairly ghastly [...] I must have the work at the right height'[46]), and Hepworth wrote, 'How on earth can I begin to thank you for all you have both done? So much of the success of the show can be attributed to your help & generosity & appreciation [...] Your keenness for sculpture generally & your understanding – & your appreciation of my own contribution means a terrific lot to me.'[47]

Her reference to Ramsden's understanding acknowledges the recently published 'The Sculpture of Barbara Hepworth' in *Polemic: A Magazine of Philosophy, Psychology, and Aesthetics*, which Hepworth described as:

> *[...] one of the nicest things you've ever written [...] So silly of*
> *me to use the word 'nice' for something which inspires me –*
> *I very nearly started a new carving after reading it because*
> *your thoughts put me easily & freely into that world into which*
> *I am constantly striving to maintain a foothold, the plane on*
> *which idea & action become one movement. If I have done*

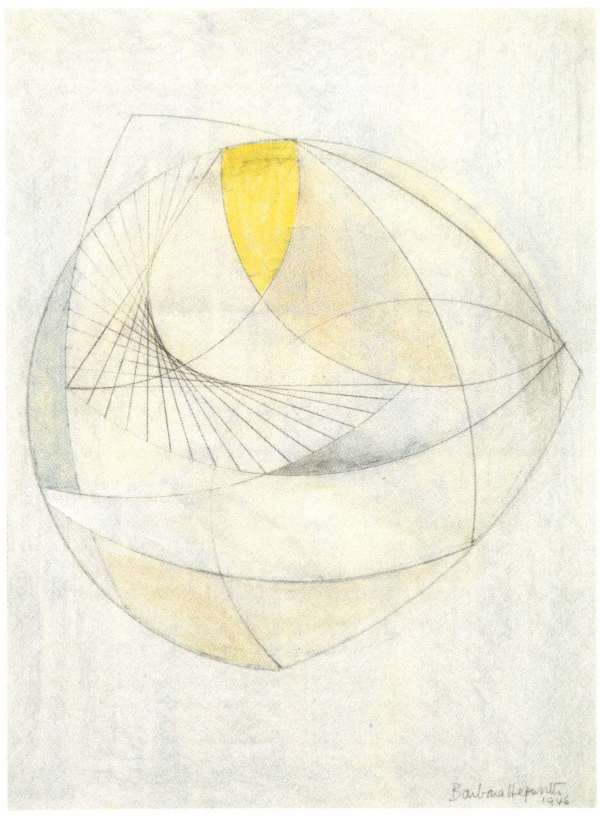

something of what you say then I am content – for the first time – because I have contacted the outside work through you. To be intelligible, to touch a plane, a phase, an idea with another human being means a lot.[48]

In the article, Ramsden relates Hepworth's work to poetry, writing, 'to recreate the patterns of experience in terms which become progressively more evanescent is for the poet sufficiently arduous a task, for the sculptor who finds himself similarly impelled the problems are immeasurably more complex, more formidable and more austere, since to him belongs the necessity of giving tangible shape to ideas and intuitions'.[49] Ramsden identifies a key characteristic of Hepworth's approach to expressing her embodied experience of landscape – the capturing of a fleeting moment in time. Rather than recreating a static object, Ramsden suggests, in Hepworth's work, as in the world, 'it is the modes of the interconnectedness of things rather than the things themselves, the evolving curve rather

ABOVE Barbara Hepworth, *Turning Form*, 1946, pencil and oil on gessoed board, 39.5 × 29 cm (15½ × 11⅜ in.)

than the completed figure, the process of "becoming" rather than the state of the "become" that is ultimately significant'.[50] Hepworth's curved and spiralling forms suggest movement and evolution, the dynamic nature of a drawing such as *Turning Form* (1946) (opposite) affirmed by its active title.

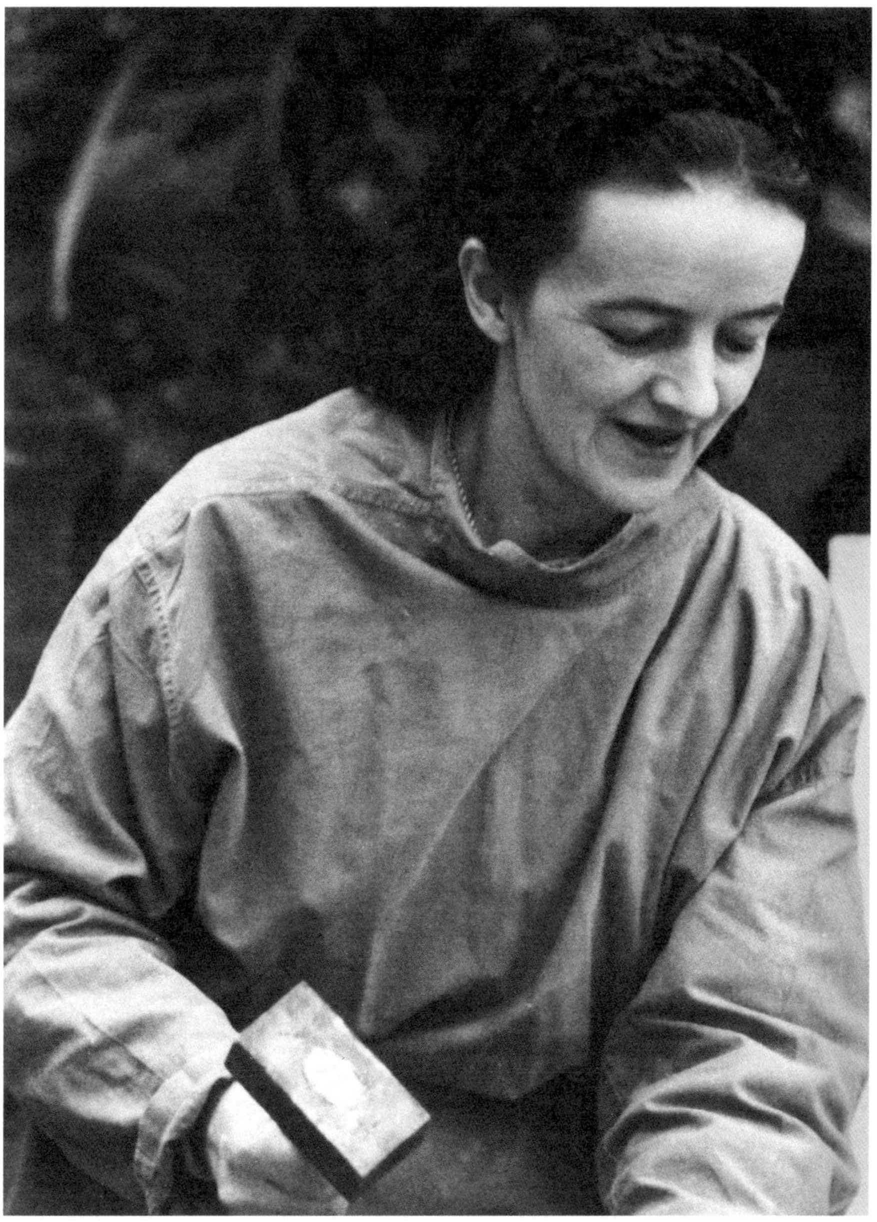

ABOVE Barbara Hepworth carving outside
Chy-an-Kerris, Carbis Bay, Cornwall, 1948

Ramsden articulated this expression of transitory nature – 'the in betweenness of things' – with quotes from Rainer Maria Rilke's *Duino Elegies*, a series of ten poems published in 1923 that were informed by Rilke's experiences during World War 1. Hepworth hugely admired this literary work, and one quote that Ramsden includes particularly resonates:

> *Between the hammers lives on*
> *Our heart, as between the teeth*
> *The tongue [...]*

A literal reading applies to Hepworth on two counts: the physical hammering of sculpture that was emotionally restorative, and the work containing inherent emotional experience born from this intense process. The passage more generally proposes persistence and continuation through adversity, pertinent not just to Hepworth but to society as a whole at the end of the war. Just as Rilke turned the trauma and frustrations of war into something productive and progressive, so Hepworth had done within her own practice. Ramsden concludes, connecting the physical properties of works such as *Pelagos*, *Wave* and *Landscape Sculpture* with a celebration of enduring life:

> *Is it not by the interpenetration of the material, the convergence and recession of the planes, the dissolving curves of the interior and exterior surfaces, the stringing and inner tensions of the configured whole that a sense of the cosmic rhythm of life which transcends all forms through which it is given is evoked? Is it not, also, by this means that the sculptor is enabled, even as 'the moaning of grief purely determines on form', to identify his own emotion not with the wave but with the curve of the wave as it flows over, unimaginably, into 'a bliss beyond the fiddle'?*[51]

Concentration, Movement & Gesture

At the end of 1946, Hepworth wrote to Margaret Gardiner about some short stories that Gardiner had written: 'these stories are to me much more abstract & much more <u>real</u> at one & the same time. I felt myself conscious of flesh & blood elements through rhythms & juxtapositions, broad forms & small accents.'[1] Hepworth could be discussing her own work, in which abstraction had always expressed a human reality. In the late 1940s, even more 'flesh & blood' elements were beginning to appear. She recalled:

> *After my exhibition in 1946 at Lefevre the abstract drawings which I did led me into new territory; the forms took on a more human aspect – forms separated as standing or reclining elements, or linked and pulled together as groups. During the early part of 1947 I had been doing the drawings and maquettes for the Waterloo Bridge competition held by the London County Council and had sat on the bridge for many hours contemplating the architectural and sculptural scale of the site in relation to the thousands of people who passed over or under the bridge.*[2]

Growing road and river traffic had necessitated a new bridge in the mid-1930s, and construction had continued during the war. The new Waterloo Bridge opened in 1944, with four plinths for sculptures, which, the LCC Town Planning committee decided, 'should be chosen on the basis of competition between sculptors of high repute'.[3] Hepworth wrote to

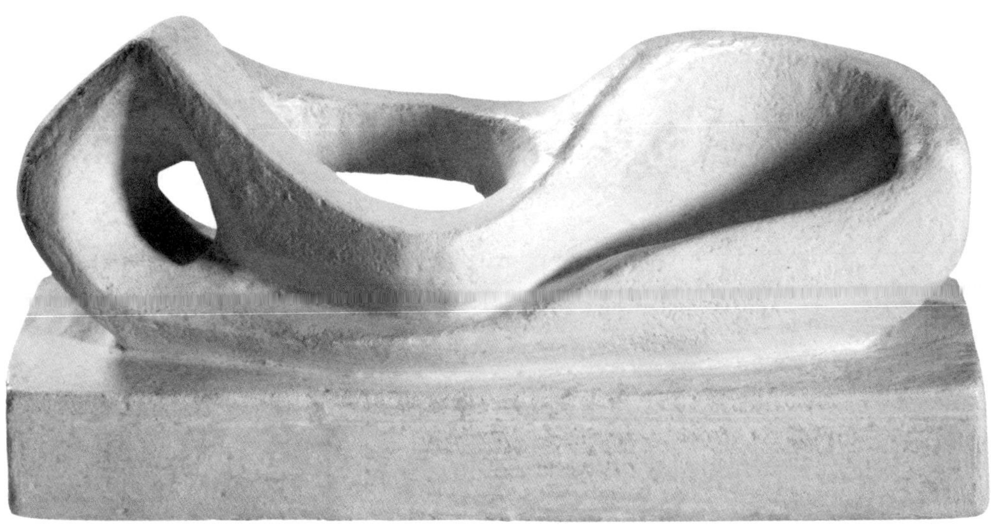

ABOVE Barbara Hepworth, *Model for 'Project for Waterloo Bridge: The River'*, 1947, plaster, height 10 cm (3⅞ in.)

Ramsden with the news: 'I shall be in London sometime for 3 or 4 days. I have been invited by L.C.C. to take part in the competition for 4 big groups for Waterloo Bridge. Shall have to come up to sit on the Bridge [...] They only give 4 months for the competition. It does not allow time for <u>anything</u> to go wrong. What a hazard life is for a woman! Moore, Dobson, Wheeler, Epstein and Kennington are the others.'[4] Nicholson recalled that Hepworth's work on the drawings and scale maquettes required for the competition 'kept her busy night and day all summer'.[5] Her designs combined the sweeping horizontal curves of *Landscape Sculpture* (see p. 128) with the complex interlacing planes of *Oval Sculpture* (see p. 109). Despite being abstract, these flowing planes (see opposite) reflect Hepworth's observation of the 'thousands of people' moving back and forth across or under the bridge. In the event, although Hepworth managed to submit her proposal by the October deadline, Moore and Epstein did not, and the competition was eventually suspended.[6]

Hepworth's interest in the relationship between architecture and sculpture had persisted from her involvement in *Unit One* and *Circle*, both of which had included architects alongside fine artists. In 1947, she wrote to architectural historian Sigfried Giedion, 'the question to be asked should not be "should the architect and sculptor collaborate from the beginning?" but "why do the architects and sculptors not collaborate from the beginning!"'[7] As the task of rebuilding the physical fabric of society following the war gained momentum, Hepworth was frustrated by the focus on technological advances in engineering and materials divorced from aesthetic sensibilities and social function. She continued to Giedion, 'During my last exhibition I found there was a keen sense, among all kinds of people, of the part that sculpture plays in life, except among the architects. They all stood with their backs to the sculpture and bewailed their lot, or chattered about new materials. I was shocked by this attitude because we are working, all of us, for something much greater than planning. We are working for a spontaneous sense of life, a unity of purpose which will give heart to the nature of our own living [...] New conditions, new materials cannot alter the basic principles.'[8]

At this time, Hepworth wrote passionately to Gardiner about the new machine age and the place of the arts within it:

> *Progress to me is*
> 1) *Acceptance & understanding of the machine & power age.*
> 2) *Research into its benefit & detriment to mass, both*
>   <u>*biologically & psychologically.*</u>

*3) Finding a true way of <u>controlling</u> the power gained in our age
by constant reference to History & Culture so that proper
understanding of all the 'needs of man' coordinates the needs
& the power.*

*I'm the last person to refute the machine – or wish to go back.
Most ardently I wish to resolve the whole thing; but I should
consider myself imbecile to accept each new discovery as good
in itself because it's new – or scientific. Hundreds have written
creatively on this subject & my limited words don't contribute
anything but in my sculpture I link up with all the discoveries
in architecture & engineering; & in art – or the realm of
aesthetics – each person is vital & the sum total is a gigantic
influence on the unconscious.*[9]

Hepworth felt that decisions being made regarding the rebuilding of
society needed to involve everyone, harnessing the power of collectivity
rather than allowing a privileged few to dictate. As she outlined: 'the only
discussion I'm interested in is the one where one accepts certain premises
& then discusses all the many possibilities of change & coordination, using
all our knowledge & not ½ of it. And using all men as being vital living
tissue (with biological needs / with individual subconscious images (as
well as archetypal)) & with anarchic individual life (as well as collective).'[10]
She elaborated, particularly taking umbrage at a suggestion by Gardiner's
partner Desmond Bernal that living in St Ives had left her out of touch:

*Des' idea of our isolation as an excuse made me smile. He
supposes that the ideas of agricultural workers, fishermen,
small town officials, local C.P members, labour members,
officials etc. as of total unimportance! I find particular
importance in the keenness of feeling in small town units.
It is more coherent & dynamic, & goodness knows I have
plenty of contact with intellectuals & all creative products.
Only one thing I lack <u>& I know it</u>, & that's contact with
factory workers – but my knowledge of the mills in Yorkshire
& 18 years intimacy with all that goes with collieries & mills
is alive in me that imagination helps me over the difficulty up
to a point. Also by living among a less mutilated set of people
(than is found in London) I have discovered how rich in response
each man really is (Londoners found that in the Blitz.) it is
all too easy to regard men in the mass as stupid.*[11]

Hepworth suffered with illness throughout 1947: rheumatism and torn muscles (described as 'occupational'), as well as 'a kind of chronic mastitis which often crops up in the 40s but has been accentuated by my work – carving – which causes considerable friction & a certain amount of bruising', which required several operations.[12] She wrote, 'I'm annoyed because I've always been rather proud of my figure, both as an efficient machine & as an inspiration to my own work! [...] a small incision is not exactly desperate! But cuts, scratches, nails, barbed wire, jagged edges or a knife on a rounded surface – all disturb intrinsic form!'[13] In addition to the personal trauma of these operations, the combined medical complaints affected Hepworth's ability to carry out the physical task of carving. She lamented to Gardiner, 'the dilemma of a woman sculptor – that at a time when my ideas & conceptions are maturing & forceful I begin to feel less physically strong. I have to use more will power – & it will be ironic if in a few years' time my ideas grow in dimensions (& given a chance) I shan't be able to carry them out! I only want to do large things now – it is an effort to contemplate small things & rheumatism in my right hand is becoming a hardship. You are lucky to be a writer. I shall have to find an apprentice to do all lifting & rough[ing out].'[14]

Her daughter Sarah had also returned to the Princess Elizabeth hospital in Exeter, and it was perhaps the combination of these personal experiences, alongside an increasing interest in all aspects of society, that led her to accept an invitation from Sarah's surgeon, Norman Capener, to observe an operation. She recalled:

In about the middle of 1947, a suggestion was made to me that I might watch an operation in a hospital. I expected that I should dislike it; but from the moment when I entered the operating theatre I became completely absorbed by two things: first, the extraordinary beauty of purpose and co-ordination between human beings all dedicated to the saving of life, and the way that unity of idea and purpose dictated a perfection of concentration, movement, and gesture, and secondly by the way this special grace (grace of mind and body) induced a spontaneous space composition, an articulated and animated kind of abstract sculpture very close to what I had been seeking in my own work.[15]

The first of these works, dated 23 November 1947, is titled *Two Figures* and shows the surgeon preparing for theatre. A characteristic that recurs throughout the many subsequent paintings is the detailed

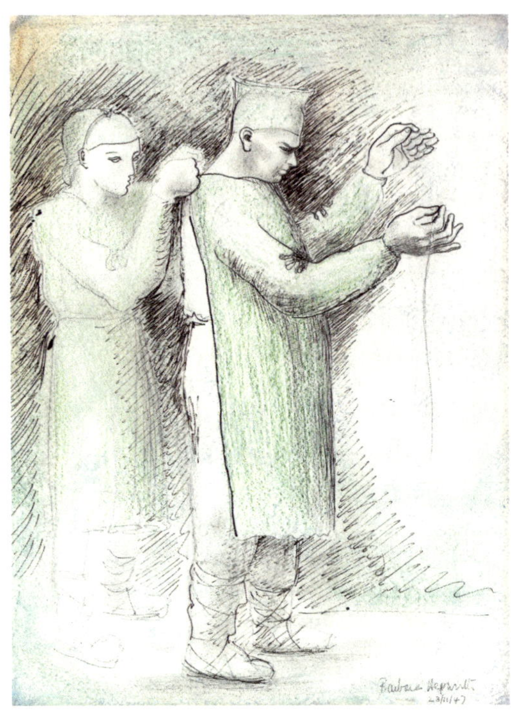

depiction of the surgeon's face and hands, the other elements receding into the background. *Two Figures* (above) is close in technique to the initial ink sketches Hepworth made in a small notebook while in the operating theatre. She said, 'I had to train myself to note only the most important things and to memorise the entire structure of the group, which was always changing as the operation proceeded. It was from notes such as these that I made my painting when I returned to the studio.'[16] Hepworth used a unique process for creating these works, building up layers of gesso and chalk on which coloured oil glaze was then painted, before rubbing and scraping at the surface with razors to reveal the white ground and brushstrokes below, giving suitable 'hardness and depth'.[17] She then drew her compositions in pencil on top, executing the faces and hands with delicate shading and detailed finish, before completing the work with colours in oil paint. In a lecture to a group of surgeons at Exeter, she described the process, noting, 'I used the colour, not in a realistic way, but in order to stress the meaning of form and light as I had seen it.'[18] Works such as *The Hands* (1948) (opposite, below) emit an ethereal glow, the surgical actors floating in a timeless space to capture, as Hepworth said of this painting, 'a very moving moment *(for me)* when

ABOVE Barbara Hepworth, *Two Figures*, 1947, green crayon and pencil, pen and black ink, 38 × 27 cm (15 × 10⅝ in.)

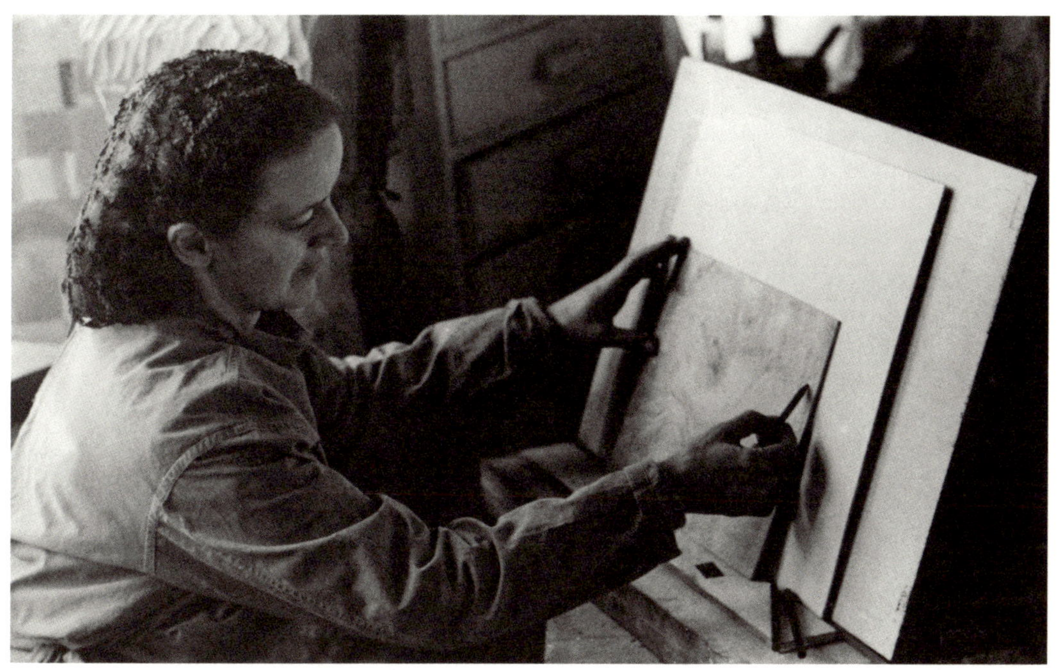

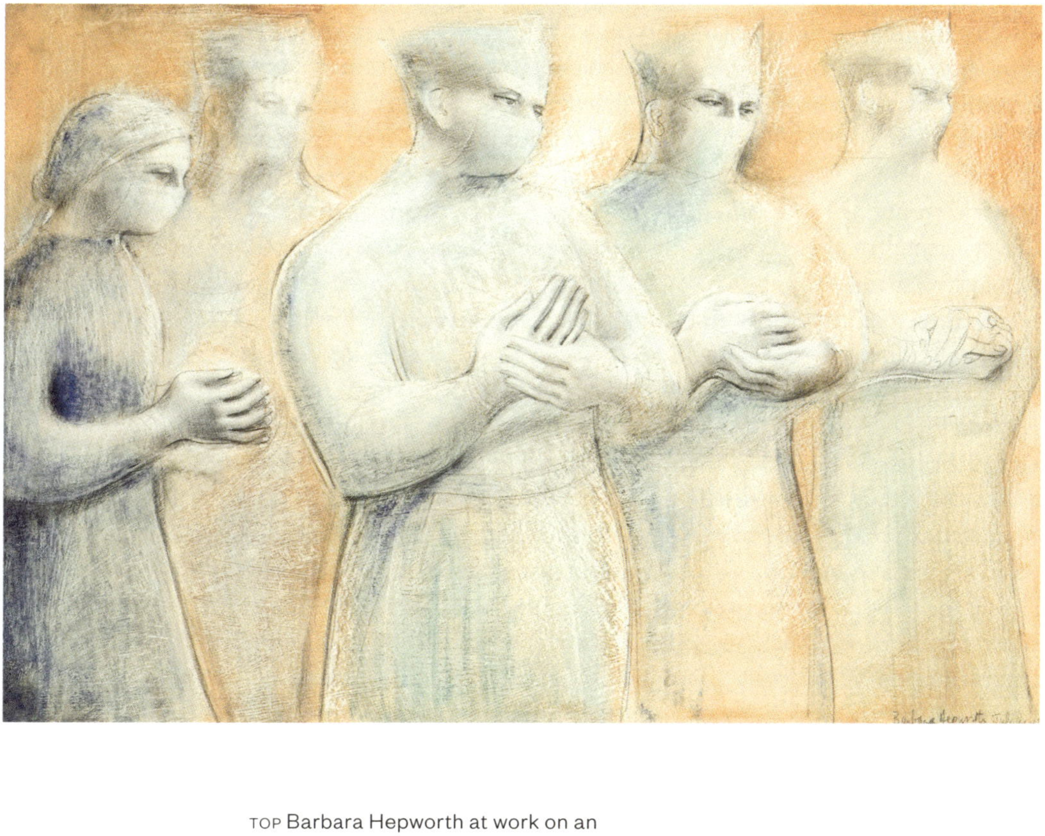

TOP Barbara Hepworth at work on an operating theatre drawing, *Quartet I (Arthroplasty)*, Chy-an-Kerris, Carbis Bay, January 1948

ABOVE Barbara Hepworth, *The Hands*, 1948, oil and pencil on gesso ground board, 38 × 51.4 cm (15 × 20¼ in.)

a group of surgeons stood together, after discussion, before commencing the operation'. She continues in describing this work, 'Here to the left you see my much loved character – the theatre sister. In her quiet stance and very tender hands I wanted to convey the whole background of incredibly intelligent and devoted work which is vested in her occupation and profession.'[19]

Hepworth made her first depictions of surgery while beginning life drawing again in her studio, drawings such as *Kneeling Woman in Armchair* (1949) (right) showing her 'renewed study of anatomy and structure'.[20] Nicholson had written to Helen Sutherland, a collector of his and Hepworth's work, in November 1947 that Hepworth had 'done some lovely new dwgs & recently some v interesting nude dwgs – we have found a particularly beautiful model here'.[21] It was perhaps due to Hepworth's physical ailments that she devoted so much time to drawing and painting in 1947, and the sculpture record that she compiled for this year lists only three sculptures.[22] Her focus on two-dimensional work was such that 1 April 1948 saw the opening of her exhibition at the Lefevre Gallery, *New Paintings by Barbara Hepworth*. In February she had written to Nicholson, 'Saw Duncan [MacDonald from Lefevre Gallery] this afternoon [...] I was nervous of his reactions after being ill so much but he liked the drawings a <u>lot</u> all of them! That was a great relief. He wants me to ask Herbert [Read] to write something definite before he leaves for America so I will do so & show Herbert the drwgs only if he feels like writing!'[23] Read did write on these works in 'Barbara Hepworth: A New Phase', an article published in *The Listener* to coincide with the exhibition and illustrated by a drawing of surgeons. He noted that the exhibited works fell into two groups – 21 studies of the female nude, and 31 hospital scenes, all figurative. Within his article, he quoted a letter from Hepworth explaining her thoughts on moving from abstraction to figuration: 'working realistically replenishes one's <u>love</u> for life, humanity & the earth. Working abstractly seems to release one's personality & sharpen the perceptions.'[24] The letter expands on the close relationship between these two modes: 'I don't feel any difference of intention or of

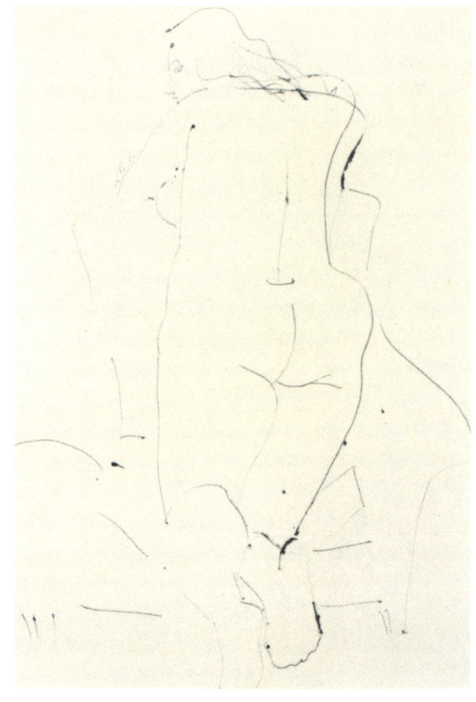

ABOVE Barbara Hepworth, *Kneeling Woman in Armchair*, 1949, ink on paper, 37 × 25 cm (14½ × 9⅞ in.)

mood when I paint (or carve) realistically or when I make abstract carvings. The two ways of working flow into each without effort. It all feels the same – the same happiness & pain, the same joy in a line, a form, a colour – the same feeling of being lost in pursuit of something. The same feeling at the end.'[25]

Over the next few years, Hepworth observed many reconstructive operations, both in Exeter and in London. She gave an explanation for her focus in the subsequent paintings on the hands and eyes of the medical professionals: 'as I became more accustomed to the various operations I began to realise how profoundly important from an artist's point of view the expression of the human hand is. Not only is it the most revealing and expressive part of the human body – it is also the visible extension of the brain and feeling generally.'[26] Drawing the eyes and hands in detail articulates this connection pictorially, and highlights the affinity that Hepworth saw between the work and approach of artists and surgeons, both seeking to restore beauty and grace through the cooperation of

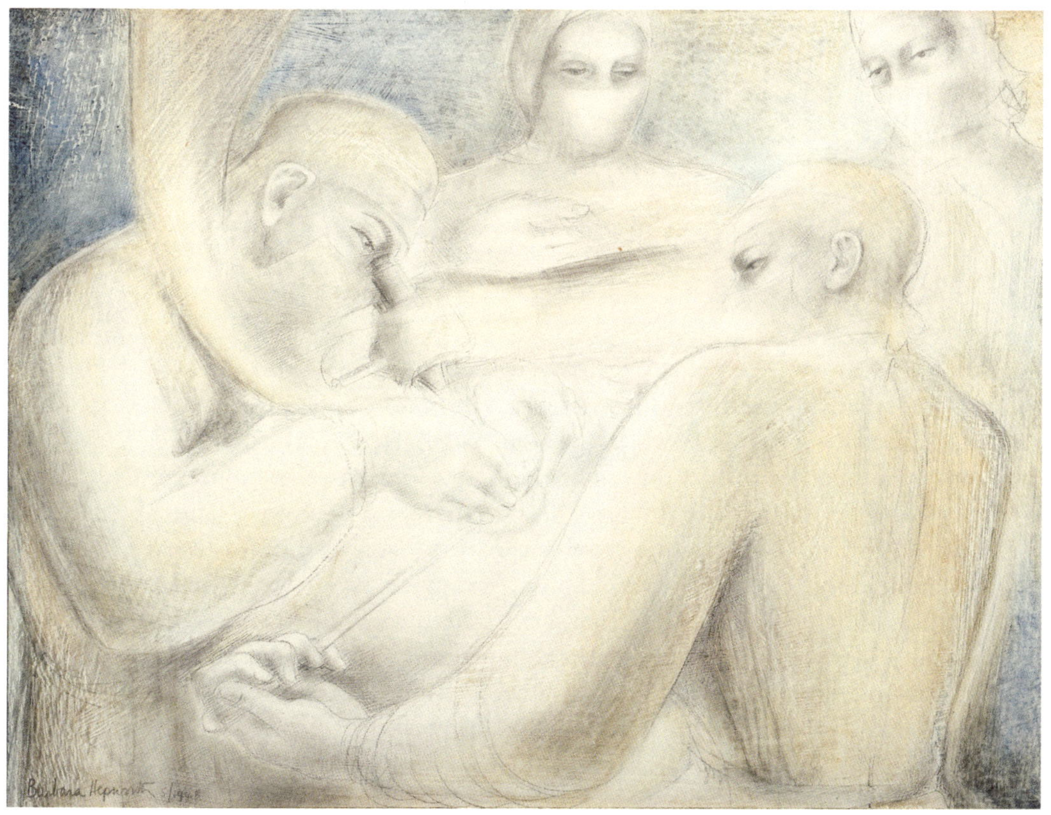

ABOVE Barbara Hepworth, *Fenestration of the
Ear (The Microscope)*, 1948, oil and pencil on
board, 34.5 × 44.5 cm (13½ × 17½ in.)

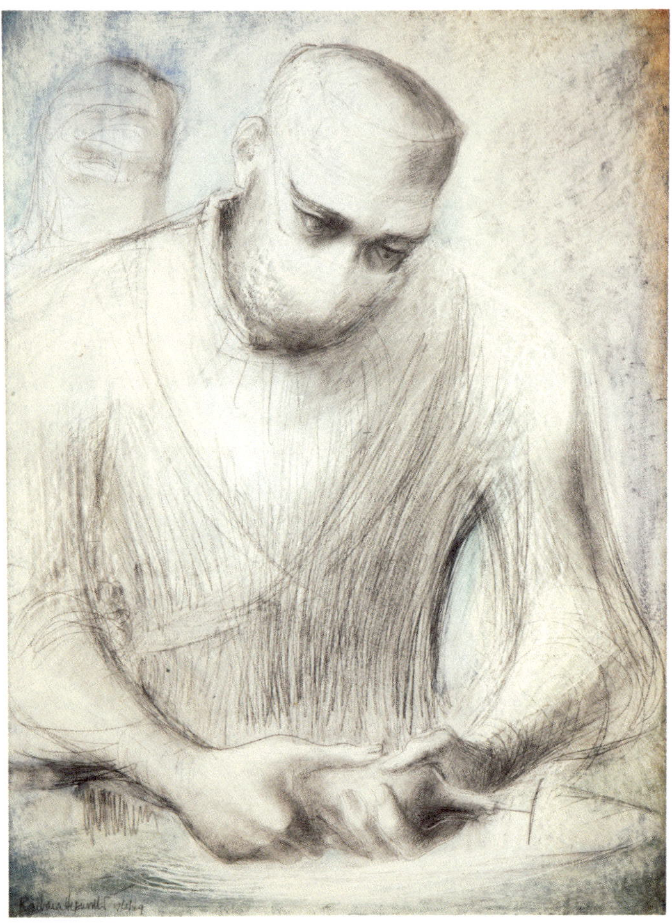

hand and eye. In 1948, she made a series of works based on the fenestration of the ear, an operation that involved making a new aperture in the
inner ear to resolve hearing loss (see previous page). Hepworth told the
surgeons in her 1953 lecture, 'You can imagine how impressed a sculptor
would be by the precision and delicacy of this particular operation! The
long concentration, the minuteness of the work and the weight of the
equipment, and the power of control behind the work, produced a very
<u>different</u> kind of composition.'[27] In this series, the three figures centred
around the subject are the focus, rather than the operation itself, the
intense concentration between them creating a circular composition. As
Hepworth noted, observing these collective actions 'ratified, moreover,
my previous ideas as a sculptor, of the basic principles of the abstract
composition, rhythm, poise, and equilibrium'.[28] Hepworth even related

above Barbara Hepworth, *Tibia Graft*, 1949,
oil and pencil on board, 52.2 × 37.3 cm
(20½ × 14⅝ in.)

the solo 'portrait' compositions, such as *Tibia Graft* (1949) (opposite), to her abstract work, noting in a letter to Read, 'I draw a surgeon with clasped hands, he is a monolith!'[29]

Hepworth's ambitions to make monumental sculptures before the war were now fuelled by an increasing investment in public sculpture post-war. She took part in the first 'Open Air Exhibition of Sculpture' in Battersea Park, from May to September 1948 and described it to Nicholson:

> *I do so wish you had been at the show this aft. It was such fun & <u>the most</u> glorious Mayday you can possibly imagine. Such heavenly trees. I'm delighted with my position – near a big early Lipchitz, & Modigliani, very good. A whole mass of bad academic work including 3 (more than anybody else) Dobsons which were awful beyond belief. Henry's things (3 graces) look fine – lovely scale. Rodin & Maillol's Despiau all look lovely. It was all beautifully done, perfectly placed – couldn't have been better but for the choice. No Brancusi, Arp, Giacometti, Calder, Gabo or Pevsner – left an awful gap!*[30]

Hepworth began to make practical steps to create work on a larger scale, and in the same letter she asks Nicholson, 'could you broach the idea to Hodge [Ethel Hodgkins, their neighbour in Carbis Bay] of me having a wee bit of field in order to do 1 large sculpture? It need only be temporary. I want to do one of 3 tons [sketch with a person to show monumental scale].'[31] However, these ambitions rose alongside continuing health problems, potentially related to the onset of menopause, which at the time was little understood.[32] This impacted her work, as she noted to Nicholson: 'I feel a bit better – but still super tired. Hope the iron & new pills take effect SOON. Don't feel a bit like ptg or drawing. Trying to carve – but it's fatiguing.'[33] Her continuing contact with Capener was a comfort: 'An occasional letter or phone call from N has been a great help. He is very kind & very sane.'[34] She also drew great solace from her friendship with Margaret Gardiner, who had had similar experiences. Hepworth wrote in May 1949: 'I expect you realise only too well what a "lever" a fluctuating temp. an uncertain pulse etc. can be under the circumstances. Even the medical confirmation that it is emotional & not organic worsens rather than alleviates the pressure. If organic then everything can be calculated. When neurotic any move – either left or right – can worsen the situation. Even if I attempt to escape into work the condition worsens.'[35]

Despite these physical challenges, Hepworth made significant sculptures in 1949, several larger in size than those of previous years and in tough materials. She recalled these 'exciting conflicts with material. The sawn cube out of which I carved *The Cosdon Head* 1949 proved to be a singularly intractable metamorphic rock – the very nature of my tussle with it gave the whole carving a quality of some giant pebble worn by centuries of waves beating on it.'[36] As with her work of the early 1930s, this

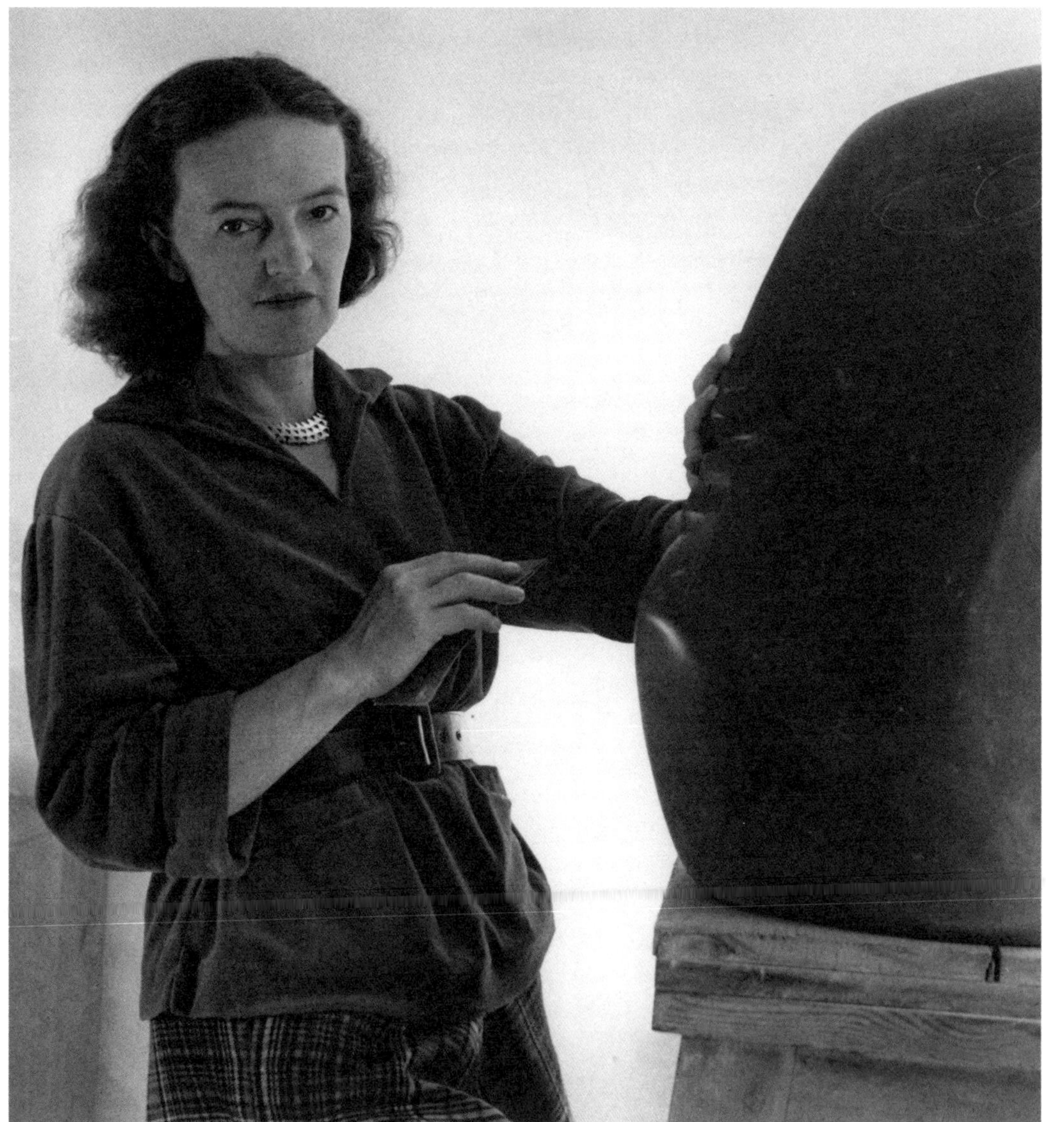

ABOVE Barbara Hepworth with *The Cosdon Head*, 1949. Photograph by Hans Wild

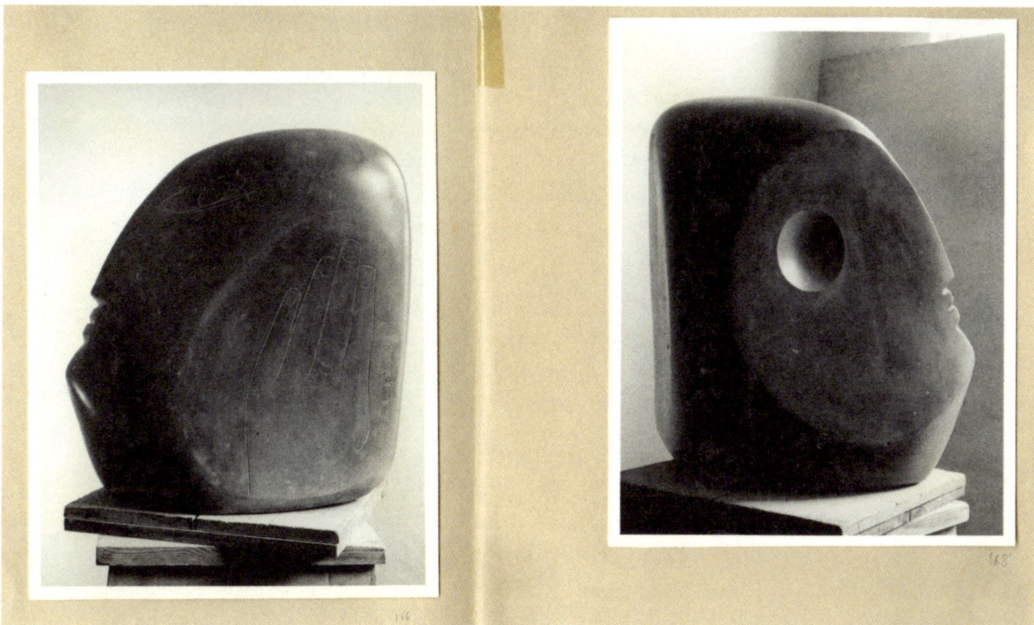

sense of an organic form rising from the earth is coupled with figurative elements. *The Cosdon Head* (see above) fuses Hepworth's abstract and figurative languages into one sculpture. The reading of an indented circle on one side as a symbolic eye is confirmed by a more realistic drawn eye incised on the other, the latter accompanied by a detailed hand. From another angle only the hand is visible, resting on the 'giant pebble'. The focus of eye and hand echoes Hepworth's hospital drawings, and a photograph of Hepworth posing with this sculpture (opposite) emphasised the affinity she felt between the surgeon and sculptor's work – her hands active, holding a sculpting tool and touching the sculpture, her eyes holding the viewer's gaze. Patrick Heron, writing in *The New Statesman*, found the combination of abstraction and figuration in *The Cosdon Head* compelling: 'in introducing the profiles of nose, lips, chin, forehead, or the engraved outline of a hand or eye, Barbara Hepworth is enhancing, not diluting, the quality and power of her own abstraction'.[37]

Not everyone felt so positive about the incorporation of representational elements within abstract sculpture, and Hepworth wrote in defence to E. H. Ramsden, 'I should like to think that you reserve judgement on my last work until you see it. 2 of the last more representational ones are more fully abstract than some of the last purely abstract ones.'[38] They evidently reached some form of accord, as she later thanked

Ramsden for her response: 'It was so nice to get your note (I thought you had abandoned me as being too anthropomorphic!)'[39] A further letter clarifies the relationship between the purely abstract work that Ramsden championed and Hepworth's recent sculptures:

I have just looked up anthropomorphic! I'm afraid I must confess that all sculpture to be good must (in my mind) be anthropomorphic to some extent. My abstracts which I think are the best are anthropomorphic – Helicoids, Elegy, Involute, Oval Form etc. I can think of only 3 exceptions /
1. Sculpture with Colour 1941 (but this was an eye a god's eye if you like)
2. The Wave (but this is 2 arms embracing)
3. Pelagos (again the arms & bosom of a goddess?)

If, instead of string & colour accents one draws an eye or carves a nose it doesn't in my opinion make a work less abstract or less 'good' of necessity.

I heartily detest any kind of limitation as to what form can or will be discovered (intuitively) by the artist to present his image or his emotion or inspiration.

Good work comes into being when the right form is discovered.[40]

While seeming to have executed a dramatic shift from earlier abstract work, Hepworth makes clear that for her the hospital drawings and subsequent more figurative sculptures are consistent explorations of sculptural form in its relation to lived experience.

1949 brought a significant change to Hepworth's working life. As her reputation grew, along with the scale of her sculptures, her studio at Chy-an-Kerris became increasingly inadequate. She wrote enviously to Ramsden and Eates about their new studio: 'if ever I make any money & can get myself a barn to convert into workshop & living quarters I shall come round begging Margot to do it for me. Frankly I am beginning to pine for my own shapes & colours, and I long for space & height!'[41] This wish was soon granted when a building in the centre of St Ives came up for sale at auction (see opposite). Hepworth recalled, 'Finding Trewyn Studio was a sort of magic. For ten years I had passed by with my shopping bags not knowing what lay behind the twenty-foot walls.'[42]

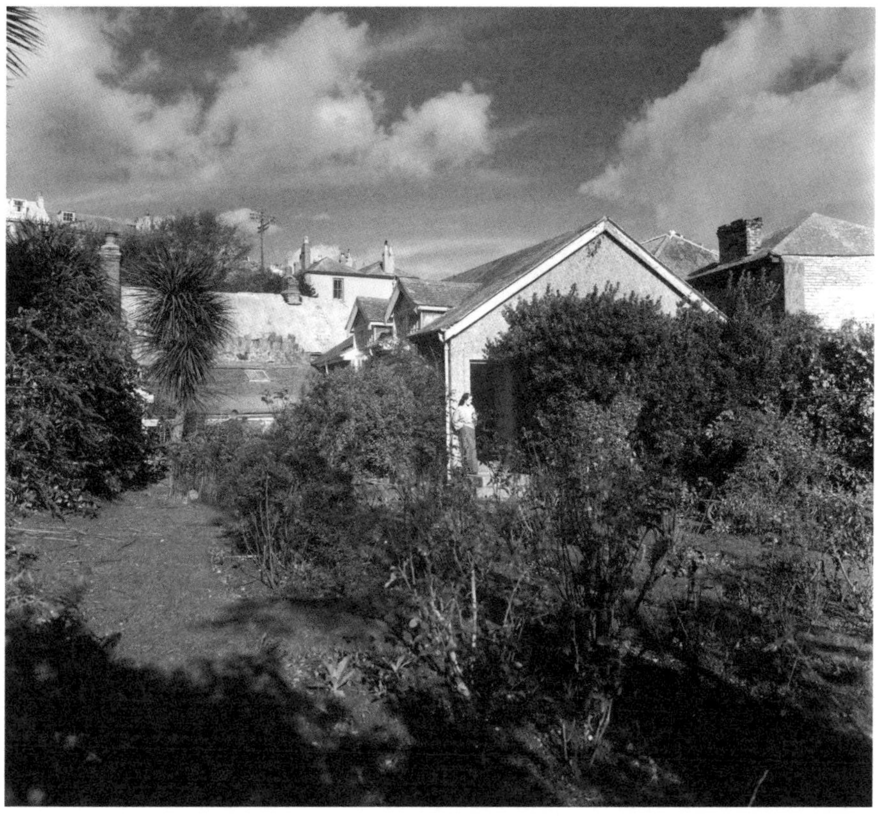

The studio comprised two rooms over two floors, the upper of which Hepworth used initially as a wood-carving and painting studio, while in the lower she installed a kitchen, bathroom and eating area. Within the walled garden, an outside store and adjacent courtyard became her main carving workshop, and she used the connected greenhouse (or upper workshop) for her drawings and early experiments in plaster. The garden itself offered a perfect setting for her sculptures.[43] The walls provided 'protection from cold winds so that I could carve out of doors nearly all the year round', and Hepworth recalled in 1952, 'the atmosphere was so ideal that I started a new carving the morning after I moved in'.[44]

ABOVE Barbara Hepworth in the garden of Trewyn Studio, October 1949. Photograph by Studio St Ives

Fierce Counterpoint

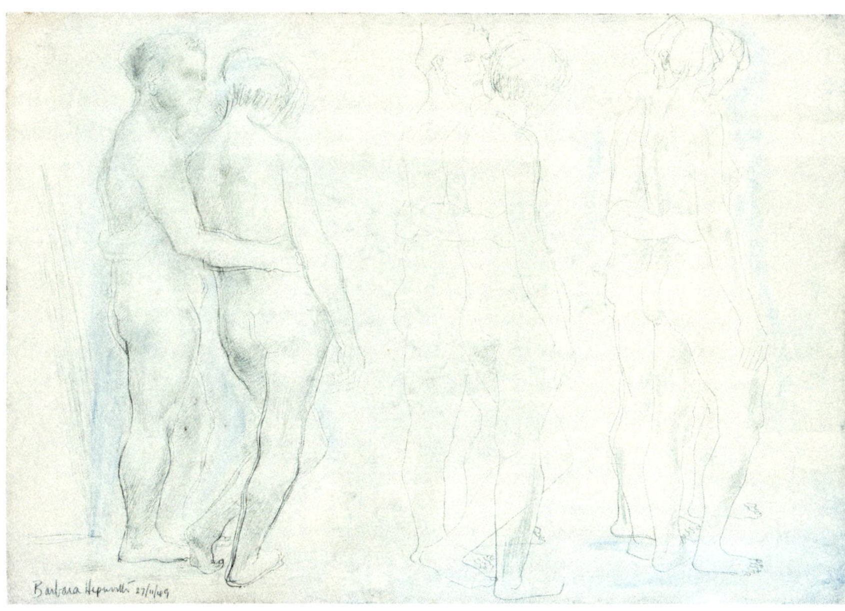

Hepworth noted that from 1947, 'for two years I drew, not only in the operating theatres of hospitals, but from groups in my studio and groups observed around me [see above]. I studied all the changes and defects which occurred in the composition of human figures when there were faulty surroundings or muddled purpose [...] I began to consider a group of separate figures as a single sculptural entity, and I started working on the idea of two or more figures as a unity, blended into one carved and rhythmic form.'[1] *Dyad* (1949) was the first of these (see following page), its title proclaiming duality. A profile is incised on one side of the uppermost protuberance, while another nestles in a hollow near the suggestion of a shoulder, echoing the intertwined male and female couple in related drawings. The impression is of two figures embracing, combined in perfect yet fluid unity. Over the next two years Hepworth's work would explore the relationship of two figures in varying degrees of contact and harmony, as her own relationship with Nicholson deteriorated and her work expanded into the public realm, reaching new audiences.

Dyad was shown at *Barbara Hepworth New Sculpture and Drawings* at Lefevre Gallery, February 1950, a time of celebration as it was announced that the British Council had selected Hepworth to represent Britain at the Venice Biennale. Hepworth had felt underrepresented by the British Council in previous years, complaining to Herbert Read that she was 'always being omitted from British Council exhibitions', a fact she

ABOVE Barbara Hepworth, *Three Groups on a Pink Ground*, 1949, oil and pencil on fibreboard, 57.3 × 74 cm (22½ × 29⅛ in.)

attributed to: '1) Being a woman, 2) Being abstract, 3) Being young and 4) Being a wife and mother etc.etc.'[2] In 1948, the British pavilion had departed from the usual practice of a group show and had exhibited works only by Turner and Henry Moore. This combination of historic and contemporary art 'created a precedent which was exceedingly well received in Venice and in other countries'.[3] Continuing this format for 1950, Hepworth was invited to represent the British section alongside Constable and contemporary painter Matthew Smith. The British Council offered two rooms to each artist and aimed, in Hepworth's case, 'to assemble about twenty sculptures and as many drawings'.[4] Hepworth initially proposed fifty-eight sculptures, writing to Read, who was on the selection committee, 'my feeling is that if 100 works are shown, or even 50 it is bound to give a fairly solid impression of the artist. But if one cuts down to as few as 25 I think it is a difficult job.'[5] She also wanted to include '50 or 60 drawings', noting to Lilian Somerville, the Director of the British Council's Fine Arts department, 'I want to present the idea of research into pure form & strings, landscape & colour, stone, wood & lastly human form and human groups.'[6] As plans progressed and the selecting committee proposed a list of under twenty sculptures they wished to show, Hepworth feared 'a small scale and pernickety exhibition [...] I like strong juxtapositions [...] something dynamic & not "discreet" & ladylike. Sculpture is exciting & forceful?'[7]

Despite these pleas, on 21 February 1950, the British Council sent a list of only eighteen sculptures to be shown, four of these to be displayed outside. The selection confirmed Hepworth's fears that the show would not convey the disparate but connected elements of her work, and she wrote to Somerville, 'I am still far from happy about the Biennale – from my point of view (the artist's!) I feel it just misses being what I would like to make it. It just lacks the fire, the imaginative juxtapositions which in my view make life worth living!' Hepworth wanted to include additional recent stone carvings that she felt were 'sharper, more arresting, more colourful' and 'some more colourful & dominant drawings in the same vein'. As she noted:

RIGHT Barbara Hepworth, *Dyad*, 1949, Himalayan rosewood, 118 × 40.5 × 22 cm (46⅜ × 15⅞ × 8⅝ in.)

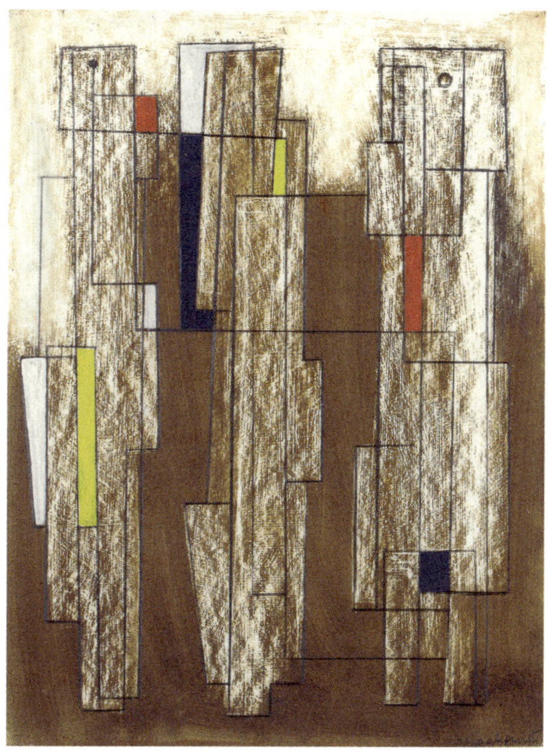

*More violent & formal – including some ink & chalk drawings
which make an <u>emphasis</u> (as well as some more violent oil
ones) and enable us, if necessary, to have a block of equal sized
drawings together in the Pavilion to balance some weight
or disposition of sculpture. These are absolutely minimum
requirements [...] my feeling for the committee is, in brief, that
they have taken the spice out of the exhibition & the result will
be damned ladylike – forgive me for being violent but I do so
hate things that haven't a kick in them [...] if the committee
want to set off those qualities of my work which give them a
feeling of satisfaction they could do it better by adding the
element of disturbance which brings out these qualities.*[8]

Hepworth's rationale shows a significant shift in her philosophy from
before the war – harmony and balance is not enough. For these qualities to exist and be appreciated they must be accompanied by violence
and discord. The 'violent oil' paintings she describes are works such as
Granite Forms, Red, Yellow and Deep Blue (1953) (above),[9] where figures

ABOVE Barbara Hepworth, *Granite Forms, Red,
Yellow and Deep Blue*, 1953, pencil and oil on
gessoed board, 35.6 × 25.4 cm (14 × 10 in.)

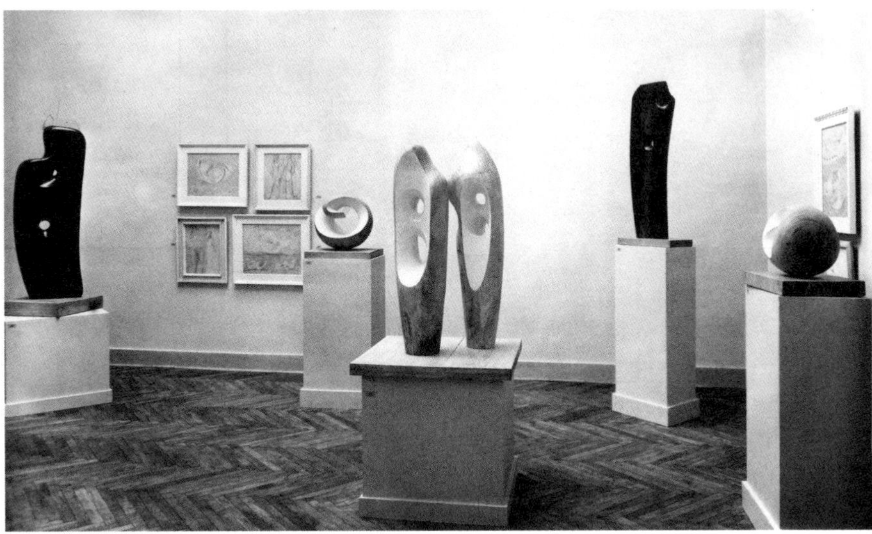

comprised of sharp, angular forms are painted vivid colours, a fierce counterpoint to both the muted, pastel curves of her post-war abstract drawings and the still serenity of her hospital drawings.

The committee were unable to accommodate all Hepworth's requests, Somerville writing, 'it is not possible to include any more sculpture', though agreeing to ship more drawings with a final decision to be made during the installation of the show.[10] While the installation photographs show that some drawings were hung in blocks, in accordance with Hepworth's wishes, her fears of a 'discreet' presentation appear to have been founded (see above). The show did not receive great press, which the British Council report attributed in part to Hepworth's 'reserved temperament' and the fact that 'her inability to speak either French or Italian meant that she could have little contact with artists or critics'.[11] However, the cause could not be purely personality as Matthew Smith also received little attention, and the language barrier does not explain the luke-warm reception to the show in the English-speaking press. Much of the coverage focused on Constable and, where mentioned, Hepworth was frequently compared with Moore – erroneously claimed to be Moore's pupil,[12] and her sculptures described as 'Moore-ish'.[13] Where her work was critiqued on its own merit, it was damned as being 'so cool, so business-like and so patiently smoothed and polished that its subtleties tend to be overlooked or misunderstood'.[14] These reviews echo critiques of earlier exhibitions, and perhaps explain the urgency with which Hepworth had campaigned Somerville for a presentation with more 'spice'.

ABOVE Barbara Hepworth's exhibition at
the British Pavilion, Venice Biennale, 1950

The works' reception did not dampen Hepworth's enthusiasm for the opportunity to exhibit in Venice, and she wrote thanking Somerville following the opening: 'I came away feeling very satisfied – indeed more than satisfied for I felt a real appreciation of my work from many people and the visit to Venice was one of the major experiences of my life.'[15] Her account to Margot Eates was more circumspect, suggesting the struggle to effectively communicate her ideas but also the inspiration she gained: 'Venice was a great experience for me. Strange & vivid – the more so because I wasn't very well & was truly unhappy. The quality of form, light & colour was incredibly moving, especially when alone.'[16] In 1952, she would recall that 'the two weeks I spent there [in Venice] were a great stimulus to the idea on which I was working at that time':

> *Whenever I could get away alone I walked and observed people in relation to the buildings. Every day I sat for a time in the Piazza San Marco, a miracle of man-made space, and wondered at the unique way in which one sensed within this opened space the closed-in space-volume of the interior of San Marco itself. One was aware of all the intricacies of height and breadth in planes and curvature [...] But the most significant observation I made for my own work was that as soon as people, or groups of people, entered the Piazza they responded to the proportions of architectural space. They walked differently, discovering their innate dignity. They grouped themselves in unconscious recognition of their importance in relation to each other as human beings.[17]*

Hepworth's letters to the British Council in the lead-up to Venice show her working concurrently on a major project that would draw upon these observations. Writing on 27 March regarding lists of work for shipping, she notes, 'I have been <u>ill</u> & only just better in time for the arrival of 9 tons of stone for the Festival job. I cannot write properly to-day as there are 12 men milling round & the business of moving the stones into the studio is formidable.'[18] Income from one project went straight into the next, as she wrote to Somerville thanking her 'for the surprise cheque. It saved my life as it has cost me over £100 to move the Festival stones from the station here into position in my garden!'[19] The 'Festival' referred to the Festival of Britain, proposed to celebrate the centenary of the Great Exhibition of 1851. Instead of exhibiting cultures from around the world, as in 1851, the Festival of Britain was more inward-looking, aiming to focus on Britain's achievements in technology, industrial design, architecture and the arts to boost public morale following the devastation of war. Twenty-three arts festivals were to be held across the UK between May and September 1951. Hepworth strongly appreciated the festival's aims, not just in its interdisciplinary approach, but also in integrating art more thoroughly into society. She wrote, 'A Festival of Art allows the impact [of creative arts] to be made upon the social structure, breaking the crust of resistance and allowing a new free growth, of interplay between the practicing artist and the rest of society, an absolute necessity if we are to maintain a proper articulation between members both of communities and of nations.'[20] *The Times* announced as early as January 1950 that Hepworth had been commissioned by the Arts Council, along with Moore and Epstein, to make new site-specific sculpture for the Festival on the South Bank in London, and 'the sites where their works will be on view have already been chosen by the sculptors'.[21]

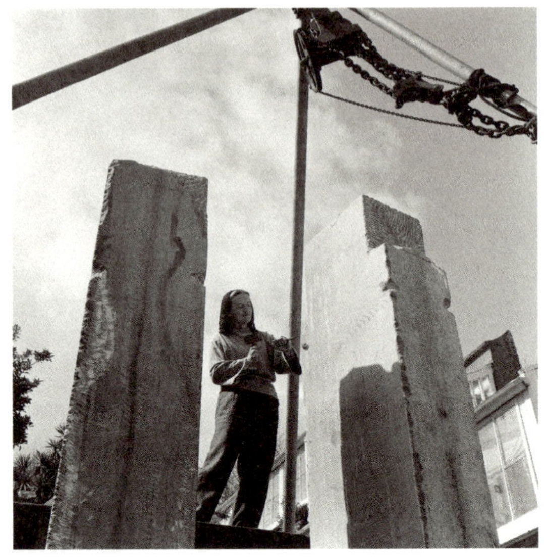

Hepworth's observations in Venice informed her ambitions for sculpture in the public realm, as she noted, 'sculpture should act not only as a foil to architectural properties but the sculpture itself should provide a link between human scale and sensibility and the greater volumes of space and mass in architecture'.[22] She began work on *Contrapuntal Forms* in the spring of 1950, again two figures but this time separate entities with corresponding forms and piercings (see above). Film footage shows Hepworth using black paint to sketch the outline of figures, similar to those in her contemporaneous paintings, onto the uncut stones, identifying where the forms would take shape.[23] The title is a musical term, 'contrapuntal' meaning that each element is the counterpoint to the other, designed to be related but distinct. Hepworth described to Margaret Gardiner, 'Yesterday we moved the 2 big stones close up together, very, very slowly. It thrilled me absolutely because as they drew together I saw all the shapes take on significance & what had been, up till now, a mental image took on reality.'[24] The physical challenge of carving such monumental work was immense, and Hepworth had taken on two assistants at the end of 1949 to work on the commission.[25] In July, she wrote that the work was complicated by 'weather so wet that I've had to design & order a most elaborate & expensive shelter for the 2 large figures. 2 more weeks of rain would set the work back so far I should never finish in time.'[26] The situation had not improved by the autumn, as Hepworth wrote to Ramsden:

It is exciting to have the sort of work one has longed for but a pity that the Festival has brought it all at once & the zero hour is oppressive, especially as I am (& I suppose everybody else)

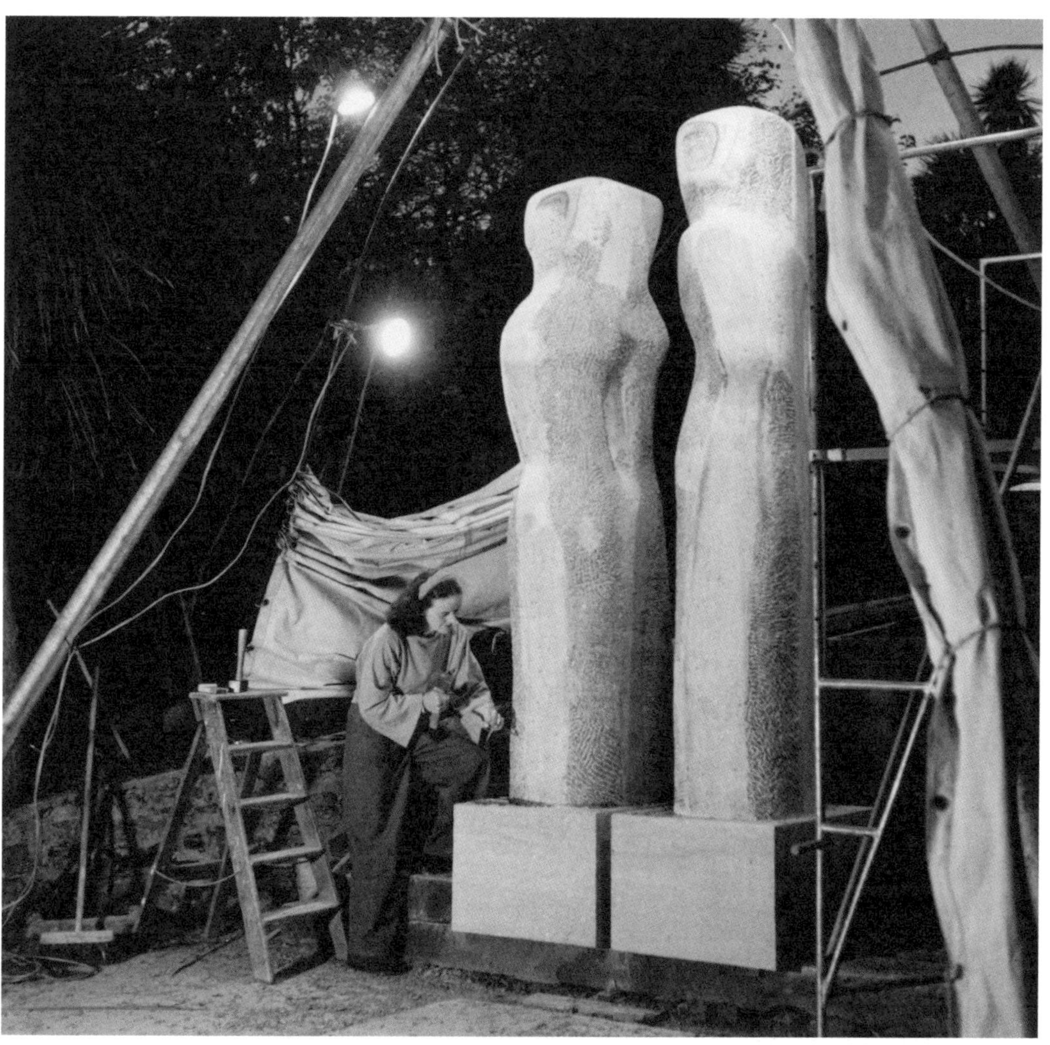

ABOVE Barbara Hepworth at work on *Contrapuntal Forms* by floodlight, 25 October 1950. Official Festival photograph

fighting the weather. Never have I seen such rain! Week after
week of it & though we've had a sort of rough shelter built it
means I can't get away & see what I'm doing [...] I think
I may need more assistance with the big stones – the weather
is so appalling that progress gets slower & slower. They are
shaping really well & I'm praying for light & <u>sun</u>.[27]

The gruelling schedule of work caused increasing friction between Hepworth and Nicholson, as Hepworth complained to Gardiner: 'I have an immense amount of thrilling work to do – but this weather (so terribly wet & unpleasant) or worry or both, makes me v. tired at times, really too tired to move. I think we ought to have some help – or some scheme for the evening meal. It is almost disastrous to cope with it when over fatigued. Ben's recipe is "give up work." Why give up real joy? In some way he wants to stop me – net result – slow wearing down process – a steady inevitable drip of water.'[28] Earlier in the year Nicholson had met someone else, and wanted to pursue the relationship with Hepworth's blessing. While agreeing with the principle ('my own', she remarked),[29] she felt their respective approaches jarred, reflecting the inherent differences between a painter and a sculptor:

Ben says the whole issue depends on how well it works for
<u>me</u> – but when asked more precisely he says that everything
must remain fluid & instinctive 'moment to moment'. I
appreciate this from a painters point of view but I have to
consider the 2 big figures, all my work commitments – being
tied to them & to Chy-an-Kerris & a thousand practical details
of finance, home, income tax etc. – none of which is solved by
instinct! [...] I have to plan, rationalise & organise in order to
do my sculpture at all – now as never before as March 31st 1951
is the zero hour for 2 large jobs.[30]

Hepworth felt she needed security and peace for the slow and persistent process of sculpting, lamenting to Eates, 'when a great love like Ben's & mine goes wrong after 19 years it can go very wrong – especially as Ben's temperament is (to me at any rate) too complicated & undisciplined. One cannot be temperamental with a piece of stone.'[31] She also felt that Nicholson was 'deeply jealous of my work but it's against his principles to be so – so he represses it & it comes out in a million unconscious acts of putting me in the wrong. The more it continues the longer it takes me to do the day's work, consequently I'm tired & his complaint that work absorbs me is true!'[32] By the end of the year their differences were irreconcilable, and the separation of the two figures from *Dyad* to *Contrapuntal Forms* transferred from art to life.

Following a month of illness, shingles followed by salmonella, Hepworth moved into Trewyn Studio, transforming the upper room into a hybrid living and working space, and writing to Gardiner, 'as far as work is concerned I feel on top of the world – the lost 4 weeks is the devil but I have gained clarity & intensity of vision so perhaps when I'm strong I shall be able to carve more decisively than ever before'.[33] She maintained good relations with Nicholson, visiting his studio just two weeks after they separated, and writing, 'it was the greatest possible delight to see the huge painting this morning. I think it is the finest thing you've ever done & the "life" & tension in it seems to have all the experience & joy of all your periods of work – both "still life" and "abstract"

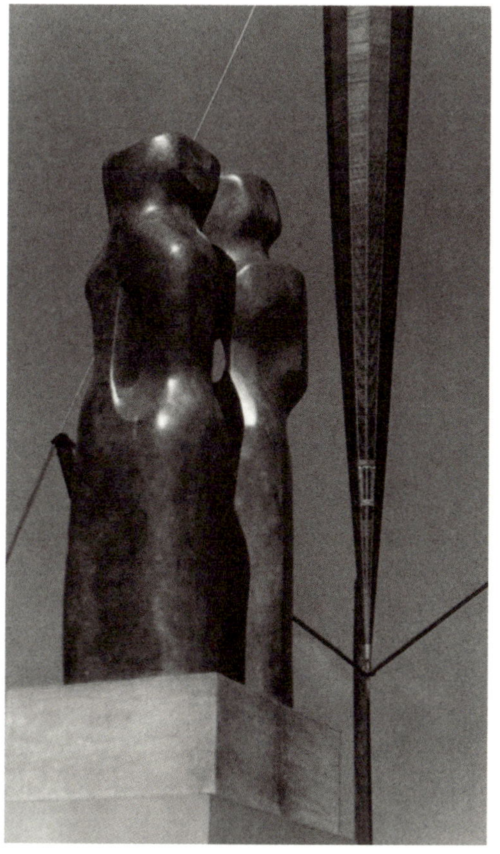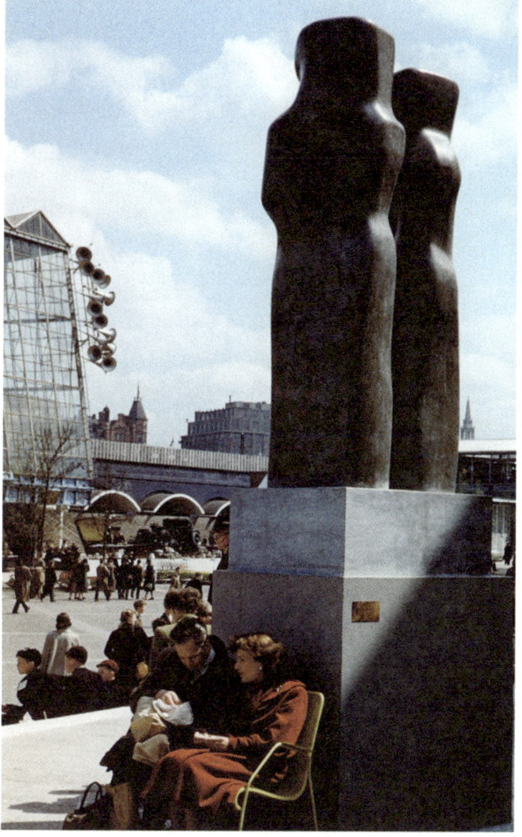

ABOVE LEFT Barbara Hepworth's *Contrapuntal Forms* at the Festival of Britain, South Bank, London, with the Skylon, 1951. Photograph by Anthony Panting

ABOVE RIGHT *Contrapuntal Forms* at the Festival of Britain, London, 1951

[...] As you know there is nothing more inspiring to me than the act of creation – & the creation of <u>your</u> work in particular.'[34] Despite the loss of their romantic relationship, Hepworth remained single-minded, writing to Gardiner, 'for myself I have only 2 thoughts! One to feel my proper strength again & two, to finish the work I have to do.'[35] She completed *Contrapuntal Forms* and a second commission, *Turning Form*, for the Riverside Restaurant that was located between the Festival Hall and Waterloo Bridge, designed by architect Jane Drew. This was a kinetic sculpture made of white-painted reinforced concrete on a metal armature that rotated every two minutes. Hepworth was delighted with both sculptures and wrote to Nicholson of 'my figures [*Contrapuntal Forms*] which I consider exactly the right size & perfectly placed on the site. The carving as well as human beings "come to life". I have just got some lovely photos of them.'[36] Photographs show the figures against the modern architecture of the Festival of Britain on the South Bank, in particular the 'Skylon', a vertical feature and engineering feat designed by architects Hidalgo Moya, Philip Powell and Felix Samuely that became a symbol of the Festival (see previous page, left). Colour documentary photographs see the sculpture surrounded by people, perhaps providing shelter, offering a point of contact between the monumental architecture and the human visitors (see previous page, right).

Hepworth's photographs of *Contrapuntal Forms* were included in her concurrent solo exhibition at Wakefield City Art Gallery, part of the Festival of Britain's programme outside of London (see opposite, right). In the round-up of 'Some Festival Exhibitions', the *Manchester Guardian* noted 'the magnificent "Contrapuntal Forms" of the South Bank exhibition (here shown in photographs) represents the limit to which she can press the explicitly human', while 'far the most satisfactory, most balanced, most perfectly achieved of the works shown, even when seen against the rather dismal Victorian-boarding-house background of the Wakefield gallery, are the strictly abstract sculptures'.[37] Advance local press shows the unpacking of *Dyad*, with the headline, 'Wakefield Show of Unusual Sculpture',[38] suggesting that however accepted by the arts establishment, Hepworth's work was still seen as avant-garde in broader circles (see opposite, left). Being part of the Festival programme seemed to have helped boost public interest, and Hepworth reported to Nicholson on the opening, 'The Wakefield show looked very good & well over 600 came yesterday afternoon.'[39]

Despite the perceived division between figurative and abstract work, Hepworth continued to merge both approaches. Her concerted

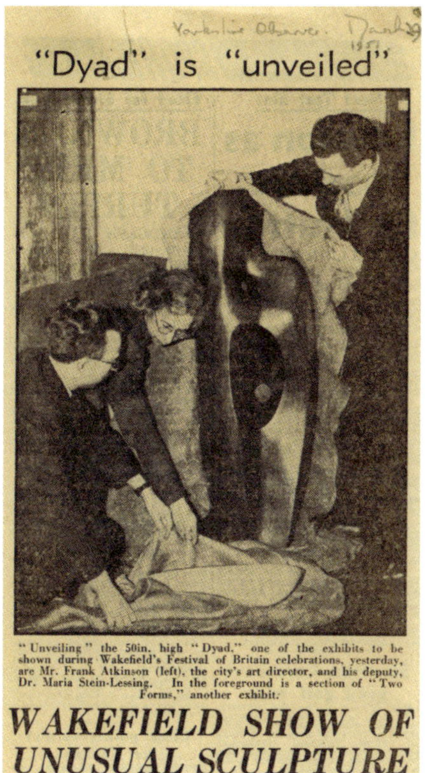

" Unveiling " the 50in. high " Dyad," one of the exhibits to be shown during Wakefield's Festival of Britain celebrations, yesterday, are Mr. Frank Atkinson (left), the city's art director, and his deputy, Dr. Maria Stein-Lessing. In the foreground is a section of " Two Forms," another exhibit.

WAKEFIELD SHOW OF UNUSUAL SCULPTURE

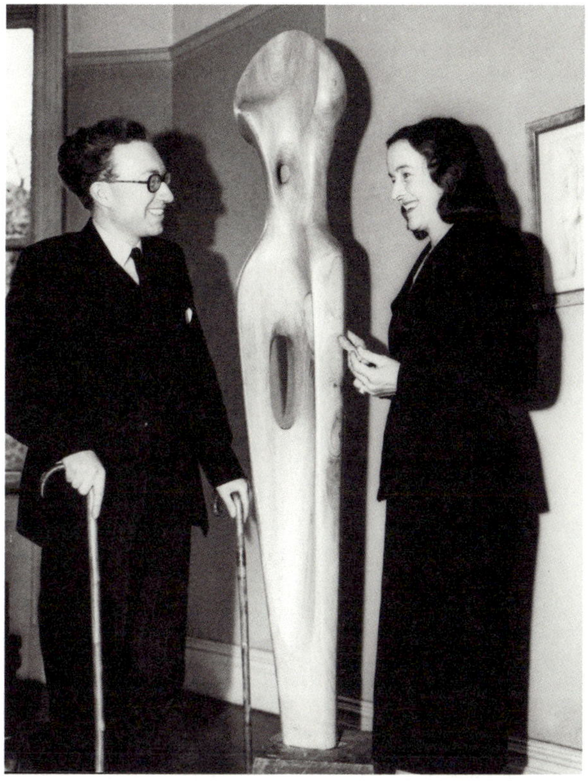

exploration of the human experience of landscape formed, in Hepworth's words, 'the apprenticeship to my present concern with an image in sculpture of the community as a unit in landscape'.[40] Hepworth traced her interest in depicting groups of figures, both abstractly and realistically, to the formation of her family, writing, 'it is an extension of the same idea which started in November 1934, but extended gradually from within outwards; through the family group and its closely knit relationship out to the larger group related to architecture'.[41] In 1951, Hepworth received her first architectural commission, *Vertical Forms*, through the architect Howard Robertson for Hatfield Technical College (now the University of Hertfordshire, Hatfield). A painting probably made to present her proposal to the commissioners shows three overlapping standing figures, broadly human-shaped, as *Dyad* and *Contrapuntal Forms*, connected by a circular piercing (see following page). Hepworth is reported as telling a journalist at the unveiling in 1952, 'I tried to express a quality of aspiration to learning.'[42] Rather than imposing a didactic depiction of education, the sculpture inspires through symbolic means, the overlapping of the figures

ABOVE LEFT Press clipping, 'Dyad is unveiled', from *Yorkshire Observer*, 29 March 1951

ABOVE RIGHT Barbara Hepworth with Frank Atkinson, Director of Wakefield Art Gallery, at her exhibition at the gallery, May 1951

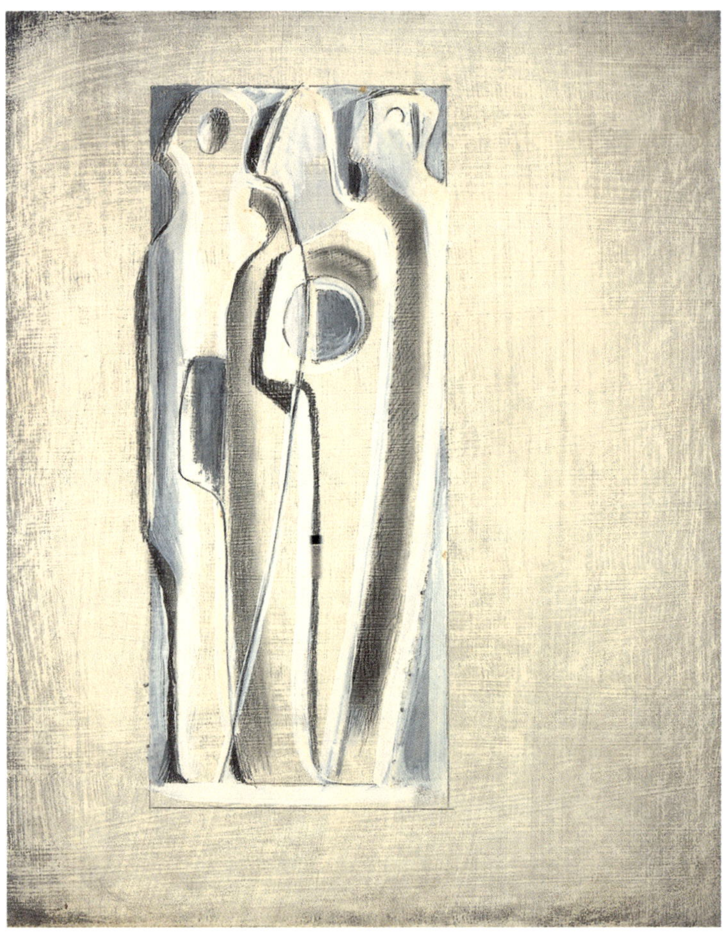

suggesting an exchange of ideas. Hepworth would note of abstraction's ability to convey meaning: 'in opposition to "social realism" I believe that meanings in sculpture emerge more powerfully when they are carried through sculpture's own silent language'.[43]

Abstract figures continued to appear in Hepworth's work through the early 1950s. In *Hieroglyph* (1953), two distinct figures are articulated by polished piercings made in Ancaster stone. While separate, they are bound within the same organic material, its geological composition visible in the varying layers of colour and pattern. These ephemeral figures made of space metaphorically convey Hepworth's belief in the strong ties between individuals embedded within the same earthly society.

Hieroglyph featured in Hepworth's next major exhibition after Venice, a complete retrospective held at the Whitechapel Art Gallery

ABOVE Barbara Hepworth, *Three Figures – Project for Sculpture* (for Hatfield Technical College), *c*. 1950, oil and pencil on board, 35.6 × 27.9 cm (14 × 11 in.)

in 1954. Installation photographs show Hepworth got her wish for a vast number of works to convey the range and disparate elements of her practice (see below). Sculptures of different materials and from different periods jostled alongside one another, while the walls were tiled with a multitude of drawings and paintings of various styles. She wrote to Nicholson, praising the understanding of curator Bryan Robertson, 'fortunately for the growth of my [Whitechapel] show Bryan is a wonderfully clear person of great integrity & purpose'.[44] Her vision paid off, as a review in *The Sunday Times* made clear: '"Chilling" and "inhuman" are the cant-words for Miss Barbara Hepworth's sculptures; and it is true that, when dumped in the conventional surroundings of a West

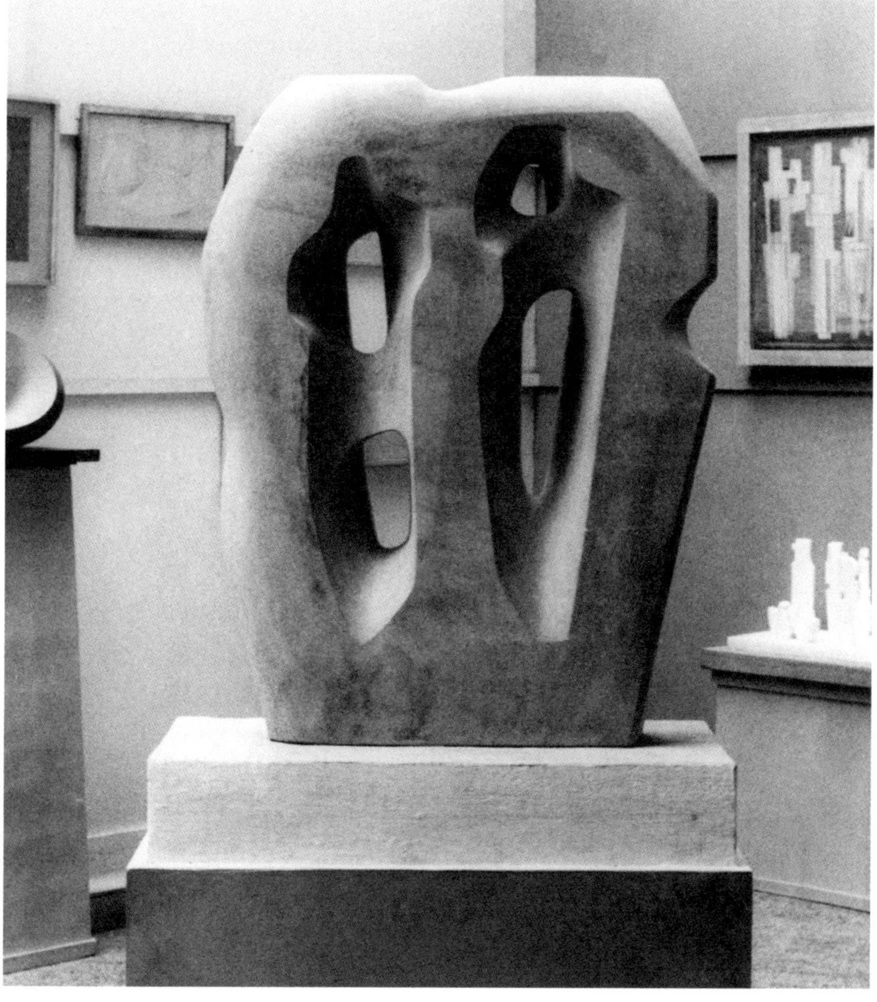

ABOVE View of Barbara Hepworth's exhibition at the Whitechapel Art Gallery, London, 1954, showing *Hieroglyph* (1953)

End gallery, they keep themselves to themselves. At the Whitechapel Art Gallery, however, where Miss Hepworth has contributed nearly two hundred items to a comprehensive survey of her career, the conditions are very different. For the first time in twenty-seven years, she has been given the chance to arrange, light and populate an enormous room.'[45] Given the opportunity, Hepworth was able to articulate the vitality and dynamism of her abstract ideals, each work forming part of a vibrant holistic experience.

The Whitechapel exhibition catalogue included statements taken from the monograph *Barbara Hepworth: Carvings and Drawings*, published in 1952, which placed Hepworth's own eloquent descriptions of the phases of her career thus far alongside carefully selected photographs of her sculptures. Here, she addressed publicly the question of gender that had been the subject of her private correspondences:

> *I have never understood why the word feminine is considered to be a compliment to one's sex if one is a woman, but has a derogatory meaning when applied to anything else. The feminine point of view is a complementary one to the masculine [...] there is no question of competition. The woman's approach presents a different emphasis.*
>
> *There is a whole range of formal perception belonging to feminine experience. So many ideas spring from an inside response to form; for example, if I see a woman carrying a child in her arms it is not so much what I see that affects me, but what I feel within my own body.*[46]

Hepworth's fight for the validity of 'the woman's approach' should be seen in the context of contemporary views. Contemporaneous press, for example, while writing positively about Hepworth, would remark, 'it might be possible to mistake the huge-browed Miss Hepworth [...] for a professional intellectual. But she is, in fact, the mother of four children,'[47] the possibility of being both intellectual and a mother unthinkable to *The Sunday Times* in 1955. Hepworth wanted to celebrate these experiences and the insight they gave her, which she communicated through her work. In the Whitechapel catalogue she goes further, stating that the female voice in art is not only 'complementary' to the masculine, but necessary: it 'completes the total experience of life'.[48] After years of being ignored or misunderstood, Hepworth was making herself heard.

Rhythmic Form

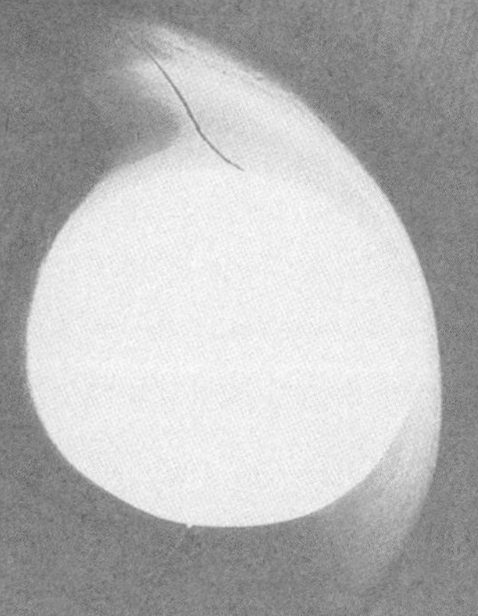

In the final section of her 1952 monograph, Hepworth reflected on her written statements, 'in these very brief notes I seem to have omitted everything that goes to make up my usual working day. These things are immensely important to me; perhaps more important than the things about which I have written. My home and my children; listening to music, and thinking about its relation to the life of forms, the need for dancing as recreation, and where dancing links with the actual physical rhythm of carving; the intense pleasure derived from tools and craftsmanship – all these things are daily expressions of the whole.'[1] Hepworth had drawn parallels between abstract art and music in the early 1930s, and rhythm had always been part of the way she wrote about and perceived the world. In the late 1940s and early 1950s these references became more overt, as she began titling her works after musical elements. The first of these, *Rhythmic Form* (1949) (right), was made the year that Hepworth met composer Priaulx Rainier, and was exhibited in the Lefevre Gallery exhibition of February 1950 after which Rainier wrote to her, 'I cannot think of other modern sculpture which contains an essence usually associated only with music of the highest abstract quality [...] You have already achieved the world towards which one struggles so hard in music.'[2]

In the summer of 1950, Hepworth invited Rainier to stay in St Ives, and wrote to Margaret Gardiner, 'my friend Priaulx Rainier is staying with us. She is a very beautiful person with a rare intelligence & astonishing creative power. She has been composing in a corner of Trewyn garden – somewhat disturbed perhaps by the odd rhythms of hammers.'[3] Rainier composed *Rhythms of the Stones* on 20 July 1950, fragments notating the sound of Hepworth and her assistants carving the two monumental figures of *Contrapuntal Forms*, and reflecting Hepworth's feeling that 'the sound of a mallet or hammer is music to my ears, when either is used rhythmically'.[4] Just as Hepworth's practice inspired Rainier's work, so too the musical term within the title of Hepworth's Festival of Britain commission, *Contrapuntal Forms*, shows Rainier's influence on Hepworth. In a letter of 1951, Hepworth asks Rainier for her opinion on

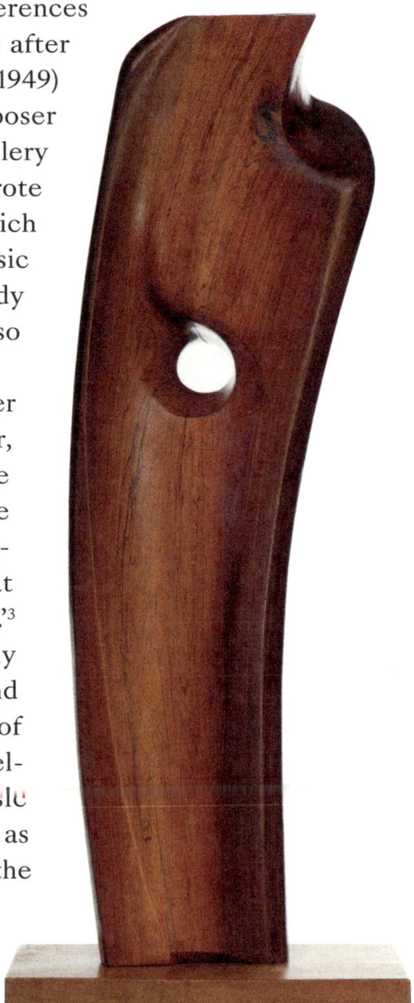

RIGHT Barbara Hepworth, *Rhythmic Form*, 1949, rosewood, 100.3 × 35 × 12.2 cm (39½ × 13¾ × 4⅞ in.)

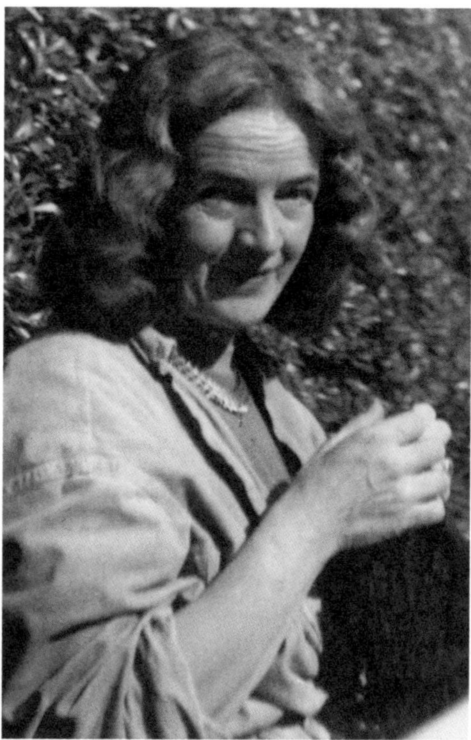

alternative titles: 'Motet (contrapuntal forms in blue limestone)' or 'Motet (Praising) blue stone figures'.[5] The 'motet' of the title seems to reference Thomas Tallis's forty-part motet *Spem in Alium*, a score and record of which Rainier had given Hepworth. In the letter enclosed with the score, Rainier writes, 'Here is the immortal masterpiece by Tallis [...] It is right that you should have the score of this miracle of architecture in sound,'[6] echoing Hepworth's drive to give tangible form to ephemeral qualities. Hepworth replied, 'I'm determined to understand something of the construction. I must unravel its simplicity and understand its complexity.'[7] For Hepworth, music offered a freer way to consider form, as she wrote to Rainier: 'how much more absolute, reliable & defined are the materials with which you create. There's nothing you cannot do with sounds – infinite relationships.'[8]

As well as creative inspiration, Rainier offered Hepworth emotional and practical support through the dissolution of her marriage to Nicholson, as Hepworth recounted: 'thank heavens Priaulx has stayed on – she is a beautiful person & Ben likes her a lot. Also she has looked after me superbly – insisting on meals & medicine at regular hours.

ABOVE Barbara Hepworth with a cat, *c.* 1950. Photograph possibly taken by Priaulx Rainier

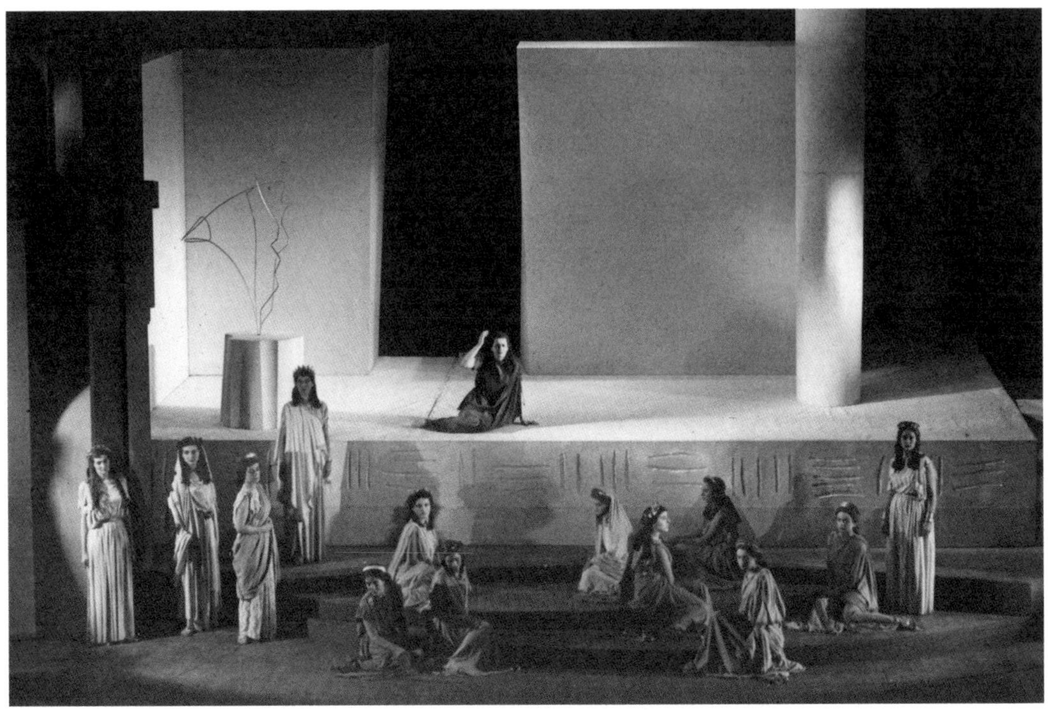

Consequently I have put on 2lbs & feel stronger. It is lovely to be in contact with music & so refreshing to talk about another medium.'[9] Rainier would visit St Ives regularly over the next few years, eventually taking a studio for herself in the town, and she dedicated several of her compositions to Hepworth.[10] When not both in St Ives, Rainier and Hepworth kept in contact through letters, exchanging reading materials – sharing a love of Rilke – and ideas on form. Rainier described her process of composition in visual terms, 'the colour changes are through "dark" and "light" toned instruments with a special orchestration for the purpose',[11] while Hepworth complimented Rainier, 'I like it when you write about my work, it teaches me a lot.'[12] In addition to records of both contemporary and early English music, Rainier gave Hepworth the composer Igor Stravinsky's book, *The Poetics of Music*, which affirmed Hepworth's belief in the proximity of music and sculpture. It became one of her favourite books, and she wrote enthusiastically in 1951, 'Stravinsky's chapter on composition corresponds so exactly to the creation of form that a mere half a dozen words only would need to be changed to make it a statement on sculpture.'[13] In the same letter, she described Rainier's composition *Sinfonia da Camera* (1947) in sculptural

ABOVE The stage set of Sophocles'
Electra at the Old Vic, London, with set
and costumes by Barbara Hepworth.
Photograph by John Vickers

terms as 'a fine & strong work – indeed very stone-like – the 4 movements in echelon with vertical blocks & integrated vertical impulses & detail which excites me profoundly'.

As Hepworth was engaging further with the discipline of music, she was also becoming involved in the world of theatre. In the summer of 1950, as Rainier composed while *Contrapuntal Forms* was carved, Hepworth wrote to Ramsden, 'I am doing the "set" for Electra at the Old Vic. Have just finished the memorial for Duncan [MacDonald], & completed the model for the Festival sculpture. Life is full & my studio is really a marvellous place.'[14] *The Times* announced in February 1951, 'before the war the Old Vic Company frequently included a Greek play in its repertory, and now that the company is back in its own theatre this practice is to be revived. The first Greek play to be given in the restored theatre will be Sophocles' *Electra*, with Miss Peggy Ashcroft in the name part. It will be produced by Mr. Michel Saint-Denis, with sets and costumes designed by Miss Barbara Hepworth.'[15] The *Daily Telegraph and Morning Post* elaborated, 'the settings for the Sophocles classic should be worth seeing. They are being done by Barbara Hepworth, who has made a name as a sculptress of the advanced school. This is her first venture in the theatre.'[16]

Perhaps fittingly, given the context, *Electra* is set in the aftermath of the Trojan War. It centres around the titular character and her brother Orestes' attempt to gain justice for their father, King Agamemnon, who was

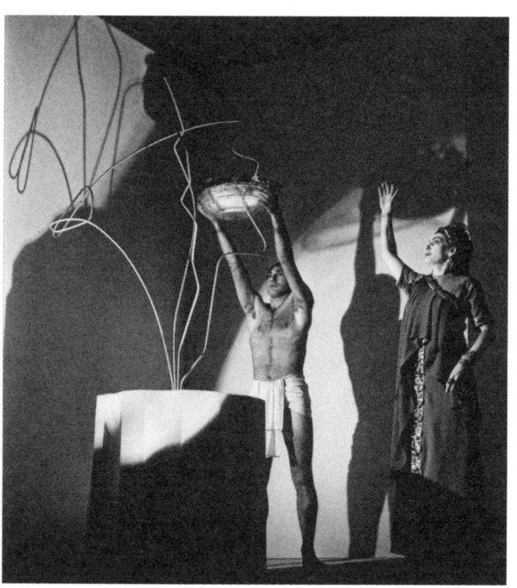

killed by their mother Clytemnestra and her new lover Aegisthus, Agamemnon's cousin, on his return from war. The role of the god Apollo is also highly significant within the drama. Sophocles' stage directions suggest that the action take place before the main gate of the palace of Mycenae, with Apollo's temple on the left. Hepworth's palace façade was rendered in minimal terms by a white square behind a taller single white column. Against this white background, she designed the draped, classical costumes for the actors in primary colours (see opposite and left). The most striking element of Hepworth's design is Apollo's temple, to the left of the set. Apollo himself is given sculptural

ABOVE Barbara Hepworth's *Apollo* (1951) on the stage of Sophocles' *Electra* at the Old Vic, London. Photograph by John Vickers

form, positioned on a tall square base with fluted corners, perhaps suggesting the temple building or altar. As the *Daily Telegraph and Morning Post* reported, 'The statue of Apollo before the Palace of Mycenae has been done in wire as Miss Hepworth, who is a sculptor of reputation, thought a normal form would dominate the stage.'[17] The wire delineates several profiles, giving the illusion of a three-dimensional entity drawn in space. Variances in lighting cast different shadowy profiles across the stage, reflecting Apollo's multifarious presence across the drama. Images of both Clytemnestra and Electra praying to Apollo illustrate Hepworth's assertion in 1952 that 'a sculpture might, and sculptures do, reside in emptiness; but nothing happens until the living human encounters the image. Then the magic occurs – the magic of scale and weight, form and texture, colour and movement, the encircling interplay and dance occurs between the object and the human sensibility.'[18] This was Hepworth's first work in metal, made in an edition of two, the wire allowing seemingly spontaneous movement, giving life to the ephemeral form of a god.

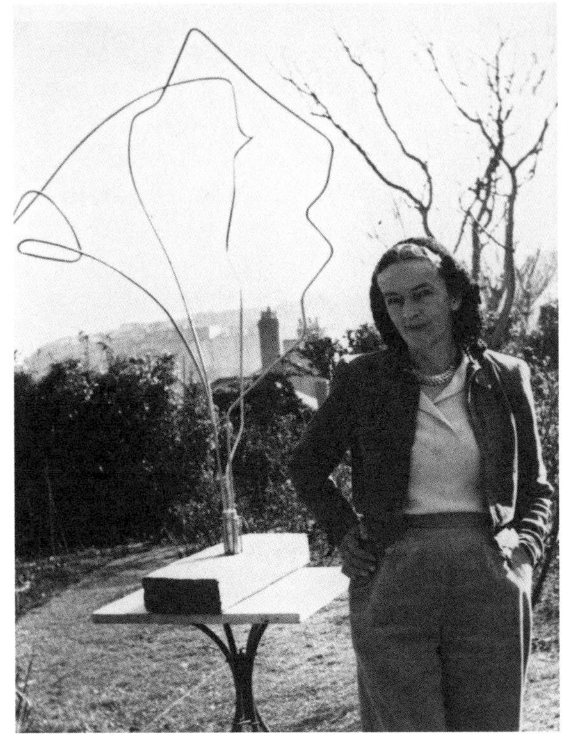

The expression of spirituality through sculptural form was a continued impulse in Hepworth's work. *Single Form (Antiphon)* (1953), a twisting and elongated biomorphic figure (opposite), combines spiritual and musical references, 'antiphon' being a short chant in Christian ritual using the texts of the biblical Psalms. This was another point of contact with Rainier, who gave Hepworth a handwritten copy of her composition *Sinfonia da Camera*, which Hepworth had complimented, inscribed with 'The meaning of the figure / The eternal beauty and mystery of the act / Of creation and spiritual soaring / Towards the Divine'.[19] In 1953, Rainier composed music for a film featuring Hepworth and her work, *Barbara Hepworth: Figures in a Landscape*, a collaborative project funded by the newly established BFI Experimental Film Fund, directed by Dudley Shaw Ashton, with words written by archaeologist and poet Jacquetta Hawkes

ABOVE Barbara Hepworth with
Apollo at Trewyn, Cornwall, 1951

(see also p. 162). Hawkes wrote a sweeping narrative of the evolution of the Cornish landscape in spiritual as well as geological terms, describing the pagans who made 'stones for dancing and stones for dying',[20] before referencing Christian landmarks, the camera juxtaposing Hepworth's totemic sculptures with the upright tower of St Ives Church. Hepworth mused on the parallels of artistic and divine creation during the 1950s, and concluded in 1959 that 'in all those works of art which move me most I find this special sense of timeless praising and affirmative creation. It is perhaps the difference between thinking one is a god or believing that one should reflect God.'[21]

The attempt to reflect God through creative acts informed another collaboration with the performing arts. Through Rainier, Hepworth met composer Michael Tippett, and together the three founded the St Ives Festival in 1953. The programme offered a celebration of the two Elizabethan ages, on the accession of Elizabeth II, by placing contemporary music alongside sixteenth-century compositions. More broadly, Hepworth noted:

> *The festival was originally conceived as an act of praise. For centuries man has tried to offer the best that he could give to God, and by joining in this act of dedication with his fellow men he has replenished his faith in the true values of life and work. In this century of great wars and political strife, men and woman have endeavoured, through such festivals, to reach a better understanding with their fellow beings. Art is a universal language – music has the power to unite us and transport our spirit.*[22]

This was part of a letter from Hepworth published in the *St Ives Times* following the festival, in which she appealed for community support: 'since the festival ended, there has been so much discussion on the material gains and losses that I feel the spiritual meaning of the festival has become obscured'.[23]

Although conceived of as an annual event, the poor attendance and high production costs meant that it was not repeated.

The festival did, however, form the starting point for a more extensive collaboration

Left Barbara Hepworth, *Single Form (Antiphon)*, 1953, boxwood, 207 × 16.6 × 14 cm (81½ × 6½ × 5½ in.)

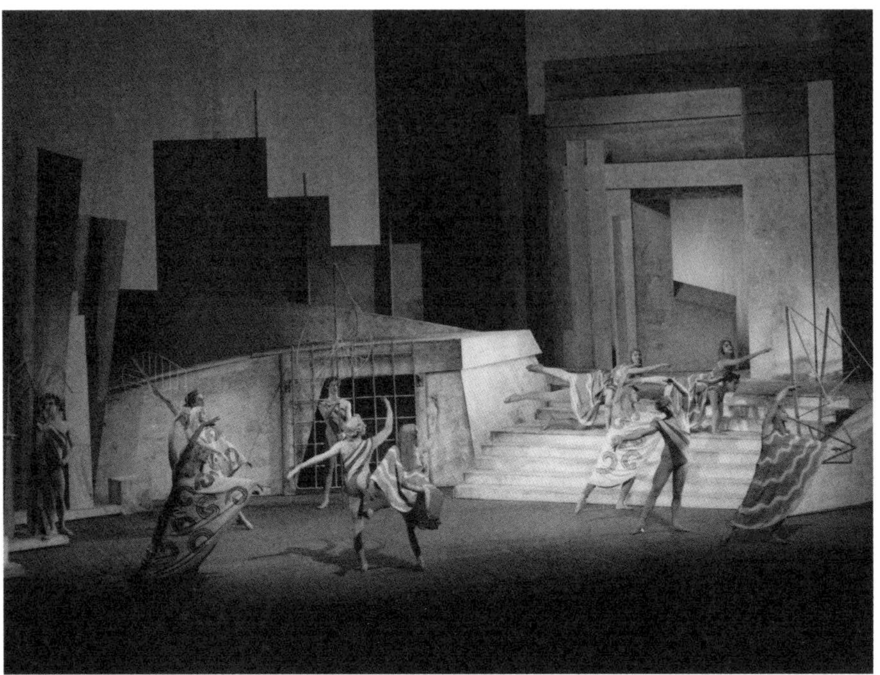

between Hepworth and Tippett. They had clearly established a relationship of mutual support and appreciation, Hepworth giving Tippett a painting, *Granite Forms, Red, Yellow and Deep Blue* (1953), following the festival, and Tippett sending Hepworth two trunks of yew in autumn of 1954, one of which may have been used in the carving *Phoenix* (1954).[24] Hepworth recalled, 'it was in 1954 that Michael approached me about the sets for *The Midsummer Marriage*. We discussed it, sitting in my garden [...] I thought that *The Midsummer Marriage* contained a new idea for opera: a concept which I felt could open the doors for a formal concept of opera in the future.'[25] In a letter to Hepworth in December 1954, Tippett wrote of the 'extraordinary degree of artistic sympathy & collaboration between us both'.[26] *The Midsummer Marriage* was Tippett's first full-scale opera, and it opened at the Royal Opera House on 27 January 1955. Based on Mozart's opera *The Magic Flute*, it followed the dual progression to marriage of two couples, one royal (Mark and Jenifer, royal names deriving from Celtic folklore to reflect Tippett's Cornish heritage) and one 'everyday' (Jack and Bella, a mechanic and 'pretty secretary'). The royal couple, in Tippett's words, 'take part in "big" supernatural manifestations', resulting in 'a collective imaginative experience dealing with the interaction of two worlds, the natural and the supernatural'.[27] The fusion

ABOVE The first production of Michael Tippett's *The Midsummer Marriage*, at the Royal Opera House, London, 1955, with set and costumes by Barbara Hepworth. Photograph by Houston Rogers

of these two realms spoke to Hepworth's enduring concerns, and the transformation of Mark and Jenifer into one natural entity in the third act drew on her earlier exploration of the interrelations of two figures. Tippett was delighted with her designs, foreseeing in their collaboration 'a unity of eye & ear which is so rare in England as to be almost non-existent'.[28]

Photographs of the production and detailed drawings show Hepworth's set and costume designs (see opposite and below). The scene is set in a woodland clearing with buildings, including a Greek temple, on one side, and a cave on the other. Hepworth conveyed the buildings and temple through a multitude of overlapping squares and coloured rectangles, and described the composition: 'the colours of the main set were white – with black lines & primary blue. The vertical rectangles were of viridian green – Indian red and venetian red with a large panel of ultramarine.'[29] The costume designs were similarly specific on colour and material ('<u>gun-metal</u> resilient silk for the grey. It must be luminous & lively'),[30] and her annotated designs reveal a sensitivity to the human form in movement. In drawing the 'water girls' costume for the Ritual Dances that take place in the second act, Hepworth notes, 'silk blue sculptured strands – Heavy – the drawing shows hem line as it would be when arm

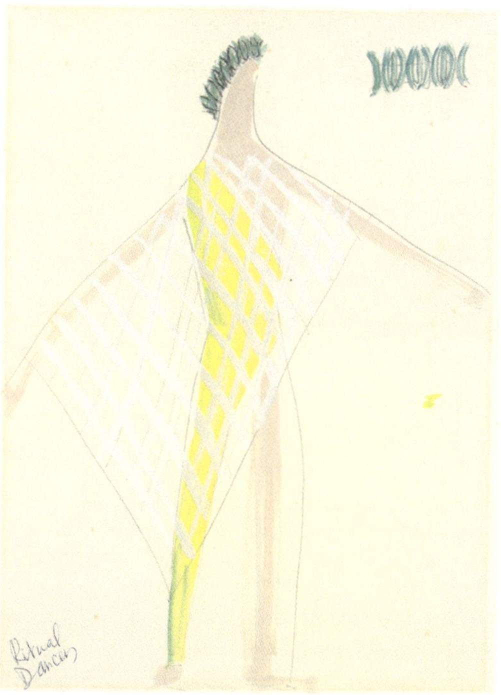

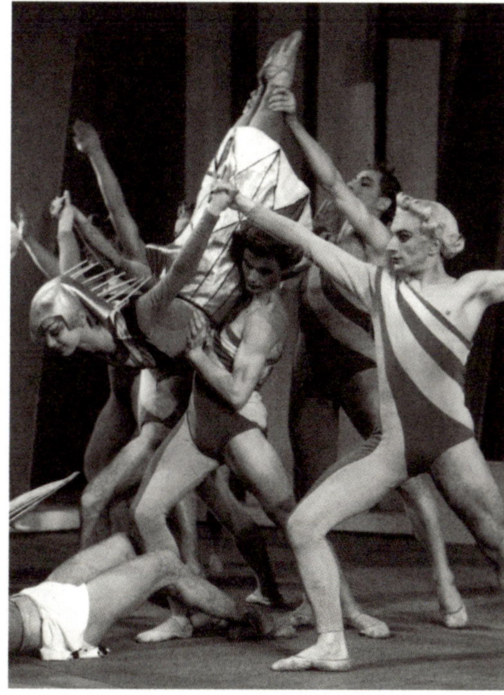

ABOVE LEFT Barbara Hepworth, costume design for a ritual dancer for *The Midsummer Marriage*, 1954

ABOVE RIGHT Set and costumes by Barbara Hepworth for the first production of Michael Tippett's *The Midsummer Marriage*, Royal Opera House, London, 1955 (detail). Photograph by Houston Rogers

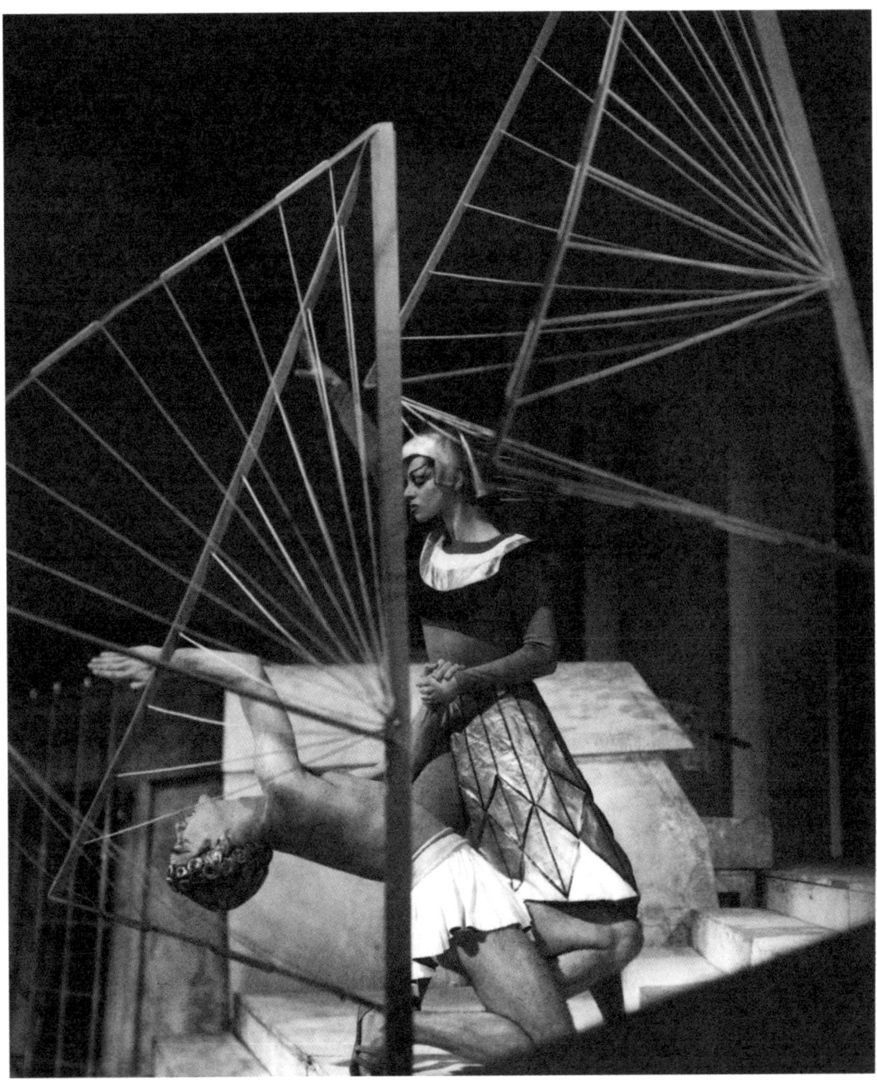

is down. When arm is up the line is a straight diagonal.'[31] The design for the mysterious character of clairvoyant Madame Sosostris echoes the upright biomorphic form of Hepworth's abstract figures, and she described the costume as 'Indigo grey drapery with white lines – the white applied & stitched according to the drawing which makes an abstract form – a sculptured form'.[32] It is during the Ritual Dances set in the woods that the most sculptural elements of Hepworth's design appear. As she wrote: 'the trees were verticals of wood with spaces for the dancers & a full play of changing light. The wood & string forms carried by the dancers were made by me in maquette form.'[33] These hand-carried props resemble Hepworth's crystalline drawings and strung forms from the 1940s (see Chapter 7), photographs of the production giving the illusion of actors captured within a giant Hepworth sculpture (see opposite).

The reviews were lukewarm, with general praise for Tippett's music tempered by persistent criticism of the incomprehensible libretto. Hepworth's modern set did not capture the critics' imagination, the *Telegraph* describing it as 'effective in an austere and angular manner though not very practicable',[34] while the *Guardian* described 'Barbara Hepworth's "mock-up" of doors and stair-ways and great curving balustrades – a temple in a wood'.[35] Undeterred, some years later Hepworth would reflect on the collaboration and on what she and Tippett were trying to achieve:

> *If this opera suffered a defeat, it was a worldly defeat [...]*
> *I think The Midsummer Marriage asked, in both its allegorical meaning and its symbolism, for a new discipline; also for a new tradition, perhaps related to the formality of Greek theatre or of the Mystery Plays. This demand should, I feel, be developed and fulfilled. On traditional lines, the unwieldy passion of the chorus could be an asset. But in unconventional presentations, musically, the chorus is needed only as a voice, and, both musically and in mass, should be as disciplined as part of an orchestra and not dramatically produced in the traditional sense.*
>
> *The English find a romantic idea easier to accept; but I still have an absolute faith in the classical development even in opera [...] but as I see it, it means a new discipline. It means a new emphasis on movement and the meaning of gesture; a new emphasis on the use of light and of darkness, and on colour and form so that the music and the composer's 'idea' can speak without dilution.*[36]

Her ambition to explore new creations of form as it relates to human experience, from movement and dance to music and spirituality, remained as fierce and determined as ever. Though now successful and entering middle age, Hepworth continued to adapt and pursue innovative creative paths.

Chapter 12

The Aegean Suite

Just as Hepworth was exploring musical, theatrical and filmic collaborations, she suffered a personal tragedy. Her elder son, Paul Skeaping, an RAF pilot, was killed in an air crash in Thailand on 13 February 1953.[1] She wrote a starkly brief note to Gardiner immediately: 'Margaret darling – a telegram has just come & Paul has been killed in Thailand. Barbara,'[2] and later, 'thank you for offering to come. I am quite useless at the moment – such unspeakable anguish. Only you could possibly understand & perhaps Rilke.'[3] Hepworth and Priaulx Rainier had discussed reading *The Selected Letters of Rainer Maria Rilke 1902–1926* in their correspondence several years earlier.[4] In Hepworth's copy, an envelope from Rainier postmarked February 1953 marked a page where Rilke writes to a friend whose sister had died:

> *The hour of death, which brings this knowledge to each of us, is only one of our hours and no exception: our life continually passes over into changes whose intensity is probably no less than the newness and successions which death brings. And so just as we have to leave one another absolutely at a certain point in that most formidable of all changes, we must, strictly speaking, give one another up every instant, let them go on and not hold them back.[5]*

Paul's sudden death left Hepworth in a state of shock. She wrote to Gardiner a week later:

> *I have been in a state of collapse where neither my head nor my knees would do what I willed. My whole being cries out against this. The vitality & radiance in Paul, the light he always brought into a room & upon which I (& SRS) seemed to depend so much, is impossible to associate with an early death [...] Rilke touches on it with some finality of truth.*
> *I found some peace this Friday after a Requiem was held for him in the church of St. Eia – the tower which dominates Trewyn & St. Ives. The unquietness round my studio was stilled. One just has to accept.[6]*

Gardiner recalled in her memoirs that Paul's death was 'a lasting grief to Barbara'.[7] Hepworth's tender *Madonna and Child* carving in his memory was unveiled in 1954, at the church in St Ives where she had found some peace following his death. That summer, in an attempt to lift her from depression, Gardiner took Hepworth to Greece.

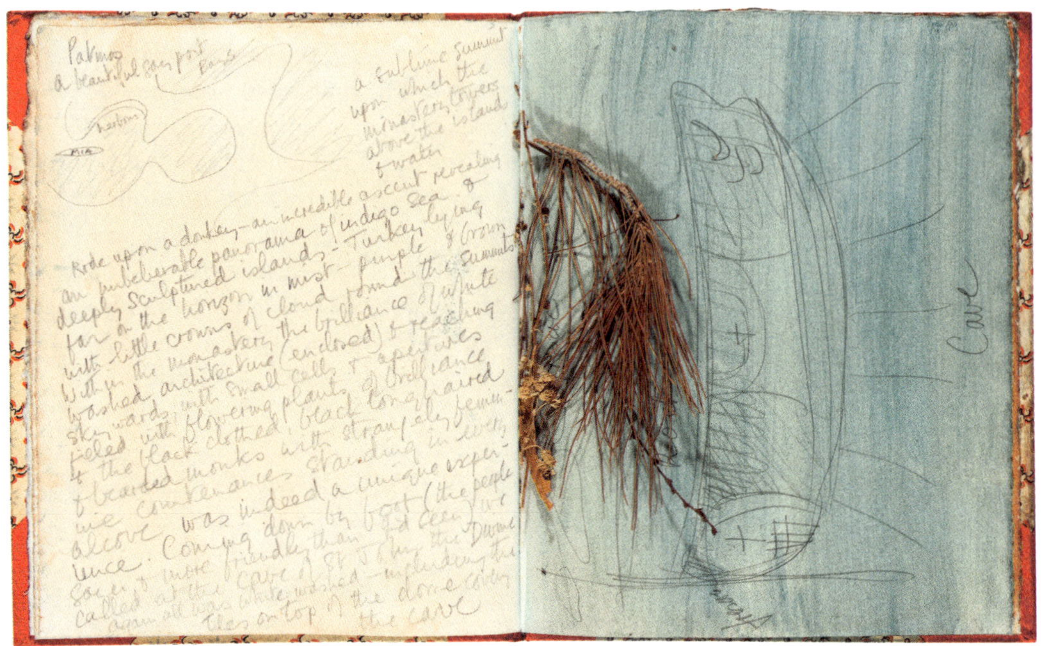

They travelled by boat, Hepworth writing to Nicholson, 'passing Salamis – Wed aboard M/v Miaollis We are approaching Athens – I have never seen such a celestial landscape [...] Beyond ones' wildest hopes. Calais to Venice just blotted out with rain – but since Sunday clear skies, indigo sea & a pink landscape.'[8] Hepworth wrote her experiences in a fragmented diary while travelling, both in a notebook Nicholson had given her for their first Christmas in Cornwall, 1940, and in a separate 'Greek sketchbook'. In the former she sets the scene:

> *I'm being antisocial – I can't help it – friends dear friends I try to escape all contact & proper human obligations. First off the boat alone, first on the site alone, escaping the lecture the arranged plan. I try to behave I can't I won't I have waited 30 yrs to see Greece. How can I be in a state of perception, walk these paths hear with my eyes & feel with my ears & think with hands with 200 1954 English figures round me. The proper corrective exists already, everywhere the taxis which brought us have their radios on. I am in this 20th century but this is Greece & in these few days I must know & find & hold all these essentials. Alas I know too little of history no dates & few facts would be nice to know – but not here! The quality of touch through feet hands*

ABOVE Barbara Hepworth, Greek Sketchbook, interleaved with pressed flowers and plants, 1954

*cheek, the rhythm of movement, the temperature of marble, the
worn path leading to somewhere & the space, volume, rhythm
weight & substance of sculpture temple or palace have a meaning
which I must find & hold in these brief hours and silent exultant
pleasure. I must be antisocial – Each morning at dawn we now
arrive at some new island.*[9]

Hepworth's annotated sketchbook (see opposite) captured fragments of these experiences as she moved from island to island around
the Aegean Sea. The texts were later published, dated and set out typo-
graphically as poems, offering a lyrical insight into her journeys.[10]

COLOURS
Indigo sea, which when light reflects from cliffs, becomes
pure cerulean.
Their Indian red and pink hills – monastral purple mountains
at sunset, which intensifies the greens to the wildest
vitality.

The Acropolis – the spaces between the columns – the depth
of flutings to touch – the breadth, weight and volume –
the magnificence of a single marble, bole up-ended.
The passionate warm colour of the marble and all-pervading
philosophic proportion and space.

25.8.54

[...]

EPIDAUROS
Olive, hill and figures
And the quality of sound.
Grey stones
grey hills
Soft grey olive trees – deep green conifers – rustle of
The wind above.
Absolute acoustics
Cross and upwards acoustics
Growth of olives
Serenity of landscape
Sacred grove & well

[...]

MYCENAE – rhythmic movement of mountains
The Royal Tombs – a vast ellipse (pit) of stones on stones.

Majestic landscape, hills purple & pink, blue & some deep red –
the lower margin of hills rhythmic with olives; the upper hills
rhythmic with folds from left to right.

The nearest hill, a high cone (many such) but this is high and
grand. Studded with stones & green mounds of low growing
verdure.

The site itself is of great beauty & majesty – a high throne
thrust from the higher hills & facing Argos plains – the
vista so great in depth & breadth that the gods command all.

[...]

26.8.54

CRETE
[...] Knossos and its intimate proportion – its sturdy gay pillars
and colour. The heavenly stone – grey striped marble –
grey stone sedimentary – sparkling quartz and the luminosity
of blocks of white mica.

Too hot to prowl like a cat above the shadowy rooms below,
where cool stone and human-sized baths and great urns abound.

But in the museum *the gaiety of forms is paramount – an art*
of non-aggression and even non-philosophical. The first room
had two magnificent cases of Cycladic figures –
...
The Neolithic case had some wonderful figures, many very tiny –
many showing the first forms of figures B.M.

two little pebbles flattened in front to create the female form.

Early terracotta (Cretan)
with hands on stomach
and breasts spouting.

27.8.54

[...]

PATMOS
a beautiful gay port.

a sublime summit upon
which the monastery towers
above the island and water.

Rode upon a donkey – an incredible ascent revealing an unbelievable
panorama of indigo sea & deeply sculptured islands – Turkey
lying far on the horizon in mist – purple & brown with little
crowns of cloud round the summits.
Within the monastery the brilliance of white-washed architecture
(enclosed) & reaching skywards, with small cells & apertures,
filled with flowering plants of brilliance & the black clothed
black long-haired & bearded monks with strangely feminine
countenances standing in every alcove was indeed a unique
experience. Coming down by foot (the people gayer and more
friendly than I'd seen) we called at the cave of St. John
the Divine. Again all was white-washed – including the tiles
on top of the dome covering the cave.

[...]

29.8.54

DELOS
Ascended Kynthes alone, the cave of Apollo – half-way magnificent
and majestic. A pool with fine fig trees nearby full of giant
(sacred?) toads – leaping and barking. Also green frogs.

Went on alone up the last steep ascent, but the wind was angry –
ferocious. I fell, my hair was nearly whisked off my head –
my clothes nearly torn off me. I bowed to the will of the gods
and descended.

Saw a magnificent Koros – tall, fierce and passionate, bigger than
life size – in the Museum. A heavenly work – the back and buttocks
in relation to the hip and waist – an inspiration. I thought the
fragment of leg and calf (attached below the knee) was falsely attributed.
...
Delos was perturbed – an angry wind – making it difficult to return
to Miaoulis

A flower of Santorin Island or Phira the town[11]

*The indescribable beauty of Santorin and the height, breadth
and depth and colour of Phira on the peak of the crater's lip
is not possible to take in from any photograph.*

*At dawn we arrived at the base of Santorin tied to the buoy
in the water filling the deep crater – the quite incredible
white bright light on Phira – 1200 ft up in the air at the
top of the crisscross mule track was almost visionary.
Behind us lay the erupting and menacing little island of
Quinica.*

*I went up alone on a very docile and friendly donkey. The
people at the top were gay welcoming and enchanting. To look
out over the sea to Asia Minor and Turkey with all the
intervening islands was breathtaking – not a word could
describe the sense of space, air and colour – or describe
the 'lightness' of this celestial view of earth and heaven.*

Sunny terraced fertile slopes of vineyards.

*The colours of the volcanic rocks and pumice beyond belief –
the whiteness 'whiter than white'.*

[...]

31.8.54

In 1964, Hepworth added a note on Delphi to these recollections:
'perhaps I did not write in my notebook about Delphi because it meant
so much to me. On a fair and glorious morning I managed to escape some
400 people and ascend the hill alone and in silence [...] standing alone in
the stadium, alone below Olympus, I felt at ease both physically and spir-
itually.'[12] Delphi was one of the first Greek locations Hepworth included
in a title, and *Curved Form (Delphi)* (1955) (see p. 7) one of the first in a
series of sculptures carved from a whole trunk of scented Guarea wood
that Hepworth procured on her return from Greece, again with Gardiner's
help.[13] As with earlier carvings, Hepworth painted the inner surface of
the form, but here, instead of colour, it is painted 'whiter than white',
referencing the white-washed buildings that struck a visual chord on her
travels. The strings, while continuing to express Hepworth's relationship
with the landscape, here have a specific Grecian reference. As well as a
god of healing, truth and light, Apollo, whose temple is at Delphi, was

the god of the arts – poetry, dance and music – and his famous lyre can be seen in the strung form of *Curved Form (Delphi).*

Hepworth wrote in 1955 that 'the great logs have set me off on a new phase of work [...] it is terribly exciting to have such enormous breadth and depth. When I have finished perhaps I shall be able to get inside it. Now I want to carve them all at once.'[14] The deep scoop of *Curved Form (Delphi)* evokes the sweep of the amphitheatre at the Temple of Apollo, a photograph of which Hepworth included in her 1966 book *Drawings from a Sculptor's Landscape.*[15] All the locations Hepworth records boast amphitheatre remains, one described by Hepworth as 'the greatest man-made concavity'.[16] The deep, bowl-like curve of *Configuration (Phira)* (1955) (below) similarly references the landscape of its title. Phira (or Fira) is the capital of the island of Santorini, a volcanic site that offers a surging landscape of craters, as Hepworth wrote: '[t]he indescribable beauty of Santorin and the height, breadth / and depth and colour of

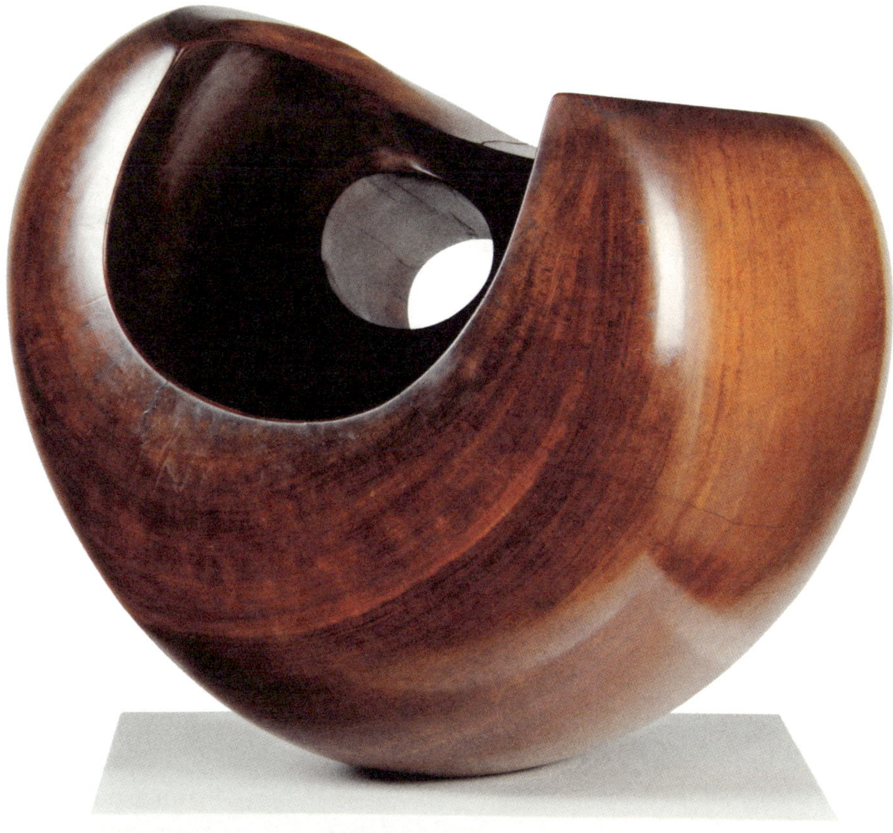

ABOVE Barbara Hepworth, *Configuration (Phira)*, 1955, scented Guarea wood, 68 × 79 × 75 cm (26¾ × 31 × 29½ in.)

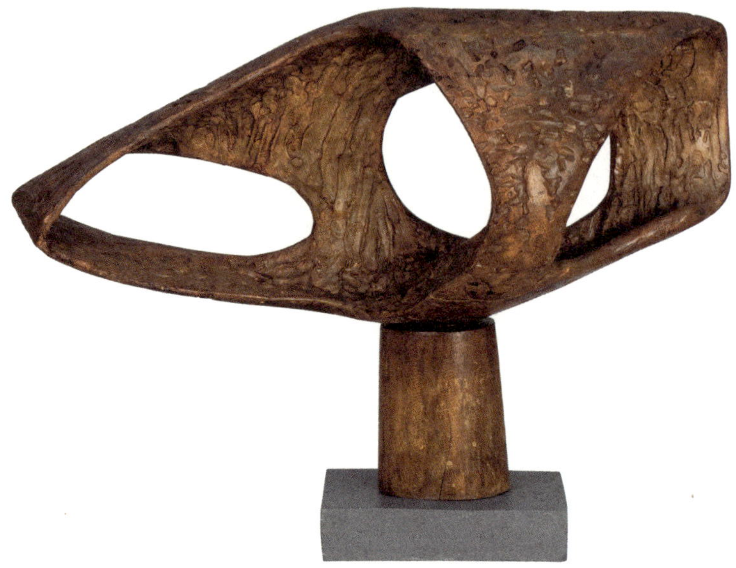

Phira on the peak of the crater's lip'.[17] An artwork from this time, *Drawing for Sculpture (Santorin)* (1955) (opposite), echoes the interlacing curves of *Configuration (Phira)*, and captures some of the vivid colours Hepworth saw in the volcanic rocks and flowers, several of which she pressed within the pages of her sketchbook.

Hepworth returned to her experiences in Greece over the next decade and beyond, writing in 1965, 'timeless and in space, pure in conception and like a rock to hold on to, these forms in Greece have been a constant source of inspiration – Patmos in particular, where the curve of the horizon was omnipotent and the islands rose up from the water like flowers in the sun'.[18] In 1962–63 she created a horizontal, curling form in plaster to be cast in bronze, *Bronze Form (Patmos)* (above). Scrim and plaster were built up on an aluminium mesh support, on which Hepworth laid layers of wet plaster with a spatula, which was subsequently carved or sanded, giving its distinctive mottled surface. The plaster – which was itself exhibited in 1968 – was painted a deep burnt umber, the same colour found in her Greek sketchbook, where, in addition to her notes on colour above, whole pages are given over to watercolour washes of specific hues. However, the paint may have been applied to make visible any damages to the carefully prepared surface that occurred during transit between studio and foundry.[19] For the cast bronze Hepworth specified a green patina, writing to Charles Gaskin at the Art Bronze Foundry that she wanted the effect of 'a kind of "rock covered with lichen"'.[20]

ABOVE Barbara Hepworth, *Bronze Form (Patmos)*, 1962–63, plaster, lacquered and painted brown, 65 × 97.5 × 34.5 cm (25½ × 38⅜ × 13½ in.). Prototype for casting in bronze

The hollows in the form mirror those in a drawing in the sketchbook of Patmos's coastline, with its undulating bays and harbour, while the careful balance between stillness and movement, constructed form and earthy surface, reflects the philosophical impact of this landscape. Hepworth recalled to J. P. Hodin:

> *I remember standing on Patmos and thinking – with that incredible stretch of sea and islands before me – how intensely a figure rising in the distance expressed that perfect elevation of the human spirit which in a way is conveyed by a powerful sculptured form. I felt that the Greek idea had something of the will, the power, the ruggedness we need; that the human spirit could overcome all the problems which beset this industrial age; that it could, as did the Greeks through art, philosophy and poetry, point a clear way to a solution and give it form through a sense of grace and rhythm.*[21]

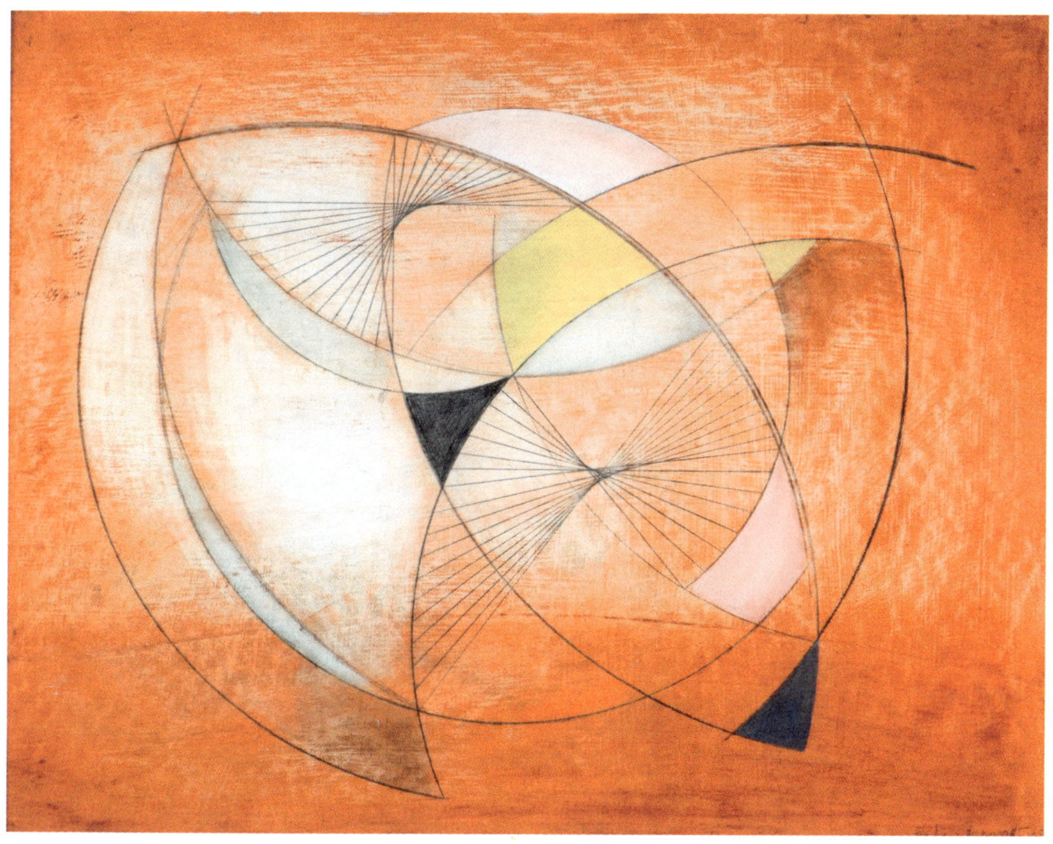

ABOVE Barbara Hepworth, *Drawing for Sculpture (Santorin)*, 1955, pencil and crayon on paper, 38 × 48.1 cm (15 × 18⅞ in.)

While most of Hepworth's 'Greek' sculptures can be loosely described as oval or spherical forms, *Two Forms with White (Greek)* (1963) conveys this sense of elevation (below). Also carved in scented Guarea wood but some years after Hepworth's return from Greece, it recalls her assertion in 1958, 'when I visited Greece and the islands of the Aegean I was greatly moved by the extraordinary power of the <u>vertical</u> in the landscape which was surrounded by the curved horizon of the sea'.[22] The two forms stand upright, Hepworth using the grain of the wood to emphasise their verticality, while incorporating the concavities of the landscape in their scooped, white-painted fronts.

Hepworth would return once more to these experiences with a set of nine lithographs collectively titled *The Aegean Suite* in 1971. Several of the individual lithographs are titled after places Hepworth wrote about, such as *Olympus* and *Delos* (opposite), both vertiginous works reflecting Hepworth's accounts of ascending the hills in both locations. The black vertical lines of *Delos* echo her steep ascent, while the repeated circles

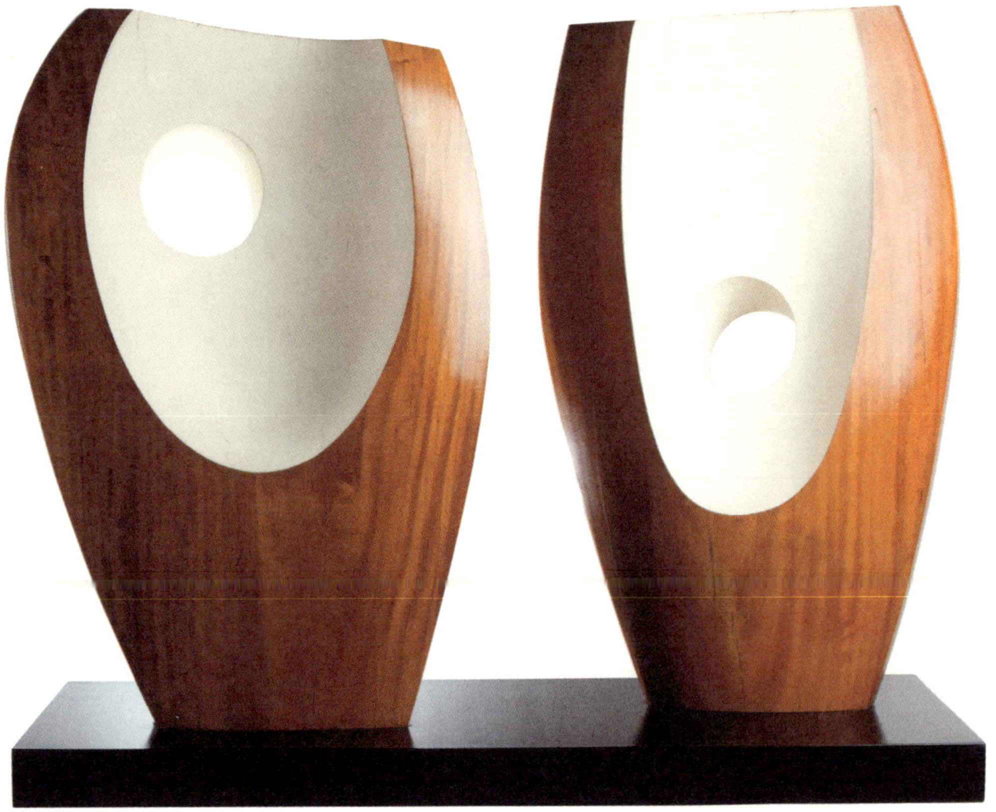

ABOVE Barbara Hepworth, *Two Forms with White (Greek)*, 1963, Guarea wood, part painted, 121.5 × 94.4 × 53 cm (47⅞ × 37⅛ × 20⅞ in.)

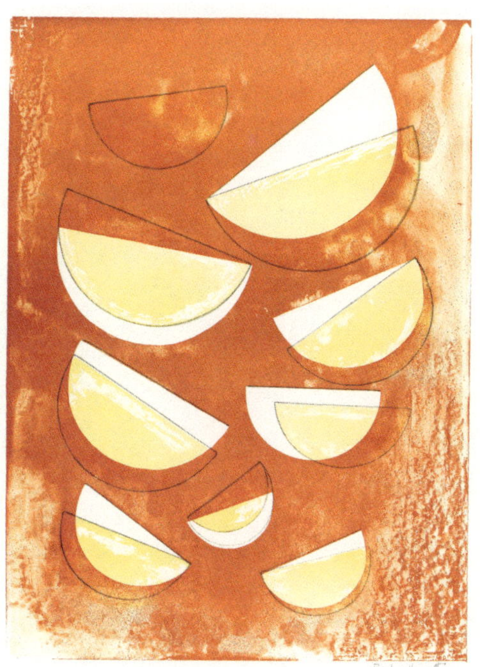

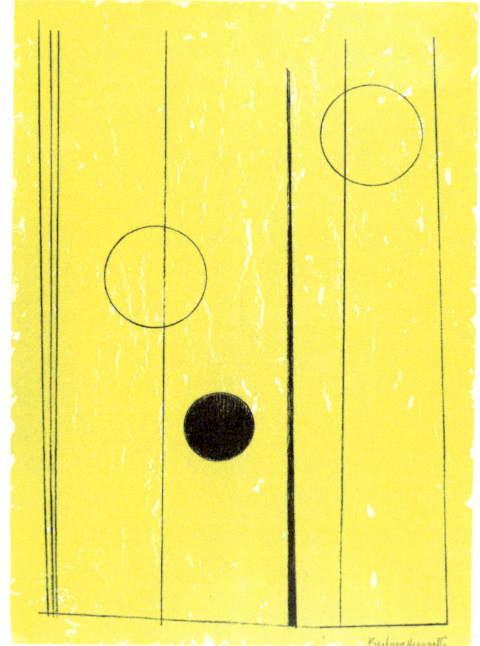

in the upper register and vivid yellow ground suggest the bright sun moving across the sky overhead. In *Olympus*, overlapping semi-circles in yellow and white cascade down a ground of the glowing 'Indian red' that Hepworth recorded. With other works given titles such as *Desert Forms*, *Sun and Water*, and *Sun and Marble*, the suite captures as a whole, like Hepworth's annotated sketchbook, snapshots of experiences and sensations still resonating years later. In writing of these experiences in a 1965 article headed 'Sculpture – An act of praise', Hepworth would note the spiritual impact that Greece had on her at the time, enabling her to rediscover 'the philosophical relationship between man and his landscape, an understanding and harmony, a maintenance of the spirit which gives power to form. Form as an affirmative image is really the tactile as well as the visual, concrete, embodiment of man's poise in relation to the universe.'[23] More than ever, for Hepworth, the physical and spiritual worlds were in close accord.

ABOVE LEFT Barbara Hepworth, *Olympus* (from *The Aegean Suite*), 1971, lithograph, 76.5 × 54 cm (30⅛ × 21¼ in.)

ABOVE RIGHT Barbara Hepworth, *Delos* (from *The Aegean Suite*), 1971, lithograph, 76.8 × 54.3 cm (30¼ × 21⅜ in.)

Chapter 13

Forms Ascending

While Hepworth had worked in metal in 1951, creating the ephemeral form of Apollo for the Old Vic in wire (see p. 176), in 1956 she returned to this medium in earnest. A younger generation of sculptors working in metal had become increasingly prominent in the early 1950s, collectively described by Herbert Read in 1952 as 'the Geometry of Fear' artists, when they exhibited at the Venice Biennale. One of these, Reg Butler, had visited Hepworth's studio the year before to record a conversation for BBC radio broadcast. Throughout their conversation, Hepworth saw no conflict between her approach as a carver and Butler's work in metal, stating, 'there's no limit to the materials one can use, but the great thing is to make this live image'.[1] She continued, 'why have the more solid properties of stone or wood become invalid? It seems to me that it's the idea that matters, not the material. I think sculpture can be expressed in absolutely any material... each of us chooses the material which will fit an idea.'[2]

Hepworth's return to making sculptures in bronze after a break of around thirty years in which she solely carved could be related to her increasing professional success. Casting in metal meant editions could be made of the same work, allowing more sculptures to be sold privately and placed in museum collections. Metal sculptures were also more durable than carvings, particularly those in wood, which were sensitive to changes in environmental conditions. This meant that they were more suitable for the 'travelling circus' of contemporary art,[3] as Hepworth explained to Read, referencing the increasing number of international exhibitions in which she was invited to take part. In addition to the many group shows that featured her work, a solo retrospective organised by Martha Jackson Gallery in New York toured to nine museums across America and Canada between 1955 and 1956.

Hepworth also found a way of working in metal that allowed her to create forms with fewer limitations. As she wrote to Read, 'the problem is, how to extend the forms beyond the capacity of stone & wood? How to swing up & outwards when feeling cannot be contained by the block?'[4] Certain ideas she wished to express called for fluid forms, like the movement of dance and music or the ephemeral nature of spirituality, and the first of these works, *Curved Form (Pavan)* (1956), takes its parenthesised title from a stately Elizabethan court dance. The skeleton of the form was made with an armature of expanded aluminium on which plaster was built up and then carved (see following page, above). Crucially, as with all Hepworth's work in bronze, the plaster prototype was made to the same scale as the resulting bronze, ensuring that the human scale

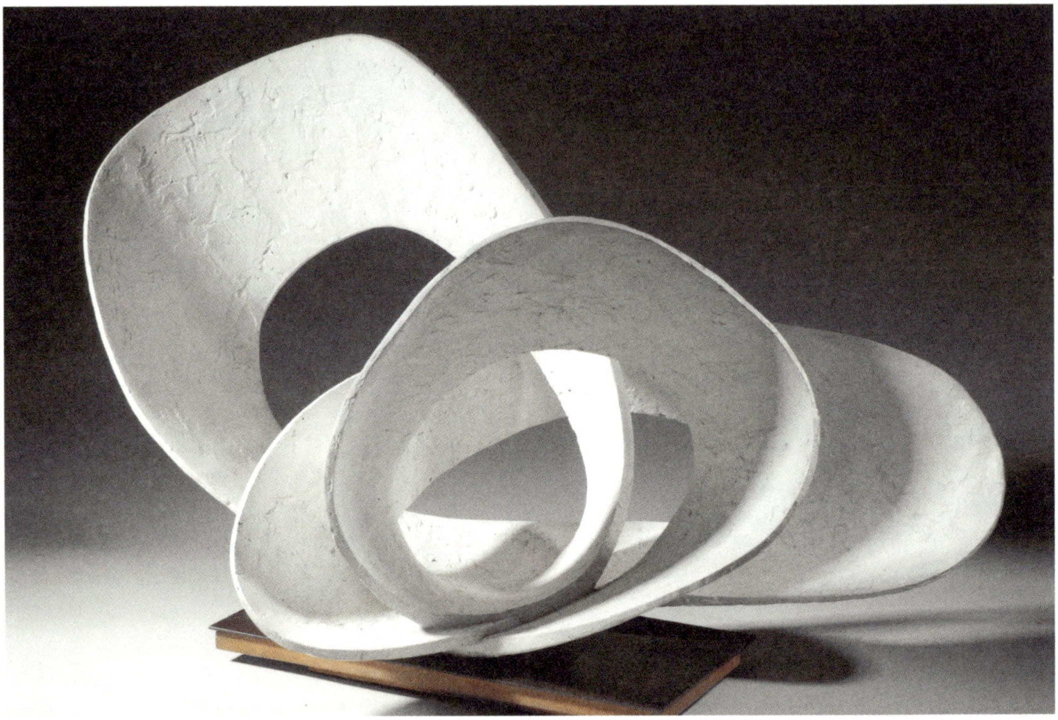

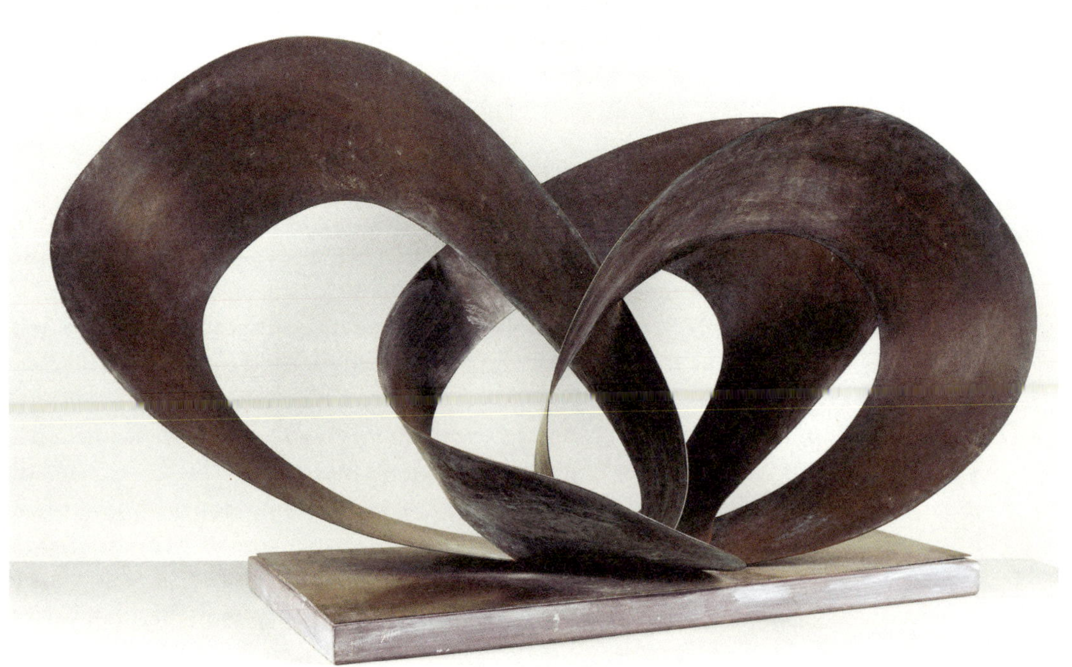

TOP Barbara Hepworth, *Curved Form (Pavan)*, 1956, metallised plaster, 55 × 37 × 83 cm (21⅝ × 14½ × 32⅝ in.)

ABOVE Barbara Hepworth, *Forms in Movement (Galliard)*, 1956, copper, length 89 cm (35 in.)

Hepworth valued in sculpture was retained. *Curved Form (Pavan)* was acquired by Wakefield City Art Gallery that year, and Hepworth wrote to the Director, Helen Kapp, about the specific technique used to create the 'metallised plaster' that gives its distinctive surface: 'the reinforced plaster was sealed and sprayed with a coating of molten zinc (an American machine and invention – then burnished & sealed with another preparation.)'[5] Hepworth remained attuned to the material, the fluidity of the sculptural form echoing the liquidity of the molten metal.

Shortly after, she made the related *Forms in Movement (Galliard)* (1956) (opposite, below) from sheets of bent copper in an edition of six.[6] In a notebook of 1961, Hepworth would identify the disparate qualities she associated with 'metal and its properties'; 'fire, running metal, molten – passionate, arrested movement – inducement of sound and resonance', distinguishing these from 'sheet under tension', which she linked to 'related rhythms of curves'.[7] She recalled making this work: 'experimenting with sheet metal, I bent and twisted the sheets under tension until I found out the nature of its construction and forced it to express what I wanted <u>by</u> its nature and not against its nature'.[8] The twisting, paper-thin sheets almost disappear at points as one moves around the sculpture, both *Curved Form (Pavan)* and *Forms in Movement (Galliard)* inviting movement from the viewer, while conveying it themselves. Galliard was also an Elizabethan dance, a lively court dance that was often paired with the pavan. Both pavans and galliards, written in memory of the Earl of Salisbury by William Byrd and Orlando Gibbons, had been included in the St Ives Festival programme three years earlier.

The first work that Hepworth had cast in bronze at this time was *Curved Form (Trevalgan)* (1956), also in an edition of six. It takes its name from a particular place in Cornwall and, in keeping with her earlier postwar work, was inspired by her experiences within this landscape, as she recalled: 'this "Curved Form" was conceived standing on the hill called Trevalgan between St. Ives and Zennor where the land of Cornwall ends and the cliffs divide as they touch the sea facing west. At this point, facing the setting sun across the Atlantic, where sky and sea blend with hills and rocks, the forms seem to enfold the watcher and lift him towards the sky.'[9] Just as *Pelagos* had done a decade before (see p. 131), this work (see following page) describes the embodied experience of being surrounded and embraced by landscape. The curved form echoes that of *Curved Form (Delphi)*, which was made the previous year (see p. 188) and was also inspired by a particular place. In Hepworth's description of Trevalgan, however, a spiritual dimension enters: the idea of ascending skywards.

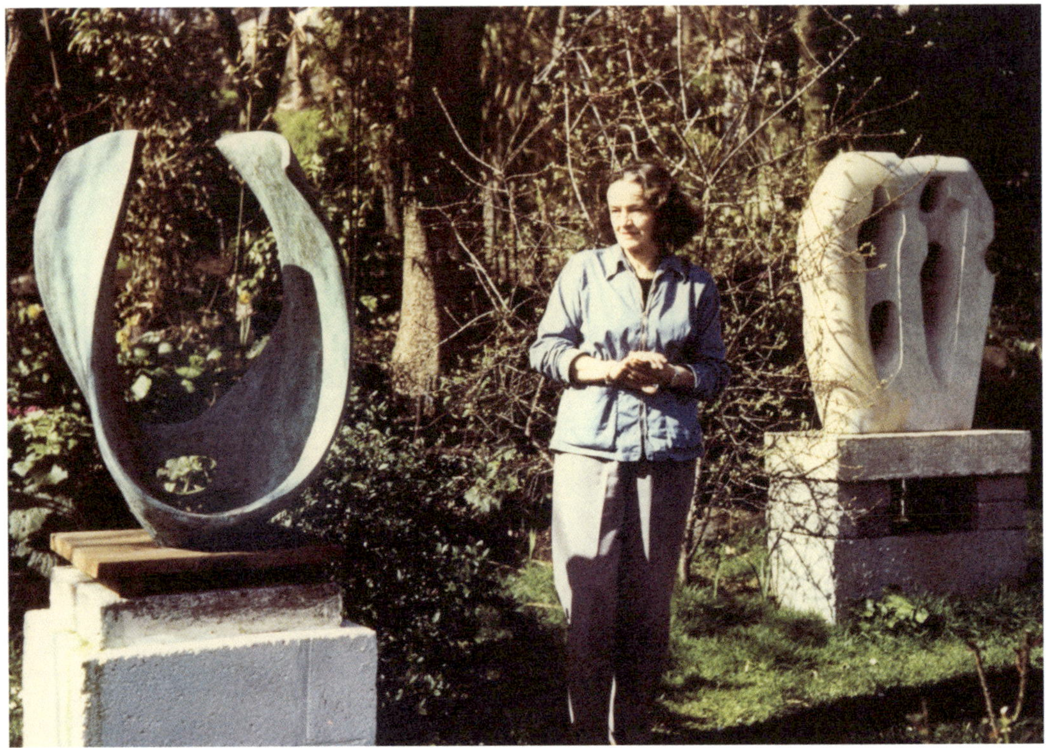

The arms of *Curved Form (Trevalgan)*, thin and sinuous, bend and reach upwards with a lightness and tension granted by the process of making in metal – again, expanded aluminium mesh forming a malleable armature on which plaster was built up and then carved back. Hepworth noted the recurrence of certain forms and wrote, 'I have found some considerable pleasure in re-interpreting forms originally carved, and which in bronze, by greater attenuation, can give a new aspect to certain themes.'[10]

Hepworth exhibited these works in her first solo show at Gimpel Fils, a gallery in London with whom she had signed a contract in 1955.[11] Run by the Gimpel brothers, the gallery was probably chosen by Hepworth for its commitment to supporting the avant-garde. As *The Times* had noted in 1952: 'how much this gallery has done in the last few years to encourage the younger or more experimental painters and sculptors of this country'.[12] Entering into a long-term agreement with a commercial gallery gave Hepworth financial stability following her divorce from Nicholson in October 1951. She negotiated a contract that allowed her to continue to make private sales from her studio, while Gimpel Fils agreed to hold regular solo exhibitions of her work and include her in group exhibitions at their gallery, as well as manage all sales and loans to exhibitions both nationally and internationally, relieving Hepworth of the weight of administration. *Recent Works by Barbara Hepworth*, held in June 1956, included Hepworth's new metal sculptures and bronze casts alongside stone and wood carvings, and paintings and drawings. She was characteristically specific about the presentation, detailing different lighting for the day-time and evening viewings, and requesting that particular plinths be borrowed from the Whitechapel Art Gallery for the exhibition, noting, 'Bryan [Robertson] had some beauties made + painted, which were specifically for my sculpture.'[13] Hepworth viewed the metal works as equal in value to her carvings, despite the fact that the latter were editioned, and comparative works such as *Curved Form (Delphi)* and *Curved Form (Trevalgan)* were priced exactly the same (£1,000 for each). Critics similarly drew little distinction between the metal and carved works, and *The Spectator* singled out *Curved Form (Trevalgan)* as 'the finest piece in the show', praising its 'movement, a pulse, a core of unsubdued energy, a heart indeed which has not before disturbed the suave stolidity of her sculpture'.[14] By 1959, Gimpel Fils had sold three of the six editions of *Curved Form (Trevalgan)*.

Bronze offered other qualities in addition to extending Hepworth's formal range and earning potential. She had always given the surface of her works great attention, from the paintings to the carvings. Now she began to think of the bronze sculptures 'in terms of molten metal, and that began to interest me because I realised that, through heat and molten metal, that one had a wide range of texture which I hadn't been able to use before'.[15] Hepworth created rough textured surfaces through manipulating wet plaster on the surface of the form, 'treating the plaster as if it were oil paint, with large flat spatulae',[16] which, when cast, gave the surface an organic impression. She was as applied and focused on detail with her bronzes as with her other sculptures, expanding and developing her technique and seeking new tools. Where successful, she passed on technical suggestions to fellow artists, for example sending Nicholson a 'Surform', a grater-like tool she used for carving into plaster, writing, 'I hoped the little surf-form plane might be of some use on large reliefs. It is newly out (I met the inventor) & I find it a joy to use in the palm of one hand.'[17] She gave precise instructions to the foundry where the bronzes were cast regarding the patination, or colour given to the surface through chemical reactions. Her colours often highlighted the distinction between the inner and outer form, as her painted concavities had done previously (see Chapter 7), but they also enhanced the impact of the surface texture. In *Involute II* (1956), the fluid form conveys a spiralling movement, the title a geometric term for a particular type of curve. The connection of this work to the shifting forms of waves is made clear by a photograph of the work staged on St Ives Bay, the sculpture framed by the sea (below). Its rough surface is given a white-grey patina, gesturing to the frothy foam of the Atlantic.

This attention to colouring the surface recalls a note written to Lilian Somerville of the British Council in 1952, in which Hepworth noted the closeness of sculpting in metal and painting: 'I feel most strongly

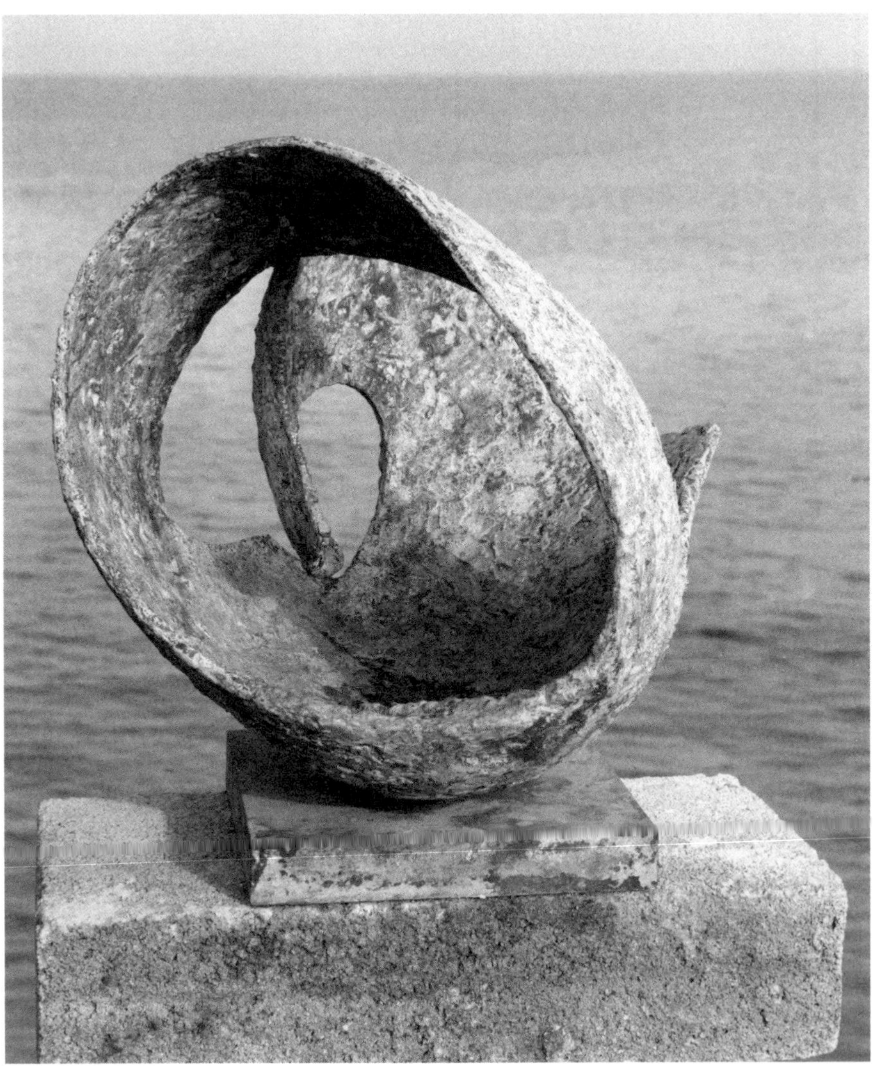

ABOVE Barbara Hepworth, *Involute II* (1956).
Photograph by Studio St Ives

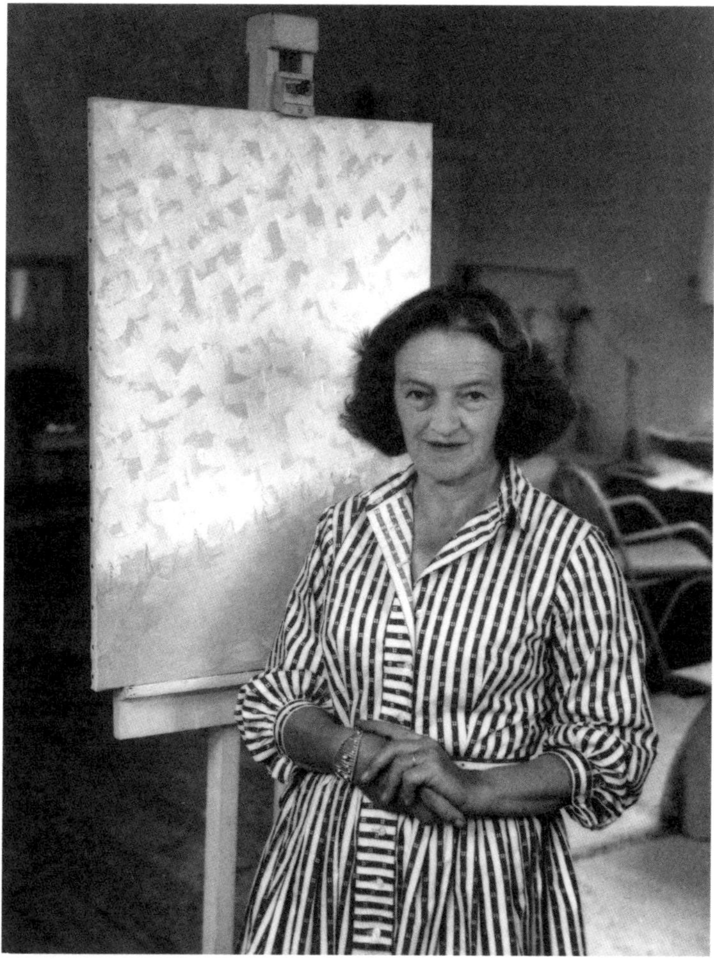

about the two mainstreams in contemporary sculpture carving on the one hand and a more fluid approach (in metal) which is perhaps nearer to the realism of painting than carving [...] both streams are facets of the sculptural idea – both essential and expanding and complementary.'[18] It is no coincidence, then, that as Hepworth begins to work in metal, her paintings and drawings take on a new character. In place of intricate 'strung' lines, the thick, black, calligraphic marks that Hepworth used to sketch out figures in the stones of *Contrapuntal Forms* (see p. 162) are deployed on paper and board. Like the fluid forms of the metal sculptures, these marks are dynamic and freely gestural. Works such as *Fantasie (Black and Grey)* (1958) (see following page) show the black lines painted swiftly over a thick ground, the process of painting evident

ABOVE Barbara Hepworth in the studio with a canvas, *c.* 1958. Photograph by Michel Ramon

in the spatters of paint and frenetic brushmarks of both the lines and the surface of the ground. Elements of metal sculptures are translated into two dimensions, the fluidity of the form depicted on the texture of the surface. That Hepworth saw herself as working across the disciplines of sculpture and painting is evident in a photograph taken at

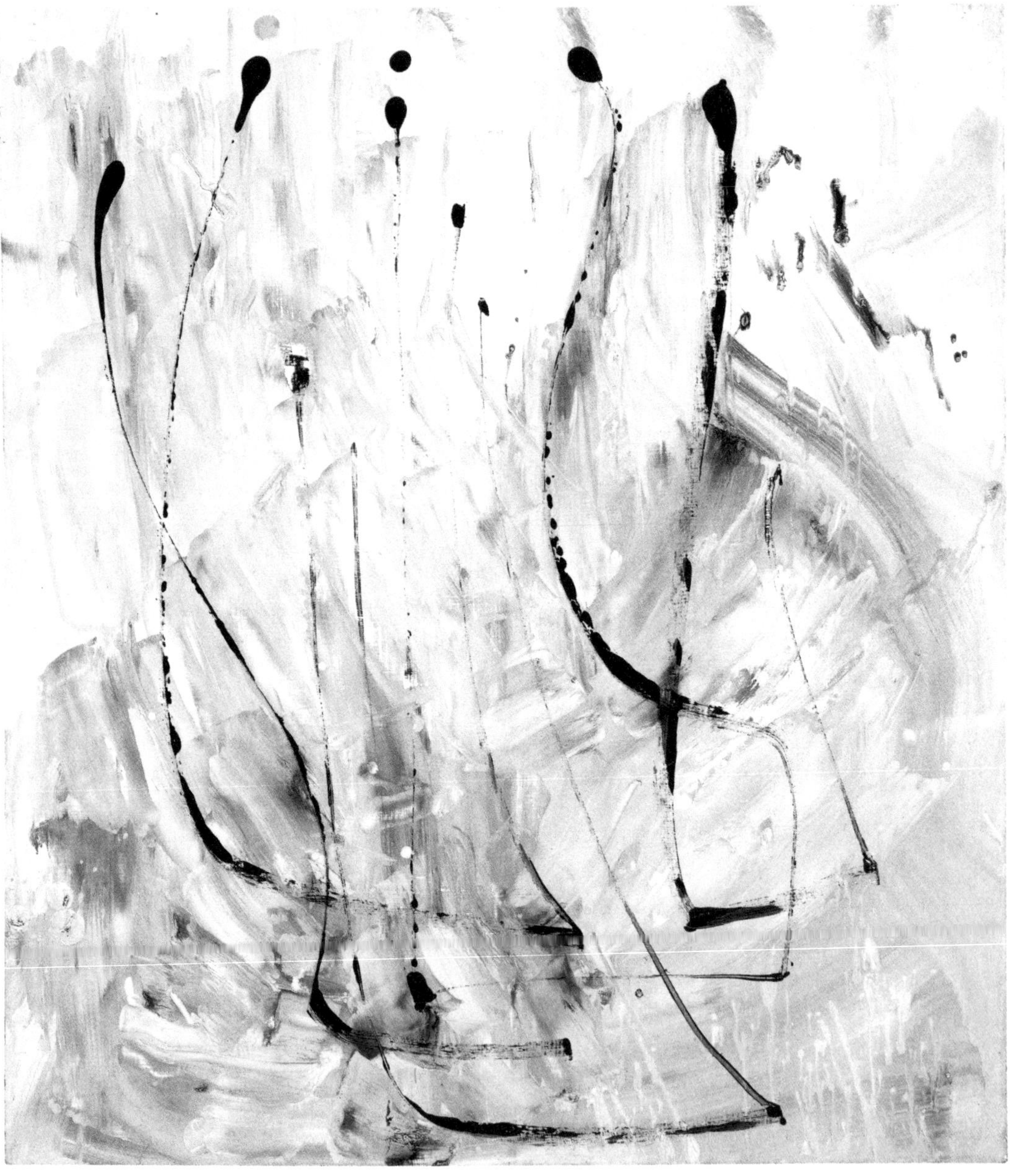

ABOVE Barbara Hepworth, *Fantasie (Black and Grey)*, 1958, oil on board, 50 × 43 cm (19⅝ × 16⅞ in.)

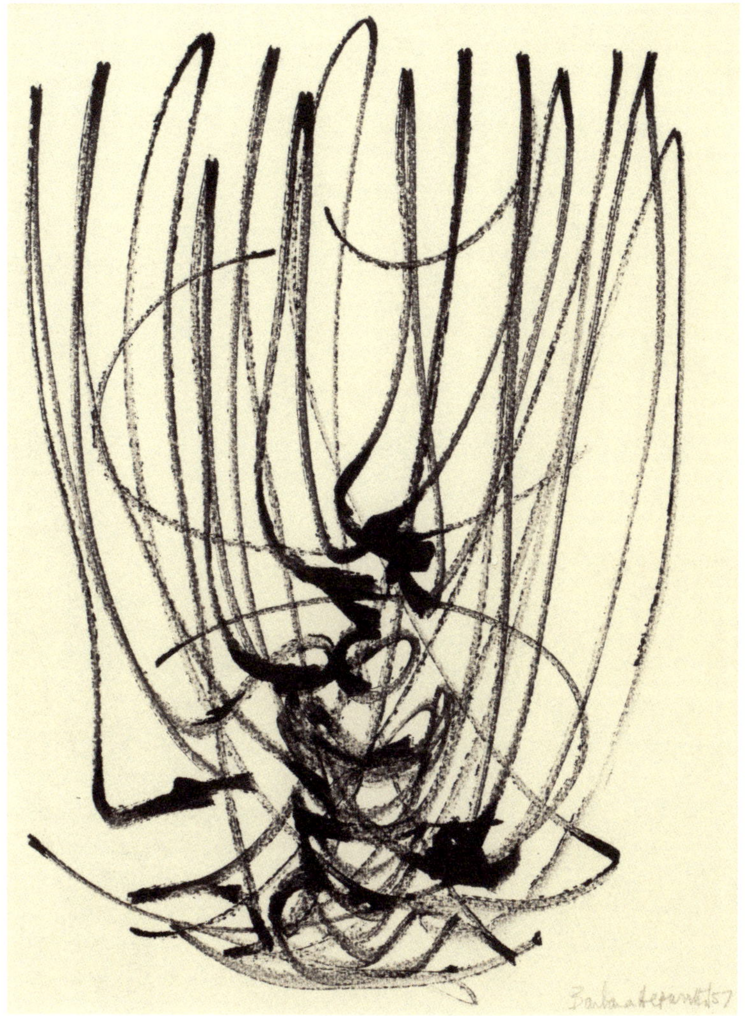

the time, where she poses in front of an easel with a painting in progress behind her (see p. 201).

As with her war-time crystalline drawings, Hepworth frequently called these works 'Project for Sculpture' without there necessarily being a direct link between a particular painting and a sculpture. She makes the connection between this style of painting and her metal work by including the medium in parenthesis in some cases, such as *The Seed (project for metal sculpture)* (1957) (above). Although not relating directly to

ABOVE Barbara Hepworth, *The Seed (project for metal sculpture)*, 1957, ink on paper, 33.6 × 25.4 cm (13⅛ × 10 in.)

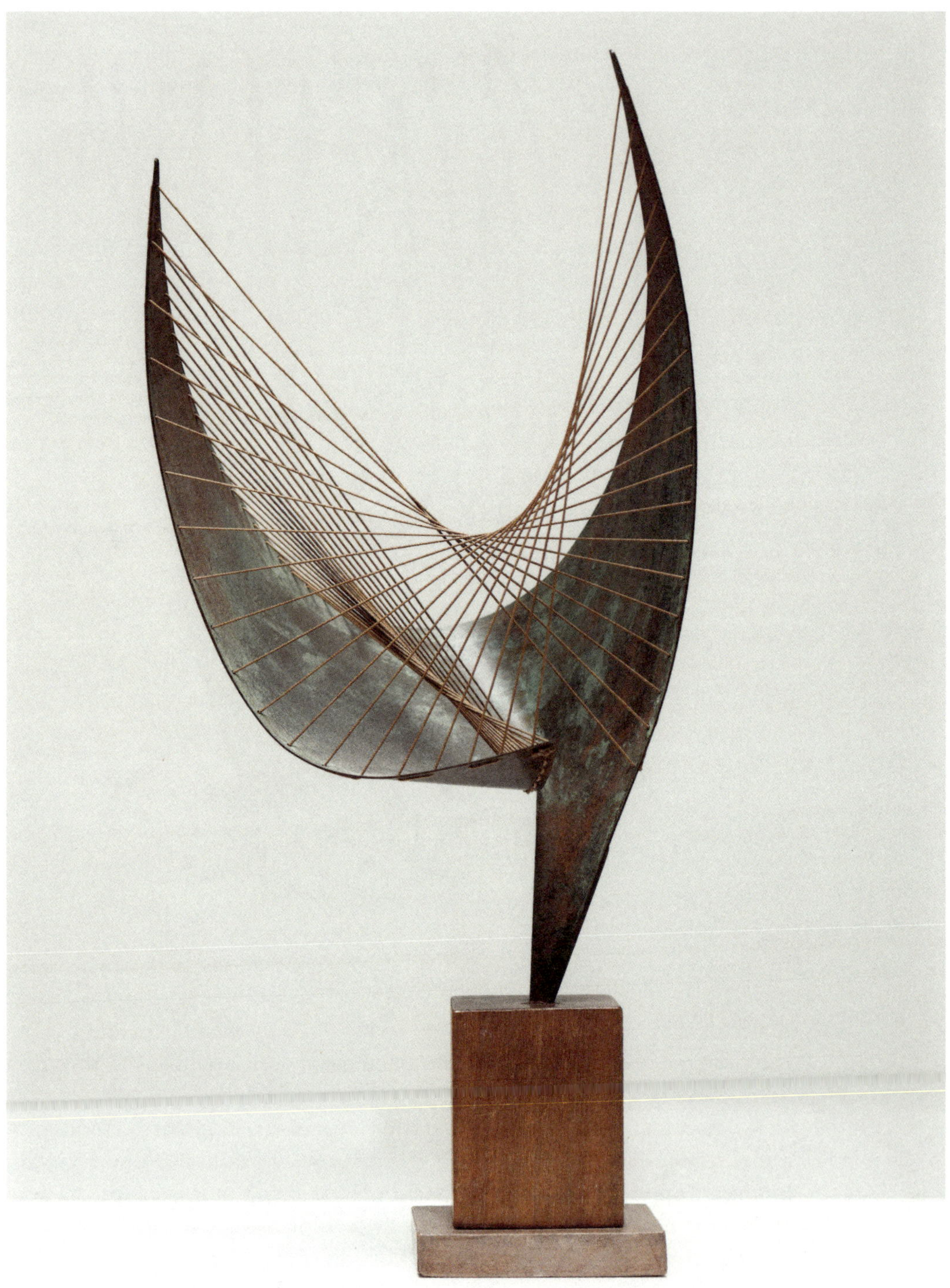

ABOVE Barbara Hepworth, *Orpheus (Maquette 1)*, 1956, brass and string, height 54 cm (21¼ in.)

a specific sculpture, the connection between this ink drawing on paper can be seen not only in the title, but also in the repeated curling lines that return to the same point at the base, mirroring in form (although multiplying in number) the metal curves of works such as *Curved Form (Pavan)* and *Forms in Movement (Galliard)* (see p. 196, above and below). In several cases, works seem to relate directly to one another across media, sculptural forms following paintings and vice versa. In 1956, Hepworth began a sculptural series prompted by a commission for the headquarters of electronics firm Mullard Ltd. The final work, *Theme on Electronics (Orpheus)*, was preceded by two maquettes increasing in size, with a third made after its completion, all created by cutting and bending cut brass sheets, the three points of the curved metal form held in tension by reddish-brown fishing line. These may have begun as experiments, but were considered successful enough that Hepworth made both *Orpheus (Maquette 1)* (opposite) and *Orpheus (Maquette 2)* into editions.[19] As the works were made in the studio rather than a foundry, the loosely brushed green patination of the inner surface would have been painted on by either Hepworth or one of her assistants, using basic patination chemicals kept within the studio. This allowed for experimentation and greater control over the surface finishes. Hepworth wrote in unpublished notes that she was 'rarely satisfied with a bronze cast unless [I] have had the opportunity to work the surface myself'.[20] The final version of *Theme on Electronics (Orpheus)* had a golden-coloured surface with white strings, and rotated on a motorised base.

As Hepworth has noted, the influence of her Greek trip in 1954 was enduring, and the experiences that brought her close to the ancient sites of Greek mythology may have led to the title 'Orpheus', after the musician and poet of the same name. Orpheus was said to have been such a great musician that he taught the god Apollo how to play the lyre, and he was also the inspiration for a collection of Rilke's poetry, *Sonnets to Orpheus*, of which Hepworth owned two copies. The poetry may have formed a direct inspiration for these works, as Sonnet I opens, 'A tree ascending. O pure transcension / O Orphic song!'.[21] Hepworth described the *Orpheus* series in similar, ascending terms: 'I found the most intense pleasure in this new adventure in material – and revelled in the lightness of poise and delicacy of forms which seemed nearer to the flight of birds and their form in flight rather than to more gravity-bound rocks and humans.'[22] A related painting made in ink on paper the following year, *Orpheus* (1957), similarly expresses this upward movement, with rapidly painted brushstrokes reaching for the sky.

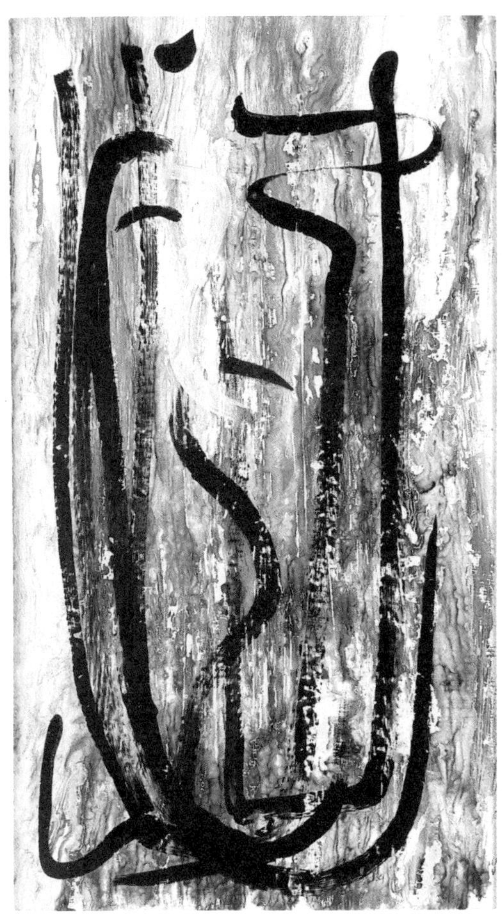

While the above shows Hepworth's sculpture informing her painting, the direction of influence also moves from painting to sculpture. In 1957, Hepworth painted *Forms Ascending* (above), another gestural oil painting with thick, black, calligraphic marks sweeping upwards on a textured white and grey ground. The following year the title was inverted in *Ascending Form (Gloria)* (1958), in which similar upward lines are articulated in bronze, patinated white-grey, and then further painted with white household paint – an unconventional technique, which allowed closer artistic control over the finished work (opposite). The pale surface and upwards thrust of *Ascending Form (Gloria)*, in conjunction with the title, give the sculpture a spiritual quality. In 1958 Hepworth's father died, perhaps prompting these religious overtones. The pair had remained close, and Hepworth credited her father for many of her inspirational

ABOVE Barbara Hepworth, *Forms Ascending*, 1957, oil on board, 56.4 × 31.1 cm (22⅛ × 12¼ in.)

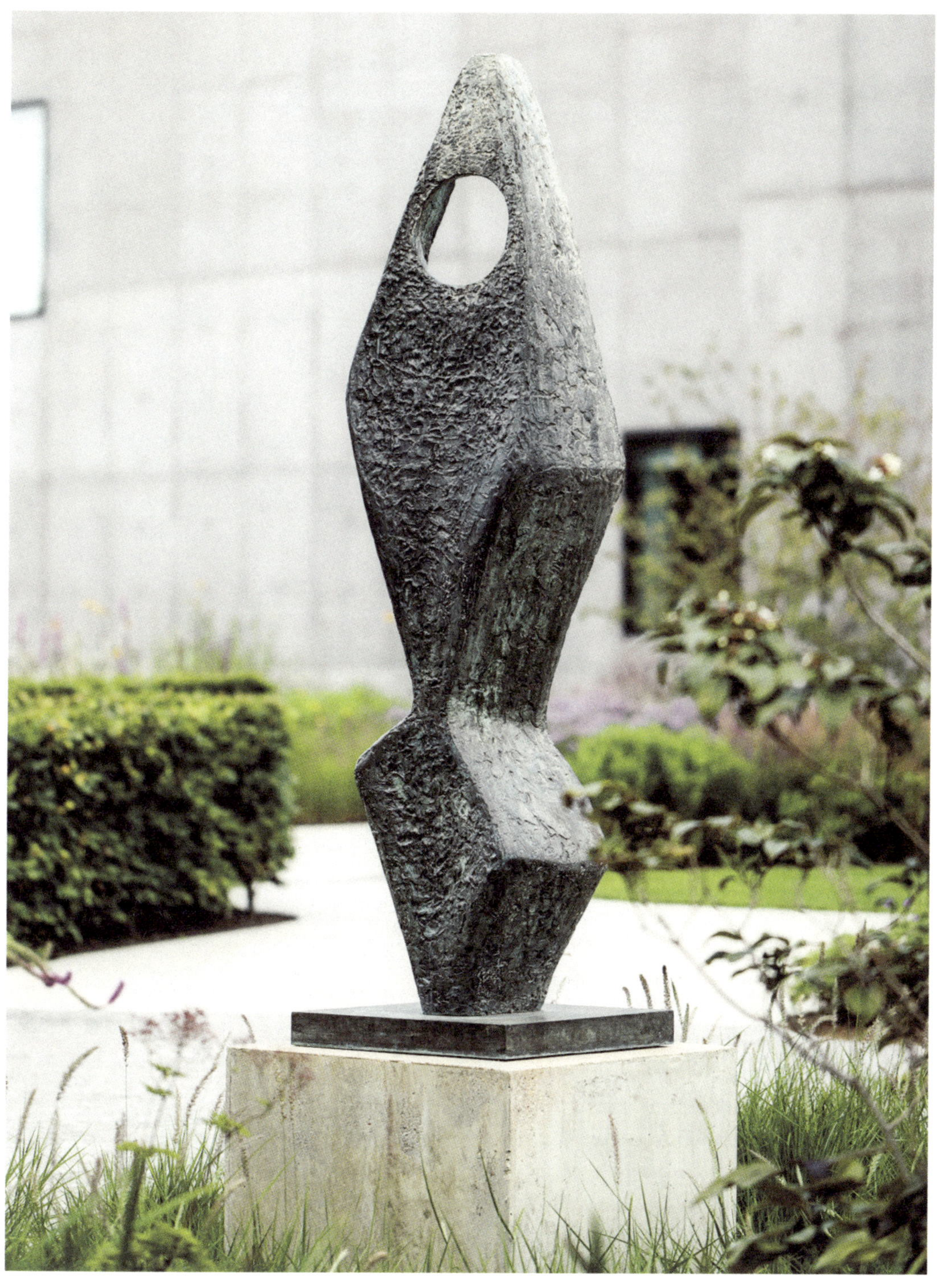

ABOVE Barbara Hepworth, *Ascending Form (Gloria)*, 1958, bronze, 195 × 53 × 50 cm (76¾ × 20⅞ × 18⅝ in.), in The Hepworth Wakefield Garden

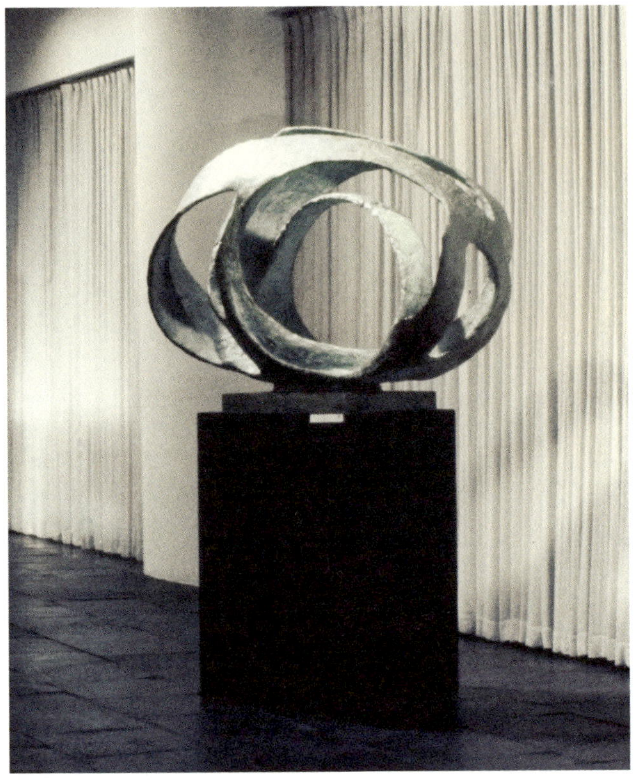

formative experiences. She wrote to Nicholson, acknowledging her father's pride in her, 'I think my "award" & seeing me on the television we gave him – was a pleasure & comfort bigger than anything any of us could understand. "a fulfilment" as you say & a fulfilment of the love he gave'.[23] The title 'Gloria' refers to the Christian hymn of praise 'Gloria in Excelsis Deo' ('Glory to God in the Highest'). Though at times she professed to be atheist, or pagan, Hepworth continued to consult a Christian Science practitioner during the 1950s, alongside increasing ties with the Anglican church, seeking solace in St Ives Parish Church following the death of Paul and becoming friends with members of the clergy. In 1959, she connected the act of artistic creation with religious faith, writing, 'suddenly, either in unconscious acknowledgement of life or in the silent tribulation of overcoming despair, one lets in the divine force and there is the work, inevitably complete, timeless and unalterable'.[24] In early notes for this text, she had written of 'God or the universal laws of evolution', the interchangeability of these concepts indicating the breadth of her spiritual beliefs.

She did relate the Christian faith with an affirmation of life, as a letter she wrote to *The Times* regarding the hydrogen bomb attests. In 1952, Britain had become the third country to have nuclear weapons, with the successful test of the atomic bomb, but the US and Soviet Union continued escalating the arms race. The issue was subject to intense political debate, with the Labour party, of which Hepworth would become a member in 1956, calling for a moratorium on nuclear testing in 1954. The decision was made to continue to develop nuclear weapons, and the H-bomb in particular, to keep up with America. Hepworth wrote in protest on 24 January 1956: 'to remain inert in this matter, or to argue over expediency, is to disbelieve in the power of good, and the moral courage generated by affirmative action. The Bishops of Chichester and Exeter have given us a lead. Our daily prayer should be that all of us face, as individuals, the situation and test our spiritual courage by relying on the power of good.'[25] In addition to the church providing positive role models in the political sphere, Hepworth found space within St Ives Parish Church for personal solace and broader philosophical reflections, writing to Nicholson on the anniversary of Paul's death in 1957, 'I went into the church today into the little chapel – it was all so quiet & peaceful. To be happy & peaceful oneself one seems to have to blend the past & future. Is this blending possible?'[26]

Certainly Hepworth's sculptures in bronze seemed to take ideas and forms from the past and push them further, opening up new avenues for artistic and philosophical exploration. At the end of the 1950s, she began to make larger and larger bronzes, recognising the potential for external display and the increasing size that these settings demanded. In writing about *Oval Form (Trezion)* (1961–63) (opposite), she moves from connecting form with landscape to thinking about sculpture as interactive and architectural, with the material of bronze being key to this shift:

> *These are all sea forms and rock forms, related to Porthcurno on the Land's End coast with its queer caves pierced by the sea. They were experiences of people – the movement of people in and out is always a part of them. They are bronze sculptures, and the material allows more openness of course. I was a comparative newcomer to bronze, so I used it extravagantly to see how far I could go [...] There is a stronger sense of participating in the form – you want to go in and out as you look at a sculpture like 'Trezion' [...] Maybe it's not big enough*

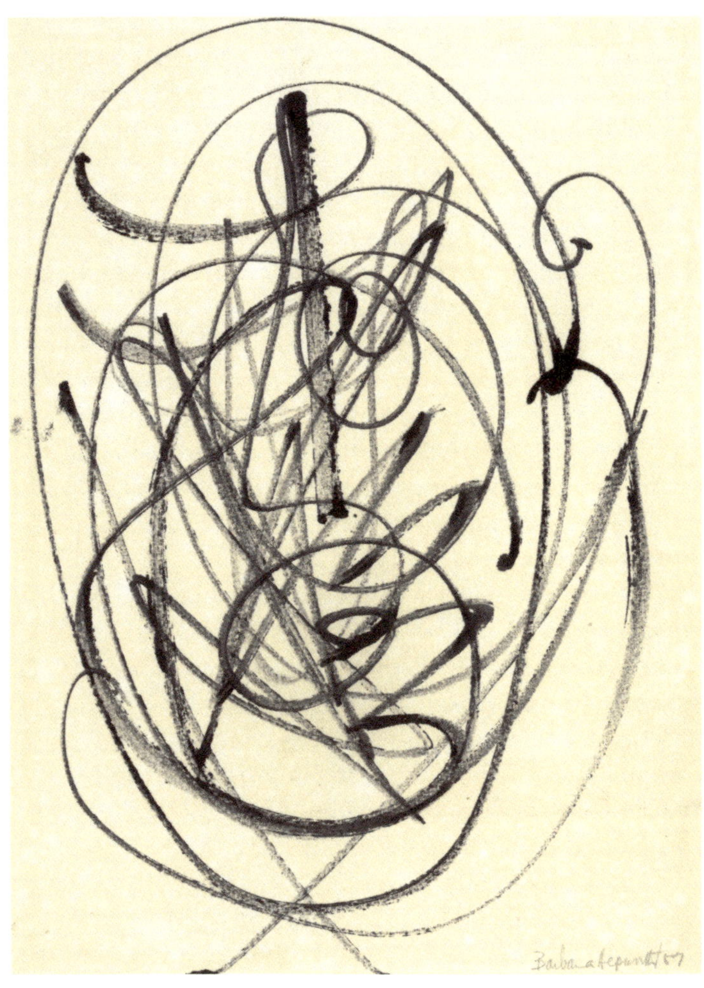

to do this, but you don't need to be physically entangled if you've got a pair of hands. If you feel something, you know what the experience is.[27]

Oval Form (Trezion) – which was preceded by a painting, the extravagantly looping *Oval Form (wire sculpture)* (1957) (above) – is one of Hepworth's most elegantly fluid bronzes, with seemingly dynamic encircling coils of metal. Although, as Hepworth notes, this work was not large enough for a person to enter, her next decade would bring monumental sculptures, participatory works, and, as she would describe, 'a greater freedom for myself'.[28]

ABOVE Barbara Hepworth, *Oval Form (wire sculpture)*, 1957, ink on paper, 36 × 25.8 cm (14⅛ × 10⅛ in.)

Chapter 14

Single Form

In 1958, just two years after returning to work in bronze, Hepworth was offered her first major public commission. She recalled in 1961 her enthusiasm for the project and initial approach:

> *In 1958 I was asked whether I would do a large bronze for*
> *State House in Holborn. I met the architect and we studied*
> *the plans and elevations – I felt very interested. This was a*
> *chance to work on a big scale and the largest commission*
> *I had so far been offered for a sculpture in bronze. After our*
> *discussion the architect [Harold Mortimer] took me to the site*
> *where the building was already nearly half-way up. I could*
> *see the approach to the place for the sculpture from the road*
> *under the first floor of the tall section of the building. In spite*
> *of the giant cranes above, the roar of machinery and pounding*
> *of cement crushers – I was able to appreciate the scale of the*
> *open space in relation to the whole building. I had a very*
> *immediate, and strong, feeling about the scale of a human*
> *being moving across this space [...] The curved wall behind*
> *the bronze was already indicated. I carried back with me to*
> *Cornwall that evening a very vivid impression of the site and*
> *a nearly-formed idea of what I would like to do [...] by the*
> *next morning I saw the sculpture in my mind quite clearly [...]*
> *I felt very prepared to carry out a large bronze which would*
> *have a rhythm of thrusts and curves as I had been working*
> *on this idea for some time previously.*[1]

Hepworth's first thoughts were of human scale and the rhythmic form of the work, which she saw as a growing, fluid line in contrast to the hardness of the concrete architecture. From this she quickly turned to the practical issue of working on such a scale, noting to Margaret Gardiner, 'I think sculptors have a specially arduous time when working on a bigger scale. Apart from the ever-lasting physical administration the conception & vitality of the idea has to be kept alive for a very long period.'[2] This problem led Hepworth to develop a particular technique to realise her dynamic 'vivid impression':

> *I used long seventeen foot timbers, steamed so that they could*
> *be curved and then clamped together – giving an immediate*
> *sense of perspective and scale. I was able to adjust the arcs quite*
> *freely and was then ready to lash the curves into solids by using*

*laths – rather like boat building. This not only gave sufficient
strength to bear the great weight of plaster which was eventually
to be carried overhead – it also allowed me to build the joints
ready for cutting up the model into nine sections ready for the
foundry. The next stage was winding the forms with hessian
soaked in Plaster of Paris – and on this I built up the surfaces
with a very large spatula. I had in mind, all the time, the living
quality of metal – the polished edges – the darkness of the hollows.[3]*

The process took longer than Hepworth had anticipated, and she
wrote to Nicholson, 'the big job for Holborn is a fantastic experience
which I would not have missed, tho' the bigger the sculpture the less
money one makes; but it is going so much slower than I anticipated. Nine
weeks have gone by & still there seems to be only the frail outline of the
forms shooting up. 15 ft & nothing tangible as yet to start putting plaster
on to. All I can say is – that one learns something!'[4] Hepworth found
beauty in the process of its construction (see following page), as she later
wrote, 'I hope to start with plaster next week (have had severe bronchial
flu for 2 wks) but the structure is so beautiful. I had it photographed this
morning just for itself. It has taken 10 weeks to cast the curves in space.'[5]

While developing the practical technique to retain both the affinity with her materials and the sense of movement that had generated
the sculpture's form, Hepworth also considered the interaction between
viewer and sculpture. She noted, 'I had to bear in mind, the many views
of the sculpture from the hundreds of windows in the building – from
the top floor to ground level – as well as the <u>distant</u> views from the main
road and the <u>close</u> approach when entering the doors with the bronze
towering above. <u>The human scale was all important</u> in the evolution of
this sculpture placed in this court where it had to be both intimate and
commanding at the same time.'[6] This account highlights central aspects
of Hepworth's practice: sensitivity to materials, the reflection of human
experience of landscape (in this case, the built-up metropolitan environment), the way sculpture was perceived, and in turn its capacity to
impact on human experience. In response to a UNESCO questionnaire
on the relationship between art and architecture, written around 1955,
Hepworth elaborated on the latter, recalling the principles for living she
had espoused in Unit One over twenty years earlier:

*All of us, architects, engineers, planners, painters, sculptors &
designers have lived through a tremendous period of discovery,*

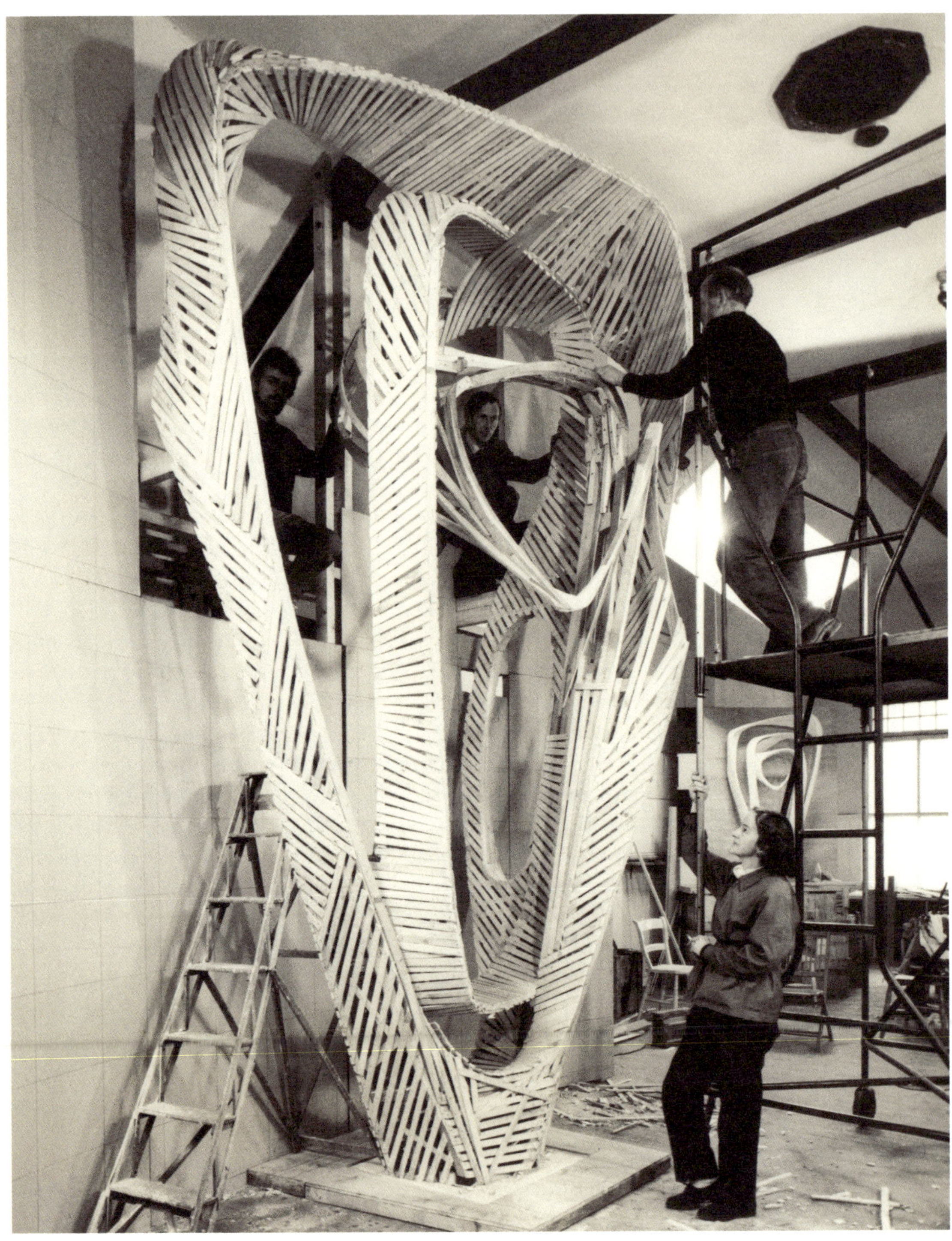

ABOVE Barbara Hepworth with the second stage
of the construction of the prototype for *Meridian*,
together with her assistants, Brian Wall (left)
and probably Keith Leonard and Dicon Nance,
January 1959. Photograph by Studio St Ives

*of experiment & of revolution [...] Paintings and sculptures
as such may change their form entirely. But painting &
sculpture as activities will always remain. They are dynamic
activities of living. In the artists they reach the ultimate form
in unconsciously registering the balancing forces required by his
time & society of spiritual growth – this activates the non-artist
to exercise his sensibilities towards creative living – in selecting,
choosing, arranging, changing his environment; in his home, his
dress, his work & his leisure so that he exists in a state of grace.*[7]

The resulting sculpture was titled *Meridian* (1958–60), which is both the imaginary arc of longitude and the highest point in the arc of the sun. As Hepworth explained to the *Daily Express*, 'it represents a series of curves in space and changes of form in movement'.[8] It was cast in Paris at Susse Frères foundry, and Hepworth went in November 1959 to oversee the finish. She wrote to her friend Dag Hammarskjöld, the United Nations Secretary-General, that it 'looked rather like a vast tiger in a cage at the foundry – but I hope that when it is sited the pure curves, rising up, will be revealed!'[9] In January 1960, Harold Mortimer raised the backing wall at Hepworth's suggestion: 'Mr. Mortimer is an angel and is most generously going to build the wall higher to make "Meridian" look perfect.'[10] The sculpture was unveiled in March 1960.

The success of *Meridian* prompted O. B. Miller, the Chairman of John Lewis Partnership, to invite Hepworth to design a sculpture for the new John Lewis department store in Oxford Street, London, which had been rebuilt following extensive bombing in the war. In his invitation, Miller quoted the purpose of the Partnership, suggesting that Hepworth's proposed work might express 'the idea of common ownership and common interest in a partnership of thousands of workers "of which the purpose is to increase the happiness of its own members while giving good service to the community"'. He also noted that the building was 'probably seen regularly by more people than any other site in the country'.[11] The opportunity both to work on a public, monumental scale and to express values that chimed with her own thoughts on community and labour was obviously appealing, and Hepworth accepted the following day. She submitted her proposal in maquette form, *Maquette, Three Forms in Echelon* (1961), in October that year. The back board is a scaled representation of the side of the building where the work would be sited, the lip at the bottom signifying the entrance canopy at the foot of the building's façade, and Hepworth included pencil lines around the three suspended

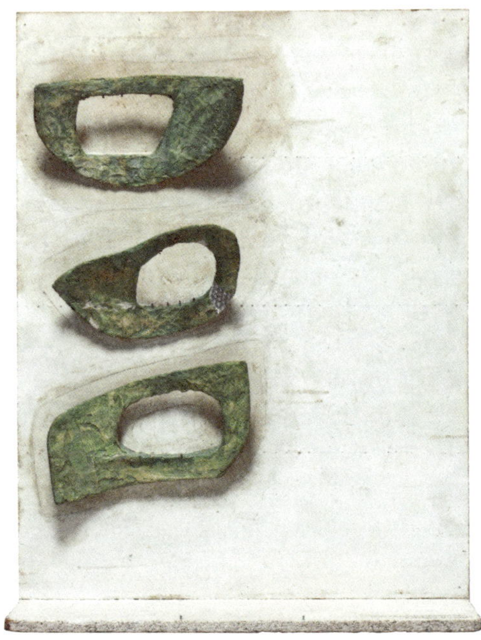

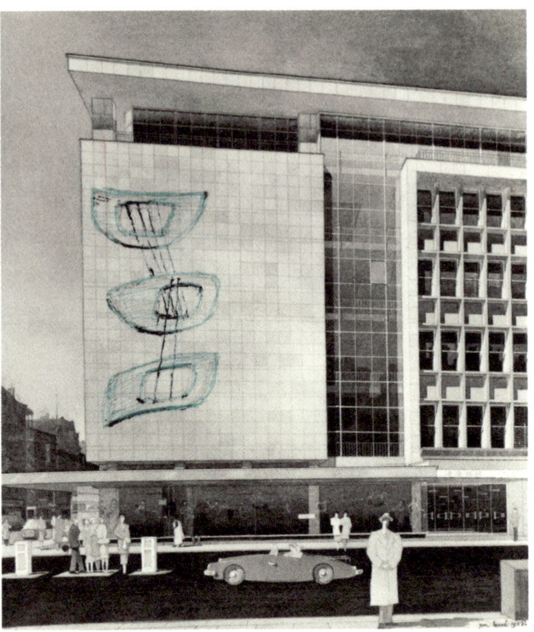

forms to show the shadows that would be cast when the sculpture was lit at night (above, left). She wrote to Miller, 'the "Three forms in echelon" with radiating strings rising upwards [connecting the three forms] is my interpretation of the John Lewis partnership, its Members and the Public',[12] suggesting that the three equal forms working in harmony reflected the interaction of these groups of people. Further, Hepworth considered that people would perceive the work as they entered 'looking upwards at the building – when naturally the forms begin to blend one with the other',[13] suggesting unity of purpose.

Despite these explanations, the design (see above, right) was rejected, Miller feeling that it neither suited the building, nor seemed characteristically 'Hepworth'. He suggested the option of an alternative derived from an existing work, and despite being disappointed that her considered proposal was rejected, Hepworth proposed enlarging and adapting an earlier work, *Winged Figure 1* (1957), to suit the space. She noted, 'I wanted to capture the greatest variety of light and shadow, from morning sun, afternoon reflected light and night floodlighting, so that visually the sculpture never remained static. The use of the apertures and stainless steel rods enabled me to get a constant "variation" of the "Winged Figure" by ever changing light and shade.'[14] The monumental final version (see p. 219) was cast in aluminium for lightness, and the

ABOVE LEFT Barbara Hepworth, prototype for *Maquette, Three Forms in Echelon*, 1961, plaster painted green, on white painted hardboard with shelf base of chipboard; strings now missing, 67.5 × 51 × 26 cm (26½ × 20 × 10¼ in.)

ABOVE RIGHT Barbara Hepworth's first scheme for the John Lewis commission, 1961. Sketch superimposed on a photograph of a line drawing by Jon Wood, an artist's impression of the new John Lewis building on Oxford Street, in green and blue ball point pen and pencil

surface was textured with 'Isopon', a polyester resin filler used in cars and boats. It was unveiled on 23 April 1963, and Hepworth wrote in *The Gazette of the John Lewis Partnership*, 'I think one of our universal dreams is to move in air and water without the resistance of our human legs. I wanted to evoke this sensation of freedom. If the Winged Figure in Oxford Street gives people a sense of being air-borne in rain and sunlight and nightlight I will be very happy.'[15]

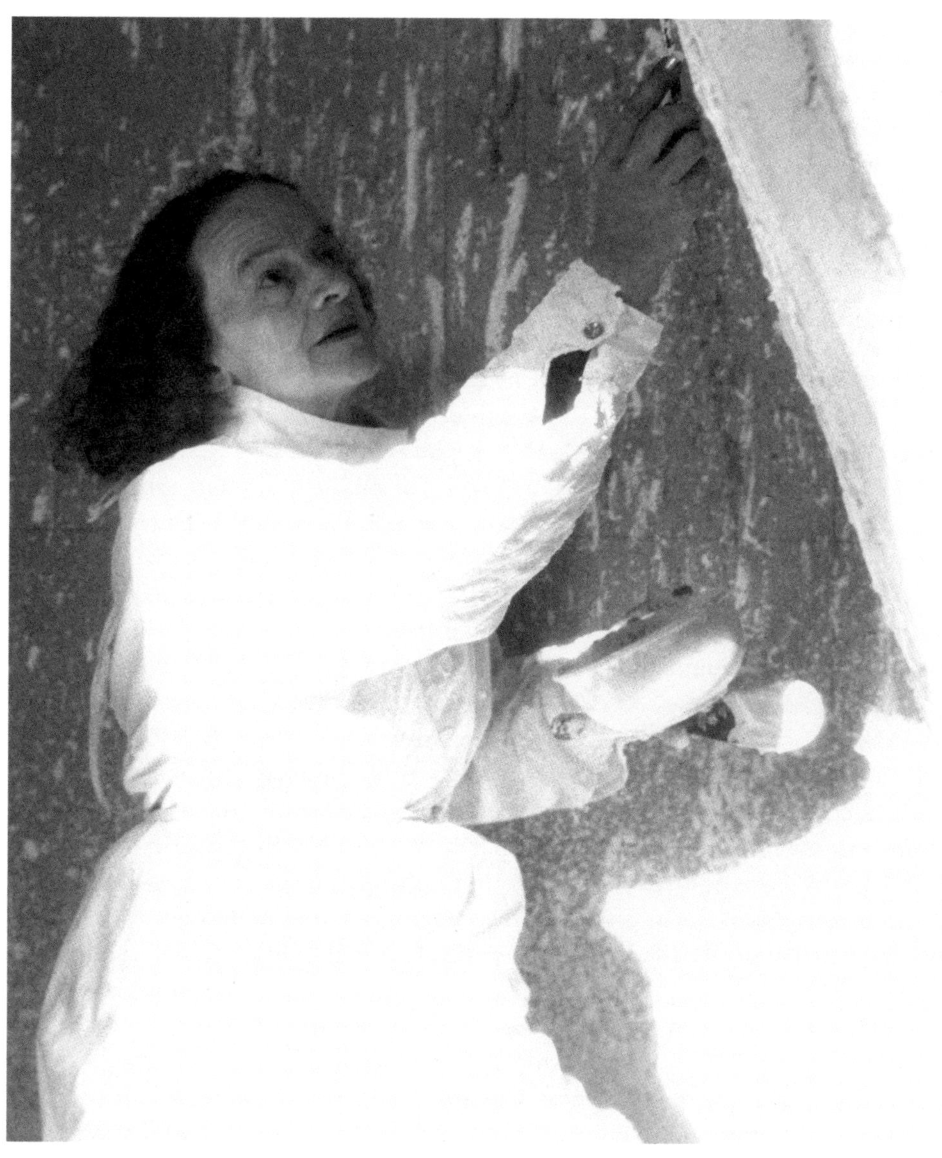

ABOVE Barbara Hepworth in Trewyn Studio, Cornwall, February 1959. Photograph by Cornel Lucas

While these public commissions in London raised her profile in Britain, Hepworth's international reputation was also growing. In September 1958, Hepworth was invited to represent Britain at the Bienal de São Paulo the following year, Lilian Somerville proposing 'a retrospective exhibition of about 20 pieces of your sculpture and about 6–13 drawings, together with exhibitions of paintings by Francis Bacon and of prints by Bill Hayter'.[16] A selection of sculpture was swiftly arrived at, but Hepworth wrote in January 1959, 'I have had all the work which is going to Sao Paolo round me now for some weeks. The more I try to visualise the total effect of the hanging, the more I feel that we need a centre piece. I feel very much that a general uniformity of size say (limited to five feet and under) gives on first impact "less of a kick" than I would like to achieve.'[17] In addition to suggesting larger sculptures for inclusion, Hepworth questioned the need for a retrospective survey, writing, 'it is my conviction that we have got a little too much emphasis on the early work of 1935–45 [...] I would like above all else to have the main stress put on the work which I am doing now!'[18]

In the end, Hepworth's São Paulo exhibition was almost entirely post-war work, with only two sculptures from the 1930s and the majority made since 1955. Photographs of the exhibition show these works rather more spaciously installed than her Venice show (see p. 160), but by this point Hepworth's ideas on the best display of modern art had shifted, as she said when interviewed in 1960: 'this overcrowding in galleries and museums deprives each work of its intended relationship to space, I mean of its ideal landscape [...] it should seem to be the centre of a globe, compelling the whole world around it to rotate, as it were, like a system of planets around a central sun. This is why each sculpture should be contemplated by itself.'[19] The show was well received and Hepworth won the prestigious Grand Prix worth around £1,600 (nearly £40,000 today), the first British artist to do so. She credited the selection of recent work as contributing to the success, telling the *Guardian*, 'I think they must have awarded me the prize for the total exhibition I gave. Some of the works were done this year.'[20] Winning this honour cemented her international reputation, in addition to easing her financial concerns, prompting Herbert Read to write, 'the prize is the great event. You need have no more worries.'[21]

Hepworth visited New York for the first time shortly after receiving news of the prize, for a solo exhibition at Galerie Chalette.[22] Perhaps surprisingly, this was only Hepworth's third solo show in New York, following an exhibition of the Hospital Drawings and other figurative works

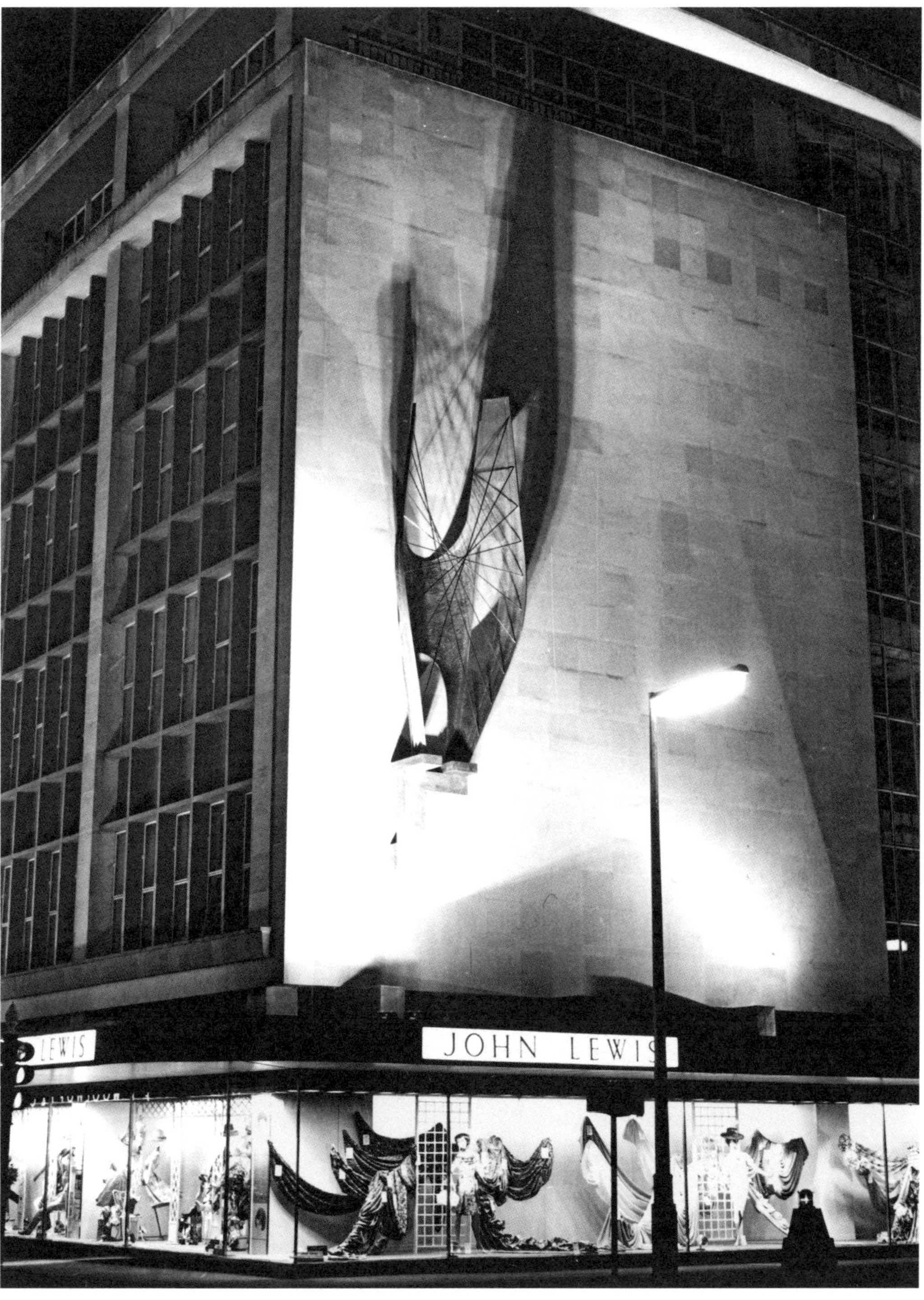

ABOVE *Winged Figure* in situ at night, April 1963

at Durlacher Brothers in 1949, and a solo show in 1956–57 with Martha Jackson Gallery, the final presentation of her American-Canadian touring exhibition (see p. 195). The latter had proved important in developing an American client base for Hepworth, including Dag Hammarskjöld, who had become a friend. Their initial contact came in 1956, when she offered to lend a sculpture for his office. He replied warmly on Christmas Day, 1956, demonstrating his knowledge of modern art: 'I have had the great pleasure of receiving your offer of one of the works belonging to you as a loan to my office at the United Nations. It is most generous of you, and I can assure you that the offer is warmly appreciated indeed, and that it will give me a constant joy to have one of your works before my eyes. I think you would approve of the setting, not only in general terms but also more specifically: on the walls you find a very good Picasso, a good Gris, a Braque and a Léger.'[23] He had previously drawn an affinity between the work of politicians and modern artists, noting in 1954, 'In modern international politics – aiming toward that world of order which now more than ever seems to be the only alternative to disruption and disaster – we have to approach our task in the spirit which animates the modern artist. We have to tackle our problems without the armour of inherited convictions or set formulas, but only with our bare hands and all the honesty we can muster'[24] – words that chimed with Hepworth's passionate belief in potential for a productive sympathy between the artist and society.

Following Hepworth's offer, Hammarskjöld visited her Martha Jackson exhibition in January 1957 and selected *Single Form* (1937–38) to borrow for his office, also purchasing a drawing himself. In 1958, he wrote a poem titled after the sculpture:

> *The breaking wave*
> *And the muscle as it contracts*
> *Obey the same law.*
>
> *An austere line*
> *Gathers the body's play of strength*
> *In a bold balance.*
>
> *Shall my soul meet*
> *This curve, as bend in the road*
> *On her way to form?*[25]

This echoes Hepworth's own interpretations of her work, drawing together natural laws and embodied experience with transcendental spirituality. The two met in person in London in April 1958, when Hammarskjöld gave an address to both houses of parliament on the UN's diplomatic role in achieving global nuclear disarmament, a subject close to Hepworth's heart, and she wrote in May, 'it was such a very great privilege, & inspiration, to be allowed to meet you'.[26]

Hepworth had remained engaged with political debates throughout the 1950s, particularly campaigning for the elimination of nuclear weapons. This was one of the primary goals of the UN, and global nuclear disarmament was the subject of the General Assembly's first resolution in 1946. In 1958, perhaps inspired by her meeting with Hammarskjöld, Hepworth drafted an unpublished text on this subject, writing, 'At this very moment we face the most momentous decisions in the history of man. We have invented the means to destroy this planet and have forced ourselves to face a total issue. It is now, therefore, that we must decide to abandon forever the old concept of power, war and destruction, and to accept in its place the real vision of constructive harmony between all men. This decision will require of us an absolute dedication to allow a peaceful world to develop.'[27] Hepworth became a sponsor for the Campaign for Nuclear Disarmament, and was quoted in *Peace News*, connecting the desire to protect life with her experience as a mother in feminist terms: 'how can any woman support the manufacture or testing of the H-bomb? It can only be that they are not yet fully emancipated and still cling to traditional ways of thinking.'[28] A later text that Hepworth and Gardiner may have worked on together suggests that the masculine-dominated field of politics could be improved by integrating the complementary feminine sensibility Hepworth had outlined earlier in the decade: 'men – and women too – should be on the lookout for these developing ideas in every sphere which are the attribute and expression of the feminine viewpoint. In so doing they will help forward a new equilibrium in our society – in the home, in politics and in statesmanship.'[29]

During Hepworth's visit to New York, Dag Hammarskjöld hosted a dinner at his private apartment, after which Hepworth wrote effusively with her thanks:

> *Thank you very much for the wonderful dinner party last night.*
> *It will always remain in my mind as a moment of great significance.*
> *Meeting you has impelled within me a tremendous*
> *reassessment of values (as it did, to a lesser degree, when I met*

*you at Lancaster House) & this re-valuation contains within
itself the innate strength to correct & confirm my ideas & go
forward with greater vitality.*

*I have tried to write to you for nearly two years to tell you
how much we, as artists, all owe to you, & depend upon you
for art itself as well as for our lives. Every morning when
I listen to the news, & read the papers, what you are doing
& saying & creating is the one 'reality' in a conflicting
nightmare of unreality & disbelief.*

*In England the artists are deeply implicated because we
are such a small & concentrated unit, & the impulse to create
depends on the ability to resolve & establish what U.N. stands
for as being an essential part of the true discipline of the
creative imagination.*

*You have the fully integrated 'vision' which demonstrates
the naturalness & beauty of the spirit of man which all of us,
in varying degrees are striving to obtain by the unity of mind &
imagination. These are halting words & I could only do better
in the quietness of my studio, where I have, for a long time,
thought of you and all you stand for, almost every day.*

*I could more easily express my thoughts by making you
something. I have always wanted Single Form to be yours
entirely [Hepworth's insertion: to give it to you] but hesitated to
speak as I do not know whether this is what you would even like.*

*An alternative idea would be to carve you a special object
just for handling, a more personal sculpture done after my
experiences here.*[30]

Hammarskjöld replied immediately, gratefully accepting the offer of
'such a beautiful – and meaningful – gift', and responding to Hepworth's
statement, 'You write very beautiful and very true words about the task
of the artist in our world of today. You have sensed the kinship with what
we try to do in our own field. I am proud that you wish to count us as
members of your fraternity.'[31]

Hepworth was hugely inspired by her trip to New York, and in
particular her interactions with Hammarskjöld. She wrote to him on her
way home, 'I came away with such a sense of the integrity at U.N., & so
fortified by your friendship towards me, that now I can only hope that
I can retain this quality of the macrocosm within this small workshop
& invest my stones with a greater purity of idea',[32] and wrote later that

year of her support for his political work: 'through the daily papers and my radio [I] will follow your work & your movements with a tremendous sense of gratitude'.[33] As her public profile increased, she used this to agitate further for nuclear disarmament, writing a statement in 1961 in consultation with John Bratby, Benjamin Britten, Herbert Read and Graham Sutherland, which was signed by fifty-nine artists, musicians and writers, and published in *The Sunday Times* and *The Times*:

> *[...] we feel that the time has come to protest against the*
> *immorality of present power politics.*
>
> *Culture means the affirmation of life. There can be no true*
> *culture while we make stock-piles of nuclear weapons – they*
> *are the negation of life.*
>
> *It is said that the bones of our children and grandchildren*
> *will be contaminated by dirty tests. But our minds are already*
> *contaminated by the present situation.*[34]

Hammarskjöld and Hepworth continued to send each other supportive letters, Hammarskjöld reinforcing the closeness of Hepworth's vision and that of the UN, writing in a letter of October 1960, 'your Single Form stands as a sentinel, representing the integrity both of the artist and of this operation', and noting of her recent work, 'my first impression is one of great beauty but also of an increasing sense of the drama of the present fight between sub-human chaos and human creative order'.[35]

They last met in June 1961, after Hepworth invited Hammarskjöld to her new Gimpel Fils exhibition, writing, 'I have a sculpture you might like – at least I feel it is good & worthy as an offering. Our thoughts have been with you daily during the trials & suffering of the last year.'[36] Hammarskjöld again affirmed their parallel intentions in writing his thanks for the sculpture, *Hollow Form (Churinga III)*: 'we shall, for our part, continue as well as we can to model in action and words what you are so fortunate to express, to perfection, visibly and tangibly'.[37] In his last letter to Hepworth, on 11 September 1961, he wrote about the successful installation of her work in his office:

> *A work of great art sets its own standard of integrity and*
> *remains a continuous reminder of what should be achieved*
> *in everything.*
>
> *So you hear that your gift gives me great joy of a kind*
> *which ultimately is of great help, whatever our specific task*

*may be. I believe that this is what you wanted to achieve
and, if so, you have indeed amply succeeded.*[38]

On 12 September, Hammarskjöld left New York for peace negotiations
in the Republic of the Congo, where civil war had raged since the country gained independence from colonial Belgian rule in 1960. He died in
a plane crash over Northern Rhodesia (now Zambia) on 18 September.

Hammarskjöld had considered commissioning a sculpture by
Hepworth for the pool in front of the UN Headquarters in New York,
and a few months before he died his colleague, Nobel Peace Prize winner Dr Ralph Bunche, had found a patron who would cover the cost.
Hepworth recounted several years later, 'we talked about the nature of
the site, and about the kind of shapes he liked. I also made [*Single Form*]
Chûn Quoit and the small walnut carving, *Single Form (September)*, with
Dag in mind', further noting of the latter, whose parenthesised title refers
to the date of Hammarskjöld's death, that 'it was such a beautiful piece of
wood, and I knew Dag loved wood. He already had two carvings of mine
in his collection, and maybe this would have ended up with them.'[39] The
composition of *Single Form (September)* (1961) (below) recalls a painting of
Hepworth's, *Incised Form (Granite)* (1960),
which Hammarskjöld had purchased, both
works sharing a shield-like shape with
a circle to one side. *Single Form (Chûn
Quoit)* (1961) (opposite) takes the same
form, its title referring to a Neolithic stone
arrangement in Cornwall. Hepworth's
choice to develop these forms for her
UN commission is perhaps explained in
her concurrent writing: 'for me sculpture
is the reassurance of the quality of things
both felt & seen. It reaffirms the nature
of our physical orientation, & reaffirms
our vitality. The essence of the materials
is a symbol of continuity – and the figure
in a landscape, the silent image, or the
standing stone is a sign of our desire for
survival and security.'[40] This echoes the
mission of the UN, and Hammarskjöld's
description of Hepworth's earlier *Single
Form* sculpture as a 'sentinel'.

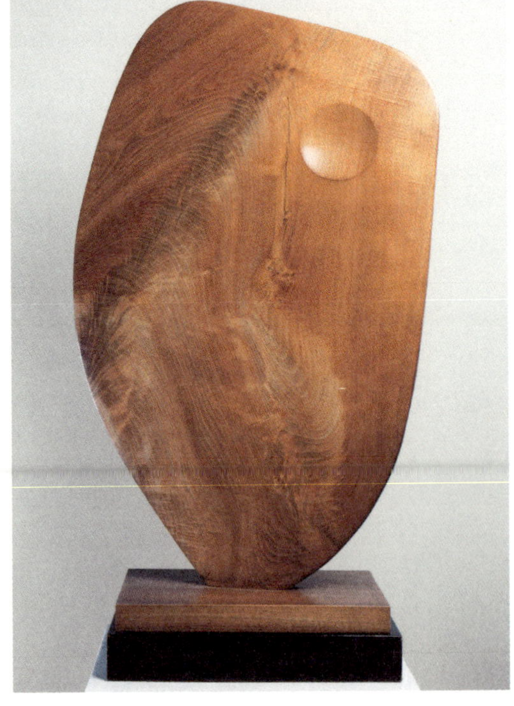

ABOVE Barbara Hepworth, *Single Form
(September)*, 1961, walnut, 82.5 × 50.8 ×
5.7 cm (32½ × 20 × 2¼ in.)

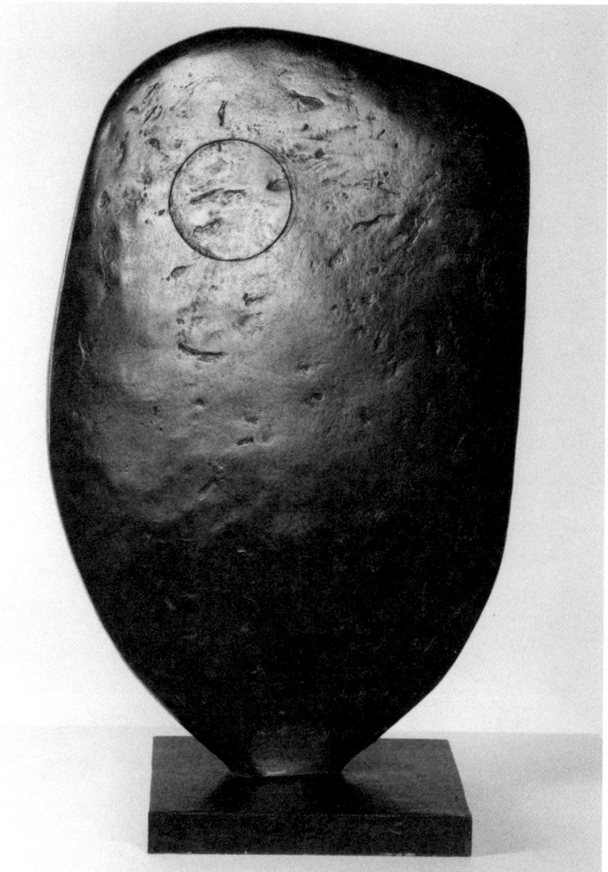

Hepworth remembered her grief on hearing of Hammarskjöld's death: 'in a kind of despair, I made the ten-foot high *Single Form (Memorial)*. This is the same theme as *September*, but the hole is moved over and now goes through the form. *Memorial* was made just to console myself, because I was so upset.'[41] With the backing of acting Secretary-General U Thant, Bunche approached Hepworth with the idea of the commission, and she replied in November 1961, 'there is no work in the world which I would like better'.[42] While her initial thoughts were for a carved stone sculpture around eight feet tall, she accepted the recommendations of the Engineering Department to enlarge the work to 15–20 feet and cast it in bronze, although noting, 'I feel that beyond twenty feet, a sculpture can become unrelated to human beings and become therefore decoration.'[43] Her ambitions for the work were tied closely to her perception of Hammarskjöld's wishes: 'He would have wanted true feeling – and would

ABOVE Barbara Hepworth, *Single Form (Chûn Quoit)*, 1961, bronze, 113 × 68 × 43 cm (44½ × 26¾ × 16⅞ in.)

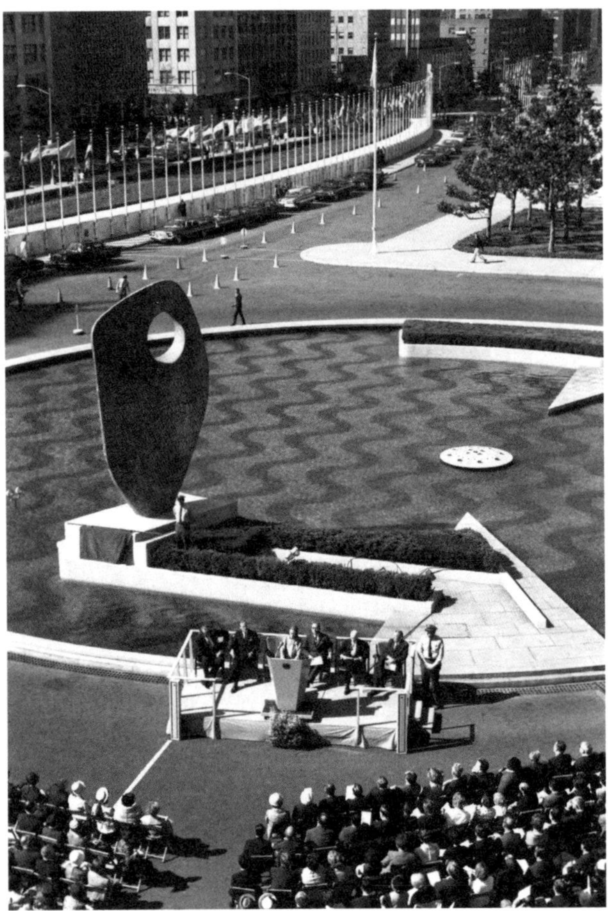

have rejected all that might veer towards the grandiose and pompous. He would have wished people to perceive, and feel, and be moved, by the intention in terms of sculpture.'[44]

Hepworth had made *Single Form (Memorial)* in plaster for bronze casting, and described the development of the sculpture to Bunche in early 1962 as 'the best work I have ever done'.[45] The plaster prototype was exhibited as simply *Single Form* in Hepworth's Whitechapel exhibition in May 1962, as the bronze had not yet been cast, and the completed bronze was shown with the subtitle '*(Memorial)*' and a dedication to Hammarskjöld at the 1963 open-air sculpture exhibition in Battersea Park.[46] Hepworth reinterpreted this work for her UN proposal (above), the larger scale requiring significant alterations, as she wrote to Bunche: 'the swellings in depth would increase – the curvatures attenuate and the circle through

ABOVE Barbara Hepworth speaking at the unveiling of the United Nations *Single Form*, New York, June 1964

OPPOSITE Barbara Hepworth with the plaster *Single Form* at the Morris Singer Foundry, May 1963. Photograph by Morgan-Wells

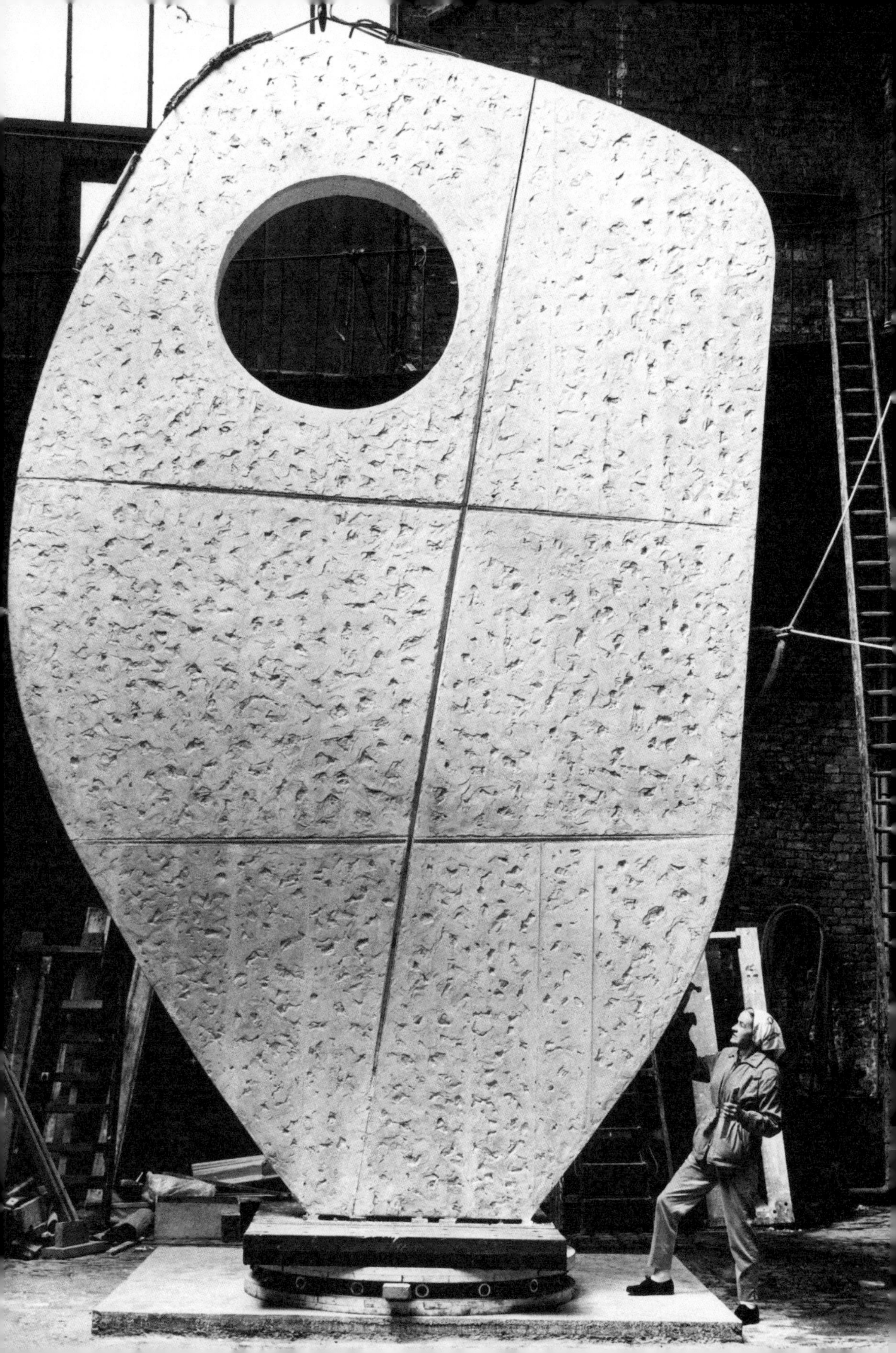

would enlarge – the surface change in texture'.[47] The design was accepted by the UN in September 1962. Working on it during the following winter, Hepworth wrote to Margaret Gardiner, 'throughout this zero weather I have continued work on the huge thing for N.Y. I am halfway through & it goes well. But it is the most arduous & exacting work of my life.'[48] She was determined to make a work that would do justice to the ideals and friendship shared with Hammarskjöld, and was unwilling to accept any compromise on the form, as she had with the John Lewis Commission, noting, 'the whole world situation seems so intensely difficult that, in this particular project so near to my heart, I could not bear any kind of contamination or blurring of the conception which must be the sort of work in the purest form which Dag Hammarskjöld would both have wished for and commanded'.[49] Hepworth oversaw every detail, creating a variety of textures on the surface by using 'axes, rakes, hatchets – different kinds in a different rhythm. You can see the axe marks where I wanted the extra vitality.'[50] The work had to be cast in seven sections, and Hepworth decided to keep the joints visible on one side of the final work to 'show aesthetically the construction, as well as indicate the powerful interior structure',[51] providing a metaphor for the strength in unity of purpose presented by the UN. She included a personal inscription in her own handwriting within the pierced circle of the sculpture: 'To the glory of God, and the memory of Dag Hammarskjöld.'

On the occasion of its unveiling in front of the UN in 1964, Hepworth gave a short speech:

> *Dag Hammarskjöld spoke to me often about the evolution of the Single Form in relation to compassion, and to courage and to our creativity. When I heard of his death, and sharing grief with countless thousands of people, my only thought was to carry out his wishes.*
>
> *Dag Hammarskjöld had a pure and exact perception of aesthetic principles, as exact as it was over ethical and moral principles. I believe they were, to him, one and the same thing, and he asked of each one of us the best we could give.*
>
> *The United Nations is our conscience. If it succeeds it is our success. If it fails it is our failure. Throughout my work on Single Form I have kept in mind Dag Hammarskjöld's ideas of human and aesthetic ideology and have tried to perfect a symbol that would reflect the nobility of his life, and at the same time give us a motive and symbol of both continuity and solidarity for the future.*[52]

Chapter 15

Affirmation of Life

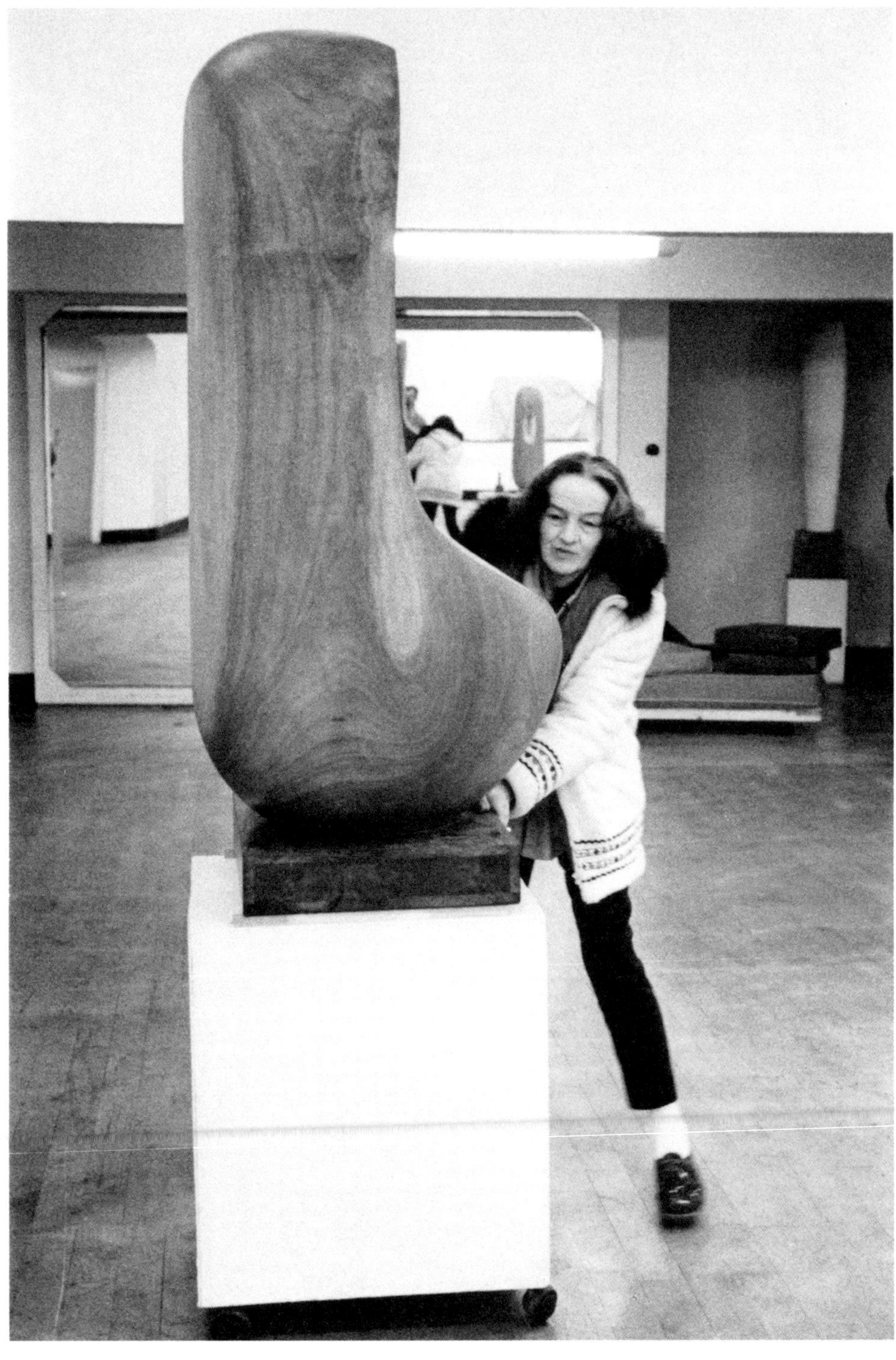

ABOVE Barbara Hepworth in her new
studio (the Palais de Danse, St Ives,
Cornwall), February 1961. Photograph
by Charles Gimpel

Alongside her major public commissions, Hepworth maintained a prolific sculptural output during the 1960s, making nearly as many sculptures in this decade as in her whole career up to this point. As the popularity of contemporary art grew, so did Hepworth's reputation. In 1961, she appeared in *Tatler* in a photo-story by Ida Kar on 'Le Quartier St. Ives', described as 'easily the district's most famous resident'.[1] The following year, *The Sunday Times* began to publish a weekend colour supplement, *The Sunday Times Magazine*, which demanded attractive visual content – ideal for introducing contemporary art to a mass audience. Hepworth appeared on the cover in 1965, photographed by Lord Snowdon on the seashore at Porthmeor Beach, St Ives, to promote the publication *Private View: The Lively World of British Art*. With photographs by Snowdon of key British artists, and texts by Whitechapel curator Bryan Robertson and art critic John Russell, the book claimed to reveal to the general public, 'just what has turned London into one of the world's three capitals of art? Who did it, and how? And what kind of people are they?'[2] Hepworth was described: 'At home, and at work, Barbara Hepworth is rather like an extremely amiable Captain Ahab, for ever in search of a particularly alluring White Whale – in her case, the next sculpture.'[3]

A show of her work from the past decade was mounted at the Whitechapel Art Gallery where, in 1954, the catalogue boasted, 'visitors to the Hepworth retrospective show saw for the first time that her sculpture was warm, eloquent, extremely sensuous, surprisingly easy to explore and experience and that above all it was beautiful'. This exhibition celebrated Hepworth's recent work, as Robertson wrote: 'the new carvings and bronzes have a strength and a presence which few earlier sculptures fully realised. They are not simply larger. They are dynamic [...] This artist is gradually encompassing the best work of her life. Already a formidable group of majestic giants has been unleashed and there is no sign of even momentary slackening in this creative drive.'[4] Hepworth had taken on a new studio in St Ives, the Palais de Danse, in 1961, to allow for these larger works, her major public commissions, and invigorated output. A former dance hall complete with large mirror on one side, the space encouraged an awareness of movement.[5] Hepworth placed her sculptures on specially made rubber-wheeled plinths, and 'danced' them around the studio (see opposite). She would later assert of her work: 'one is physically involved and this is sculpture [...] It's rhythm and dance and everything.'[6]

A key characteristic that Robertson noted of the recent works was their colour, both in painted carvings and in the patination of bronzes.

He wrote, 'the colour of the recent work is extremely varied, and extends an innate feeling for the formal and atmospheric properties of colour which has always distinguished Hepworth's work'.[7] *The Times* reviewer concurred, noting that the first impression was 'of colour. Colour and then massiveness [...] the natural tones of wood, from pale buff to dark, rich red-brown; the blacks, blackish-greens and viridians of unpolished bronze, and the bright gold of it polished; white marble and the unexpected pink plaster of "Single Form, 1962" [...] Hepworth's practice of painting the inner cavities of her carvings seems to have grown steadily more sharp and dramatic in the contrast it makes (and therefore colouristic effect) between interior and exterior forms.'[8] *Oval Form (Penwith Landscape)* (1955–56) typifies this practice (below), with two hollowed-out circles painted blue and white, respectively. Colour encourages the movement that Hepworth thought the viewing of sculpture required, the painted circles shifting in form when seen from different angles. Walls lined with pale blue and vivid ultramarine fabric in the exhibition provided contrasting backgrounds for pierced sculptures, emphasising this dynamism and foreshadowing Hepworth's later practice of photographing work against colourful painted backdrops on wheels, which she designed and kept in the Palais.[9]

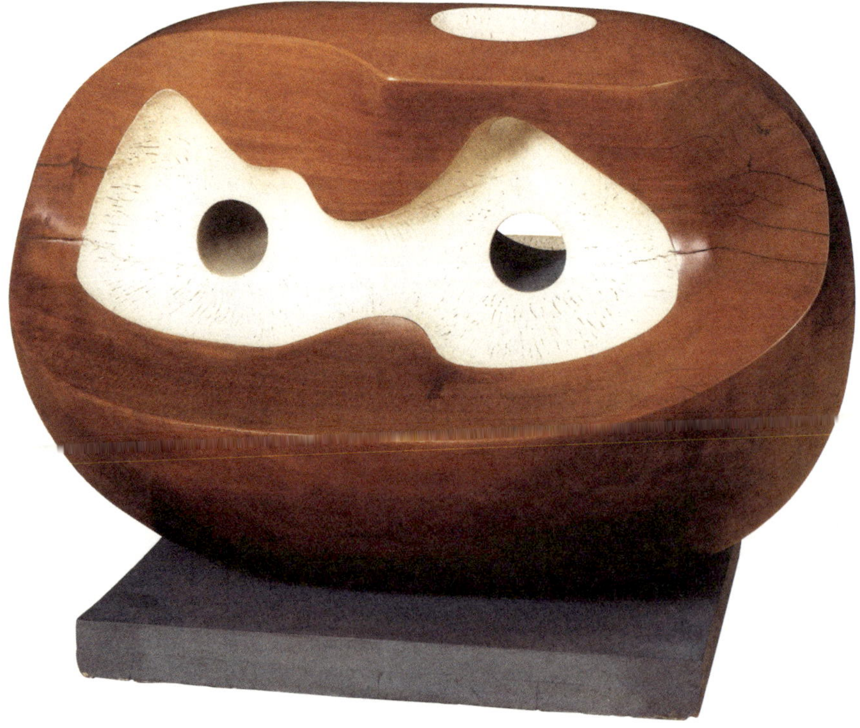

ABOVE Barbara Hepworth, *Oval Form (Penwith Landscape)*, 1955–56, scented Guarea wood, concavities painted blue and white, length 121.9 cm (48 in.)

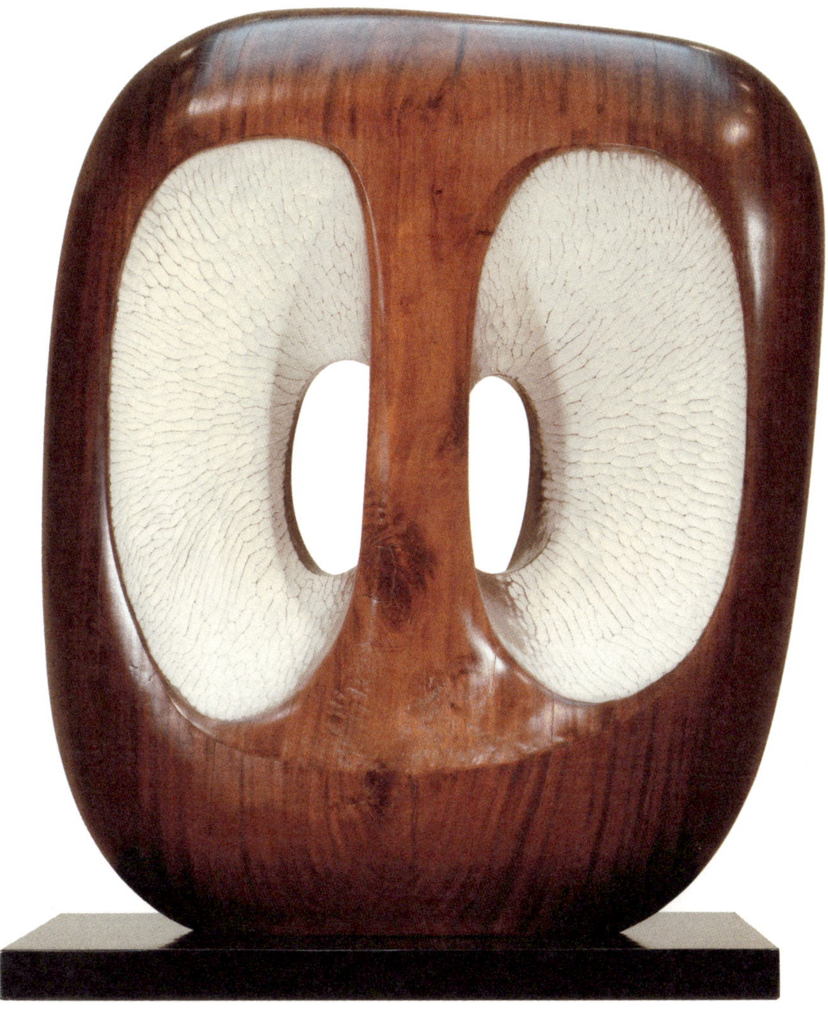

As the decade progressed, Hepworth became more explicit about the way in which sculpture encouraged physical engagement from the viewer, noting in 1968, 'there's no fixed point for a sculpture, there's no fixed point at which you can see it, there's no fixed point of light in which you can experience it, because it's ever-changing and it's a sensation which cannot be replaced'.[10] A sculpture such as *Hollow Form with White Interior* (1963) (above) transforms as it is encircled, the piercings seeming to morph and change shape. *Oval Form (Penwith Landscape)* again supports this statement. From one view, the oval wooden form is indented by a corresponding oval scoop, painted white and pierced by coloured circles. These connect to the white-painted hollow of the other

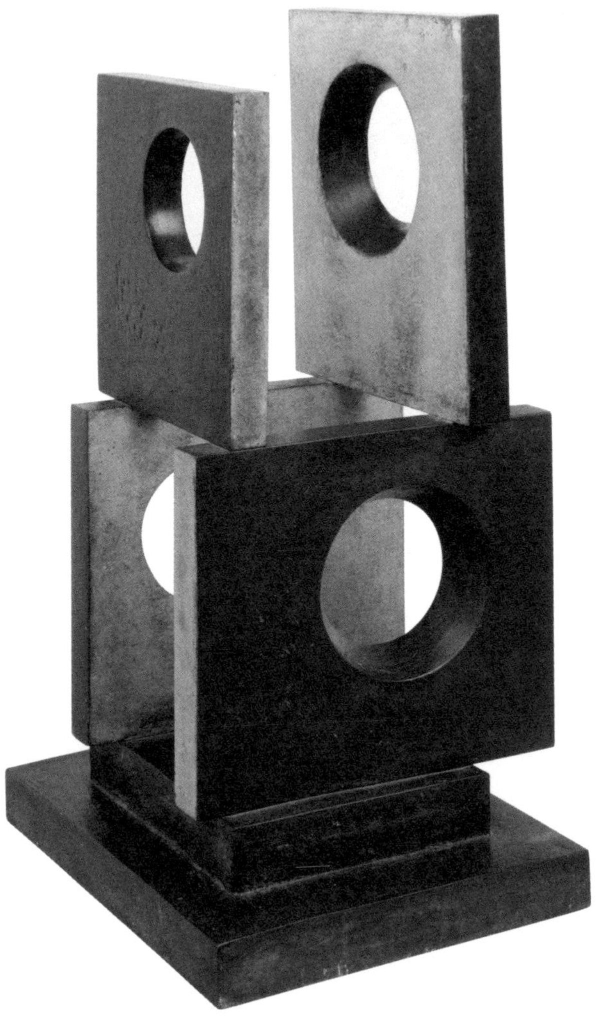

side, which, instead of the geometric simplicity of an oval, is carved into a biomorphic shape that suggests a reclining figure or rocky landscape, reminiscent of Hepworth's 'turbulent' forms of the 1930s (see p. 68). The sculpture offers different but connected aspects of Hepworth's ideology from different viewpoints, demonstrating her assertion that sculpture demands to be experienced rather than simply seen. Working on a variety of scales heightened this sense, as Hepworth saw specific physical interactions inherent in each sculpture. She wrote in 1966, 'sculpture is to me an affirmative statement of our will to live: whether it be small, to rest in the hand; or larger, to be embraced; or larger still, to force us to move around it and establish our rhythm of life'.[11] Scale did not always

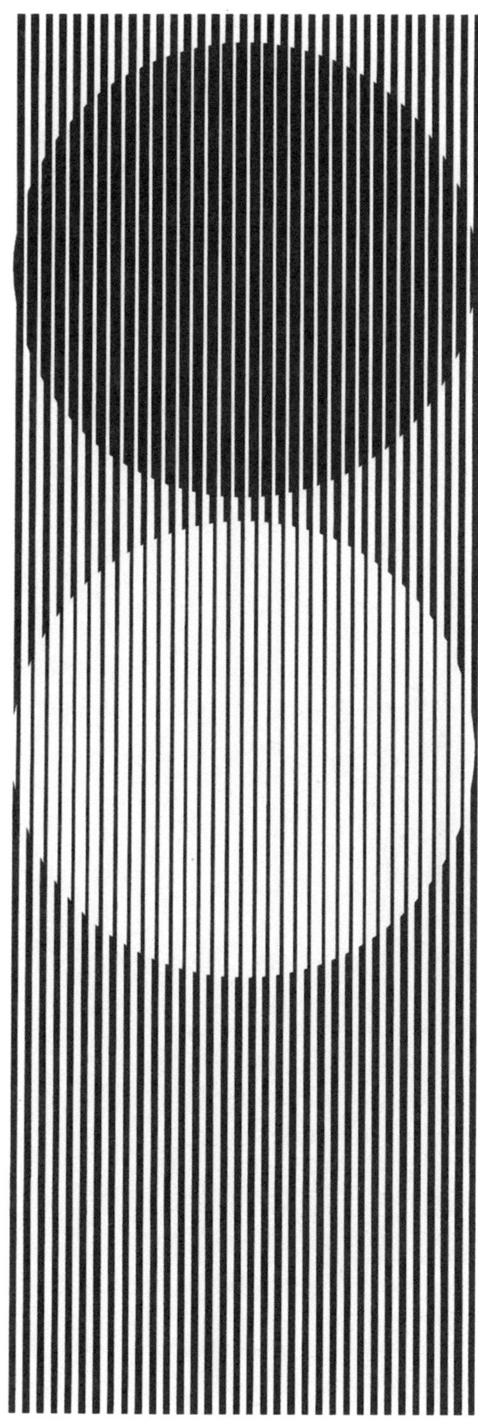

equate to size: several works Hepworth titled *Hand Sculpture* in the 1960s are too large to be held, yet evoke in the viewer how it would feel to hold them through their form.

Hepworth's continued focus on viewer participation and dynamism within her work had particular resonance in the 1960s. There was an increase in participatory art practices, such as installation art in which the viewer experienced the work as a physical environment, while a new generation of sculptors were eliminating plinths. Bryan Robertson wrote of British sculptor Anthony Caro's new work in an exhibition at the Whitechapel Art Gallery shortly after Hepworth's, 'Caro's sculptures stand on the floor without the intervention of pedestals or bases. Their impact is direct and immediate. Caro dislikes the idea of sculpture presented with artificial aids, separate from the ground – and from life.'[12] These new concerns chimed with Hepworth, who had always paid close attention to the way in which her works were presented, using different styles and heights of plinths to engage the viewer, and, in the case of larger works, placing them directly on the floor to create this immediacy as early as 1932. She wrote to Nicholson in 1969 of her approval: 'I like the new sculpture, King, Caro, Wall, Turnbull. The young generation.'[13] Alongside these developments in sculpture, there was also the emergence of Op Art, in which geometric forms were used to create dynamic optical effects, often using a formal language of circles and squares to which Hepworth was increasingly returning (see opposite). Hepworth was attuned to these new developments, becoming the

ABOVE Bridget Riley, *Echo*, 1962, oil on board, 129.5 × 43.2 cm (51 × 17 in.)

first female Tate Trustee from 1965 until 1972.[14] This meant monthly trips to London to discuss acquisitions, among other items, at a time when works by leading Op Art painter Bridget Riley (see previous page), Caro and others were entering the Tate collection.[15] Riley wrote to Hepworth after a visit to her studio some years later, 'as an artist, your example has always been a source of encouragement and your great achievements I deeply respect. So it was a great pleasure for me to see you so serene and radiating a spiritual strength which is quite overwhelming.'[16] Hepworth replied, saying how nice it was to see Riley again: 'you must know I have always been a great admirer of your work'.[17]

Riley and Hepworth had exhibited together in April 1964 in a major exhibition at the Tate, *Painting and Sculpture of a Decade '54–'64*, one of the largest surveys of post-1945 painting and sculpture to be held at that point, and one which attracted over 95,000 visitors. They were two of only eight women in this expansive group show of 170 artists, evidencing the truth behind Hepworth's statement in 1966 that, even at this time of female emancipation, 'there is a deep prejudice against women in art'.[18] Hepworth's example encouraged a younger generation of female artists to fight this prejudice, and in 1974 Hepworth agreed to a request from American artist Judy Chicago to reproduce an image of her work in Chicago's seminal feminist text, *Through the Flower: My Struggle as a Woman Artist* (1975). Chicago writes, 'the experience of comparing my work to that of other women and of sharing my perception contributed to my belief that, as Barbara Hepworth said, "The woman's approach presents a different emphasis. I think that women will contribute a great deal ... to the visual arts, and perhaps to sculpture, for there is a whole range of formal perception belonging to the feminine experience..." But how could we make the contribution that Hepworth described if those aspects of our womanhood that *were* expressed in our art were not even acknowledged.'[19] Chicago continues, echoing Hepworth's statements of the early 1950s, 'Once I began to examine women's work independently of men's, it became obvious that what some women had been trying to say about themselves as women in their art actually *constituted a challenge to male perception* of women and exposed male art as only a *partial*, rather than a universal, perception of reality [...] Asserting their own self-definition was an implicit step toward challenging the culture and demanding that it adjust its definition of women to correspond to the reality of women's lives, a demand that was not even apprehended, much less met.'[20] Between 1974 and 1979 Chicago made *The Dinner Party*, a landmark in feminist art, to celebrate the history of women's achievements. Thirty-nine significant women from throughout history were each represented by a place-setting in vulva form on a triangular table, while a further 999 women, including Hepworth, had their names inscribed on the ceramic 'heritage' floor.

Hepworth continued to speak loudly about the injustices she wished to fight, not restricting herself to her own personal struggles as a woman. In 1961, the *Daily Express* included her in their 'Woman-to-Woman' feature, which aimed to find 'the real person behind the public face'.[21] The writer, Sally Vincent, sets the scene of her meeting with Hepworth, who foregrounds her political stance:

> *'"We'll have such a nice chat", she said cosily, "I was a bit afraid of it at first, so what I've done", she went on, "I've made a list of my convictions to help you".*
>
> *She took up a piece of paper and read from the bold, black letters she had made.*
>
> *"I am a pacifist and an ardent supporter of the United Nations. And of nuclear disarmament.*
>
> *I am against capital punishment and I support the Treason Trial Fund of South Africa"*[22]
>
> *The dark glasses turned twinklingly in my direction, "I thought we might as well get that straight at the start", she concluded.'*[23]

Vincent goes on to note of Hepworth, 'what she does and what she is, she explained early on, were inseparable. And she is a woman who works in hard materials. As a sculptor she bites into stone, marble, and the hardest of woods, and loves the life she finds in them.' Vincent draws parallels, as Hepworth did, between her work and her activism, both as a feminist and a political campaigner: 'it is not surprising, perhaps, that as a woman she has found the world as recalcitrant as the materials she works with. And it makes her militancy a gentle and wonderful thing when she is prepared to hack at the wrong she sees in the world with as much faith and optimism as she feels when she takes a chisel to a huge block of granite.' Hepworth incited the (largely female) readers to direct action, suggesting that they 'write to politicians, ring up the B.B.C. – write to Mr. Kennedy if you like. But just keep on and on saying, "we will not have it, we will not have it."'[24]

In addition to her efforts for the CND, Hepworth donated many works to a wide range of charitable causes, including auctions for Save the Children Fund,[25] and also lent her support to Margaret Gardiner's appeal for peace in Vietnam. She wrote to Gardiner of the latter, 'I can well appreciate that it takes 330 letters to get 30 signatures. I am glad the advert may be Dec 10 as I feel that world issues are changing so rapidly.'[26] The advert in the end appeared in *The Times* on 23 December, paid for by the thirty-eight signatories, Hepworth listed alongside luminaries from a range of fields, including composer Benjamin Britten and author Graham Greene. The advert stated, 'We are disturbed at reports of the further escalation of the United States military commitments in Vietnam', and concluded presciently, 'it is our deep belief that for the United States to seek to achieve a solution in Vietnam on solely military terms and at the expense of continued suffering both to Vietnamese and to Americans, will vitiate whatever victory might be achieved and incur a generation of bitterness and distrust'.[27]

While battling against world events, Hepworth also entered a period of ill health. In 1965 she was diagnosed with cancer of the tongue, writing to Gardiner at the end of the year, 'Pain gets harder & harder to bear.'[28] Her cancer treatment was lengthy and draining, as she wrote

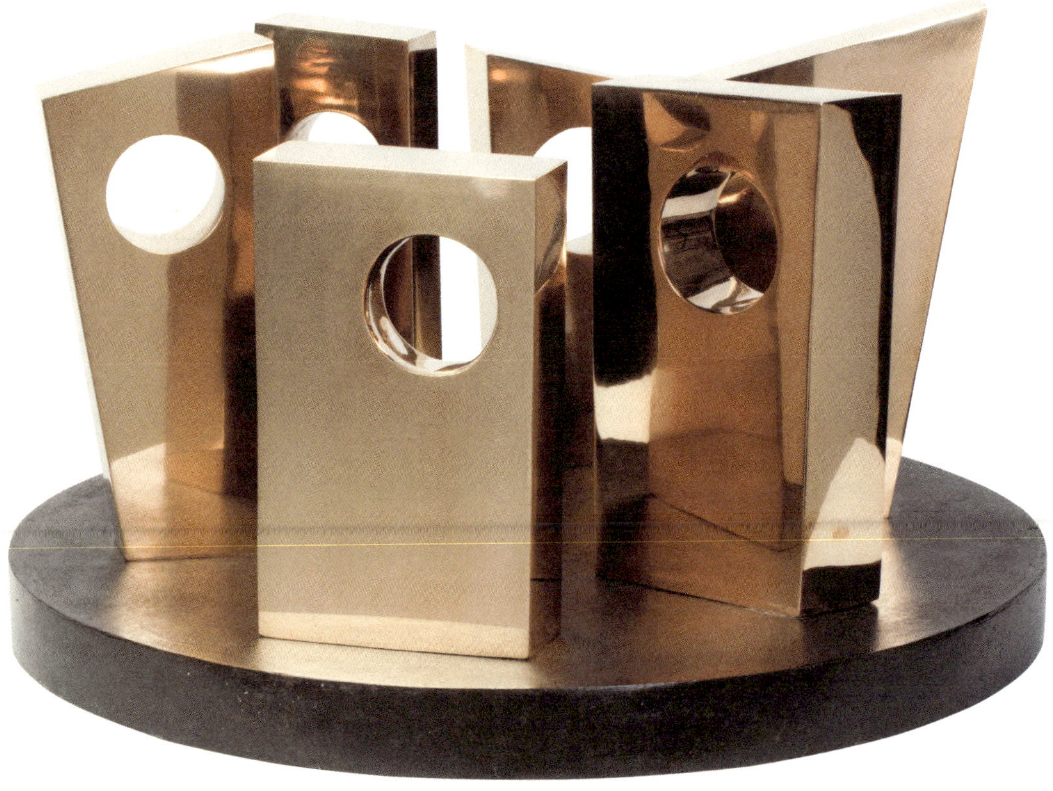

ABOVE Barbara Hepworth, *Six Forms on a Circle*, 1967, polished bronze, 31.7 × 61 × 61 cm (12½ × 24 × 24 in.)

to Nicholson in 1966: 'the last six months have been trying. The treatment (radium) for cancer seems to sap one's vitality & give one terrible fatigue. Even worse I could not eat anything & so got very weak. But I am pulling up now & my surgeon is pleased with me. I have worked – meanwhile – & I think well.'[29] Though she acknowledged to Nicholson that at times she felt 'this awful fright that I was not beating cancer', Hepworth also reflected that 'through all these health troubles one learns to live each hour with gratitude & open eyes'.[30] While still in recovery, she had another setback, breaking her leg in June 1967 while climbing aboard a helicopter on holiday in the Isles of Scilly. She complained to Nicholson at the end of the year, 'I hope to feel more myself when I can walk again. Being crippled does not really suit a sculptor.'[31]

Hepworth's injury did not halt her prolific output, and she recalled in 1969, 'even breaking my leg was a good thing because it made me extend my arms as far as I could'.[32] Physical impediment prompted further reflections on the bodily relationship to sculpture, and writing to Nicholson in late 1967 under the heading 'Circles & ½ Circles', she noted, 'so much depends, in sculpture, on what one wants to see through a hole! Maybe, in a big work I want to see the sun or moon. In a smaller work I may want to lean in the hole. In a "six forms on a circle" I may want to see every form all at once![33] I don't care whether they end up spiral, oblique or straight through. It is the physical sensation of piercing & sight which I want. I like to be free & at the moment I have 20 "collared doves" flying through 4 giant holes in my "walk through" sculpture. I just love it.'[34]

From the monumental 'walk through' *Four-Square (Walk Through)* (1966) to the polished bronze *Six Forms on a Circle* (1967) that could be surveyed 'all at once' (opposite), a complete range of Hepworth's work was included in her next major exhibition, a retrospective held at Tate Gallery in April 1968. Photographs of Hepworth next to the towering *Four-Square (Walk Through)*, still on crutches, appeared in the press (see following pages). The show had been confirmed in early 1967, and much of the year was spent gathering work, eventually totalling 186 sculptures. Hepworth worked with architect Michael Brawne to design the exhibition, dividing the grand neoclassical architecture of Tate's Duveen Gallery using white angular screens. Similar screens had been used by architects Peter and Alison Smithson for *Painting and Sculpture of a Decade 1954–1964*, in which Hepworth had featured a few years earlier, and reviews of that exhibition had remarked, 'the booming halls of the Tate have been cleverly, if rather plainly, brought down to human scale by mazes of screens'.[35] Within the newly created spaces, Hepworth placed sculptures on plinths made of

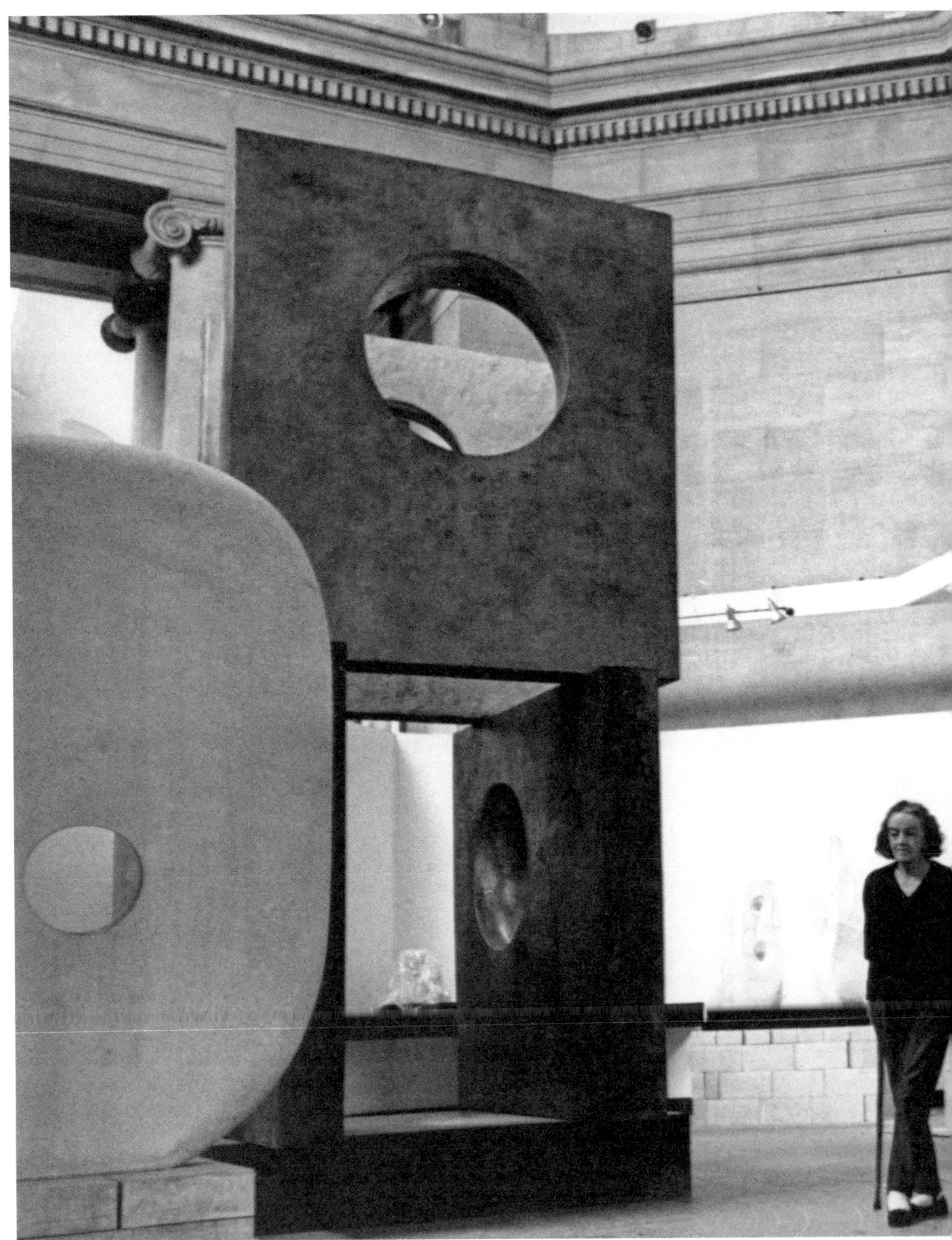

 Barbara Hepworth preparing for
her retrospective exhibition at Tate Gallery,
London, 21 March 1968

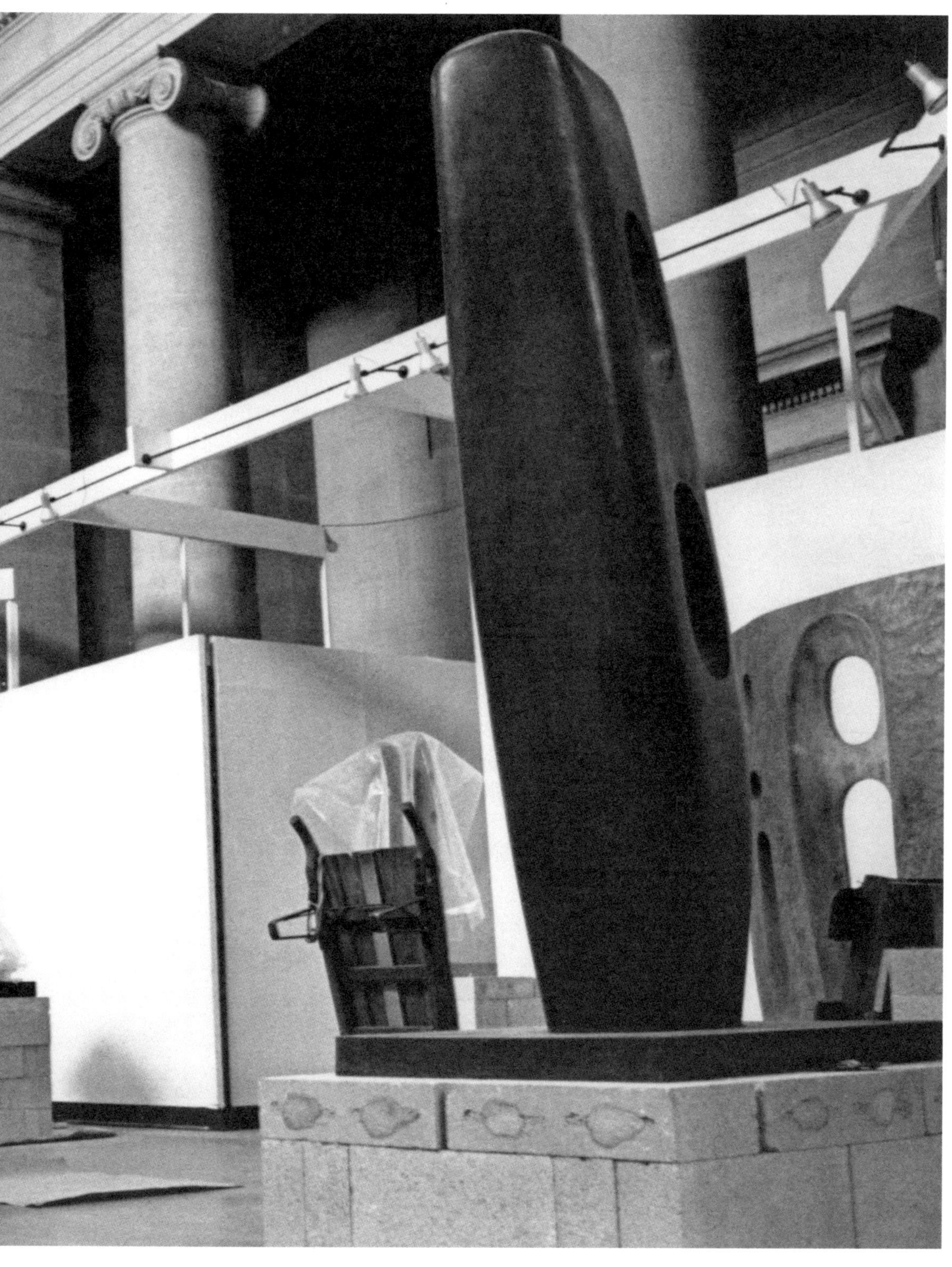

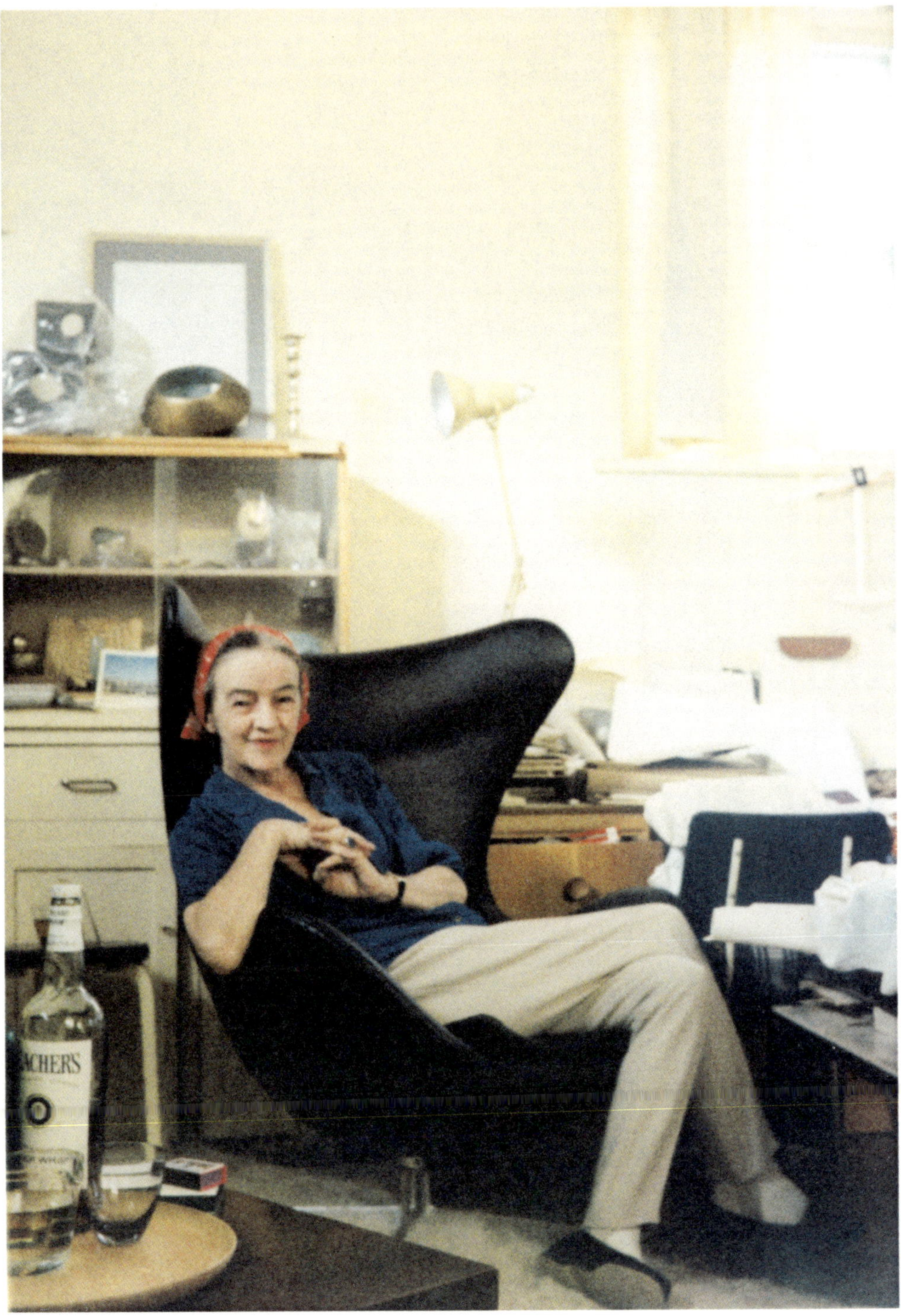

ABOVE Barbara Hepworth in the studio, 1966

concrete blocks, and positioned others directly on the floor, interspersed with pot plants.[36] The plinths and plants could have been inspired by the Trewyn Studio garden, where photographs show concrete block plinths being used as early as 1956. Hepworth's work had also been shown on concrete block plinths at the Rietveld Pavilion, a modernist structure originally built in 1955 for the *Third International Sculpture Exhibition* in The Netherlands, and permanently sited at the Kröller-Müller Museum in 1965 with Hepworth's show as the inaugural exhibition. She clearly felt these modernist architectural materials provided a good foil for her work, writing, 'never again will I see my work in such perfect and wonderful conditions and surroundings'.[37]

At Tate it was the range of work, rather than the exhibition design, that caused most comment in the press. Guy Brett in *The Times* noted of the number of works, 'this crowded effect seems at once the right sort of installation; partly because most of her sculptures, with their hollowed-out interiors, focus the attention inward, and partly because it suggests her teeming production over the past 10 years',[38] while Norbert Lynton in the *Guardian* praised, 'this is only a fraction of her output, of course, but as full and cheering an account of her life's work as one could hope to find'.[39] Hepworth was delighted with the exhibition, writing to Nicholson, 'I have myself been richly rewarded by the high attendance at the Tate & the huge sale of catalogues. Also by so many moving letters from strangers all of whom loved "touching" the sculpture altho' against orders.'[40] As the decade drew to a close, she continued to create monumental works for national and international settings, writing to Nicholson about a sculpture for her 1970 exhibition at Hakone Open-Air Museum in Japan, 'I'm just finding the strength to finish a huge one for a glorious site. It's a "walk-into" – a starred maze – a moon form. You'll hate it no doubt. But it gives me spiritual & physical joy [...] You never like arrogant sculpture nor fierce forms – but I do.'[41] Having now the space and opportunity to create a range of work in a range of materials, Hepworth recognised the formal connections of her later work with earlier sculptures, the re-appearance of geometric forms and circular piercings that characterised her work of the late 1930s. In an interview in 1969, she reflected, 'I don't think anyone realises how much the last ten years has been a fulfilment of my youth.'[42] Though now nearing her seventieth birthday, she wrote to Nicholson, 'I have never <u>never</u> never felt bored with my work or in working. In fact I get such intense & sensuous pleasure out of it that it is almost a Yorkshire sin!'[43]

Chapter 16

Sun &
Moon

Hepworth lived through an astonishing array of technological advances and believed that these should necessarily inform the creative arts. She wrote in 1958, 'the new forms in painting and sculpture are capable, in my opinion, of infinite development and extension for the artist because they are the result of man's increasing awareness of the fundamental truths concerning the universe which are being discovered with the greatest rapidity during this century'.[1] The development of aviation was a case in point, from the first passenger transatlantic flights in the 1930s to the beginnings of space exploration in the 1960s. Hepworth noted at the end of the decade, 'Man's discovery of flight has radically altered the shape of our sculpture, just as it has altered our thinking.'[2] She had first-hand experience of the visual impact of this discovery, as she recalled in 1971:

> *Coming back from America after one of my visits, I became so unutterably bored by the false surroundings in the aircraft, the colour T.V., cigar smoke and champagne that I begged permission to go into the cockpit and make a drawing of the sunrise. Permission was granted and it was one of the great experiences of my life.*
>
> *The pilot said, quite frankly, that he thought I was a bit silly and that he, personally, was tired of sun-rises. But quite apart from the super-natural colours and shapes, and the sense of real flying, I think I was even more deeply impressed by the utter ease of the movement by pilot and co-pilot and navigator in such an incredibly restricted space.*
>
> *To go on seemed sensible. To descend a very hard discipline. I would like to be an astronaut and go round the moon, and maybe remain in orbit forever [...] my son Paul once told me that there was a new aesthetic in flying and space...*[3]

In 1959, the USSR had landed the first unmanned aircraft on the moon. Over the next decade, the public's imagination was captured by the 'space race' between America and the USSR to put the first man on the moon.

Space exploration also offered technological advances in telecommunications. While the BBC's first television broadcast was in 1936, by the early 1950s there was still only one black and white channel, and most households did not own a television set. This changed dramatically during the 1950s and '60s, with the arrival of commercial television channels in 1954, BBC 2 in 1964 and colour television in 1967. In 1962, NASA launched Telstar 1 into orbit around the Earth, a communications satellite that

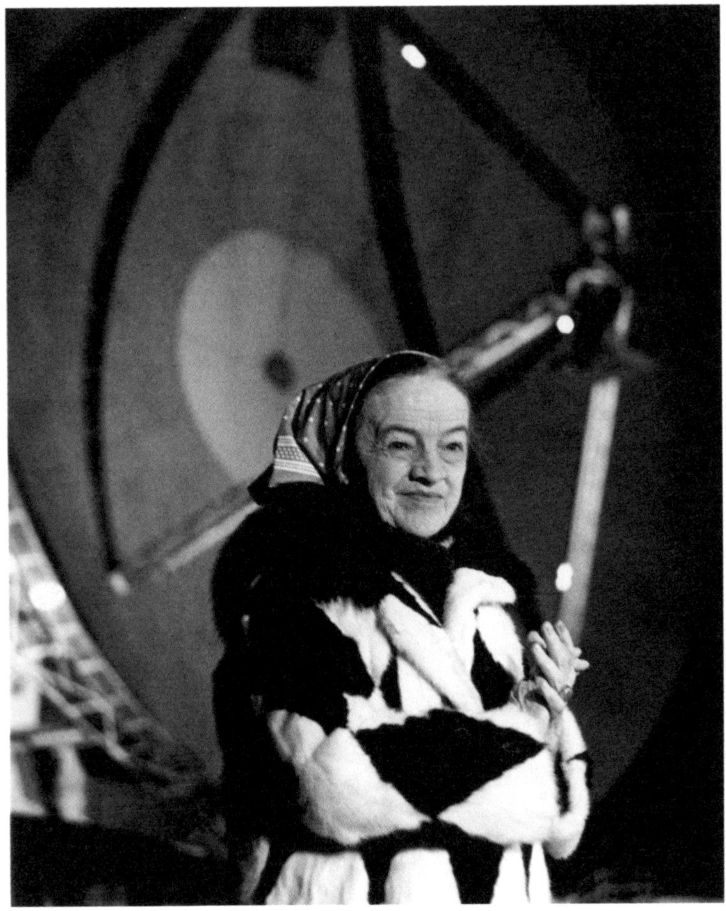

successfully relayed television, radio and telegraph signals through space, and allowed the first live broadcast of television images between America and Europe. The same year, the Goonhilly Satellite Earth Station was established in Cornwall, run by the General Post Office, with enormous satellite dishes to communicate with Telstar. Hepworth recalled visiting the site in 1963: 'I was invited on board the first one [dish] when it began to go round, and it was so magical and strange. I find such forms of our technology very exciting and inspiring.'[4] A wood carving made the same year, *Pierced Hemisphere (Telstar)* (opposite), offers a proxy for the dish in its white-painted, scooped interior, the string suggesting lines of communication. Hepworth translated her experiences into other sculptures, noting, 'you might say that the Four Hemispheres equals the dishes at Goonhilly and the trackers of the sky'.[5] Carved in Seravezza marble in

 Barbara Hepworth at Goonhilly Satellite Station, near Helston, Cornwall, *c.* 1966. Photographed by Ander Gunn during filming for a Westward Television documentary (Goonhilly footage unused)

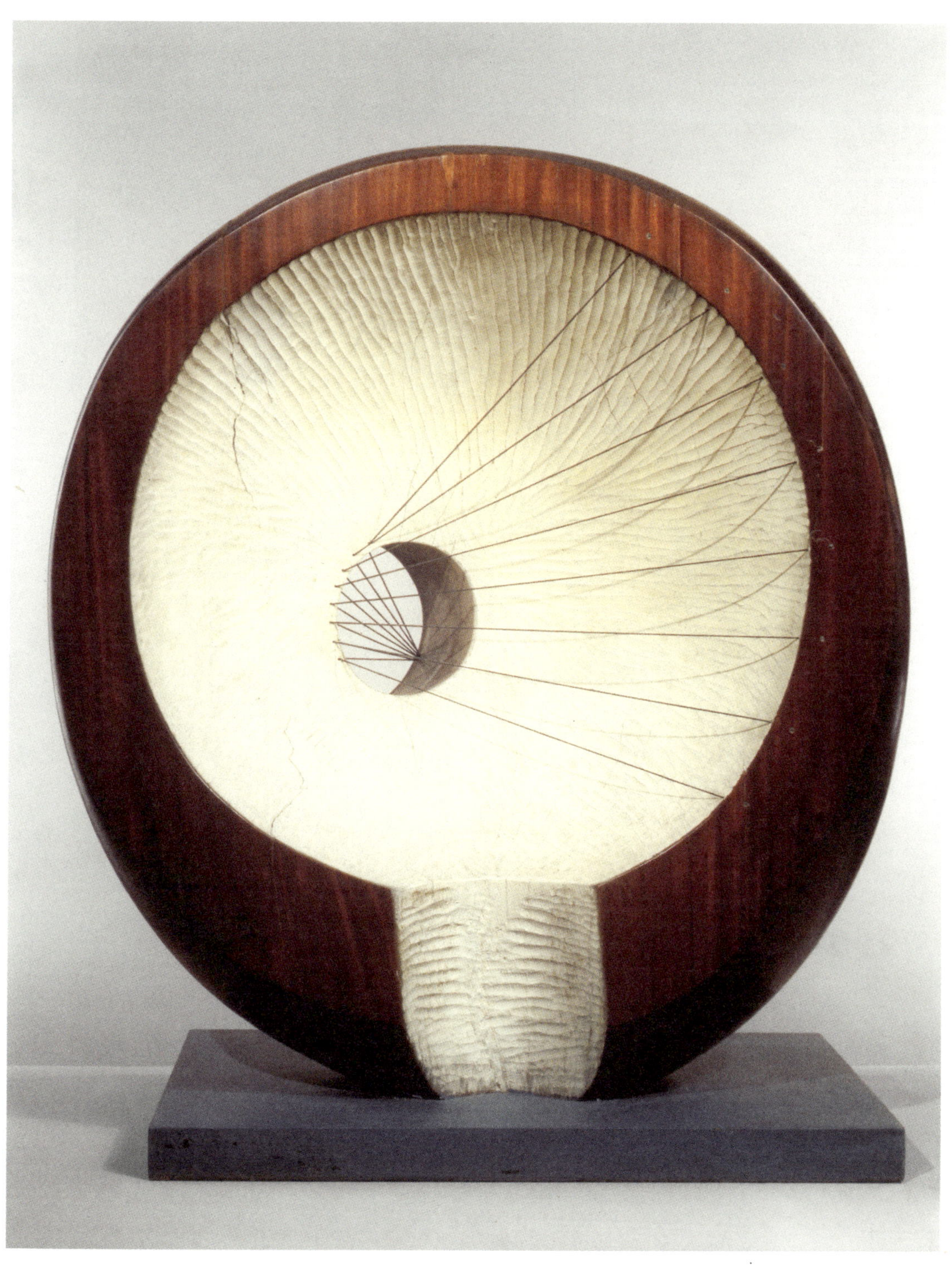

ABOVE Barbara Hepworth, *Pierced
Hemisphere (Telstar)*, 1963, Guarea wood
with strings and colour, 97 × 62 × 92 cm
(38⅛ × 24⅜ × 36⅛ in.)

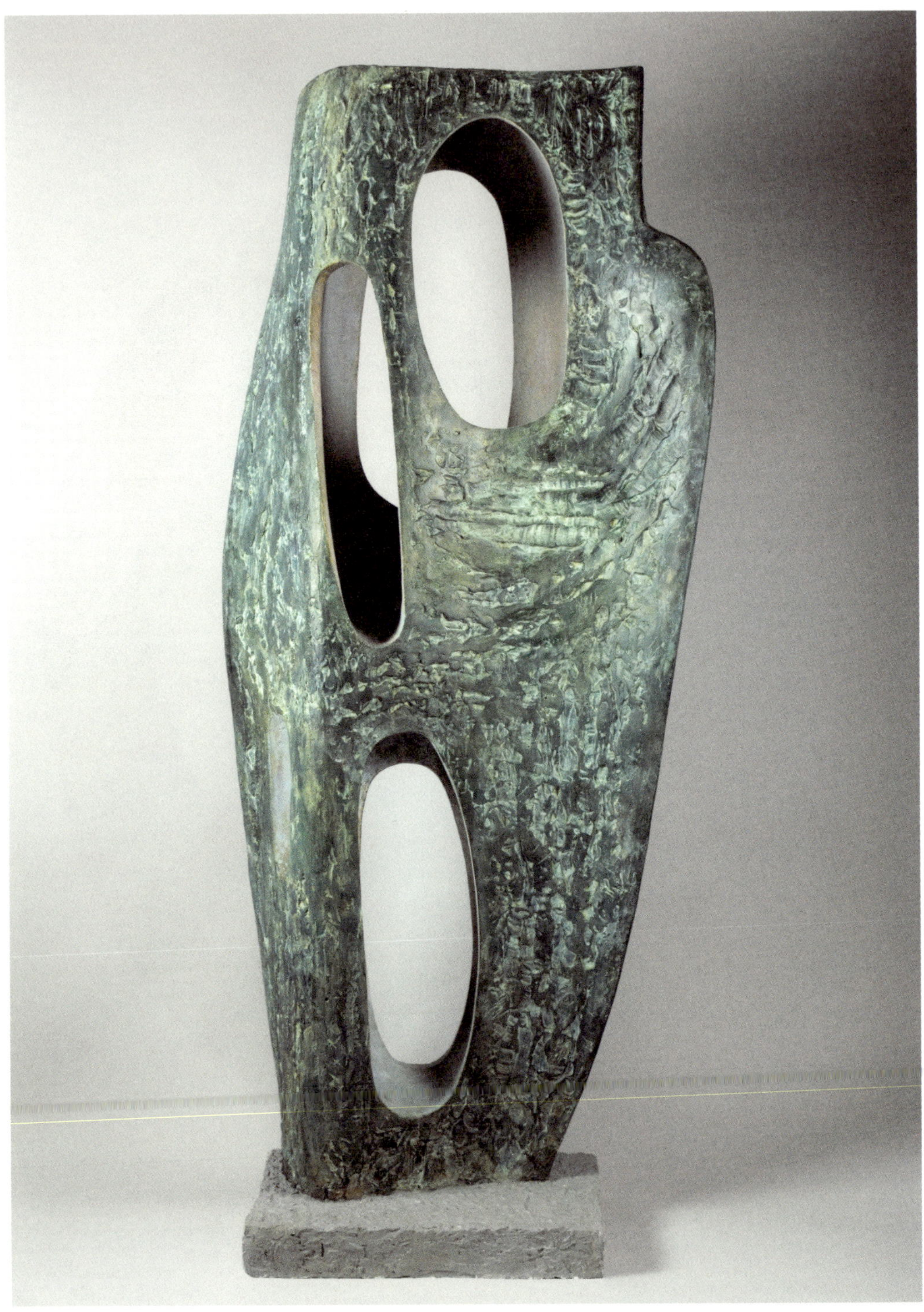

ABOVE Barbara Hepworth, *Rock Form (Porthcurno)*, 1964, painted plaster on painted wooden base coated with plaster, 255.8 × 109.5 × 65 cm (100⅝ × 43⅛ × 25½ in.). Prototype for casting in bronze

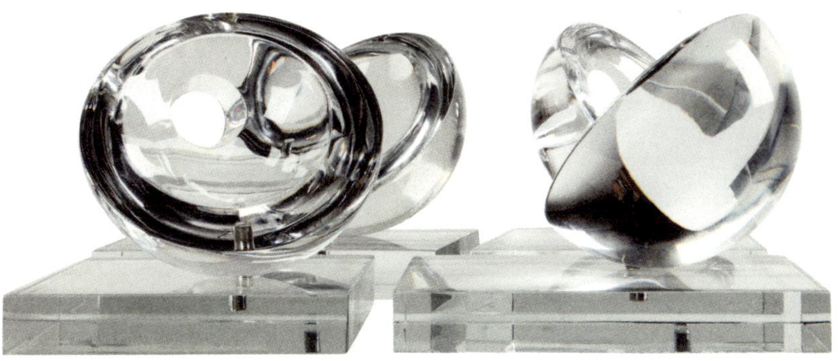

1969, *Four Hemispheres* was also cast in lead crystal in 1970. At the opening of her exhibition that year at Marlborough Fine Art, London,[6] she said her work was 'becoming more fluid and experimental, and may well involve new materials'.[7] The four half-sphere elements of the lead crystal *Four Hemispheres* (above) were independent and could be rearranged to communicate with one another in different configurations. A variation on this theme, *Three Hemispheres* (1967) (below), was created using plastic bowls to cast half-spheres in plaster, two of which were then carved with circular reliefs, in one consecutively deeper circles eventually piercing the sphere entirely.[8] The plaster prototype was then cast in highly reflective, polished bronze.

While she was still making works with explicit reference to particular landscapes, such as *Rock Form (Porthcurno)* (1964) (opposite), Hepworth's notes show her connecting her earthly experiences with the new discoveries of space exploration, writing of this work, 'the light pouring through a hole, whether sun or moon: the texture of sea, sand or land: the colour of dawn or sunset; all put into the poise of the human response to our environment and the expanding universe'.[9] In 1969 the first manned lunar landing took place, with astronaut Neil Armstrong famously proclaiming as he set foot on the moon, 'That's one small step for man, one giant leap for mankind.' The Apollo 11 mission was televised in Britain, with the BBC providing twenty-seven hours of coverage over a ten-day period, culminating in the UK's first all-night broadcast. It is little wonder that celestial bodies, and particularly the moon, appear with increasing regularity in Hepworth's work from this time. In 1969, she made *Disc with Strings (Moon)* in aluminium, the

TOP Barbara Hepworth, *Four Hemispheres*, 1970, lead crystal, each 16 cm (6⅜ in.) high, including bases

ABOVE Barbara Hepworth, *Three Hemispheres*, 1967, plaster, each 13.7 cm (5⅜ in.) in diameter. Prototype for casting in bronze

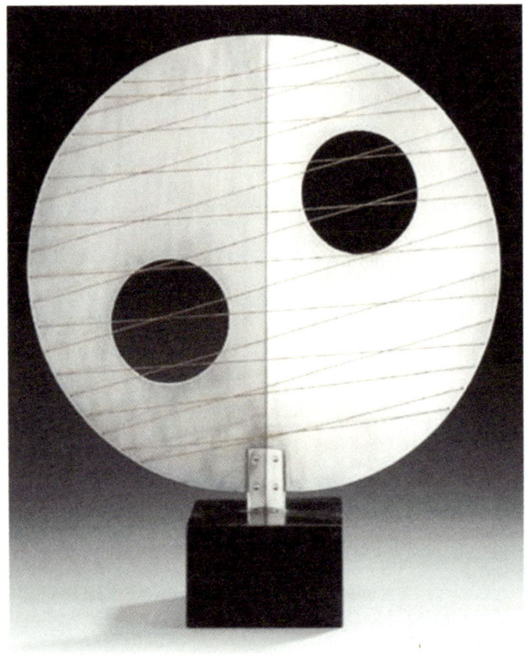

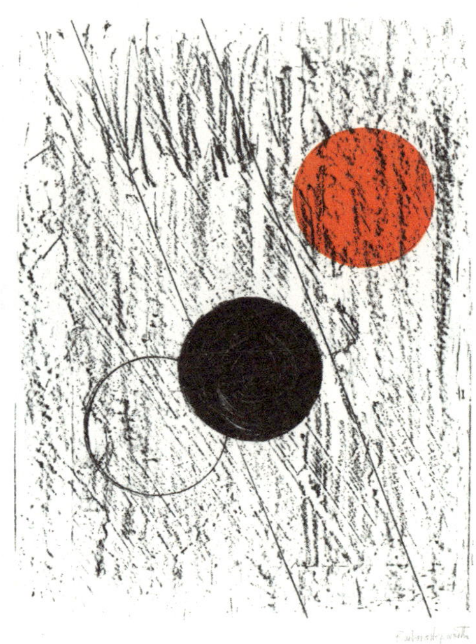

soft silver metal adding to its space-age sensibility, divided into geometric shapes by interlacing strings (above, left). Two circles puncturing the surface could be moon craters, or the moon and sun moving across the sky. Hepworth also made her first suite of prints this year, titled *Twelve Lithographs*, several of which pick up this theme, such as *Sun and Moon* (above, right), in which red and black circles float on a shadowy background. Hepworth had been persuaded to make lithographs by Herbert Simon, the director of the printmaking studio Curwen Press, on the grounds that it would enable 'people of modest means to own something by Barbara Hepworth and secondly because I suspect you would enjoy working on stone and find you have a real affinity for it'.[10]

In a note written in 1966 titled 'The Sun and Moon', Hepworth reflects that observing these bodies and interpreting their light effects in her work 'expresses my deep interest in a new sense of poetry in our scientific age'.[11] The same circular forms of 'Sun and Moon' appeared in a painting, *Genesis III* from 1966 (opposite, above), floating amid a cosmic background of spattered ink.[12] Its biblical title suggests a connection between the forms that Hepworth related to space exploration and spirituality. The same year, she began the monumental *Construction (Crucifixion)* (1966–67) (opposite, below), making a prototype in aluminium

ABOVE LEFT Barbara Hepworth, *Disc with Strings (Moon)*, 1969, aluminium and strings, 59 × 47 × 15 cm (23⅛ × 18½ × 5⅞ in.)

ABOVE RIGHT Barbara Hepworth, *Sun and Moon*, 1969, lithograph, 74 × 55.6 cm (29⅛ × 21⅞ in.)

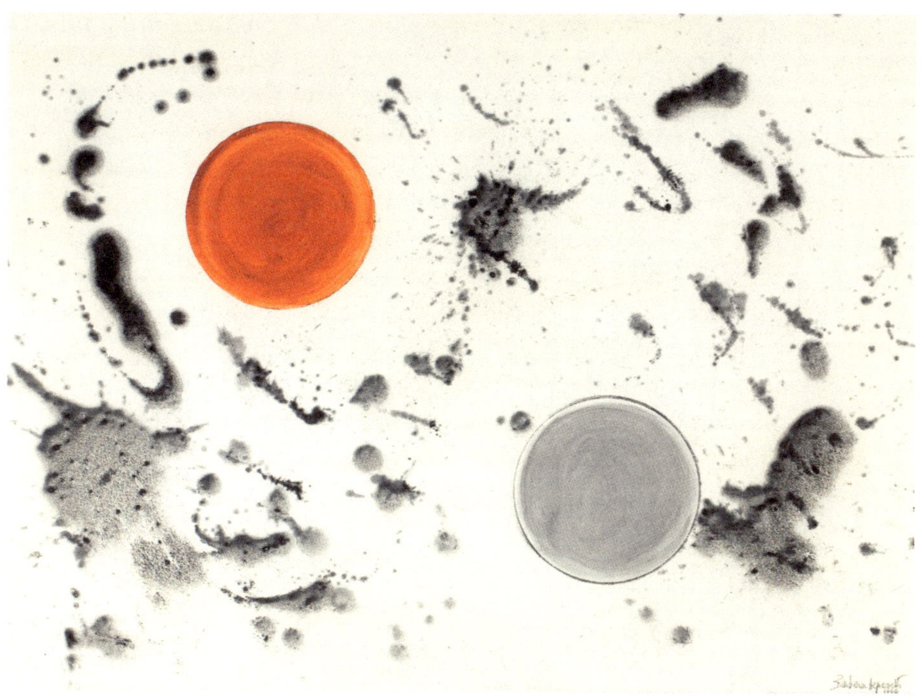

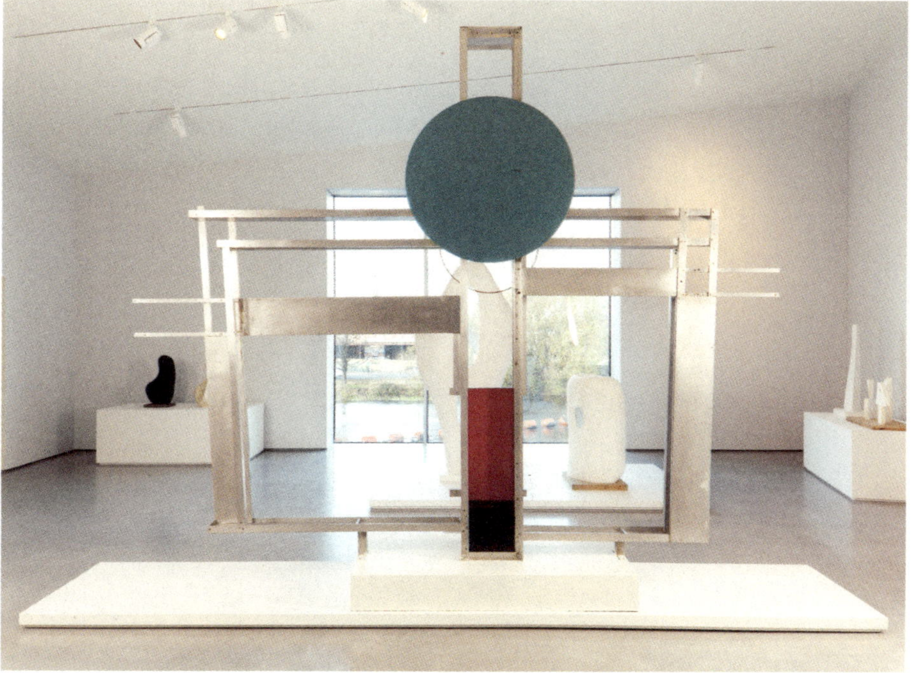

TOP Barbara Hepworth, *Genesis III*, 1966, oil and pencil on board, 76 × 102 cm (29⅞ × 40⅛ in.)

ABOVE Barbara Hepworth, *Construction (Crucifixion)*, 1966–67, aluminium, part painted, 391 × 471.3 × 92 cm (153⅞ × 185½ × 36⅛ in.). Prototype for casting in bronze, on display in The Hepworth Family Gift at The Hepworth Wakefield

to be cast in bronze, an abstract crucifixion which contains three circles – a blue circle viewed from one side and yellow from the other, with a gold-painted steel circle outline hung slightly lower.[13] Hepworth saw this as furthering her experimentation with colour, as well as comprising an overtly religious work that she related to her period of illness.[14] In *Science and Health*, the Christian Science text that Hepworth owned and consulted, Mary Baker Eddy writes that 'the circle represents the infinite without beginning or end'.[15] The synthesising of scientific advances with spirituality is typical of Hepworth's inclusive philosophy, and she noted in an interview of May 1966, 'I regard the present era of flight and projection into space as a tremendous expansion of our sensibilities, and space sculpture and kinetic forms are an expression of it; but in order

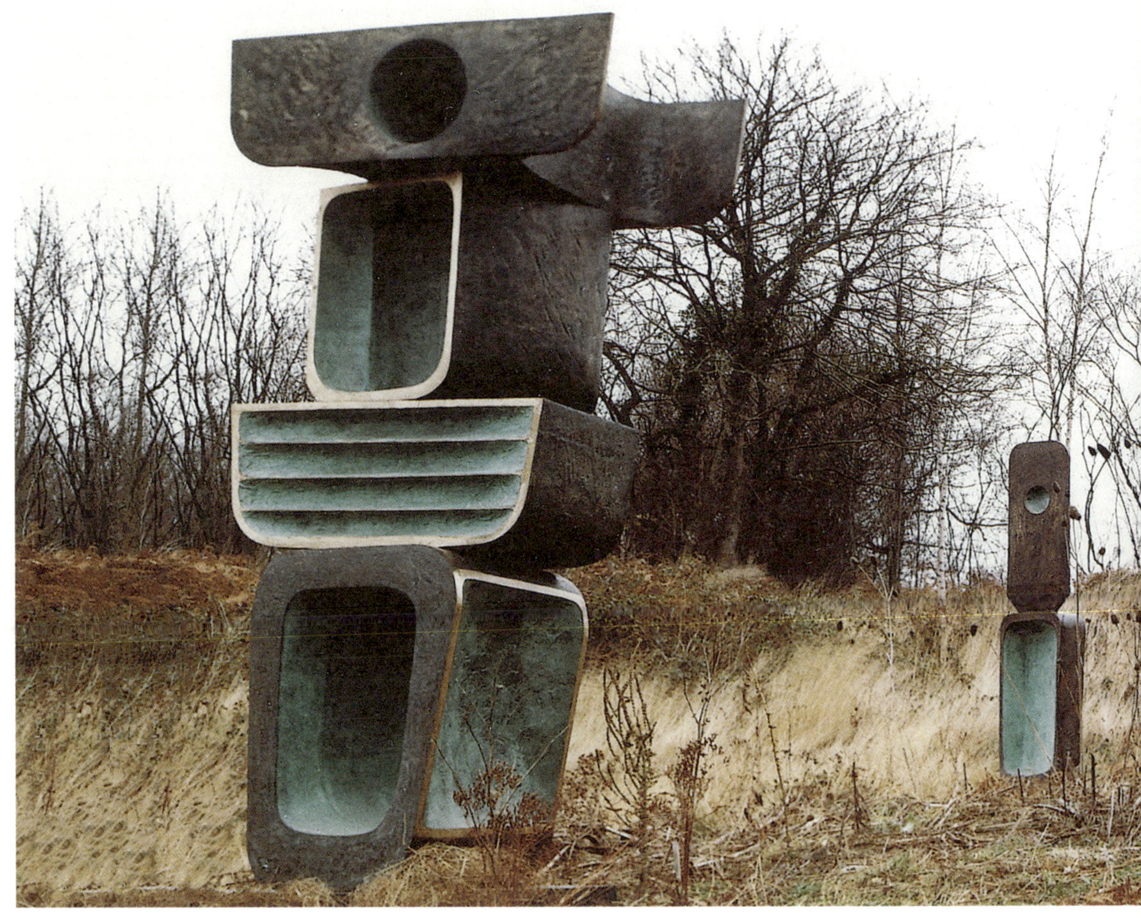

ABOVE Barbara Hepworth, *The Family of Man* (1970), bronze. Photograph taken by Foresees outside the Morris Singer Foundry, January 1972

to appreciate this fully I think that we must affirm some ancient stability.'[16] At this time Hepworth wrote to Nicholson, relaying her heightened awareness of astronomical forms through her worldly surroundings:

It is midnight 4th May & full moon! I have just been in the garden & in this light everything is strange & new. The flowering cherries & bushes are like stars. The sculptures strangely huge & ethereal. The moon is at right angles to my new 'thinking room' (no stone dust allowed!) & the fierce & gorgeous moonlight gives a new dimension to all things. It is warm with a clear & wonderful sky. A night never to forget.[17]

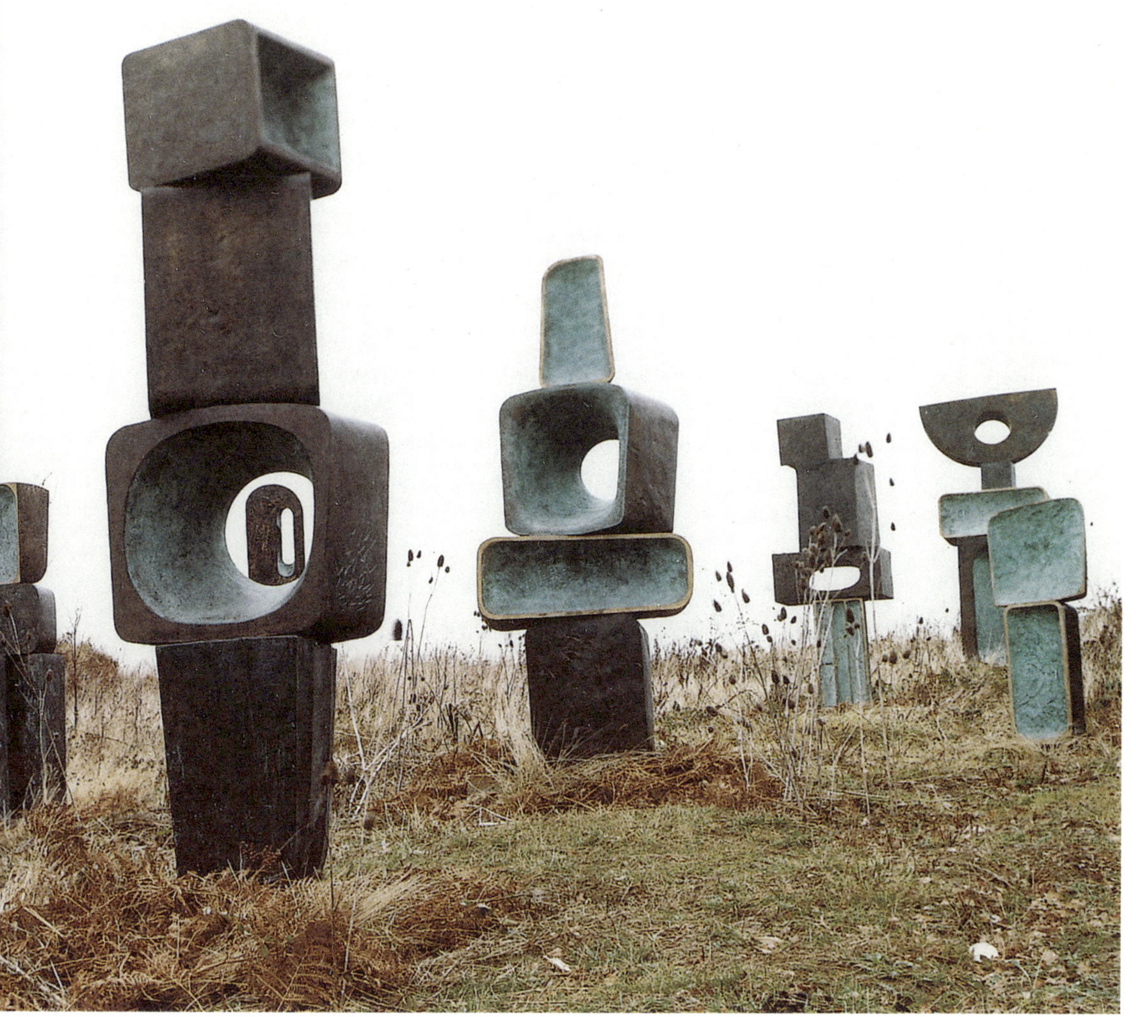

Hepworth's deep connection to St Ives was affirmed in 1968 when she was given the Honorary Freedom of the Borough, along with potter Bernard Leach, in recognition of their contribution to the arts. She was made a Bard of Cornwall and took the Cornish name 'Gravyor' in a ceremony led by the Grand Bard of Cornwall. She wrote in 1971, 'I shall never forget the sound of singing voices, the cadences of the Cornish language, the sound of pipes, horn and harp. I think the name "Gravyor" suits me and could well go on my headstone as showing my love for this land and its people.'[18] She had begun to 'dream of a new big sculpture – nine figures walking up a hill. It's an idea that has been boiling for years, now it's boiled and I'm starting.'[19] Originally intended for a Cornish hillside, the expansive *Family of Man* (1970) (see previous pages) offers the 'ancient stability' Hepworth sought through nine individual but connected bronze sculptures that represent the human figure across generations: *Ancestor I*, *Ancestor II*, *The Bride*, *The Bridegroom*, *Parent I*, *Parent II*, *Youth*, *Young Girl*, and *Ultimate Form*. Each is comprised of multiple stacked elements that repeat and gain in complexity from the *Youth* to the *Ancestors*, suggesting the evolution of humanity in both universal and personal terms. Hepworth wished viewers to 'identify themselves' with the sculptures, and related the 'Ancestors' to both her great-great-grandmother and 'ancient Britons'.[20] Of the concluding *Ultimate Form*, she explained:

> *All, from the Ancestor to the Young Girl, have an Ultimate*
> *Form in view of some kind. We all have an aspiration which we*
> *share. They may be different aspirations, but they are still hopes*
> *for the future, a belief in the future, a belief in the children that*
> *are going to be born. And the Ultimate Form has this kind of*
> *serenity saying, 'Go on working, here I am'.*[21]

In the 1970s, Hepworth continued to expand on her uses of new materials, while consistently returning to the forms that had had special meaning for her since childhood. In one of her last interviews, she noted her continued aim 'for certain basic things which I feel very strongly about like single forms and oval forms and finding all the possible variations – one could really do with 10 lifetimes to express the variations and subtleties which one lifetime can give'.[22] Both the single form and the oval form expressed for Hepworth the experience of the human figure in the landscape,[23] but the landscape had expanded to include the infinite universe, and the experience was one not only seen but also felt, of transitory moments made enduring and timeless. Two works completed in 1973 show the breadth of the visual language that Hepworth had now developed for expressing these ideas. *Cone and Sphere* (below) is carved in marble, the first stone that captured Hepworth's enthusiasm in the 1920s, and which she returned to with zeal in later life. *The Sunday Times* critic John Russell would note of her 'white marbles' exhibited at Marlborough Fine Art, London, in 1972, that the 'slow-flowing movement of the rounded and hollowed forms has never looked better'.[24] A single form or standing figure, *Cone and Sphere* married the pure geometry of Hepworth's earlier work with her later concerns, evoking shifting celestial bodies through incised, overlapping circles orbiting the seemingly balanced sphere. The form recalls a line from *Science and Health* that Hepworth wrote out in a notebook of the time, that the divine Mind – the spiritual entity of which all true existence is a part – 'is in perpetual motion. Its symbol is the sphere. The rotations and revolutions of the universe of Mind go on eternally.'[25] *Sphere* (1973) (see following page) incorporated bright primary colours and was developed from a sculpture, *Sphere with Inside and Outside Colour* (1967), which Hepworth had made in aluminium, a material that had only recently been used by a younger generation of sculptors, such as Anthony Caro.[26] The spherical form that had appeared in Hepworth's earlier carvings is made ephemeral through the lightness of thin metal bands encircling the space within, reflecting bouncing light.

By this time Hepworth was beginning to struggle with her continued illness, having periodically returned to hospital, and had written with dark humour to Nicholson at the end of the 1960s, 'I work, but live week to week medically [...] I love life and nature so much it is a bore to think of being "snuffed".'[27] In 1973, she celebrated

LEFT Barbara Hepworth, *Cone and Sphere*, 1973, white marble, 105 × 500 × 380 cm (41⅜ × 196⅞ × 149⅝ in.)

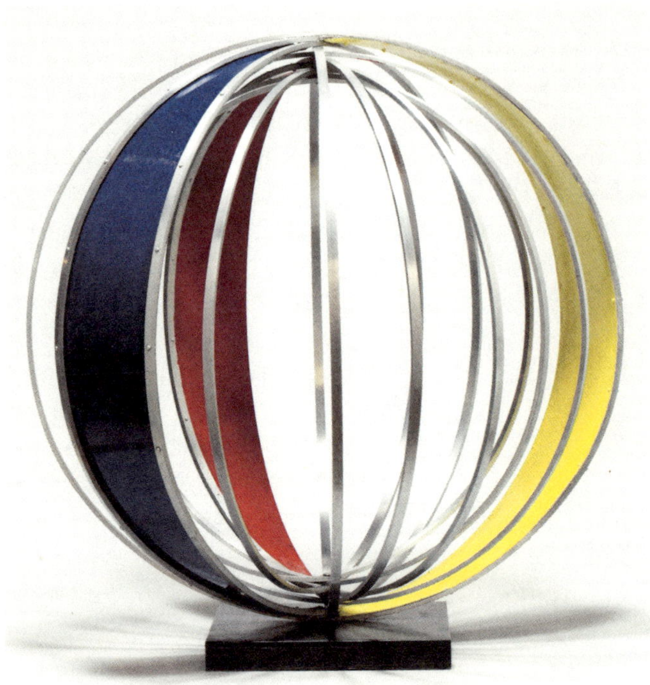

her seventieth birthday in St Ives, the *Guardian* reporting the attendance of 150 guests. Hepworth wrote to Margaret Gardiner following the event, 'I gather champagne was served from Paddington to St. Erth and brandy from St. Erth to Paddington!! [...] it really wouldn't have been so thrilling for me if you hadn't been able to come and I very much appreciate it. It was the first time I had ever seen all the grandchildren together and that was very exciting; I would like to live it all again in slow motion. I have now got back to work, thank goodness.'[28] When asked of her future plans by the *Guardian* at the event, Hepworth said, 'I detest a day of no work, no music, no poetry [...] It's all brewing in my mind, all I want is time.'[29] By 1974 she was largely confined to the upper room at Trewyn Studio where she slept, worked and lived, continuing to make sculpture with the aid of a few trusted assistants. She died in an accidental fire at the studio the following year.

Epilogue

In her last decade, Hepworth began to consider the future of Trewyn Studio. In 1965 she wrote to her solicitor that her son-in-law, Alan Bowness, a significant art historian and curator who would become Director of the Tate in 1980, 'had an idea that perhaps my studio here, Trewyn, might be a permanent site for the work'.[1] There were various precedents for artist studio museums, particularly the example of Romanian sculptor Constantin Brancusi, whose studio had made a profound impression on Hepworth when she had visited in 1933. Brancusi had left his studio to the French government on his death in 1956, and a partial reconstruction had opened to the public in 1962.[2] By 1972 Hepworth had written a memorandum to the Trustees of her Estate that they should consider:

> *establishing a permanent exhibition of some of my works in Trewyn Studio and its garden. I favour such an idea possibly with small sculptures, carvings and drawings being shown on the first floor, my working studio being shown as closely as possible as it had been in my lifetime and a few large works being shown in the garden.*[3]

The Barbara Hepworth Museum opened in April 1976, adhering to these wishes with a display of works in the upper room, the carving workshop retained as it was at her death to give a sense of her working process, and a selection of larger sculptures shown in the garden, for the most part in the specific locations that Hepworth had placed them herself.[4]

The museum proved popular with the public, receiving 10,000 visitors in just over four months. While initially run by the Hepworth Estate, in 1979 the museum was gifted to the nation and the management was taken over by Tate, who continue to run it to this day. Tate St Ives opened nearby in 1993 and, showing Hepworth's work held in the Tate Collection alongside other artists who had been based in St Ives, consolidated her association with the area. A major retrospective of Hepworth's work was curated in 1994 by Penelope Curtis and Alan Wilkinson, presented at Tate Liverpool and the Art Gallery of Ontario, Toronto, touring to the Yale Center for British Art in New Haven. Suggesting that since her death 'Barbara Hepworth and her work have become less well known to the general public', the thoroughly researched exhibition and catalogue aimed to 'reintroduce Hepworth to a wider audience'. In the accompanying 'Critical Forum' reader published by Liverpool University, Curtis wrote:

> *There has been a tendency to infer from Hepworth's work that she was a cool and disciplined person. However, if we were able to start instead with the person, we might be persuaded to discard this traditional reading, and infer from her personality that her work is about passion and zeal [...] She is both passionate and precise. She is extremely loyal to friends and to causes, energetic in making sure the right thing is done, intelligent but realistic. She cares about the detail as much as the wider cause, and one perceives the place of the detail within the lifestyle as a whole.*[5]

Curtis's subsequent monograph on Hepworth in 1998 as part of Tate's 'St Ives' Artists' series was followed in 1999 with a catalogue, *Barbara Hepworth: Works in the Tate Gallery Collection and the Barbara Hepworth Museum St Ives*, compiled by Matthew Gale and Chris Stephens. This looked at seventy-six works in depth, bringing together art historical information on their creation and reception with detailed analysis of their physical make-up and production. In 2003 a joint 'Centenary' exhibition was staged at Tate St Ives and Yorkshire Sculpture Park, with a concurrent exhibition of Hepworth's late polished bronze sculptures held at Wakefield Art Gallery.

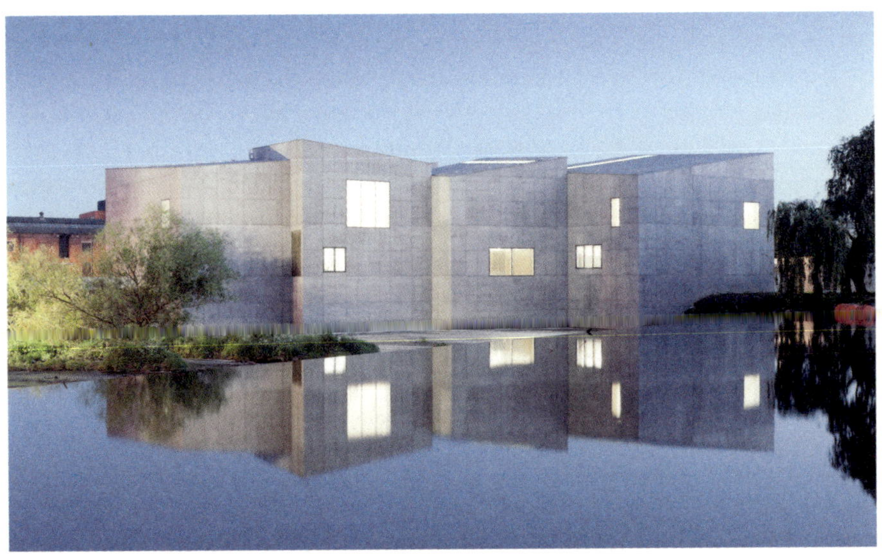

ABOVE The Hepworth Wakefield, designed
by David Chipperfield Architects.
Photograph by Iwan Baan

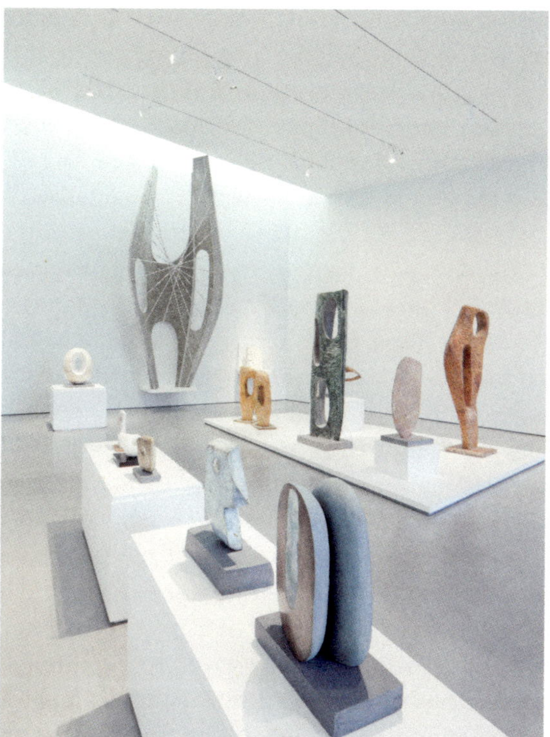

The same year, Wakefield Council launched an international RIBA (Royal Institute of British Architects) competition to find an architect to design a new art gallery for Hepworth's hometown of Wakefield. A new home for the Wakefield Permanent Art Collection had been sought for some time, as the facilities at Wakefield Art Gallery were increasingly inadequate. In 1997 Bowness had offered, on behalf of the Hepworth Estate trustees, a major gift of Hepworth's plaster and aluminium prototypes from which her bronze sculptures had been cast, provided they could be housed in 'a building of architectural distinction and museum standard'.[6] David Chipperfield Architects were selected to design the building, RIBA praising the 'human scale' of their proposal, while Chipperfield noted that 'the sculptural form of the museum may be seen as paying homage to Barbara Hepworth'.[7] In 2011 The Hepworth Wakefield opened, presenting the Wakefield Permanent Art Collection, which included works by Hepworth, the first acquired in 1940, alongside The Hepworth Family Gift of forty-four plaster and aluminium prototypes, a number of unfinished works and fragments, studio materials, tools and templates to present her working process.

ABOVE The Hepworth Family Gift gallery at The Hepworth Wakefield. Photograph by Iwan Baan

Since 2011, The Hepworth Wakefield's exhibition programme has brought contemporary art in dialogue with the permanent display of Hepworth's work. Hepworth always remained interested in younger artists, and in an interview shortly before her death she affirmed her engagement with the next generation: 'I think one must do all one can in painting and carving and music to make a link which is handed on.'[8] These dialogues, while existing in her lifetime, were continued posthumously. Between 1998 and 2000, Montserrat-born British artist Veronica Ryan undertook an artist residency based at the Palais de Danse,[9] and created new sculptures from some of Hepworth's unused marble which she was given by the Hepworth Estate.[10] Ryan described Hepworth as 'a friendly muse',[11] and found inspiration not only in her materials but also in her tools on view at the Barbara Hepworth Museum. A whisk in an overall pocket that Hepworth used to get air bubbles out of plaster suggested resourcefulness and a closeness of domestic labour and sculptural practice present in Ryan's own practice, which previously incorporated baby-wipe containers and continues to include textiles using techniques she learned from her mother.[12] Ryan also found inspiration in Hepworth's garden, particularly the magnolia pods growing there that reminded her of soursop fruits from Montserrat. She has recently returned to these, beginning to cast in plaster and suspend the forms, which she connects to Hepworth's irregular organic structures, as well as her own personal history.

Hepworth's studios in St Ives have continued to inspire contemporary artists. In 2009 sculptor Alice Channer wrote about Hepworth's garden, 'while moving around Barbara Hepworth's sculptures and writing about them, I am aware of them framing me as I am framing them. What interests me in Hepworth's work now is the way in which it can make relationships like these between people and objects happen in the present.'[13] The same year, collage and performance artist Linder was invited to visit the garden of Trewyn at night and recalled, 'we were encouraged to discover the sculptures purely through touch. Hepworth once said that every piece must be touched – that it was part of the way in which she made her work. So be it, Juno! Through stroking her sculptures in the dark, I fell in love.'[14] In 2012, inspired by Hepworth's *Family of Man*, and in the spirit of her musical and theatrical collaborations, Linder worked with Northern Ballet and The Hepworth Wakefield to create *The Ultimate Form* ballet. A major retrospective held at Tate Britain in 2015 aimed to reclaim Hepworth as a sculptor of international standing and toured to the Kröller-Müller Museum in Otterlo, The Netherlands, where Hepworth had particularly liked her exhibition in 1965, and to the Arp Museum in

Rolandseck, Germany. This was accompanied at Tate Britain by a commission from artist Charlotte Moth, whose archival intervention for the exhibition included a film she made of the Palais de Danse, intrigued by Hepworth's specific decisions relating to the display of her sculptures.

In 2016, The Hepworth Prize for Sculpture was established at The Hepworth Wakefield to honour artists making a significant contribution to the field of sculpture. Several of the inaugural nominees recognised the influence of Hepworth in different ways. Sculptor Phyllida Barlow, who represented Britain at the Venice Biennale the following year, admired the way in which Hepworth set up the physical interaction with the viewer, saying, '[she] teases us, restricting our view as we move around her protective surfaces, shielding forms within forms', while multi-media artist and musician Steve Claydon noted, 'her kind of modernism is bound up with cataclysmic events, with world wars and the fall of empire. It looks very solid but it's punctured with views into other spaces. It aspires to a kind of primitivism, but it's technological too.'[15] In 2019, artist Rosanne Robertson related their exploration of water and stone in connection with nature and queer bodies to Hepworth's interest in the human figure in the landscape, and recalled, 'I always thought of her figures as genderless.'[16] The diversity and range of these artistic interpretations of Hepworth speak to the breadth and complexity of her expansive philosophy and practice, its astonishing physical variety and universal reach. Her continued relevance to contemporary practice is fitting for an artist who ceaselessly sought to affirm the importance to sculpture of the present moment.

> *'What is the meaning of art, of sculpture in our time?',*
> *she suddenly asked. And she replied in these words –*
> *'Today when we are all conscious of the expanding universe,*
> *the forms experienced by the sculptor should express not*
> *only this consciousness but should, I feel, emphasize also the*
> *possibilities of new developments of the human spirit, so that*
> *it can affirm and continue life in its highest form. The story*
> *is still the same as that of the Greek or of any other culture.*
> *I mean – it does not matter what philosophy or which religion*
> *is involved; the point is that we must be aware of this extension*
> *of our knowledge of the universe and must utilize it in the*
> *service of the continuity of the human spirit.'[17]*

Notes

Introduction

1   *Barbara Hepworth: A Retrospective Exhibition of Carvings and Drawings from 1927 to 1954*, Whitechapel Art Gallery exh. cat., texts by Hepworth, section I, reprinted in Sophie Bowness (ed.), *Barbara Hepworth: Writings and Conversations* (London: Tate Publishing, 2015), p. 95. This compendium of Hepworth's writings and interviews, compiled by her granddaughter, provides an invaluable and easily accessible resource for further reading. Where original sources are reprinted here, I have given this as reference.

2   Gardiner published some of these letters in two memoirs, *Barbara Hepworth: A Memoir* (Edinburgh: The Salamander Press, 1982) and *A Scatter of Memories* (London: Free Association Books, 1988), both now out of print. The letters were acquired by Tate Archive in 2020 and assigned the reference TGA 202016, as yet uncatalogued. Here they join Hepworth's archive of letters from numerous correspondents (left by Hepworth in her will and deposited in batches from 1996, catalogue completed in 2014), her notebooks and manuscripts gifted in 2015, Nicholson's archive (TGA 8717) acquired in 1987, which includes over 350 letters from Hepworth, and Ramsden's archive (TGA 9310), which also includes significant correspondence from Hepworth and was acquired in 1993. Texts have been printed in this present volume with original spellings, grammar, punctuation and underlining; any editorial clarifications appear in square brackets.

3   Interview with Cindy Nemser, 1973, printed in C. Nemser (ed.), *Art Talk: Conversations with 15 Women Artists* (New York: IconEditions, 1975), p. 14, reprinted in S. Bowness (ed.), *Writings and Conversations*, op. cit., p. 251.

4   Ibid., p. 252.

5   Letter from Hepworth to E. H. Ramsden, October/ November 1944, Tate Archive TGA 9310.1.1.32.

6   Letter from Hepworth to Margaret Gardiner, 5 July 1944, TGA 202016.

7   *Barbara Hepworth: A Pictorial Autobiography* (Bath: Adams and Dart, 1970, extended ed. 1978, reprinted by Tate Publishing, 1985), p. 17.

8   'Yorkshire Couple's Daring Sculpture', *Yorkshire Evening News*, review of *An Exhibition of Sculpture by John Skeaping and Barbara Hepworth* held at Arthur Tooth & Sons gallery, 15 October–15 November 1930, cutting on display at Barbara Hepworth Museum.

9   F. W., 'Two Yorkshire Artists: London Painting and Sculpture Exhibitions', *The Yorkshire Post*, 29 September 1937, p. 5.

10   'In the Picture: Barbara Hepworth', *The Observer*, 13 May 1962, p. 26.

11   Cited in Robert Hughes, 'About Nothing Except Love: Visiting Barbara Hepworth in Cornwall', *The Bulletin*, Sydney, 19 May 1966, reprinted in S. Bowness (ed.), *Writings and Conversations*, op. cit., p. 189.

12   Letter from Hepworth to Gardiner, 'Mon'/'Tues' [probably 10/11 March 1947, dates suggested by Alan Bowness, 2005], TGA 202016.

13   'Two Conversations with Barbara Hepworth: Art and Life', dated 18 August 1959, printed in J. P. Hodin, *Barbara Hepworth* (London: Lund Humphries, 1961), p. 23, reprinted in S. Bowness (ed.), *Writings and Conversations*, op. cit., p. 126.

14   Conversation with Reg Butler, recorded on 28 September 1951 and broadcast on 26 August 1952 on the BBC Third Programme, 'Artists on Art', printed in S. Bowness (ed.), *Writings and Conversations*, op. cit., p. 52.

15   J. P. Hodin, 'Barbara Hepworth and the Mediterranean Spirit', *Marmo*, Milan, no. 3 (December 1964). Quotations from Hepworth of June 1963 also reprinted in S. Bowness (ed.), *Writings and Conversations*, op. cit., p. 171.

Chapter 1

1   B. Hepworth, 'Section I: 1927–1931', in *Barbara Hepworth: A Retrospective Exhibition of Carvings and Drawings from 1927 to 1954*, Whitechapel Art Gallery exh. cat., reprinted in S. Bowness (ed.), *Writings and Conversations*, op. cit., p. 94.

2   *Barbara Hepworth: Drawings from a Sculptor's Landscape* (London: Cory, Adams and Mackay, 1966), pp. 9–10.

3   *Pictorial Autobiography*, op. cit., p. 7.

4   Ibid., p. 11.

5   Lucy Kent, '"An Act of Praise": Religion and the Work of Barbara Hepworth', in Penelope Curtis and Chris Stephens (eds.), *Barbara Hepworth: Sculpture for a Modern World*, exh. cat. (London: Tate Publishing, 2015), p. 37.

6   *Drawings from a Sculptor's Landscape*, op. cit., p. 9.

7   *Pictorial Autobiography*, op. cit., p. 9.

8   Letter from Hepworth to Gardiner, undated [22 June 1950, date suggested by Alan Bowness, 2005], TGA 202016.

9   These photographs were commissioned in 1964 for the book *Drawings from a Sculptor's Landscape*, op. cit., in which Hepworth highlighted the impact of particular landscapes, including Yorkshire, on her work.

10   Letter from Hepworth to Ramsden, 'Saturday' [c. June 1943], TGA 9310.1.1.20.

11   *Pictorial Autobiography*, op. cit., p. 11.

12   Hodin, *Barbara Hepworth*, op. cit., p. 11.

13 *Pictorial Autobiography*,
    op. cit., p. 7.
14 Interview with Alan Wilkinson,
    quoted in A. Wilkinson, *The
    Drawings of Barbara Hepworth*
    (Farnham and Burlington:
    Lund Humphries, 2015), p. 14.
15 Recollections of Raymond
    Coxon, quoted in Gillian
    Spencer (foreword) and Alan
    Bowness (introduction),
    Barbara Hepworth: Early Life,
    exh. cat. (Wakefield: Wakefield
    Art Gallery, 1985), p. 11.
16 Alan Wilkinson (ed.),
    *Henry Moore: Writings and
    Conversations* (Farnham:
    Lund Humphries, 2002),
    pp. 42–3.
17 *Drawings from a Sculptor's
    Landscape*, op. cit., p. 10.
18 Ibid.
19 F. Rutter, 'New English Art
    Club', *The Sunday Times*,
    31 December 1922, p. 17.
20 'Restoring a Reputation', *The
    Telegraph*, 10 May 1974, p. 16.
21 *Pictorial Autobiography*,
    op. cit., p. 11.

Chapter 2

1   Editorial, 'The Shock of the
    Old: "Manet and the Post-
    Impressionists," 1910', *The
    Burlington Magazine*, vol. 152,
    no. 1293 (December 2010): 779.
2   P. G. Konody, 'Art Notes: Post-
    Impressionists at the Grafton
    Galleries', *The Observer*,
    13 November 1910, p. 9.
3   J. B., 'The Post-Impressionists',
    The Manchester Guardian,
    11 November 1910, p. 14.
4   R. E. Fry, 'Modern Art',
    Cambridge, Lecture I, 1920–29.
    Cambridge, King's College
    Archive Centre, Roger Elliot
    Fry Papers, REF1/92, quoted
    in Elizabeth Berkowitz,
    'The 1910 "Manet and the Post-
    Impressionists" Exhibition:
    Importance and Critical
    Issues.' *BRANCH: Britain,
    Representation and Nineteenth-
    Century History*. Dino Franco
    Felluga (ed.), Extension of
    *Romanticism and Victorianism
    on the Net*. Web 9 July 2020.
5   L. Housman, 'The Post-
    Impressionist Exhibition',
    The Manchester Guardian,
    4 October 1912, p. 10.
6   Alan Wilkinson (ed.),
    *Henry Moore: Writings and
    Conversations* (Farnham:
    Lund Humphries, 2002), p. 47.
7   Interview with Alan
    Wilkinson, quoted in
    Wilkinson, *The Drawings of
    Barbara Hepworth*, op. cit.,
    p. 19.
8   Ibid., p. 18.
9   Hepworth's report from
    Royal College of Art, for
    period ending July 1922.
    Royal College of Art Archive.
10 Sophie Bowness (ed.), *Barbara
    Hepworth: The Plasters. The
    Gift to Wakefield* (Farnham
    and Burlington: Lund
    Humphries, 2011), p. 34.
11 William Ordway Partridge,
    The Technique of Sculpture
    (first published 1895; reprinted
    Whitefish, MT: Kessinger
    Publishing, 2010), pp. 91–4.
12 Ann Compton, 'Crafting
    Modernism: Hepworth's
    Practice in the 1920s', in
    Curtis and Stephens (eds.),
    Sculpture for a Modern World,
    op. cit., p. 16; also Penelope
    Curtis, 'Barbara Hepworth
    and the Avant Garde of the
    1920s', in Penelope Curtis and
    Alan Wilkinson (eds.), *Barbara
    Hepworth: A Retrospective*, exh.
    cat. (London: Tate Publishing,
    1994), p. 12, fn. 3.
13 Hodin, *Barbara Hepworth*,
    op. cit., p. 11. Sophie Bowness
    points out that *Cahiers d'Art*
    began publication in 1926,
    so Hepworth could not
    have read it at this time.
    However, this later inaccurate
    recollection to Hodin is
    telling in reflecting the strong
    impression that French
    contemporary art had on her
    and her peers at this time.
14 'Leeds Art Students: Two
    in Final Examination for
    Rome Scholarships', from our
    London Correspondent, *Leeds
    Mercury*, 23 February 1924.
15 Quoted in P. Curtis, 'Barbara
    Hepworth and the Avant
    Garde of the 1920s', in Curtis
    and Wilkinson (eds.), *A
    Retrospective*, op. cit., p. 12.
16 *Daily Chronicle*, 7 March 1925.
17 *Barbara Hepworth: Carvings
    and Drawings* (London: Lund
    Humphries, 1952), section 1.
18 S. Bowness (ed.), *The Plasters*,
    op. cit., p. 102.
19 Leo Walmsley, *So Many Loves*
    (London: Collins, 1944; 2nd ed.,
    1969), p. 47. Hepworth thought
    this book was sensationalist
    trash, but it does provide
    enticing descriptions of her
    early years.
20 *Carvings and Drawings*,
    op. cit., section 1.

Chapter 3

1   Walmsley, *So Many Loves*,
    op. cit., p. 252.
2   See P. Curtis, 'Barbara
    Hepworth and the Avant
    Garde of the 1920s', in Curtis
    and Wilkinson (eds.), *A
    Retrospective*, op. cit., p. 19.
3   *Mamua* (*c.* 1926), by Alfred
    James Oakley, was acquired
    from the Royal Academy
    exhibition in 1926.
4   *Pictorial Autobiography*,
    op. cit., p. 13.
5   R. Bedford, 'Chinese Animal
    Sculpture', *Old Furniture* IV,
    August 1928: 223, quoted in
    P. Curtis, 'Barbara Hepworth
    and the Avant Garde of the
    1920s', in Curtis and Wilkinson
    (eds.), *A Retrospective*, op. cit.,
    p. 16.
6   For further description of
    The Mall Studios, see
    Caroline Maclean, *Circles
    and Squares: The Lives and Art
    of the Hampstead Modernists*
    (London: Bloomsbury, 2020),
    p. 15.
7   'Beaux Arts Gallery', *The
    Times*, 13 June 1928, p. 14.
8   Listed in the catalogue as
    Female Torso (cat. 11).
9   'Beaux Arts Gallery', *The
    Times*, op. cit.
10 *Carvings and Drawings*,
    op. cit., section 1.
11 Cats. 14–23. The titles all refer
    to figures, except for cat. 16
    (*Study for Light and Shadow*)
    and cat. 17 (*Study for Sculpture*).
    Alan Wilkinson notes, 'all
    but two of the ten are almost
    certainly life drawings'.
    Wilkinson, *The Drawings*

of Barbara Hepworth, op. cit., p. 25.

12 John Skeaping recalls in his autobiography, 'the exhibition was a sell-out, but more than that it brought considerable recognition'. Skeaping, *Drawn From Life: An Autobiography* (London: HarperCollins, 1977), quoted in ibid.

13 'Modern and African Sculpture' in *The Times*, 26 November 1928, p. 12. While the nine European artists were individually named, the African works were designated by their originating tribe or broad location, e.g., 'Bakota "Mask"', or 'Gabon "Head"'.

14 *Pictorial Autobiography*, op. cit., p. 17.

15 John Skeaping, *Drawn From Life: An Autobiography*, quoted in Wilkinson, *The Drawings of Barbara Hepworth*, op. cit., p. 31.

16 Letter from Hepworth to Ben Nicholson, describing Happisburgh when the group repeated the trip the following year, postmarked 14 August 1931, TGA 8717.1.1.46.

17 Hepworth refers to renegotiating her contract following her separation from Skeaping in 1931 (see also p. 50): letter from Hepworth to Nicholson, postmarked 2 October 1931, TGA 8717.1.1.56.

18 F. Rutter, 'Modern British Sculpture', *The Sunday Times*, 26 October 1930, p. 5.

19 Wood carvings were *Torso* (1929) (cat. 43), *Torso* (1929) (cat. 44), *Mask* (cat. 47), *Standing Figure* (cat. 40) and *Infant* (cat. 35).

20 Ann Compton, 'Crafting Modernism: Hepworth's Practice in the 1920s', in Curtis and Stephens (eds.), *Sculpture for a Modern World*, op. cit., p. 17.

21 B. Hepworth, 'Contemporary English Sculptors', *The Architectural Association Journal*, London, vol. XLV, no. 518 (April 1930), reprinted in S. Bowness (ed.), *Writings and Conversations*, op. cit., p. 14.

22 Ibid.

23 Wilkinson, *The Drawings of Barbara Hepworth*, op. cit., pp. 32–3.

24 *Carvings and Drawings*, op. cit., section 1.

Chapter 4

1 Letter from Hepworth to Nicholson, postmarked 13 December 1933, TGA 8717.1.1.161.

2 Letter from Hepworth to Nicholson, postmarked 14 August 1931, TGA 8717.1.1.46.

3 Beaux Arts Gallery in 1928, and Arthur Tooth & Sons in 1929. Nicholson had been invited into The Seven & Five exhibiting society by Hitchens in 1924 and had become its chair in 1925.

4 Letter from Hepworth to Nicholson, undated [summer 1931], TGA 8717.1.1.45.

5 Lucy Kent, '"An Act of Praise": Religion and the Work of Barbara Hepworth', in Curtis and Stephens (eds.), *Sculpture for a Modern World*, op. cit., fn. 15.

6 Maclean, *Circles and Squares*, op. cit., pp. 6–7.

7 Both copies are now held in Tate Archive, along with the rest of Hepworth's personal library.

8 Letter from Hepworth to Nicholson, postmarked 14 August 1931, TGA 8717.1.1.46.

9 *Pictorial Autobiography*, op. cit., p. 19.

10 Letter from Hepworth to Nicholson, postmarked 14 August 1931, TGA 8717.1.1.46.

11 Letters from Hepworth to Ben (TGA 8717.1.1.49 [*c.* 16 September 1931]) and Winifred (TGA 8717.1.4.25 [early August 1931]).

12 Letter from Hepworth to Nicholson, postmarked 24 September 1931, TGA 8717.1.1.50.

13 Letter from Hepworth to Nicholson, postmarked 29 September 1931, TGA 8717.1.1.52.

14 Letter from Hepworth to

Nicholson, postmarked 2 October 1931, TGA 8717.1.1.56.

15 Letter from Hepworth to Nicholson, postmarked 5 October 1931, TGA 8717.1.1.58.

16 Letter from Hepworth to Nicholson, postmarked 16 May 1932, TGA 8717.1.1.68.

17 Letter from Hepworth to Nicholson, postmarked 14 May 1932, TGA 8717.1.1.66.

18 Letter from Hepworth to Nicholson, 'Saturday', postmarked 24 March 1934, TGA 8717.1.1.175.

19 Letter from Hepworth to Nicholson, postmarked 2 April 1934, TGA 8717.1.1.181.

20 Letter from Hepworth to Nicholson, postmarked 22 July 1932, TGA 8717.1.1.82.

21 Letter from Hepworth to Nicholson, postmarked 22 July 1932, TGA 8717.1.1.82.

22 The latter was exhibited as *Woman* (cat. 2).

23 Letter from Hepworth to Nicholson, postmarked 3 September 1932, TGA 8717.1.1.102.

24 Letter from Hepworth to Nicholson, postmarked 7 September 1932, TGA 8717.1.1.106.

25 'The Aim of the Modern Artist: Barbara Hepworth, Ben Nicholson', *Studio*, London, vol. 104 (December 1932), reprinted in S. Bowness (ed.), *Writings and Conversations*, op. cit., p. 17.

26 Jim Ede wrote the foreword to Nicholson's paintings.

27 Read had already written an article on Moore's work, published in *The Listener*, 22 April 1931.

28 H. Read, 'Foreword', in *Carvings by Barbara Hepworth, Paintings by Ben Nicholson*, exh. cat. (London: Arthur Tooth & Sons Galleries, 1932), unpaginated.

29 Ibid.

30 P. Nash, 'Goings On: A Painter and a Sculptor', *Weekend Review*, 19 November 1932, p. 613.

31 Read, 'Foreword', in *Carvings by Barbara Hepworth, Paintings by Ben Nicholson*, op. cit.

32 Letter from Hepworth to

Nicholson, postmarked 27 December 1932, TGA 8717.1.1.125.

33 *Pictorial Autobiography*, op. cit., pp. 22–3.

34 Letter from Hepworth to Nicholson, undated [18 December 1933, date suggested by Alan Bowness, 2005], TGA 8717.1.1.165.

35 Sophie Bowness, 'Barbara Hepworth et Paris', in *Barbara Hepworth*, exh. cat. (Paris: Musée Rodin, 2019), p. 34.

36 New translation of an untitled text in *Abstraction-Création: art non-figuratif*, Paris, no. 2 (1933), published in S. Bowness (ed.), *Writings and Conversations*, op. cit., pp. 18–19. Hepworth's original text in English does not exist.

37 Letter from Hepworth to Nicholson, postmarked 8 December 1933, TGA 8717.1.1.157.

38 Letter from Nicholson to Hepworth, 22 December 1933, quoted in S. Bowness, 'Barbara Hepworth et Paris', in *Barbara Hepworth*, op. cit., p. 35.

39 Letter from Hepworth to Nicholson, postmarked 8 December 1933, TGA 8717.1.1.157.

40 The first exhibition staged by the newly reopened London gallery was *An Exhibition of Recent Paintings by English, French and German Artists*, and it included work by Miró, Arp, Picasso and Braque alongside Moore and Nash, among others.

41 Letter from Hepworth to Nicholson, postmarked 25 November 1933, TGA 8717.1.1.147.

42 Letter from Hepworth to Nicholson, postmarked 17 December 1932, TGA 8717.1.1.114.

43 Letter from Hepworth to Nicholson, postmarked December 1932, TGA 8717.1.1.128.

44 Letter from Hepworth to Nicholson, postmarked 17 December 1932, TGA 8717.1.1.114.

45 Letter from Hepworth to Nicholson, undated [*c*. June 1932, so dated due to the Diamond print reference], TGA 87171.1.74.

46 Letter from Hepworth to Nicholson, undated [July or September 1932], TGA 8717.1.1.97.

47 Letter from Hepworth to Nicholson, postmarked 19 December 1932, TGA 8717.1.1.116.

48 P. Nash, 'Unit One: A New Group of Artists', in Letters to the Editor, *The Times*, 12 June 1933.

49 Letter from Hepworth to Nicholson, postmarked 14 December 1933, TGA 8717.1.1.162.

50 Letter from Hepworth to Nicholson, postmarked 11 December 1933, TGA 8717.1.1.160.

51 Letter from Hepworth to Nicholson, postmarked 17 December 1933, TGA 8717.1.1.163.

52 Letter from Hepworth to Nicholson, postmarked 23 March 1934, TGA 8717.1.1.173.

53 Letter from Hepworth to Nicholson, postmarked 28 March 1934, TGA 8717.1.178.

54 B. Hepworth in *Unit One*, reprinted in *Pictorial Autobiography*, op. cit., p. 30.

Chapter 5

1 A. Stokes, 'Miss Hepworth's Carvings', *The Spectator*, 3 November 1933, reprinted in *Pictorial Autobiography*, op. cit., p. 29.

2 Letter from Hepworth to E. H. Ramsden, 4 April 1943, TGA 9310.1.1.15.

3 Letter from Hepworth to Gardiner, 19 February 1945, TGA 202016.

4 Letter from Hepworth to Nicholson, postmarked 17 May 1932, TGA 8717.1.1.72.

5 Letter from Hepworth to Nicholson, 'Sunday' [13 May 1934, date suggested by Alan Bowness, 2005], TGA 8717.1.1.189.

6 *Pictorial Autobiography*, op. cit., p. 31.

7 *Carvings and Drawings*, op. cit., section 2.

8 Letter from Hepworth to Ramsden, 4 April 1943, TGA 9310.1.1.15.

9 Letter from Hepworth to Nicholson, postmarked 20 December 1934, TGA 8717.1.1.197.

10 Ibid.

11 Letter from Hepworth to Nicholson, 'Friday' [postmarked 21 December 1934], TGA 8717.1.1.198.

12 Ibid.

13 Letter from Hepworth to Nicholson, postmarked 4 January 1935, TGA 8717.1.1.201.

14 Letter from Hepworth to Nicholson, postmarked 15 January 1935, TGA 8717.1.1.204.

15 Letter from Hepworth to Nicholson, postmarked 4 January 1935, TGA 8717.1.1.201.

16 Letter from Hepworth to Nicholson, 'Thursday' [postmarked 17 January 1935], TGA 8717.1.1.206.

17 Letter from Hepworth to Nicholson, postmarked 4 January 1935, TGA 8717.1.1.201.

18 *Carvings and Drawings*, op. cit., section 3.

19 For an account of how *Axis* was established, see Maclean, *Circles and Squares*, op. cit., p. 180.

20 Letter from Hepworth to Nicholson, 'Sat' [4 May 1935, after *Axis 2* published], TGA 8717.1.1.209.

21 H. Frankfort, 'New Works by Barbara Hepworth', *Axis*, no. 3 (July 1935): 16.

22 Letter from Hepworth to Nicholson, postmarked 20 December 1935, TGA 8717.1.1.214. Summerson married Hepworth's sister Elizabeth in March 1938.

23 New translation of an untitled text in *Abstraction-Création: art non-figuratif*, Paris, no. 2 (1933), published in S. Bowness (ed.), *Writings and Conversations*, op. cit., pp. 18–19.

24 *Carvings and Drawings*, op. cit., section 3.

25 Letter from Hepworth to Nicholson, postmarked 16 January 1935, TGA 8717.1.1.205.

26 Letter from Hepworth to Nicholson, postmarked 12 January 1935, TGA 8717.1.1.203.

27 New translation of an untitled text in *Abstraction-Création: art non-figuratif*, Paris, no. 2 (1933), published in S. Bowness (ed.), *Writings and Conversations*, op. cit., pp. 18–19.

28 Hepworth describes meeting a number of those listed in a letter to Nicholson, postmarked 21 December 1935, TGA 8717.1.1.215, among other items of correspondence.

29 Letter from Hepworth to Nicholson, 'Monday', postmarked 13 January 1936, TGA 8717.1.1.231.

30 Letter from Hepworth to Nicholson, postmarked 2 January 1936, TGA 8717.1.1.222.

31 Letter from Hepworth to Nicholson, postmarked 22 January 1936, TGA 8717.1.1.233. She continues: 'I had 22 telephone calls yesterday – nearly all business – I saw 11 people & made 16 calls myself! Today nearly as bad. Could you please tell me how your insurance stands for work for the Abstract show – is it covered for all journeys? The insurance we have to see to Nic says.'

32 Letter from Hepworth to Nicholson, undated [before 24 January 1936], TGA 8717.1.1.235.

33 'The Machine Age: Artistic Reactions', *The Times*, 24 April 1936, p. 21.

34 'London Art Shows: Impressionist and Abstract', *The Manchester Guardian*, 24 April 1936, p. 16.

35 T. W. Earp, 'Geometry in Colours: The Art of Squares and Circles', *The Daily Telegraph*, 28 April 1936, p. 22.

Chapter 6

1 N. Gabo, 'Constructive Art', *The Listener*, 4 November 1936: 846.

2 Ibid.

3 H. Read, 'The First British Artists' Congress', *The Listener*, 28 April 1937: 816.

4 G. Lansbury, 'My Meeting with Hitler', *The Listener*, 28 April 1937: 818.

5 *Carvings and Drawings*, op. cit., section 3.

6 Letter from Hepworth to Nicholson, 12 May 1937, TGA 8717.1.1.240. The book was published to coincide with an exhibition, *Constructive Art*, at the London Gallery, which had recently been established by Hepworth's neighbour, Roland Penrose, and his fellow surrealist, E. L. T. Mesens.

7 Gropius's wife, Ise, was Jewish, and the Nazi authorities suspected Gropius of 'disloyalty and embezzlement'; see Maclean, *Circles and Squares*, op. cit., p. 88.

8 N. Gabo, L. Martin and B. Nicholson (eds.), *Circle: International Survey of Constructive Art* (London: Faber and Faber, 1937; repr. 1971), p. 113.

9 Ibid.

10 Ibid., p. 115.

11 Ibid.

12 Ibid., p. 116.

13 Ibid.

14 Ibid.

15 Letter from Hepworth to Nicholson, 12 May 1937, TGA 8717.1.1.240.

16 Gabo, Martin and Nicholson (eds.), *Circle*, op. cit., p. 121.

17 Ibid., pp. 151–53.

18 Letter from Hepworth to Nicholson, postmarked 30 December 1935, TGA 8717.1.1.221. Hepworth's remark relates to John Desmond ('Des') Bernal and Margaret ('Marg.') Gardiner.

19 J. D. Bernal, 'Foreword', in *Catalogue of Sculpture by Barbara Hepworth*, exh. cat. (London: Alex Reid & Lefevre Ltd, 1937).

20 Ibid.

21 Hepworth's papers held in Tate Archive include several pages of ball-point drawings of geometric, crystalline forms alongside their proper names, e.g., 'orthorhombic bi-sphenoid' or 'icositetrahedron'; TGA 201518.

22 Bernal, 'Foreword', in *Catalogue of Sculpture*, op. cit.

23 Ibid.

24 Letter from Hepworth to Nicholson, postmarked 12 October 1937, TGA 8717.1.1.243.

25 'For Intellectual Liberty', *Nature* 139, 30 January 1937: 188; see https://doi.org/10.1038/139188c0

26 Bernal, 'Foreword', in *Catalogue of Sculpture*, op. cit.

27 Ibid.

28 Ibid.

29 'Art Out-of-Doors', *Architectural Review*, April 1939, p. 200, quoted in Matthew Gale and Chris Stephens, *Barbara Hepworth: Works in the Tate Gallery Collection and the Barbara Hepworth Museum St Ives* (London: Tate Publishing, 1999), p. 71.

30 *Pictorial Autobiography*, op. cit., p. 39.

31 *Carvings and Drawings*, op. cit., section 3.

32 Quoted in Sophie Bowness, 'Mondrian in London: Letters to Ben Nicholson and Barbara Hepworth', *The Burlington Magazine*, vol. 132, no. 1052 (November 1990): 783.

33 *Carvings and Drawings*, op. cit., section 3.

34 Ibid.

35 S. Bowness (ed.), *Writings and Conversations*, op. cit., p. 29.

36 Quoted in E. H. Ramsden, *An Introduction to Modern Art* (London, New York, Toronto: Oxford University Press, 1940), p. 4. Hepworth wrote to Ramsden praising this book; see letter from Hepworth to Ramsden, 7 May 1940, TGA 9310.1.1.3.

37 *Pictorial Autobiography*, op. cit., p. 41.

38 Letter from Mondrian to Hepworth, dated 12 November 1939, reproduced

in Sophie Bowness, 'Mondrian in London: Letters to Ben Nicholson and Barbara Hepworth', *The Burlington Magazine*, vol. 132, no. 1052 (November 1990): 784.
39 S. Bowness (ed.), *Writings and Conversations*, op. cit., p. 29.

Chapter 7

1 *Carvings and Drawings*, op. cit., section 3. This first *Sculpture with Colour (Deep Blue and Red)* (BH 113A) was broken up after being cast in bronze in 1961. Then came a further five plaster carvings, *Sculpture with Colour (Deep Blue and Red)* (BH 117 A–D 1940, BH 117 E 1942). The final *Sculpture with Colour (Deep Blue and Red)* (BH 118 1943) was larger and carved in wood.
2 Lawrence Gowing (ed.), *The Critical Writings of Adrian Stokes: Vol. II, 1937–58* (London: Thames & Hudson, 1978), p. 36.
3 *Carvings and Drawings*, op. cit., section 4. This association perhaps came later, as she wrote in 1943 that she had 'carved a larger version in wood (painted), I should love to make it larger against the sea & sky as we have it here'. Letter from Hepworth to Ramsden, 4 April 1943, TGA 9310.1.1.15.
4 Letter from Hepworth to Read, 29 November 1940, Herbert Read Archive, University of Victoria, British Columbia, Special Collections, HR/BH-9.
5 *Pictorial Autobiography*, op. cit., p. 42.
6 Letter from Hepworth to Nicholson [Christmas 1939/40], TGA 8717.1.1.244.
7 Letter from Hepworth to Nicholson, undated [2 October 1941, as the letter refers to birth of triplets; '7 years ago tonight since we went to the pictures before I produced three babies'], TGA 8717.1.1.256.
8 Letter from Hepworth to Nicholson, undated [21 September 1941, date suggested by Alan Bowness, 2005], TGA 8717.1.1.248.
9 Moore moved out of London in autumn 1940 after the studio was bombed, resulting in the destruction of several of Hepworth's sculptures that had been left.
10 Ramsden, 'Preface', in *An Introduction to Modern Art*, op. cit., n.p.
11 Letter from Hepworth to Ramsden, 7 May 1940, TGA 9310.1.1.3.
12 Letter from Hepworth to Ramsden, undated [late November 1941?], TGA 9310.1.1.7.
13 *Carvings and Drawings*, op. cit., section 4.
14 Letter from Hepworth to Nicholson, undated [25 September 1941, date suggested by Alan Bowness, 2005], TGA 8717.1.1.251.
15 Letter from Hepworth to Nicholson, undated [13 October 1941, date suggested by Alan Bowness, 2005], TGA 8717.1.1.263.
16 Letter from Hepworth to Nicholson, undated [13 October 1941, date suggested by Alan Bowness, 2005], TGA 8717.1.1.264.
17 Letter from Hepworth to Nicholson, undated [7 May 1942, date suggested by Alan Bowness, 2005], TGA 8717.1.1.269.
18 *Carvings and Drawings*, op. cit., section 5.
19 *Carvings and Drawings*, op. cit., section 5.
20 Letter from Hepworth to Nicholson, undated [26 September 1941, date suggested by Alan Bowness, 2005], TGA 8717.1.1.252.
21 Letter from Hepworth to Nicholson, undated [13 October 1941, date suggested by Alan Bowness, 2005], TGA 8717.1.1.263.
22 Letter from Hepworth to Eates, undated, TGA 9310.1.1.7.
23 Letter from Hepworth to Gardiner, 'Mon'/'Thurs' [September 1942, date suggested by Alan Bowness, 2005], TGA 202016.
24 Letter from Hepworth to Nicholson, postmarked 4 May 1942, TGA 8717.1.1.266.
25 W. S. Churchill, 'Alliance with Russia', 22 June 1941; see https://winstonchurchill.org/resources/speeches/1941-1945-war-leader/the-fourth-climacteric/ [accessed 5 May 2019].
26 Letter from Hepworth to Nicholson, undated [26 September 1941, date suggested by Alan Bowness, 2005], TGA 8717.1.1.252.
27 Letter from Hepworth to Nicholson, undated [7 May 1942, date suggested by Alan Bowness, 2005], TGA 8717.1.1.268. She continues, 'Could you arrange something for me? I don't know what you've done with my various carvings – but the ones I should like to show are (1) Conicoid (teak) [sketch] (which you were taking to Leslie) because I think it might sell, (2) [sketch of *Three Forms*] which Brumwell has if he ever uses his car & could deliver it at 113 High Holborn (3) & then I'll send a drawing.'
28 Letter from Hepworth to Nicholson, postmarked 4 May 1942, TGA 8717.1.1.266.
29 Letter from Hepworth to Gardiner, undated [early 1943, date suggested by Alan Bowness, 2005], TGA 202016.
30 Ibid.
31 Letter from Hepworth to Gardiner, 'Thurs' [May or June 1943, dates suggested by Alan Bowness, 2005], TGA 202016.
32 *Carvings and Drawings*, op. cit., section 4.
33 Letter from Hepworth to Ramsden, undated [*c.* 1943, re. *New Movements in Art*, written from Chy-an-Kerris], TGA 9310.1.1.12.
34 Letter from Hepworth to Ramsden, undated [early 1943], TGA 9310.1.1.13.
35 Letter from Hepworth to Ramsden, undated [June 1943, re. Temple Newsam exhibition], TGA 9310.1.1.20.
36 W. Gibson, 'Modern Art at Temple Newsam', *The Listener*, 20 May 1943: 606.

37 Letter from Hepworth to Ramsden, undated [June 1943, re. Temple Newsam exhibition], TGA 9310.1.1.20.

38 Ibid.

39 Ibid. Ramsden preferred to use her ungendered second name, 'Hartley'.

40 Letter from Hepworth to Gardiner, 'Thurs' [May or June 1943, dates suggested by Alan Bowness, 2005], TGA 202016.

41 Ibid.

42 Letter from Hepworth to Ramsden, 8 March 1944, TGA 9310.1.1.25.

43 Letter from Hepworth to Gardiner, 'Thursday' [24 June 1943, date suggested by Alan Bowness, 2005], TGA 202016.

44 Ibid.

45 'Approach to Sculpture', *The Studio*, London, vol. CXXXII, no. 643 (October 1946): 97–8.

46 Ibid.: 101.

47 'Living British Artists', *The Yorkshire Post*, 16 May 1936, p. 16.

48 Letter from Hepworth to Musgrave, 7 December 1942, Wakefield Art Gallery Archive, THW 1/2/3/1 Box 12.

49 Letter from Hepworth to Musgrave, 31 January 1944, Wakefield Art Gallery Archive, THW 1/2/3/1 Box 12.

50 Letter from Hepworth to Musgrave, 22 February 1944, Wakefield Art Gallery Archive, THW 1/2/3/1 Box 12.

51 Letter from Hepworth to Ramsden, undated [*c.* spring 1944], TGA 9310.1.1.26.

52 Letter from Hepworth to Eates, 21 November [1944? as the letter mentions the publishing of Leo Walmsley's *So Many Loves*], TGA 9310.1.1.33.

53 Letter from Hepworth to Gardiner, 17 May 1944, TGA 202016.

54 Ibid.

55 Letter from Hepworth to Ramsden, 'Thurs' [October or November 1944], TGA 9310.1.1.32.

56 Referring to the Normandy landings of 6 June 1944.

57 Letter from Hepworth to Gardiner, 10 July 1944, TGA 202016.

58 Letter from Hepworth to Nicholson, undated [September 1943, date suggested by Alan Bowness, 2005; the letter mentions the Wakefield exhibition, which took place February–March 1944], TGA 8717.1.1.278.

59 Letter from Hepworth to Ramsden, undated [late summer 1944], TGA 9310.1.1.31.

60 This was around the time of the Normandy landings. Hepworth possibly alludes to the 'Careless Talk Costs Lives' propaganda campaign, which discouraged writing about specific political events for fear of information being intercepted by enemy spies.

61 Letter from Hepworth to Gardiner, 'Sunday' [refers to 'mid-June': 11 or 18 June 1944, dates suggested by Alan Bowness, 2005], TGA 202016.

62 Letter from Hepworth to Ramsden, undated [late summer 1944], TGA 9310.1.1.31.

63 Hepworth considered joining the Communist Party, but was put off by several points: 'If I could see the faintest glimmer of hope that the C.P. could offer creative integrity to the artist I should endeavour to work my passage to be a P. member. I don't see it & so I can work more clearly "free" & through my own sculptural integrity.' Letter from Hepworth to Gardiner, dated 'Nov. 5th' [1944, date suggested by Alan Bowness, 2005], TGA 202016; 'Yes, I would like to join the Party but for 3 things (1) I have a primary allegiance – to aesthetics – & it would always come first (2) I don't know how it would affect my relationship with Ben (3) I can't make up my mind whether I'm emotionally stable – that is, should I want to be free the moment I gave my word to a set thing which I could not control?' Letter from Hepworth to Gardiner, dated 'Wed 13th' [December 1944, date

suggested by Alan Bowness, 2005], TGA 202016.

64 Letter from Hepworth to Ramsden, undated [late summer 1944], TGA 9310.1.1.31.

65 Letter from Hepworth to Gardiner, 17 May 1944, TGA 202016.

66 Letter from Hepworth to Gardiner, 5 July 1944, TGA 202016.

67 *La Libération de Paris* (The Liberation of Paris), a short historical documentary shot in secret by small units of the French Resistance during the Battle for Paris in August 1944.

68 Letter from Hepworth to Gardiner, 'Sunday' [8 or 15 October 1944, dates suggested by Alan Bowness, 2005], TGA 202016.

69 *Carvings and Drawings*, op. cit., section 4.

70 Letter from Hepworth to Gardiner, 'Fri' [8 December 1944, date suggested by Alan Bowness, 2005], TGA 202016.

71 Ibid.

72 Letter from Hepworth to Gardiner, 'Mon' [19 February 1945, date suggested by Alan Bowness, 2005], TGA 202016.

73 Letter from Hepworth to Gardiner, '3 February' [1945, based on the possible Tate Acquisition, date suggested by Alan Bowness, 2005], TGA 202016.

74 Letter from Hepworth to Nicholson, undated [before 11 May 1945], TGA 8717.1.1.287.

75 Letter from Hepworth to Nicholson '11 May' [1945; Hepworth sees the Belsen film], TGA 8717.1.1.288.

76 Letter from Hepworth to Gardiner, 'Tues' [15 May 1945, date suggested by Alan Bowness, 2005], TGA 202016.

77 Letter from Hepworth to Nicholson, '11 May' [1945], TGA 8717.1.1.288.

Chapter 8

1 Description taken from a compendium of *World Review* articles, *This Changing World*

(London: Routledge, 1945), title page.

2 Letter from Hepworth to Ramsden, 25 June 1941, TGA 9310.1.1.5.

3 Letter from Hepworth to Ramsden, 4 April 1943, TGA 9310.1.1.15.

4 Ibid.

5 Ibid.

6 Edouard Roditi, 'Barbara Hepworth' (interview), in *Dialogues on Art*, London, 1960, reprinted in S. Bowness (ed.), *Writings and Conversations*, op. cit., p. 134.

7 Letter from Hepworth to Ramsden, dated 28 April [1943], TGA 9310.1.1.16.

8 Letter from Hepworth to Ramsden, undated [1943], TGA 9310.1.1.17.

9 E. H. Ramsden, 'Barbara Hepworth: Sculptor', *Horizon*, vol. 7, no. 42 (June 1943): 419.

10 Letter from Hepworth to Ramsden, undated [1943], TGA 9310.1.1.18.

11 *Carvings and Drawings*, op. cit., section 4.

12 Ibid.

13 Letter from Hepworth to Gardiner, 24 September [1943, date suggested by Alan Bowness, 2005], TGA 202016.

14 'The Sculptor Speaks', recorded talk for the British Council, 8 December 1961, printed in S. Bowness (ed.), *Writings and Conversations*, op. cit., p. 155.

15 H. Read (foreword), *Exhibition of Sculpture and Drawings by Barbara Hepworth*, Wakefield Art Gallery exh. cat., reprinted in *Pictorial Autobiography*, op. cit., p. 46.

16 Letter from Hepworth to Ramsden, undated [*c.* 1945?], TGA 9310.1.1.35.

17 Letter from Hepworth to Nicholson, 12 May 1945, TGA 8717.1.1.289.

18 Ibid.

19 *Carvings and Drawings*, op. cit., section 4.

20 *Barbara Hepworth: A Retrospective Exhibition of Carvings and Drawings from 1927 to 1954*, Whitechapel Art Gallery exh. cat., texts by Hepworth, section I, reprinted

21 E. H. Ramsden, *Sculpture: Theme and Variations. Towards a Contemporary Aesthetic* (London: Lund Humphries, 1953), p. 42.

22 Text on Ascher scarf design, 'Landscape Sculpture', dated June 1947, printed in S. Bowness (ed.), *Writings and Conversations*, op. cit., p. 38.

23 Letter from Hepworth to Nicholson, undated [October 1945, before Nicholson's Lefevre exhibition], TGA 8717.1.1.294.

24 S. Bowness (ed.), *Writings and Conversations*, op. cit., p. 34.

25 *Carvings and Drawings*, op. cit., section 4.

26 Read, 'Introduction', in ibid., p. x.

27 *Barbara Hepworth: A Retrospective Exhibition of Carvings and Drawings from 1927 to 1954*, Whitechapel Art Gallery exh. cat., texts by Hepworth, section I, reprinted in S. Bowness (ed.), *Writings and Conversations*, op. cit., p. 95.

28 In speaking of the unconscious, Hepworth was perhaps informed by her reading of Jung, as she noted to Gardiner, 'there was that fine talk by Jung – printed in this last week's Listener. Have you read it? I found it quite remarkable & intensely reassuring. I have scored it all over.'

29 Letter from Hepworth to Ramsden, undated [*c.* 1946], TGA 9310.1.1.39.

30 Letter from Hepworth to Gardiner, 'Friday' [21 or 28 February 1947, dates suggested by Alan Bowness, 2005], TGA 202016.

31 Letter from Hepworth to Nicholson, undated [September 1945, date suggested by Alan Bowness, 2005], TGA 8717.1.1.291.

32 Letter from Hepworth to Nicholson, undated [October 1945], TGA 8717.1.1.295.

33 Letter from Hepworth to Nicholson, undated

in S. Bowness (ed.), *Writings and Conversations*, op. cit., p. 95.

[October 1945, suggested by reference to Nicholson exhibition at Lefevre Gallery], TGA 8717.1.1.298.

34 Letter from Hepworth to Nicholson, undated [October 1945, date suggested by Alan Bowness, 2005], TGA 8717.1.1.299.

35 Letter from Hepworth to Ramsden, undated [1946?], TGA 9310.1.1.46.

36 Letter from Hepworth to Gardiner, 'Tues night' [3 or 10 September 1946, dates suggested by Alan Bowness, 2005], TGA 202016.

37 Letter from Hepworth to Ramsden, undated [*c.* May/June 1946], TGA 9310.1.1.43.

38 S. Bowness (ed.), *Writings and Conversations*, op. cit., p. 37.

39 Letter from Hepworth to Ramsden, undated [*c.* May/June 1946], TGA 9310.1.1.43.

40 The work was eventually titled *Elegy*.

41 Letter from Hepworth to Ramsden, undated [*c.* August 1946, as the letter mentions a storm, also mentioned to Gardiner in a letter postmarked 10 August], TGA 9310.1.1.45.

42 W. Lewis, 'Henry Moore and Barbara Hepworth', *The Listener*, 17 October 1946: 506.

43 E. Newton, 'The Sculptor Returns', *The Sunday Times*, 10 October 1946, p. 3.

44 M. Collis, 'Old Masters and New', *The Observer*, 6 October 1946, p. 2.

45 Letter from Hepworth to Ramsden, undated [*c.* November 1946], TGA 9310.1.1.50.

46 Letter from Hepworth to Eates, undated [*c.* 30 September 1946 re. delivery of artwork for exhibition], TGA 9310.1.1.48.

47 Letter from Hepworth to Ramsden, undated [*c.* October/November 1946], TGA 9310.1.1.49.

48 Letter from Hepworth to Ramsden, undated [*c.* October 1946], TGA 9310.1.1.47.

49 E. H. Ramsden, 'The Sculpture of Barbara Hepworth', *Polemic: A Magazine of Philosophy,*

Psychology, and Aesthetics, no. 5
(September–October 1946): 33.
50 Ibid.
51 Ibid.: 34.

Chapter 9

1 Letter from Hepworth
to Gardiner, 'Sunday'
[10 November 1946, date
suggested by Alan Bowness,
2005], TGA 202016.
2 *Carvings and Drawings*,
op. cit., section 5.
3 Quoted in Gale and Stephens,
*Works in the Tate Gallery
Collection and the Barbara
Hepworth Museum St Ives*,
op. cit., p. 102.
4 Letter from Hepworth to
Ramsden, undated [*c.* June 1947],
TGA 9310.1.1.57. The sculptors
listed are Henry Moore, Frank
Dobson, Charles Wheeler, Jacob
Epstein and Eric Kennington.
5 Letter from Nicholson to
Helen Sutherland, postmarked
27 November 1947, quoted in
Gale and Stephens, *Works in
the Tate Gallery Collection and
the Barbara Hepworth Museum
St Ives*, op. cit., p. 105.
6 The assessors wrote in
November 1947, 'we do not
consider that any of the four
schemes submitted can be
adjudged suitable for the
position that they are intended
to occupy'. They suggested
extending the deadline to
allow Epstein and Moore
to complete their entries,
but by 2 February 1948 it
was decided 'that no action
be taken' to further the
competition. Quoted in Gale
and Stephens, ibid., p. 104.
The plinths remain empty.
7 Letter from Hepworth to
Giedion, 10 September 1947,
printed in S. Bowness (ed.),
Writings and Conversations,
op. cit., p. 40.
8 Ibid.
9 Letter from Hepworth to
Gardiner, 'Mon'/'Tues'
[10/11 March 1947, date
suggested by Alan Bowness,
2005], TGA 202016.
10 Ibid.
11 Ibid.

12 Writing to Gardiner, 'I'm
bored because I may have to
go into hospital again – (same
thing the other side, damn
it) – & it will break the
threads of my work.' Letter
from Hepworth to Gardiner,
'Wed' [19 March 1947, date
suggested by Alan Bowness,
2005], TGA 202016.
13 Letter from Hepworth to
Gardiner, 'Mon'/'Tues'
[10/11 March 1947, date
suggested by Alan Bowness,
2005], TGA 202016.
14 Letter from Hepworth
to Gardiner, 'Thurs'
[27 March 1947, date
suggested by Alan Bowness,
2005], TGA 202016.
15 *Carvings and Drawings*,
op. cit., section 5.
16 Quoted in Nathaniel Hepburn,
*Barbara Hepworth: The
Hospital Drawings* (London:
Tate Publishing, 2012), p. 84.
17 Gale and Stephens, *Works in
the Tate Gallery Collection and
the Barbara Hepworth Museum
St Ives*, op. cit., p. 110.
18 B. Hepworth, 'The Artist's
View of Surgery', quoted
in Hepburn, *The Hospital
Drawings*, op. cit., p. 86.
19 Ibid., p. 97.
20 *Carvings and Drawings*,
op. cit., section 5.
21 Gale and Stephens, *Works in
the Tate Gallery Collection and
the Barbara Hepworth Museum
St Ives*, op. cit., p. 107.
22 This may also have been due
to time spent on the Waterloo
Bridge commission, for which
she made five sculptures,
which are included in the
catalogue raisonne, though not
listed in the sculpture record.
Other works are double dated.
23 Letter from Hepworth to
Nicholson, undated [late
January 1948, date suggested
by Alan Bowness, 2005],
TGA 8717.1.1.320.
24 Quoted in H. Read, 'Barbara
Hepworth: A New Phase', *The
Listener*, 8 April 1948: 592.
25 Letter from Hepworth to
Read, 6 March 1948, Herbert
Read Archive, HR/BH-99-102.
26 Quoted in Hepburn, *The
Hospital Drawings*, op. cit., p. 81.

27 Ibid., pp. 114–15.
28 Ibid., p. 81.
29 Letter from Hepworth to Read,
6 March 1948, Herbert Read
Archive, HR/BH-99-102.
30 Letter from Hepworth
to Nicholson, undated
[May 1948, date suggested by
Alan Bowness, 2005], TGA
8717.1.1.328.
31 Ibid.
32 Hormone Replacement
Therapy (HRT), now used
to ameliorate the effects
of the menopause, was not
introduced until 1960.
33 Letter from Hepworth to
Nicholson, undated
[summer 1948, suggested
by Alan Bowness, 2005],
TGA 8717.1.1.331.
34 Letter from Hepworth to
Gardiner, 'Tues'/'Wed'
[26/27 April 1949, dates
suggested by Alan Bowness,
2005], TGA 202016.
35 Letter from Hepworth to
Gardiner, '26 May' [1949,
date suggested by Alan
Bowness, 2005], TGA 202016.
36 *Carvings and Drawings*,
op. cit., section 5.
37 P. Heron, 'The Return of the
Image', *The New Statesman*,
18 February 1950.
38 Letter from Hepworth
to Ramsden, undated [*c.*
June 1949], TGA 9310.1.1.60.
39 Letter from Hepworth to
Ramsden, undated [1949, as
the letter refers to Duncan
MacDonald's death],
TGA 9310.1.1.62.
40 Letter from Hepworth to
Ramsden, undated [*c.* 1950?],
TGA 9310.1.1.65.
41 Letter from Hepworth
to Ramsden, undated
[June 1949, date suggested
by Alan Bowness, 2005],
TGA 9310.1.1.61.
42 *Pictorial Autobiography*,
op. cit., p. 52.
43 For more on the history,
development and different
usages of the spaces in Trewyn
Studio, see Sophie Bowness,
The Sculptor in the Studio
(London: Tate Publishing,
2017).
44 *Carvings and Drawings*,
op. cit., section 5.

Chapter 10

1 *Carvings and Drawings,*
op. cit., section 5.

2 Letter from Hepworth to
Read [written 12 January 1943,
datable by Hepworth's
reference to her recent
fortieth birthday], Herbert
Read Archive, HR/BH-55,
quoted in Penelope Curtis,
'What is Left Unsaid', in
David Thistlewood (ed.),
Barbara Hepworth Reconsidered
(Liverpool: Liverpool
University Press, 1996), p. 158.

3 Letter from Lilian
Somerville, Director of Fine
Arts Department, British
Council, to Hepworth,
2 December 1949, National
Archives, GB/641/43c(1).

4 Letter from Somerville to
Philip James, Art Director of
the Arts Council requesting
work for loan to the exhibition,
27 January 1950, GB/641/43c(1).

5 Letter from Hepworth to Read,
12 January 1950, GB/641/43c(1).

6 Letter from Hepworth to
Somerville, 9 December 1949,
GB/641/43c(1).

7 Letter from Hepworth to
Somerville, 18 January 1950,
GB/641/43c(1).

8 Letter from Hepworth to
Somerville, 17 March 1950,
GB/641/43c(1).

9 Hepworth specifically requests
Drawing for Stone Sculpture
(1947), one of the first of this
body of work.

10 Letter from Somerville to
Hepworth, 30 March 1950,
GB/641/43c(1).

11 British Council 'Report of the
British Participation in the
25th Biennale Art Exhibition
Venice, June–October, 1950',
p. 3, GB/641/43c(1).

12 'The Venice Biennale –
Wanted, A Patron', *The
Manchester Guardian,*
24 August 1950, p. 4.

13 'Constable Attracts Italian
Crowds', *The Manchester
Guardian,* 9 June 1950, p. 10.

14 Eric Newton, 'Venetian
Biennale', *The Sunday Times,*
25 June 1950, p. 4.

15 'Extract from a personal letter
from Barbara Hepworth to

Mrs. Somerville about the
Venice Biennale, 1950', dated
5 June 1950, GB/641/43c(1).

16 Letter from Hepworth to
Eates, 28 July 1950 (from
Trewyn Studio; address on
paper circled in pen), TGA
9310.1.1.63.

17 *Carvings and Drawings,*
op. cit., section 6.

18 Letter from Hepworth to
Miss McLeod, Secretary for
the Exhibition in Venice,
27 March 1950, GB/641/43c(1).

19 Letter from Hepworth to
Somerville, 4 April 1950,
GB/641/43c(1).

20 'Text for broadcast in USA',
printed in S. Bowness (ed.),
Writings and Conversations,
op. cit., p. 49.

21 'Festival of Britain Sculpture',
The Times, 16 January 1950,
p. 2.

22 *Carvings and Drawings,*
op. cit., section 6.

23 Dudley Shaw Ashton (dir.),
*Barbara Hepworth: Figures
in a Landscape,* 1953, https://
player.bfi.org.uk/free/film/
watch-figures-in-a-landscape-
1953-online [accessed
21 August 2020].

24 Letter from Hepworth to
Gardiner, 24 August 1950,
TGA 202016.

25 Her first assistants were
artists John Wells and Denis
Mitchell. They were joined
in October 1950 by another
artist, Terry Frost. Hepworth
painted the outline of
the forms she wanted the
assistants to 'rough out' onto
the large stones 'using a brush
tied to a long bamboo stick';
S. Bowness, *The Sculptor in
the Studio,* op. cit., p. 37. This
process can be seen in the film
*Barbara Hepworth: Figures in a
Landscape* (1953).

26 Letter from Hepworth to
Gardiner, 19 July 1950, TGA
202016.

27 Letter from Hepworth
to Ramsden, undated
[*c.* September 1950],
TGA 9310.1.1.66.

28 Letter from Hepworth to
Gardiner, 24 August 1950,
TGA 202016.

29 When Hepworth and

Nicholson first began their
relationship while both
married to other people,
Hepworth had characterised
the situation in Christian
Science terms, noting,
'I'm not "another woman",
we are all "ideas" of God's';
letter from Hepworth
to Nicholson, 'Friday'
[postmarked 12 January 1935],
TGA 8717.1.1.203.

30 Letter from Hepworth
to Gardiner, postmarked
27 September 1950,
TGA 202016.

31 Letter from Hepworth
to Eates, undated
[*c.* September 1950],
TGA 9310.1.1.67.

32 Letter from Hepworth
to Ramsden, undated
[*c.* September 1950],
TGA 9310.1.1.66.

33 Letter from Hepworth to
Gardiner, 29 November 1950,
TGA 202016.

34 Letter from Hepworth to
Nicholson, 28 December 1950,
TGA 8717.1.1.339.

35 Letter from Hepworth to
Gardiner, 16 December 1950,
TGA 202016.

36 Letter from Hepworth to
Nicholson, dated '19th May 1951
1.30 am from Leeds', TGA
8717.1.1.341.

37 John Willett, 'Some Festival
Exhibitions', *The Manchester
Guardian,* 6 August 1951, p. 4.

38 *Yorkshire Observer,*
29 March 1951, cutting from
Wakefield Art Gallery Archive,
THW 1/2/4/2 Box 13.

39 Letter from Hepworth to
Nicholson, dated '19th May 1951
1.30 am from Leeds', TGA
8717.1.1.341

40 *Carvings and Drawings,*
op. cit., section 6.

41 *Carvings and Drawings,*
op. cit., section 4.

42 *The Star,* London,
20 December 1952, quoted
in Sophie Bowness, *Barbara
Hepworth: Artist in Society
1948–53,* exh. cat. (St Albans:
St Albans Museum + Gallery,
2019).

43 *Carvings and Drawings,*
op. cit., section 6.

44 Letter from Hepworth to

Nicholson, undated [*c*. mid-1953, date suggested by Sophie Bowness to the author], TGA 8717.1.1.344.

45 John Russell, 'Sculptress', *The Sunday Times*, 18 April 1954, p. 11.

46 *Carvings and Drawings*, op. cit., section 6.

47 'Sculptress', *The Sunday Times*, 23 January 1955, p. 3.

48 *Barbara Hepworth: A Retrospective Exhibition of Carvings and Drawings from 1927 to 1954*, Whitechapel Art Gallery exh. cat., texts by Hepworth, section VI, reprinted in S. Bowness (ed.), *Writings and Conversations*, op. cit., p. 98.

Chapter 11

1 *Carvings and Drawings*, op. cit., section 6.

2 Quoted in Sophie Bowness, '"Rhythms of the Stones": Hepworth and Music', in Chris Stephens (ed.), *Barbara Hepworth: A Centenary* (London: Tate Publishing, 2003), p. 23, fn. 3.

3 Letter from Hepworth to Gardiner, 19 July 1950, TGA 202016.

4 *Pictorial Autobiography*, op. cit., p. 49.

5 Letter from Hepworth to Rainier, 4 February 1951, Royal Academy of Music Archive, IPR 3/36/2/12. I am grateful to Dr Clare Nadal, whose excellent PhD thesis on Hepworth's personal library contains references to this correspondence.

6 Letter from Rainier to Hepworth, 26 June 1950, TGA 20132.1.164.19. Nadal notes, 'Many of the scores owned by Hepworth were sent by Rainier, including both scores of early music and of Rainier's own compositions. See TGA 20132.4.6.8 for Rainier's scores owned by Hepworth', in C. Nadal, 'The Personal Library of Barbara Hepworth: A Case Study in the Curation and Interpretation of Artists' Libraries', unpublished PhD thesis.

7 Letter from Hepworth to Rainier, 16 August 1950, Royal Academy of Music Archive, IPR 3/36/1/25.

8 Letter from Hepworth to Rainier, 28 November 1950, quoted in S. Bowness, '"Rhythms of the Stones"', op. cit., p. 23.

9 Letter from Hepworth to Gardiner, 27 July 1950, TGA 202016.

10 Sophie Bowness notes that these include 'a short piano piece', which was subsequently featured in *Five Keyboard Pieces*, 1955, and the orchestral suite *Aequora Lunae* (The Seas of the Moon), 1966–7; S. Bowness, '"Rhythms of the Stones"', op. cit., p. 24.

11 Letter from Rainier to Hepworth, 24 March 1950, TGA 20132.1.164.6.

12 Letter from Hepworth to Rainier, undated, Royal Academy of Music Archive, IPR 3/36/1/12.

13 Letter from Hepworth to Rainier, 28 March 1951, Royal Academy of Music Archive, IPR 3/36/2/31.

14 Letter from Hepworth to Ramsden, 28 July 1950, TGA 9310.1.1.63.

15 'Sophocles at the Old Vic', *The Times*, 6 February 1951, p. 10.

16 'Young and Old Vic', *The Daily Telegraph and Morning Post*, 13 January 1951, p. 4.

17 'Wire Apollo', *The Daily Telegraph and Morning Post*, 13 March 1951, p. 4.

18 *Carvings and Drawings*, op. cit., section 4.

19 Handwritten copy of *Sinfonia da Camera* by Priaulx Rainier in Hepworth's collection, TGA 20132.4.6.8.1. I am grateful to Dr Clare Nadal for this reference.

20 Dudley Shaw Ashton (dir.), *Barbara Hepworth: Figures in a Landscape*, 1953, https://player.bfi.org.uk/free/film/watch-figures-in-a-landscape-1953-online

21 Statement in *Moments of Vision*, exh. cat., with an introduction by Herbert Read, Rome-New York Art Foundation, Rome, July–November 1959, reprinted in S. Bowness (ed.), *Writings and Conversations*, op. cit., p. 124.

22 Letter from Hepworth to the editor, *The St Ives Times*, St Ives, 9 October 1953, reprinted in S. Bowness (ed.), *Writings and Conversations*, op. cit., p. 83.

23 Ibid.

24 As recounted in S. Bowness, '"Rhythms of the Stones"', op. cit., pp. 26–7.

25 'Tribute to Michael Tippett, January 1964', in Ian Kemp (ed.), *Michael Tippett: A Symposium on his 60th Birthday* (London, 1965), reprinted in S. Bowness (ed.), *Writings and Conversations*, op. cit., pp. 179–80.

26 Letter from Tippett to Hepworth, 'Wed' (*c*. 29 December 1954), quoted in S. Bowness, '"Rhythms of the Stones"', op. cit., p. 27.

27 M. Tippett, *Moving into Aquarius* (London: Paladin Books, 1974; repr. 1984), p. 62.

28 Letter from Tippett to Hepworth, undated [*c*. 29 December 1954], quoted in S. Bowness, '"Rhythms of the Stones"', op. cit., p. 27.

29 Handwritten note sent from Hepworth to Miss W. A. Ward at the British Council regarding the São Paulo Theatre Biennale, 9 June 1959, National Archives, BRA/181/58. When discussing the possibility of exhibiting the costume sketches Hepworth insisted that they be accompanied by photographs of the performance and a description of the colour.

30 'Twenty-three designs, notes and swatches for Sir Michael Tippett's opera, "The Midsummer Marriage"', TGA 20159.

31 Ibid.

32 Handwritten note sent from Hepworth to Miss W. A. Ward at the British Council, 9 June 1959, National Archives, BRA/181/58.

33 Ibid.

34 Martin Cooper, 'Opera Marred by Obscurity: The Midsummer Marriage', *The Daily Telegraph and Morning Post*, 28 January 1955, p. 9.

35 Philip Hope-Wallace, '"The Midsummer Marriage": First Performance of Michael Tippett's New Opera', *The Manchester Guardian*, 28 January 1955, p. 7.

36 'Tribute to Michael Tippett, January 1964', reprinted in S. Bowness (ed.), *Writings and Conversations*, op. cit., pp. 179–80.

Chapter 12

1 Skeaping was flying patrols over Malaysia, which did not gain independence from British rule until 1957.

2 Letter from Hepworth to Gardiner, 13 February [1953], TGA 202016.

3 Letter from Hepworth to Gardiner, 'Sunday' [15 February 1953, date suggested by Alan Bowness, 2005], TGA 202016.

4 For example, 'The "Warser" letter is a strange one observing the psychological differences between bird and man owing to the early stages of growth in man inside the womb and bird an outside womb in the form of a nest. I believe this could be linked somewhere to the idea you presented to me in a few words in the train. There is also one on p.315 speaking of ultimately the <u>one</u> conflict in life: to reconcile life with work.' Letter from Rainier to Hepworth, 18 March 1950, TGA 20132.1.164.5. I am grateful to Dr Clare Nadal for this reference.

5 Letter from Rilke to Elisabeth Freiin Schenk zu Schweinsberg, 1909, in *The Selected Letters of Rainer Maria Rilke 1902–1926* (London: Macmillan, 1946), p. 175. I am grateful to Dr Rachel Smith for this reference. See R. Smith, 'Hepworth Reading Rilke',

in *Barbara Hepworth* (Paris: Musée Rodin, 2019), p. 56.

6 Letter from Hepworth to Gardiner, 'Sunday' [22 February 1953, date suggested by Alan Bowness, 2005], TGA 202016. The service was held in St Ia's church, the parish church of St Ives.

7 M. Gardiner, *Barbara Hepworth: A Memoir* (Edinburgh: The Salamander Press, 1982), p. 18.

8 Letter from Hepworth to Nicholson, undated [August 1954], TGA 8717.1.1.345.

9 Dunluce notebook, TGA 201518, printed in S. Bowness (ed.), *Writings and Conversations*, op. cit., p. 100.

10 'Greek Diary: 1954–64', in Walter Kern (ed.), *J. P. Hodin: European Critic. Essays by Various Hands Contributed in Honour of his Sixtieth Birthday* (London: Cory, Adams and Mackay, 1965), pp. 19–24, reprinted in S. Bowness (ed.), *Writings and Conversations*, op. cit., pp. 102–8. Hodin, who was a significant writer on Hepworth's work, specifically requested that the Greek Sketchbook notes be included.

11 Hepworth refers to the pressed flowers, leaves and grasses she placed between the pages of the original sketchbook, now in Tate Archive.

12 'Greek Diary: 1954–64', op. cit., p. 24.

13 Hepworth recalled, 'a friend had asked for *samples* of Nigerian wood to be sent to me. Suddenly I got a note from the docks to say that 17 tons of wood had arrived at Tilbury Docks and would I please collect.' *Pictorial Autobiography*, op. cit., p. 72. Gardiner recounts that she had requested this sample from a Nigerian plantation owner through family contacts (Gale and Stephens, *Works in the Tate Gallery Collection and the Barbara Hepworth Museum St Ives*, op. cit., p. 140). Hepworth made

thirteen Guarea sculptures between 1954 and 1963.

14 Letter from Hepworth to Abraham Marie Hammacher, February 1955, quoted in A. M. Hammacher, *Barbara Hepworth* (London: Thames & Hudson, 1968), p. 115.

15 *Drawings from a Sculptor's Landscape*, op. cit., p. 12.

16 Dunluce notebook, TGA 201518.

17 'Greek Diary: 1954–64', op. cit., p. 23.

18 *Drawings from a Sculptor's Landscape*, op. cit., p. 12.

19 Jackie Heuman, 'The Conservation of the Gift', in S. Bowness (ed.), *The Plasters*, op. cit., p. 189. This work was also exhibited at the *Penwith Past and Present* exhibition, Penwith Gallery, St Ives, in 1968 as part of the celebrations of Hepworth and Bernard Leach being honoured with the Freedom of St Ives. Sophie Bowness notes that some of the plasters exhibited at this time were 'coloured "similar to the bronze sculptures" by Morris Singer' for this display; letter from Eric Gibbard [manager of the Morris Singer foundry] to Hepworth, 1 August 1968, quoted in S. Bowness, 'Barbara Hepworth's Studio Practice: Plaster for Bronze', in *The Plasters*, op. cit., p. 59.

20 Letter from Hepworth to Gaskin, 27 January 1964, quoted in S. Bowness (ed.), *The Plasters*, op. cit., p. 132.

21 Hodin, *Barbara Hepworth*, op. cit., p. 10.

22 S. Bowness (ed.), *Writings and Conversations*, op. cit., p. 116.

23 B. Hepworth, 'The Artist on his Work – no. 4: "Sculpture – An act of praise"', in *The Christian Science Monitor*, 13 July 1965, p. 9, reprinted in S. Bowness (ed.), *Writings and Conversations*, op. cit., pp. 185–88.

Chapter 13

1 Conversation with Reg Butler, recorded on 28 September 1951

and broadcast on 26 August 1952 on the BBC Third Programme, 'Artists on Art', printed in S. Bowness (ed.), *Writings and Conversations*, op. cit., p. 49.
2 Ibid., p. 53.
3 Letter from Hepworth to Read, 29 October 1961, quoted in S. Bowness (ed.), *The Plasters*, op. cit., p. 38.
4 Letter from Hepworth to Read, 1961, quoted in S. Bowness (ed.), *The Plasters*, op. cit., p. 40.
5 Letter from Hepworth to Kapp, 11 November 1956, quoted in S. Bowness (ed.), *The Plasters*, op. cit., p. 111.
6 Only four of the six were actually made.
7 Pages of notes from sketchbook related to British Council lecture, 1961, Tate Archive, reprinted in S. Bowness (ed.), *Writings and Conversations*, op. cit., p. 161.
8 'The Sculptor Speaks', in S. Bowness (ed.), *Writings and Conversations*, op. cit., p. 158.
9 *Pictorial Autobiography*, op. cit., p. 75.
10 'Artist's notes on technique', in Michael Shepherd, *Barbara Hepworth* (London: Methuen, 1963), p. 1.
11 Hepworth's arrangement with Alex Reid & Lefevre Ltd had been on an exhibition-by-exhibition basis. In 1953, the gallery directors decided to revert to their earlier specialism of French painting. For a detailed account of Hepworth's arrangement with Gimpel Fils, see Alice Correia, 'Gimpel Fils, Barbara Hepworth and the Promotion of British Sculpture in the 1950s', *Sculpture Journal*, vol. 24, no. 1 (2015): 97–112.
12 'Gimpel Fils' summer exhibition', *The Times*, 30 July 1952, p. 9.
13 Letter from Hepworth to Peter Gimpel, 3 May 1956, quoted in Correia, 'Gimpel Fils', op. cit., p. 104.
14 Basil Taylor, 'Contemporary Arts', *The Spectator*, 15 June 1956, press cutting, Gimpel Fils archive, quoted in Correia, 'Gimpel Fils', op. cit., p. 106.
15 Westward Television Film, *Barbara Hepworth* (1967), quoted in S. Bowness (ed.), *The Plasters*, op. cit., p. 40.
16 'The Sculptor Speaks', in S. Bowness (ed.), *Writings and Conversations*, op. cit., p. 159.
17 Letter from Hepworth to Nicholson, 'Christmas day 1958', TGA 8717.1.1.361.
18 Letter from Hepworth to Somerville, 6 April 1952, National Archives, GB/652/25.
19 *Orpheus (Maquette 1)* (1956) is an edition of eight; *Orpheus (Maquette 2) (Version I)* (1956) is an edition of eight; *Orpheus (Maquette 2) (Version II)* (1956–59) is an edition of three.
20 Text on working practice, *c.* 1959, unpublished typescript, printed in S. Bowness (ed.), *Writings and Conversations*, op. cit., p. 130.
21 Rainer Maria Rilke, *Sonnets to Orpheus*, trans. J. B. Leishman (London: Hogarth Press, 1946, 2nd ed.), p. 35. I am grateful to Dr Clare Nadal for this suggestion in her unpublished PhD thesis, 'The Personal Library of Barbara Hepworth: A Case Study in the Curation and Interpretation of Artists' Libraries'.
22 'The Sculptor Speaks', in S. Bowness (ed.), *Writings and Conversations*, op. cit., p. 158.
23 Letter from Hepworth to Nicholson, undated [1958], TGA 8717.1.1.360. Hepworth was created CBE (Commander of the Order of the British Empire) in 1958.
24 Printed in *Moments of Vision*, Rome-New York Art Foundation exh. cat., 1959, reprinted in S. Bowness (ed.), *Writings and Conversations*, op. cit., p. 124. Versions of the finished text are held in Tate Archive, TGA 201518.
25 Letter to *The Times*, 24 January 1956, unpublished typescripts, reprinted in S. Bowness (ed.), *Writings and Conversations*, op. cit., p. 113.
26 Letter from Hepworth to Nicholson, 'Feb 12th midnight' [1957], TGA 8717.1.1.359. The 'little chapel' refers to the Lady Chapel, where her sculptural tribute to Paul, *Mother and Child* (1954), is located.
27 Alan Bowness (ed.), *The Complete Sculpture of Barbara Hepworth 1960–69* (London: Lund Humphries, 1971), p. 12.
28 'The Sculptor Speaks', in S. Bowness (ed.), *Writings and Conversations*, op. cit., p. 155.

Chapter 14

1 'The Sculptor Speaks', in S. Bowness (ed.), *Writings and Conversations*, op. cit., pp. 151–52.
2 Letter from Hepworth to Gardiner, 'Monday' [23 or 30 November 1959, date suggested by Alan Bowness, 2005, who notes the mention of the John Moores Painting Prize won by Patrick Heron], TGA 202016.
3 'The Sculptor Speaks', in S. Bowness (ed.), *Writings and Conversations*, op. cit., pp. 152–53.
4 Letter from Hepworth to Nicholson, 'Christmas day 1958', TGA 8717.1.1.361.
5 Letter from Hepworth to Nicholson, undated [late 1958; Sophie Bowness notes that the photographs mentioned are dated], TGA 8717.1.1.362.
6 'The Sculptor Speaks', in S. Bowness (ed.), *Writings and Conversations*, op. cit., p. 153.
7 B. Hepworth, 'Towards an open architecture', *c.* 1955, unpublished notes, printed in S. Bowness (ed.), *Writings and Conversations*, op. cit., pp. 111–12.
8 John Rydon, 'Bronze Meridian is so Abstract', *Daily Express*, 18 March 1960, p. 9.
9 Letter from Hepworth to Hammarskjöld, 5 December 1959, 'The Dag Hammarskjöld–Barbara Hepworth Letters', in *Development Dialogue*, no. 1 (2001): 51, http://www.daghammarskjold.se/wp-content/uploads/2001/08/

DD2001_1.pdf [accessed
2 October 2020].

10 Letter from Hepworth to
Gimpel Fils, 20 January 1960,
quoted in Penelope
Curtis, 'The Artist in Post-
War Society', in Curtis
and Wilkinson (eds.), *A
Retrospective*, op. cit., p. 155.

11 Quoted in S. Bowness (ed.),
The Plasters, op. cit., p. 71.

12 Quoted in Gale and Stephens,
*Works in the Tate Gallery
Collection and the Barbara
Hepworth Museum St Ives*,
op. cit., p. 210.

13 Ibid.

14 Text on *Winged Figure*
(1961–63, aluminium, BH
315), 4 July 1963, unpublished
typescript sent to J. P. Hodin,
printed in S. Bowness (ed.),
Writings and Conversations,
op. cit., p. 172.

15 *The Gazette of the John Lewis
Partnership*, 27 April 1963,
pp. 304–5, quoted in
S. Bowness (ed.), *The Plasters*,
op. cit., p. 77.

16 Letter from Somerville to
Hepworth, 26 September 1958,
PRO GB/641/133c.

17 Letter from Hepworth to
Somerville, 13 January 1959,
PRO GB/641/133c.

18 Ibid.

19 Edouard Roditi, 'Barbara
Hepworth' (interview), in
Dialogues on Art, London, 1960,
reprinted in S. Bowness (ed.),
Writings and Conversations,
op. cit., p. 142.

20 'Brazilian Award for Barbara
Hepworth', *The Guardian*,
18 September 1959, p. 11.

21 Letter from Read to Hepworth,
9 November 1959, TGA
2032.1.167.571092.

22 For details on Hepworth's
struggles to find a suitably
effective American dealer,
see Emma Roberts,
'Representation and
Reputation: Barbara
Hepworth's Relationships
with her American and British
Dealers', in *Tate Papers*,
no. 20 (Autumn 2013), https://
www.tate.org.uk/research/
publications/tate-papers/20/
representation-and-
reputation-barbara-hepworths-

relationships-with-her-
american-and-british-dealers
[accessed 5 August 2020].

23 Letter from Hammarskjöld to
Hepworth, 25 December 1956,
'The Dag Hammarskjöld–
Barbara Hepworth Letters',
op. cit., p. 44.

24 Quoted in Manuel Fröhlich,
'A Fully Integrated Vision:
Politics and the Arts in the
Dag Hammarskjöld–Barbara
Hepworth Correspondence',
Development Dialogue, no. 1
(2001): 18.

25 D. Hammarskjöld, *Markings*
(New York: Vintage Books,
1964; repr. 2006), p. 171.

26 Letter from Hepworth to
Hammarskjöld, 22 May 1958,
'The Dag Hammarskjöld–
Barbara Hepworth Letters',
op. cit., p. 44.

27 Unpublished text on new
developments in art and
society, 1958, manuscript
and typescripts, printed in
S. Bowness (ed.), *Writings and
Conversations*, op. cit., p. 118.

28 Interview with Margaret Tims,
'A Sculptor's Philosophy: A PN
Profile of Barbara Hepworth',
in *Peace News*, London,
16 January 1959, reprinted in
S. Bowness (ed.), *Writings and
Conversations*, op. cit., p. 120.

29 Text on women's art, *c.*
late 1950s, unpublished
manuscript and typescripts,
printed in S. Bowness (ed.),
Writings and Conversations,
op. cit., p. 131. Bowness notes:
'among Hepworth's papers
is a manuscript of the text in
Margaret Gardiner's hand,
suggesting that they may have
worked on it together'.

30 Letter from Hepworth
to Hammarskjöld,
16 October 1959, 'The Dag
Hammarskjöld–Barbara
Hepworth Letters', op. cit.,
p. 46.

31 Letter from Hammarskjöld to
Hepworth, 16 October 1959,
ibid.

32 Letter from Hepworth
to Hammarskjöld,
21 October 1959, ibid., p. 49.

33 Letter from Hepworth
to Hammarskjöld,
5 December 1959, ibid., p. 51.

34 'Statement on nuclear
weapons', *The Sunday Times*,
1 October 1961, and *The Times*,
2 October 1961.

35 Letter from Hammarskjöld to
Hepworth, 15 October 1960,
'The Dag Hammarskjöld–
Barbara Hepworth Letters',
op. cit., p. 52. Hepworth had
sent a supportive letter and a
new catalogue of her work on
25 September 1960.

36 Letter from Hepworth to
Hammarskjöld, 11 May 1961,
ibid., p. 53.

37 Letter from Hammarskjöld to
Hepworth, 3 June 1961, ibid.,
p. 54.

38 Letter from Hammarskjöld to
Hepworth, 11 September 1961,
ibid., p. 56.

39 Interview with Alan Bowness,
in A. Bowness (ed.), *Complete
Sculpture*, op. cit., p. 10.

40 Notes relating to Hepworth's
contribution to John
Read's BBC film, *Barbara
Hepworth* (1961), printed in
S. Bowness (ed.), *Writings and
Conversations*, op. cit., p. 146.

41 Interview with Alan Bowness,
in A. Bowness (ed.), *Complete
Sculpture*, op. cit., p. 10.

42 Letter from Hepworth to
Bunche, 23 November 1961
(UNA DAG –1/2.3 Box 321),
quoted in Fröhlich, 'A Fully
Integrated Vision', op. cit.,
p. 36.

43 Letter from Hepworth to
Bunche, 22 May 1962 (UNA
DAG –1/2.3 Box 321), ibid.

44 Letter from Hepworth to
Bunche, 19 June 1962 (UNA
DAG –1/2.3 Box 321), ibid.

45 Letter from Hepworth to
Bunche, 24 January 1962 (UNA
DAG –1/2.3 Box 321), ibid.

46 The dedication to Dag
Hammarskjöld was included in
the plaster but covered up for
the Whitechapel exhibition,
as the UN commission had
not yet been announced.
Hepworth's 'bond' with
Hammarskjöld was referenced
by curator Bryan Robertson in
the catalogue.

47 Letter from Hepworth to
Bunche, 24 January 1962,
quoted in S. Bowness, 'Barbara
Hepworth's Studio Practice:

Plaster for Bronze', in *The Plasters*, op. cit., p. 80.

48 Letter from Hepworth to Gardiner, 'Sun' [December 1962 or January 1963, dates suggested by Alan Bowness, 2005], TGA 202016.

49 Letter from Hepworth to Bunche, 1 January 1962 (UNA DAG –1/2.3 Box 321), quoted in Fröhlich, 'A Fully Integrated Vision', op. cit., p. 76.

50 Interview with Alan Bowness, in A. Bowness (ed.), *Complete Sculpture*, op. cit., p. 15, quoted in S. Bowness, 'Barbara Hepworth's Studio Practice: Plaster for Bronze', in *The Plasters*, op. cit., p. 82.

51 Letter from Hepworth to Bunche, 24 February 1964, quoted in S. Bowness (ed.), *The Plasters*, op. cit., p. 82.

52 Speech made at the unveiling of the United Nations *Single Form* on 11 June 1964, reprinted in S. Bowness (ed.), *Writings and Conversations*, op. cit., p. 181.

Chapter 15

1 'Le Quartier St. Ives', *The Tatler*, 26 July 1961, p. 171.

2 'Private View', *The Sunday Times Magazine*, 26 September 1965, p. 12.

3 Ibid.

4 B. Robertson, 'Preface', in *Barbara Hepworth: An Exhibition of Sculpture from 1952–1962*, exh. cat. (London: Whitechapel Art Gallery, 1962), unpaginated

5 Hepworth had frequently danced at the Palais in its former life, 'on what was said to be the best-sprung dance floor in the South West'; S. Bowness, *The Sculptor in the Studio*, op. cit., p. 61.

6 Interview with Cindy Nemser, 1973, printed in C. Nemser (ed.), *Art Talk*, op. cit., p. 21.

7 Robertson, 'Preface', in *An Exhibition of Sculpture from 1952–1962*, op. cit.

8 'Ten Years of Sculpture by Miss Barbara Hepworth', *The Times*, 16 May 1962, p. 5.

9 Sara Matson, 'The Palais de Danse', at the Hepworth Research Network Launch, The Hepworth Wakefield, 12–13 March 2020. Sophie Bowness notes these backdrops came later, as the colours are those of *Sphere* (1967) and *Crucifixion* (1966–67): in conversation with the author, email 21 September 2020.

10 Conversation with Edwin Mullins for 'The Lively Arts', broadcast on BBC's Third Programme (Radio 3), 8 May 1968, printed in S. Bowness (ed.), *Writings and Conversations*, op. cit., p. 212.

11 *Drawings from a Sculptor's Landscape*, op. cit., p. 13.

12 B. Robertson, *Anthony Caro: Sculpture, 1960–1963*, exh. cat. (London: Whitechapel Art Gallery, 1963), p. 1.

13 Letter from Hepworth to Nicholson, 21 January 1969, TGA 8717.1.1.377. The sculptors listed are Phillip King, Anthony Caro, Brian Wall and William Turnbull.

14 'Chronology', in S. Bowness (ed.), *Writings and Conversations*, op. cit., p. 294.

15 For example, Riley's *Late Morning* (1967–68) was purchased in 1968, and Caro's *Early One Morning* (1962) was acquired through the Contemporary Art Society in 1965. Both artists' use of abstract form and colour to evoke phenomenological experience is another point of commonality with Hepworth.

16 Letter from Riley to Hepworth, 26 January 1975, TGA 965.2.19.58.1.

17 Letter from Hepworth to Riley, 6 February 1975, TGA 965.2.19.58.2.

18 Robert Hughes, 'About Nothing Except Love: Visiting Barbara Hepworth in Cornwall', *The Bulletin*, Sydney, 19 May 1966, reprinted in S. Bowness (ed.), *Writings and Conversations*, op. cit., p. 189.

19 J. Chicago, *Through the Flower: My Struggle as a Woman Artist* (New York: Anchor Press/ Doubleday, 1975), p. 144.

20 Ibid., p. 158.

21 S. Vincent, 'Woman to Woman: Barbara Hepworth', *Daily Express*, 3 October 1961, p. 6, reprinted in S. Bowness (ed.), *Writings and Conversations*, op. cit., pp. 265–67.

22 The Treason Trial Fund supported the defendants of the so-called 'Treason Trial' of anti-apartheid protestors in South Africa, including Nelson Mandela. The trial began in 1956 and concluded in 1961, when all defendants were found not guilty.

23 Vincent, 'Woman to Woman', op. cit., p. 6, reprinted in S. Bowness (ed.), *Writings and Conversations*, op. cit., pp. 265–67.

24 Ibid.

25 For example, Hepworth donated a bronze sculpture to Save the Children Fund and Children and Youth Aliyah, Christies Charity Sale, 22 May 1963; Peter Turks, 'Charity Sale Makes £12,718', *The Daily Telegraph*, Thursday 23 May 1963, p. 19.

26 Letter from Hepworth to Gardiner, 'Fri' [26 November 1965, date suggested by Alan Bowness, 2005], TGA 202016.

27 Advertisement, *The Times*, 23 December 1965, p. 5.

28 Letter from Hepworth to Gardiner, 'Fri' [26 November 1965, date suggested by Alan Bowness, 2005], TGA 202016.

29 Letter from Hepworth to Nicholson, 26 February 1966, TGA 8717.1.1.363.

30 Letter from Hepworth to Nicholson, 30 March 1966, TGA 8717.1.1.364.

31 Letter from Hepworth to Nicholson, 22 December 1967, TGA 8717.1.1.371.

32 Interview with Alan Bowness, in A. Bowness (ed.), *Complete Sculpture*, reprinted in S. Bowness (ed.), *Writings and Conversations*, op. cit., p. 238.

33 'Six forms on a circle' may refer to the slate carving *Six Forms on a Circle* (1967)

(BH449) or the polished bronze *Six Forms on a Circle* (1967) (BH454), or to the form of both.

34 Letter from Hepworth to Nicholson, 22 December 1967, TGA 8717.1.1.371.

35 Guy Brett, 'Gulbenkian Exhibition', *The Guardian*, 23 April 1964, p. 9.

36 For more on the exhibition design, see Eleanor Clayton, '"The Whole Question of Plinths" in Barbara Hepworth's 1968 Tate Retrospective', *Tate Papers*, no. 25 (Spring 2016), https://www.tate.org.uk/research/publications/tate-papers/25/whole-question-of-plinths [accessed 7 August 2020].

37 Letter from Hepworth to Warren Forma, 11 May 1965, TGA 965.18.18.8, quoted in Penelope Curtis, 'From Bridgwater to Otterlo', in Curtis and Stephens (eds.), *Sculpture for a Modern World*, op. cit., p. 103, fn. 7. Forma was an American author and filmmaker, whose book *5 British Sculptors Work and Talk* (1964) and film of the same name (1966) featured Hepworth.

38 G. Brett, 'Themes of Barbara Hepworth', *The Times*, 3 April 1968, p. 14.

39 N. Lynton, 'Family Reunion', *The Guardian*, 3 April 1968, p. 8.

40 Letter from Hepworth to Nicholson, 9 May 1968, TGA 8717.1.1.373.

41 Letter from Hepworth to Nicholson, 21 January 1969, TGA 8717.1.1.377. The sculpture referred to is *Three Obliques (Walk In)* (1970).

42 Interview with Alan Bowness, in A. Bowness (ed.), *Complete Sculpture*, reprinted in S. Bowness (ed.), *Writings and Conversations*, op. cit., p. 238.

43 Letter from Hepworth to Nicholson, 21 January 1969, TGA 8717.1.1.377.

Chapter 16

1 Unpublished text on new developments in art and society, 1958, printed in S. Bowness (ed.), *Writings and Conversations*, op. cit., p. 118.

2 Edwin Mullins, *Barbara Hepworth*, exh. cat., Hakone Open-Air Museum, 1970, which includes quotations by Hepworth from letters to and conversations with Mullins, 1969–70, reprinted in S. Bowness (ed.), *Writings and Conversations*, op. cit., p. 223.

3 *Pictorial Autobiography*, op. cit., p. 81.

4 Interview with Alan Bowness, in A. Bowness (ed.), *Complete Sculpture*, reprinted in S. Bowness (ed.), *Writings and Conversations*, op. cit., p. 240.

5 Ibid.

6 In 1965, Hepworth had begun working with Marlborough Fine Art, who had galleries in London, New York and Zurich, to support her international exhibitions and sales. She formally moved all her activity from Gimpel Fils to Marlborough in 1971. For details of this, see Roberts, 'Representation and Reputation', *Tate Papers*, op. cit.

7 'The Times Diary', *The Times*, 13 February 1970, p. 10.

8 S. Bowness, 'Barbara Hepworth's Studio Practice: Plaster for Bronze', in *The Plasters*, op. cit., p. 47.

9 Note on Porthcurno, dated 22 March 1967, TGA 201518, printed in S. Bowness (ed.), *Writings and Conversations*, op. cit., p. 204.

10 Letter from Simon to Hepworth, 30 August 1966, Curwen Studio records, quoted in Gale and Stephens, *Works in the Tate Gallery Collection and the Barbara Hepworth Museum St Ives*, op. cit., p. 276. Hepworth made two further series of prints: a suite of screenprints, *Two Opposing Forms*, in 1970, and another group of lithographs, *The Aegean Suite*, in 1971.

11 'The Sun and Moon', signed Barbara Hepworth and dated June 1966, TGA 201518, printed in S. Bowness (ed.), *Writings and Conversations*, op. cit., p. 201.

12 In 1963 Hepworth had bought a studio flat on Porthmeor Beach with expansive views of the sea and horizon, specifically for painting and drawing. For more on Hepworth's studios, see S. Bowness, *Barbara Hepworth: The Sculptor in the Studio*, op. cit.

13 Specific material shown through recent analysis of the cast owned by Salisbury Cathedral, carried out by conservator Tessa Jackson; I am grateful to Sophie Bowness for this new information.

14 See A. Bowness (ed.), *Complete Sculpture*, op. cit., p. 13.

15 Quoted in Lucy Kent, '"An Act of Praise": Religion and the Work of Barbara Hepworth', in Curtis and Stephens (eds.), *Sculpture for a Modern World*, op. cit., p. 48.

16 Edwin Mullins, 'Hepworth at Home', *The Daily Telegraph Supplement (Weekend Telegraph)*, 20 May 1966, reprinted in S. Bowness (ed.), *Writings and Conversations*, op. cit., p. 197.

17 Letter from Hepworth to Nicholson, undated [19 May 1966; five days before the Gimpel exhibition opened on 24 May], TGA 8717.1.1.366.

18 *Pictorial Autobiography*, op. cit., p. 117.

19 William Wordsworth (ed.), *Women and Men's Daughters: Portrait Studies by Zsuzsi Roboz*, typescript in Tate Archive, 8 June 1970, reprinted in S. Bowness (ed.), *Writings and Conversations*, op. cit., p. 226. Hepworth noted the connection between this work and her pre-war ambitions for monumental, multi-part sculptures like *Project – Monument to the Spanish War* (1938–39).

20 Interviewed for the film *Barbara Hepworth: Sculptress* (1972) by John Stapleton, Pathé films, https://www.youtube.com/watch?v=2qLDOcUlEhE [accessed 4 October 2020]. See also Edwin Mullins, 'Barbara Hepworth's "Family"', *Daily Telegraph Magazine*, London, 7 April 1972, reprinted

in S. Bowness (ed.), *Writings and Conversations*, op. cit., pp. 248–50.

21 Interviewed for the film *Barbara Hepworth: Sculptress* (1972) by John Stapleton, Pathé films.

22 Susanne Puddefoot, 'A Totem, a Talisman, a Kind of Touchstone…', *The Times*, 3 April 1968, p. 13, reprinted in S. Bowness (ed.), *Writings and Conversations*, op. cit., pp. 284–87.

23 Hepworth wrote in 1951 of 'the standing form (which is the translation of my feeling towards the human being standing in landscape)' and 'the "closed form", such as the oval, spherical or pierced form (sometimes incorporating colour) which translates for me the association of meaning of gesture in landscape'; see Introduction, p. 8.

24 J. Russell, 'The Life of Colour', *The Sunday Times*, 16 April 1972, p. 36.

25 Hepworth notebook, TGA 201518.

26 BH 444 is the aluminium sculpture of 1967, now destroyed, while a smaller variation, *Sphere with Inside and Outside Colour* (1967) (BH 445), in aluminium with painted panels, exists in an edition of six.

27 Letter from Hepworth to Nicholson, 11 October 1969, TGA 8717.1.1.383.

28 Letter from Hepworth to Gardiner, 26 January 1973, TGA 202016.

29 Judith Rich, 'Hepworth at 70', *The Guardian*, 17 January 1973, p. 8.

Epilogue

1 Letter from Hepworth to Anthony Lousada, 19 May 1965, quoted in S. Bowness, *The Sculptor in the Studio*, op. cit., p. 87.

2 Brancusi bequeathed his entire studio (completed works, sketches, furniture, tools, library, record library, photographs, etc.) to the French state, on condition that it undertook to reconstruct the studio just as it was at the artist's death. After an initial partial reconstruction in 1962 within the museum collections at the Palais de Tokyo, its exact replica was produced in 1977, opposite the Centre Pompidou. After being flooded in 1990, it was closed to the public. The present reconstruction, built by the architect Renzo Piano, is presented as a museum space containing the studio: https://www.centrepompidou.fr/en/Collections/Brancusi-s-Studio [accessed 7 October 2020].

3 B. Hepworth, 'Memorandum to Trustees', 20 February 1972, quoted in S. Bowness, *The Sculptor in the Studio*, op. cit., p. 87.

4 For full details of the changes made to the studio before it opened as the Barbara Hepworth Museum, see S. Bowness, *The Sculptor in the Studio*, op. cit., pp. 87–128.

5 Penelope Curtis, 'What is Left Unsaid', op. cit., p. 156.

6 Alan Bowness to Gordon Watson, 2 October 1997, The Hepworth Wakefield Archive, THW 1/2/10/2.

7 David Chipperfield, 'The Hepworth Wakefield', in S. Bowness (ed.), *The Plasters*, op. cit., p. 24.

8 Quoted in Susan Bradwell, 'Barbara Hepworth', *Arts Review*, London, 30 May 1975, Obituary: based on an interview with Hepworth shortly before her death, reprinted in S. Bowness, *Writings and Conversations*, op. cit., p. 288.

9 At this time Tate St Ives shared the workshop space with the Hepworth Estate. The Palais was formally given to Tate in 2015.

10 The works are *Quoit Montserrat* (1998) and *Mango Reliquary* (2000).

11 Veronica Ryan, *Veronica Ryan – Artist in Residence: Quoit Montserrat*, exhibition leaflet, Tate St Ives, 2000, p. 2.

12 In conversation with the author, 7 September 2020.

13 Alice Channer, 'Inside Out', *The Coelacanth Journal*, London, no. 3, 2009, p. 15. I am grateful to Sophie Bowness for this reference.

14 Linder, 'Discovering the Essence of Hepworth', *Tate Etc.*, 17 August 2015, https://www.tate.org.uk/tate-etc/issue-34-summer-2015/discovering-essence-hepworth [accessed 7 October 2020].

15 Quoted in Mark Hudson, 'Does this really qualify as sculpture?', *The Daily Telegraph*, 3 November 2016, p. 26.

16 Quoted in Charlotte Jansen, 'What We Learned at the First Yorkshire Sculpture International', *Elephant Magazine*, 26 June 2019, https://elephant.art/learned-first-yorkshire-sculpture-international/ [accessed 7 October 2020].

17 J. P. Hodin, 'Barbara Hepworth and the Mediterranean Spirit', *Marmo*, Milan, no. 3 (December 1964). Quotations from Hepworth of June 1963 also reprinted in S. Bowness (ed.), *Writings and Conversations*, op. cit., p. 171.

Bibliography

J. D. Bernal (foreword), *Catalogue of Sculpture by Barbara Hepworth*, exh. cat. (London: Alex Reid & Lefevre Ltd, 1937)

Alan Bowness (ed.), *The Complete Sculpture of Barbara Hepworth 1960–69* (London: Lund Humphries, 1971)

Sophie Bowness, '"Rhythms of the Stones": Hepworth and Music', in Chris Stephens (ed.), *Barbara Hepworth: A Centenary* (London: Tate Publishing, 2003)

——, *The Sculptor in the Studio* (London: Tate Publishing, 2017)

—— (ed.), *Barbara Hepworth: The Plasters. The Gift to Wakefield* (Farnham and Burlington: Lund Humphries, 2011)

—— (ed.), *Barbara Hepworth: Writings and Conversations* (London: Tate Publishing, 2015)

Alice Correia, 'Gimpel Fils, Barbara Hepworth and the Promotion of British Sculpture in the 1950s', *Sculpture Journal* vol. 24, no. 1 (2015)

Penelope Curtis and Chris Stephens (eds.), *Barbara Hepworth: Sculpture for a Modern World*, exh. cat. (London: Tate Publishing, 2015)

Penelope Curtis and Alan Wilkinson (eds.), *Barbara Hepworth: A Retrospective*, exh. cat. (London: Tate Publishing, 1994)

Sally Festing, *Barbara Hepworth: A Life of Forms* (Middlesex: Viking Press, 1995)

Manuel Fröhlich, 'A Fully Integrated Vision: Politics and the Arts in the Dag Hammarskjöld–Barbara Hepworth Correspondence', *Development Dialogue*, no. 1 (2001)

N. Gabo, L. Martin and B. Nicholson (eds.), *Circle: International Survey of Constructive Art* (London: Faber and Faber, 1937; repr. 1971)

Matthew Gale and Chris Stephens, *Barbara Hepworth: Works in the Tate Gallery Collection and the Barbara Hepworth Museum St Ives* (London: Tate Publishing, 1999)

'Greek Diary: 1954–64', in Walter Kern (ed.), *J. P. Hodin: European Critic. Essays by Various Hands Contributed in Honour of his Sixtieth Birthday* (London: Cory, Adams and Mackay, 1965)

'The Dag Hammarskjöld–Barbara Hepworth Letters', *Development Dialogue*, no. 1 (2001)

Nathaniel Hepburn, *Barbara Hepworth: The Hospital Drawings* (London: Tate Publishing, 2012)

Barbara Hepworth, exh. cat. (Paris: Musée Rodin, 2019)

Barbara Hepworth: A Pictorial Autobiography (Bath: Adams and Dart, 1970; extended ed., prepared under the direction of Alan Bowness, published Bradford-on-Avon: Moonraker Press, 1978; reprinted London: Tate Publishing, 1985)

Barbara Hepworth: A Retrospective Exhibition of Carvings and Drawings 1927–1954, exh. cat. (London: Whitechapel Art Gallery, 1954)

Barbara Hepworth: Carvings and Drawings (London: Lund Humphries, 1952)

Barbara Hepworth: Drawings from a Sculptor's Landscape (London: Cory, Adams and Mackay, 1966)

J. P. Hodin, *Barbara Hepworth* (London: Lund Humphries, 1961)

Caroline Maclean, *Circles and Squares: The Lives and Art of the Hampstead Modernists* (London: Bloomsbury, 2020)

Cindy Nemser (ed.), *Art Talk: Conversations with 15 Women Artists* (New York: IconEditions, 1975)

E. H. Ramsden, *An Introduction to Modern Art* (London, New York, Toronto: Oxford University Press, 1940)

Herbert Read (foreword), *Carvings by Barbara Hepworth, Paintings by Ben Nicholson*, exh. cat. (London: Arthur Tooth & Sons Galleries, 1932)

Emma Roberts, 'Representation and Reputation: Barbara Hepworth's Relationships with her American and British Dealers', *Tate Papers*, no. 20 (Autumn 2013)

Bryan Robertson (preface), *Barbara Hepworth: An Exhibition of Sculpture from 1952–1962*, exh. cat. (London: Whitechapel Art Gallery, 1962)

Michael Shepherd, *Barbara Hepworth* (London: Methuen, 1963)

Gillian Spencer (foreword) and Alan Bowness (introduction), *Barbara Hepworth: Early Life*, exh. cat. (Wakefield: Wakefield Art Gallery, 1985)

Sally Vincent, 'Woman to Woman: Barbara Hepworth', *Daily Express*, 3 October 1961

Leo Walmsley, *So Many Loves* (London: Collins, 1944; 2nd ed., 1969)

Alan Wilkinson, *The Drawings of Barbara Hepworth* (Farnham and Burlington: Lund Humphries, 2015)

Acknowledgments

I am grateful to the many people who have supported the creation of this book.

Dr Sophie Bowness, whose extensive research on Hepworth provided an invaluable foundation for my work, was kind enough to read and comment on initial drafts, offering additional insight. Through Sophie I was able to access Hepworth's letters to Margaret Gardiner, since acquired by Tate Archive. Sir Alan Bowness's years of meticulous research into Hepworth's vast correspondences, including these, have provided important information for future researchers like myself.

Dr Penelope Curtis, in addition to writing key texts and curating major exhibitions on Hepworth for over thirty years, also commented on initial drafts, clarifying the development of the field of Hepworth studies.

I was aided in my research by Adrian Glew and his team at Tate Archive, Karen Atkinson and the Henry Moore Institute Research Library, and Rodney French at The National Archives, assisted further in the latter by Mary Clayton.

The continually expanding Hepworth Research Network – a network of artists, art historians, conservators and curators founded by The Hepworth Wakefield with Professor Michael White at the University of York and Dr Anneke Pettican at the University of Huddersfield – provided important background to my ambition to combine Hepworth's physical practice with her broader philosophy. I was guided in this by conservator Laura Davies, whose knowledge of Hepworth's practical creative processes is constantly enlightening.

Several researchers have shown new pathways to understanding Hepworth's work, notably Dr Lucy Kent, Dr Rachel Smith and Dr Clare Nadal. I am deeply indebted in particular to Clare, who provided crucial editorial support. The engagement of artists Veronica Ryan and Rosanne Robertson in revealing their individual responses to Hepworth has offered more alternative approaches.

My colleagues at The Hepworth Wakefield, especially Andrew Bonacina and Nicola Freeman, were vitally supportive in giving me the time and space to write. I am also grateful to Roger Thorp, Mohara Gill, Jenny Wilson, Anna Perotti, Sadie Butler and all at Thames & Hudson for their patience and collaboration.

I would like to thank the supporters of the major exhibition at The Hepworth Wakefield timed to coincide with the publication of this book: The Headley Trust, Henry Moore Foundation, New Art Centre – Roche Court Sculpture Park, Offer Waterman, the Hepworth Estate, Stuart & Trish Fletcher, Alice Rawsthorn, The Porthmeor Fund, and those who wish to remain anonymous. I am also grateful to the many lenders to the exhibition.

Thanks are due, too, to the many private individuals who have permitted their works to be reproduced in the book, and in many cases supplied the images. I am also grateful to all the institutions who have provided information and images: the Arts Council; the Ashmolean Museum, University of Oxford; Birmingham Art Gallery, Bolton Library and Museum Services, Bristol Museum and Art Gallery; the British Council; The Cecil Higgins Art Gallery (The Higgins Bedford); Christie's; the Courtauld Institute; David Wade Fine Art Ltd; Getty Images; Hazlitt Holland-Hibbert; the Ingram Collection; Leeds Museums and Galleries; Cornel Lucas Collection; Marlborough Fine Art; the National Galleries of Scotland; the Pier Arts Centre; and the Research and Cultural Collections, University of Birmingham; Rugby Art Gallery and Museum; Tate; the University of Leeds Art Collection; Victoria and Albert Museum; Offer Waterman; and The Whitworth, University of Manchester. Above all, I am hugely grateful for the generosity of the Bowness family in granting permission to reproduce Hepworth's works, and the many images reproduced from the Hepworth Photograph Collection.

I would like to thank Sarah Beckett, Ruth Baker and Emily Sas for their encouragement throughout. Final thanks must go to my husband Matthias Pierce for his unwavering support.

Illustration Credits

Works by Barbara Hepworth
© Bowness

2 The Hepworth Photograph
Collection. Photograph:
Studio St Ives © Bowness
7 The Hepworth Photograph
Collection. Photograph:
Charles Gimpel.
© E. R. Gimpel Estate
15 Private collection
16 The Hepworth Photograph
Collection
17 The Hepworth Photograph
Collection. Photographs of
Yorkshire commissioned by
Barbara Hepworth in 1964.
Photograph: Lee Sheldrake/
Penwith Photo Press
18 The Hepworth Photograph
Collection
19 (left) Wakefield Permanent
Art Collection (The Hepworth
Wakefield). Presented by the
artist's daughters, Rachel Kidd
and Sarah Bowness, through
the Trustees of the Barbara
Hepworth Estate and the Art
Fund, 2011
19 (right) Wakefield Permanent
Art Collection (The Hepworth
Wakefield). Purchased 1982
20 The Hepworth Photograph
Collection
21 Wakefield Permanent
Art Collection (The
Hepworth Wakefield).
Presented by Ms Stoton
and Ms Devine in 2015 in
accordance with the wishes
of Mrs Ovenden, Barbara
Hepworth's nanny
22 Wakefield Permanent Art
Collection (The Hepworth
Wakefield). Presented by
Madeleine Therese Wagner
in memory of her grandparents,
Robert and Donna Hjort, 2015.
© The Estate of Ethel Walker/
Bridgeman Images
24 The Hepworth Photograph
Collection
26 Wakefield Permanent
Art Collection (The Hepworth
Wakefield). Purchased
with aid from the MLA/V&A
Purchase Grant Fund, 2006
27 Private collection
28 Private collection. © 2020
Christie's Images Limited
29 The Hepworth Photograph
Collection. Photograph:
probably Raymond Coxon

30 The Hepworth Photograph
Collection
31 The Hepworth Photograph
Collection; on loan to
The Hepworth Wakefield
32 The Hepworth Photograph
Collection
33 (left) The Hepworth
Photograph Collection
33 (right) Wakefield Permanent
Art Collection (The Hepworth
Wakefield). Presented by the
artist's daughters, Rachel Kidd
and Sarah Bowness, through
the Trustees of the Barbara
Hepworth Estate and the Art
Fund, 2011. Photograph: Jerry
Hardman-Jones
37 Wakefield Permanent Art
Collection (The Hepworth
Wakefield). Presented by Sir
George Hill, 1947
38 Victoria and Albert Museum,
London
40 The Hepworth Photograph
Collection
42 Photograph: Nick Singleton
43 Courtesy of The Whitworth,
The University of Manchester
44 Courtesy of the Pier
Arts Centre Collection.
Photograph: Alistair Peebles
45 Courtesy of the Pier
Arts Centre Collection.
Photograph: David Lambert/
Rod Tidnam
46 The Hepworth Photograph
Collection
48 Private collection.
Photographs by Ben Nicholson
© Angela Verren Taunt. All
rights reserved, DACS 2021
50 The Hepworth Photograph
Collection
51 Photographs (of sculptures):
Paul Laib. Gift to The
Hepworth Wakefield from
the Hepworth Estate, 2013.
© The de Laszlo Foundation.
Courtesy of The Courtauld
Institute of Art, London
53 Wakefield Permanent Art
Collection (The Hepworth
Wakefield). Purchased with
aid from the Wakefield Art
Fund, V&A Purchase Grant
Fund, Wakefield Corporation
and Wakefield Girls' High
School. Photograph: Jerry
Hardman-Jones
54 The Hepworth Photograph
Collection. Works by Ben
Nicholson © Angela Verren
Taunt. All rights reserved,
DACS 2021

57 Photograph (of sculpture):
Paul Laib. Gift to The
Hepworth Wakefield from
the Hepworth Estate, 2013.
© The de Laszlo Foundation.
Courtesy of The Courtauld
Institute of Art, London
58 (above) Private collection.
Image courtesy of Offer
Waterman
58 (below) Private collection.
Image courtesy of Lund
Humphries
59 Photograph: Paul Laib.
© The de Laszlo Foundation.
Courtesy of The Courtauld
Institute of Art, London
61 Manchester City Galleries.
Photograph: Michael Pollard
62 Henry Moore Institute
Research Library
66 Wakefield Permanent Art
Collection (The Hepworth
Wakefield). Purchased by
Wakefield Corporation,
1951. Photograph: Jerry
Hardman-Jones
67 Courtesy of the Pier Arts
Centre Collection. Photograph:
Mike Davidson
68 Private collection. © 2020
Christie's Images Limited
69 The Hepworth Photograph
Collection
72 Private collection.
Photograph: Lewis Ronald
73 Photograph (of sculpture):
Barbara Hepworth. Gift to
The Hepworth Wakefield from
the Hepworth Estate, 2013
76 The Hepworth Photograph
Collection. Photograph:
Barbara Hepworth. Work
by Ben Nicholson © Angela
Verren Taunt. All rights
reserved, DACS 2021
77 The Hepworth Photograph
Collection. Photograph: Arthur
Jackson. Works by Mondrian
© 2021 Mondrian/Holtzman
Trust. Works by Ben Nicholson
© Angela Verren Taunt. All
rights reserved, DACS 2021
80 Tate: Purchased 1982.
Photo © Tate
81 The Hepworth Photograph
Collection. Photograph: Hans
Erni © Doris Erni
84 Reproduced from *Circle:
International Survey of
Constructive Art*, 1937,
© Faber and Faber
85 Wakefield Permanent Art
Collection (The Hepworth
Wakefield). Presented by

Mr H. R. Hepworth Esq., 1940. Photograph: Jerry Hardman-Jones

86 Reproduced from *Circle: International Survey of Constructive Art*, 1937, © Faber and Faber

87 (left) Bought with the aid of grants from the Henry Moore Foundation and the National Heritage Memorial Fund, 190 (Leeds Museums and Galleries)

87 (right) Hepworth Estate

88 The Hepworth Photograph Collection. Photograph: Barbara Hepworth

89 (above) Private collection. Photograph: Andy Smart (A.C. Cooper)

89 (below) Gift to The Hepworth Wakefield from the Hepworth Estate, 2013

91 Photo © Tate. Presented by the artist, 1964

92 Photograph: Barbara Hepworth. Gift to The Hepworth Wakefield from the Hepworth Estate, 2013

95 Private collection. Courtesy of Hazlitt Holland-Hibbert

96 The Hepworth Photograph Collection. Photograph: Barbara Hepworth. The Work of Naum Gabo © Nina & Graham Williams/Tate, 2021

100 University of Leeds Art Collection

101 Wakefield Permanent Art Collection (The Hepworth Wakefield). Presented by Mr W. H. Hepworth Esq., 1944. Photograph: Jerry Hardman-Jones

102 © Trustees of the Cecil Higgins Art Gallery (The Higgins Bedford)

103 Bought from the artist, 1943 (Leeds Museums and Galleries)

109 Courtesy of the Pier Arts Centre Collection. Photograph: David Lambert/Rod Tidnam

111 (above) Private collection

111 (below) Courtesy of the Pier Arts Centre Collection. Photograph: Alistair Peebles

121 Photograph: Barbara Hepworth

124 National Galleries of Scotland. Purchased with support from the Heritage Lottery Fund, Art Fund and the Henry Moore Foundation, 1999

125 Henry Moore Institute Research Library

127 The Hepworth Photograph Collection

128 Hepworth Estate. Photograph: Jerry Hardman-Jones

129 Wakefield Permanent Art Collection (The Hepworth Wakefield). Gift of the Hepworth Estate, 2013. Photograph: Jerry Hardman-Jones

130 Tate: Presented by the artist, 1964. Photo © Tate

132 Courtesy of the British Council Collection. Photo © The British Council

136 The Hepworth Photograph Collection

138 Courtesy of the British Council Collection. Photo © The British Council

139 The Hepworth Photograph Collection

142 Wakefield Permanent Art Collection (The Hepworth Wakefield). Presented by the Trustees of the Hepworth Estate, 2003

146 Image courtesy of The Ingram Collection

147 (above) The Hepworth Photograph Collection

147 (below) Bristol Culture: Bristol Museum and Art Gallery

148 Wakefield Permanent Art Collection (The Hepworth Wakefield). Gift of Dr Alan Wilkinson, in honour of Sir Alan and Lady Bowness

149 Bought by the Leeds Art Fund, 1948 (Leeds Museums and Galleries)

150 Wakefield Permanent Art Collection (The Hepworth Wakefield). Purchased by Wakefield Corporation, 1951. Photograph: Jerry Hardman-Jones

152 The Hepworth Photograph Collection. Photograph: Hans Wild

153 Photographs (of sculptures): Studio St Ives © Bowness. Gift to The Hepworth Wakefield from the Hepworth Estate, 2013

155 The Hepworth Photograph Collection. Photograph: Studio St Ives © Bowness

157 Rugby Art Gallery and Museum, Rugby Borough Council

158 National Galleries of Scotland

159 Image courtesy of The Ingram Collection

160 Part of the British Council, London collection, Tate Archive. Presented by Clive

Phillpot, on behalf of the British Council, July 2003. Photo © Tate

162 The Hepworth Photograph Collection. Photograph: Peter Keen, Pictorial Press Ltd

163 Official Festival Photograph. National Archives

165 (left) The Hepworth Photograph Collection. Photograph: Anthony Panting

165 (right) Photograph: Hulton Archive/Getty Images

167 (left) Wakefield Art Gallery Archives, The Hepworth Wakefield

167 (right) The Hepworth Photograph Collection

168 Wakefield Permanent Art Collection (The Hepworth Wakefield). Presented by the artist's daughters, Rachel Kidd and Sarah Bowness, through the Trustees of the Barbara Hepworth Estate and the Art Fund, 2011

169 The Hepworth Photograph Collection

172 Courtesy of the British Council Collection. Photo © The British Council

173 The Hepworth Photograph Collection

174 The Hepworth Photograph Collection. Photograph: John Vickers

175 The Hepworth Photograph Collection. Photograph: John Vickers

176 The Hepworth Photograph Collection

177 Ashmolean Museum, University of Oxford

178 The Hepworth Photograph Collection. Photograph: Houston Rogers. © Houston Rogers/Victoria and Albert Museum, London

179 (left) Victoria and Albert Museum

179 (right) The Hepworth Photograph Collection. Photograph: Houston Rogers. © Houston Rogers/Victoria and Albert Museum, London

180 The Hepworth Photograph Collection. Photograph: Houston Rogers. © Houston Rogers/Victoria and Albert Museum, London

184 Part of the Dame Barbara Hepworth collection, Tate Archive. Presented by Alan Bowness, 2015. Photo © Tate

189 Bought by the Leeds Art Fund, 1958 (Leeds Museums and Galleries)

190 Wakefield Permanent Art Collection (The Hepworth Wakefield). Presented by the artist's daughters, Rachel Kidd and Sarah Bowness, through the Trustees of the Barbara Hepworth Estate and the Art Fund, 2011. Photograph: Mark Heathcote

191 Wakefield Permanent Art Collection (The Hepworth Wakefield). Presented by Mrs Hazel McKinley, 1956. Photograph: Norman Taylor

192 Wakefield Permanent Art Collection (The Hepworth Wakefield). Accepted by the Commission of the Inland Revenue in lieu of tax, 2013. Photograph: Jonty Wilde

193 (left) Wakefield Permanent Art Collection (The Hepworth Wakefield). Presented by the artist's daughters, Rachel Kidd and Sarah Bowness, through the Trustees of the Barbara Hepworth Estate and the Art Fund, 2011

193 (right) Wakefield Permanent Art Collection (The Hepworth Wakefield). Presented by the artist's daughters, Rachel Kidd and Sarah Bowness, through the Trustees of the Barbara Hepworth Estate and the Art Fund, 2011

196 (above) Wakefield Permanent Art Collection (The Hepworth Wakefield). Purchased with aid from National Art Collections Fund and V&A Purchase Grant Fund, 1956

196 (below) Private collection. Photo © Ioana Marinescu

198 The Hepworth Photograph Collection

200 The Hepworth Photograph Collection. Photograph: Studio St Ives © Bowness

201 The Hepworth Photograph Collection. Photograph: Michel Ramon

202 Private collection. Image courtesy of Lund Humphries

203 Wakefield Permanent Art Collection (The Hepworth Wakefield). Presented by the artist's daughters, Rachel Kidd and Sarah Bowness, through the Trustees of the Barbara Hepworth Estate and the Art Fund, 2011. Photograph: Lewis Ronald

204 Accepted under the Cultural Gifts Scheme by HM Government from Kate Ashbrook and allocated to The Hepworth Wakefield, 2019. Photograph: Lewis Ronald

206 Courtesy of the Pier Arts Centre Collection. Photograph: Alistair Peebles

207 Photograph: Nick Singleton. Wakefield Permanent Art Collection (The Hepworth Wakefield). Donated by Eric and Jean Cass through the Contemporary Art Society, 2010

208 The Hepworth Photograph Collection

210 Hepworth Estate

214 The Hepworth Photograph Collection. Photograph: Studio St Ives © Bowness

216 (left) Wakefield Permanent Art Collection (The Hepworth Wakefield). Presented by the artist's daughters, Rachel Kidd and Sarah Bowness, through the Trustees of the Barbara Hepworth Estate and the Art Fund, 2011. Photograph: Mark Heathcote

216 (right) John Lewis Archives

217 The Hepworth Photograph Collection. Photograph: Cornel Lucas. © Cornel Lucas Collection

219 The Hepworth Photograph Collection

224 Tate: Presented by the executors of the artist's estate, 1980. Photo © Tate

225 Hepworth Estate. Photograph: Jerry Hardman-Jones

226 UN Photo/Teddy Chen

227 The Hepworth Photograph Collection. Photograph: Morgan-Wells

230 The Hepworth Photograph Collection. Photograph: Charles Gimpel. © E. R. Gimpel Estate

232 Private collection

233 Private collection. Courtesy of Hazlitt Holland-Hibbert

234 Hepworth Estate. Photograph: Lewis Ronald

235 Private collection. © Bridget Riley 2020. All rights reserved

238 Hepworth Estate. Photograph: Jerry Hardman-Jones

240–41 Photograph: Central Press/Hulton Archive/Getty Images

242 The Hepworth Photograph Collection

246 Photograph: Ander Gunn

247 Private collection. Courtesy of Pace Gallery, New York

248 Wakefield Permanent Art Collection (The Hepworth Wakefield). Presented by the artist's daughters, Rachel Kidd and Sarah Bowness, through the Trustees of the Barbara Hepworth Estate and the Art Fund, 2011

249 (above) Private collection. Courtesy of Marlborough Fine Art

249 (below) Wakefield Permanent Art Collection (The Hepworth Wakefield). Presented by the artist's daughters, Rachel Kidd and Sarah Bowness, through the Trustees of the Barbara Hepworth Estate and the Art Fund, 2011. Photograph: Mark Heathcote

250 (left) Private collection

250 (right) Wakefield Permanent Art Collection (The Hepworth Wakefield). Presented by the artist's daughters, Rachel Kidd and Sarah Bowness, through the Trustees of the Barbara Hepworth Estate and the Art Fund, 2011

251 (above) Wakefield Permanent Art Collection (The Hepworth Wakefield). Purchased with aid from National Art Collections Fund and the Department of Education and Science, 1979

251 (below) Wakefield Permanent Art Collection (The Hepworth Wakefield). Presented by the artist's daughters, Rachel Kidd and Sarah Bowness, through the Trustees of the Barbara Hepworth Estate and the Art Fund, 2011. Photograph: Mark Heathcote

252–53 The Hepworth Photograph Collection. Photograph: Foresees

255 Hepworth Estate. Photograph: Jerry Hardman-Jones

256 Wakefield Permanent Art Collection (The Hepworth Wakefield). Presented by the artist's daughters, Rachel Kidd and Sarah Bowness, through the Trustees of the Barbara Hepworth Estate and the Art Fund, 2011. Photograph: Mark Heathcote

258 Photograph: Iwan Baan

259 Photograph: Iwan Baan

Index

Page references in *italic*
refer to illustrations